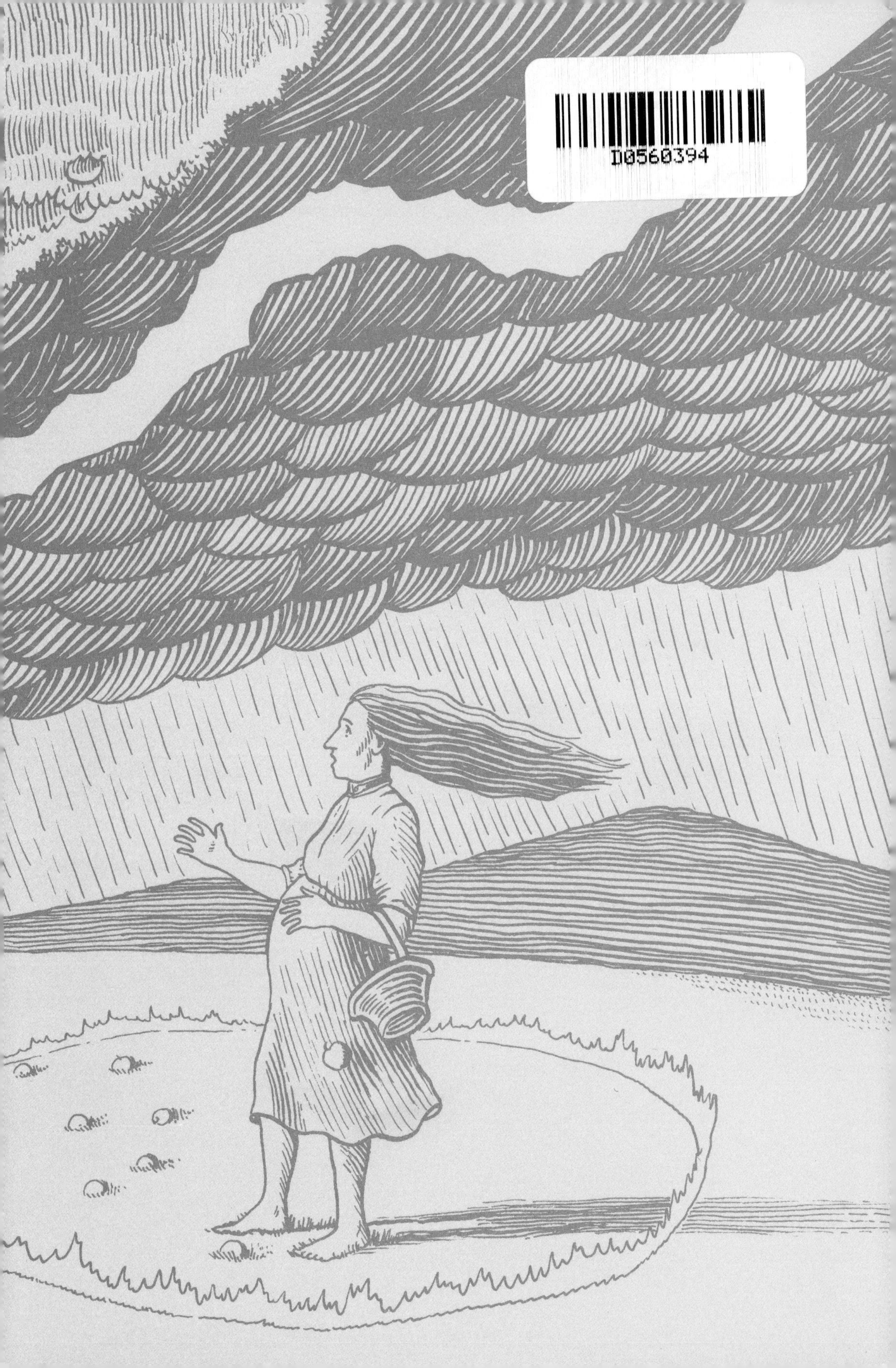

The CARTER FAMILY

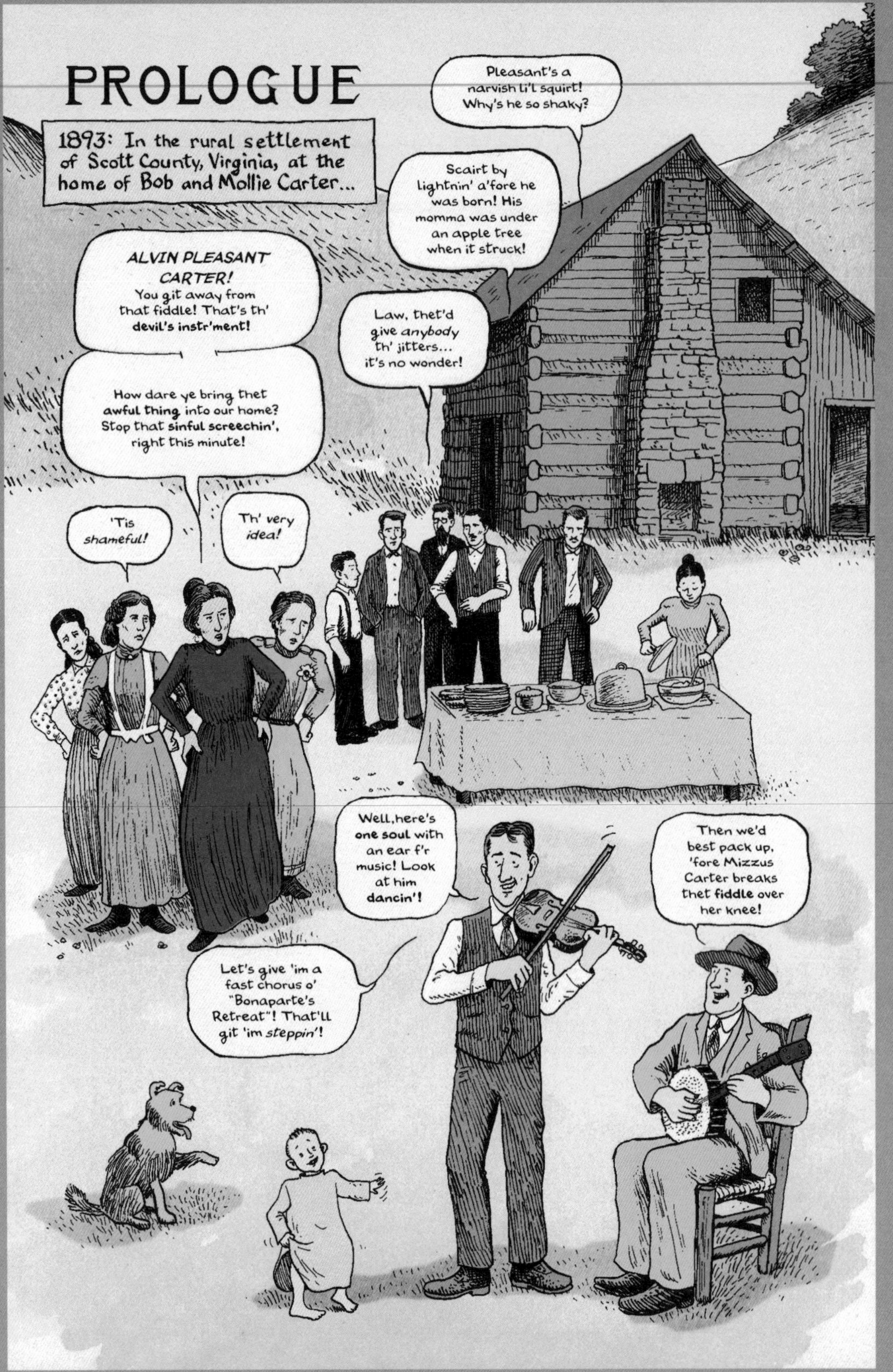
PROLOGUE
1893: In the rural settlement of Scott County, Virginia, at the home of Bob and Mollie Carter...
Pleasant's a narvish li'l squirt! Why's he so shaky?
Scairt by lightnin' a'fore he was born! His momma was under an apple tree when it struck!
ALVIN PLEASANT CARTER! You git away from that fiddle! That's th' devil's instr'ment!
How dare ye bring thet awful thing into our home? Stop that sinful screechin', right this minute!
Law, thet'd give anybody th' jitters... it's no wonder!
'Tis shameful!
Th' very idea!
Well, here's one soul with an ear f'r music! Look at him dancin'!
Then we'd best pack up, 'fore Mizzus Carter breaks thet fiddle over her knee!
Let's give 'im a fast chorus o' "Bonaparte's Retreat"! That'll git 'im steppin'!

The CARTER FAMILY

Don't Forget This Song

SUMMER 1898

I'm goin' down... to the river of Jordan...

Rock of ages, cleft for me...

Y'got a fine singin' voice, son...lemme hear another hymn!

WINTER 1900

Editor: Charles Kochman
Designers: Sara Corbett and Neil Egan
Managing Editor: Tamara Arellano
Production Manager: Alison Gervais

Cataloging-in-Publication Data has been applied
for and may be obtained from the Library
of Congress.

ISBN: 978-0-8109-8836-1

Copyright © 2012 Frank M. Young and David Lasky

Chapter 16, "Wildwood Flower," first appeared
in a completely different form in volume 4 of
Kramers Ergot, published by Avodah Books in 2003.

Abrams ComicArts is a registered trademark
of Harry N. Abrams, Inc., registered in the U.S.
Patent and Trademark Office.

Printed and bound in China
10 9 8 7 6 5 4 3 2 1

Abrams ComicArts books are available at
special discounts when purchased in quantity
for premiums and promotions as well as
fundraising or educational use. Special editions
can also be created to specification. For details,
contact specialsales@abramsbooks.com or
the address below.

ABRAMS
THE ART OF BOOKS SINCE 1949

115 West 18th Street
New York, NY 10011
www.abramsbooks.com

SPRING 1902

WINTER 1908

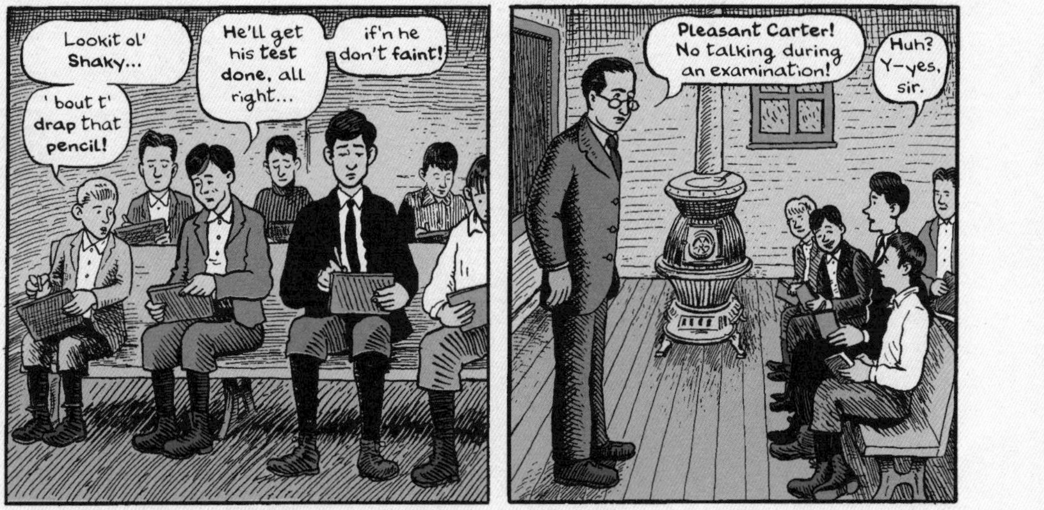
Lookit ol' Shaky...
'bout t' drap that pencil!
He'll get his test done, all right...
if'n he don't faint!
Pleasant Carter! No talking during an examination!
Huh? Y-yes, sir.

The authors wish to dedicate this book
to Rita Forrester, and to the memory of Mike Seeger.

Chapter Thirteen, "The Storms Are on the Ocean,"
is dedicated to the memory of Dylan Williams.

FALL 1909

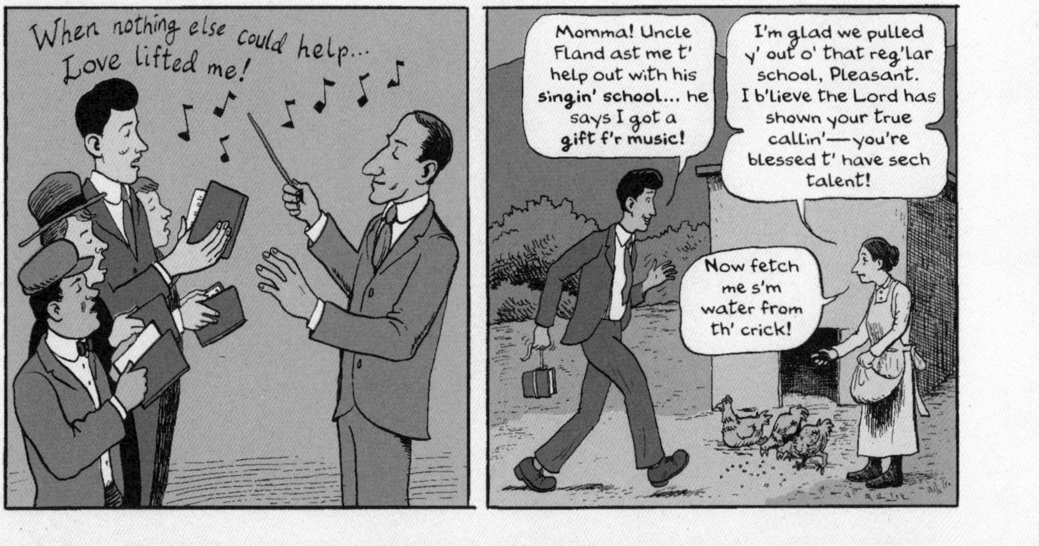
When nothing else could help... Love lifted me!
Momma! Uncle Fland ast me t' help out with his singin' school... he says I got a gift f'r music!
I'm glad we pulled y' out o' that reg'lar school, Pleasant. I b'lieve the Lord has shown your true callin'—you're blessed t' have sech talent!
Now fetch me s'm water from th' crick!

CONTENTS

FAMILY TREE

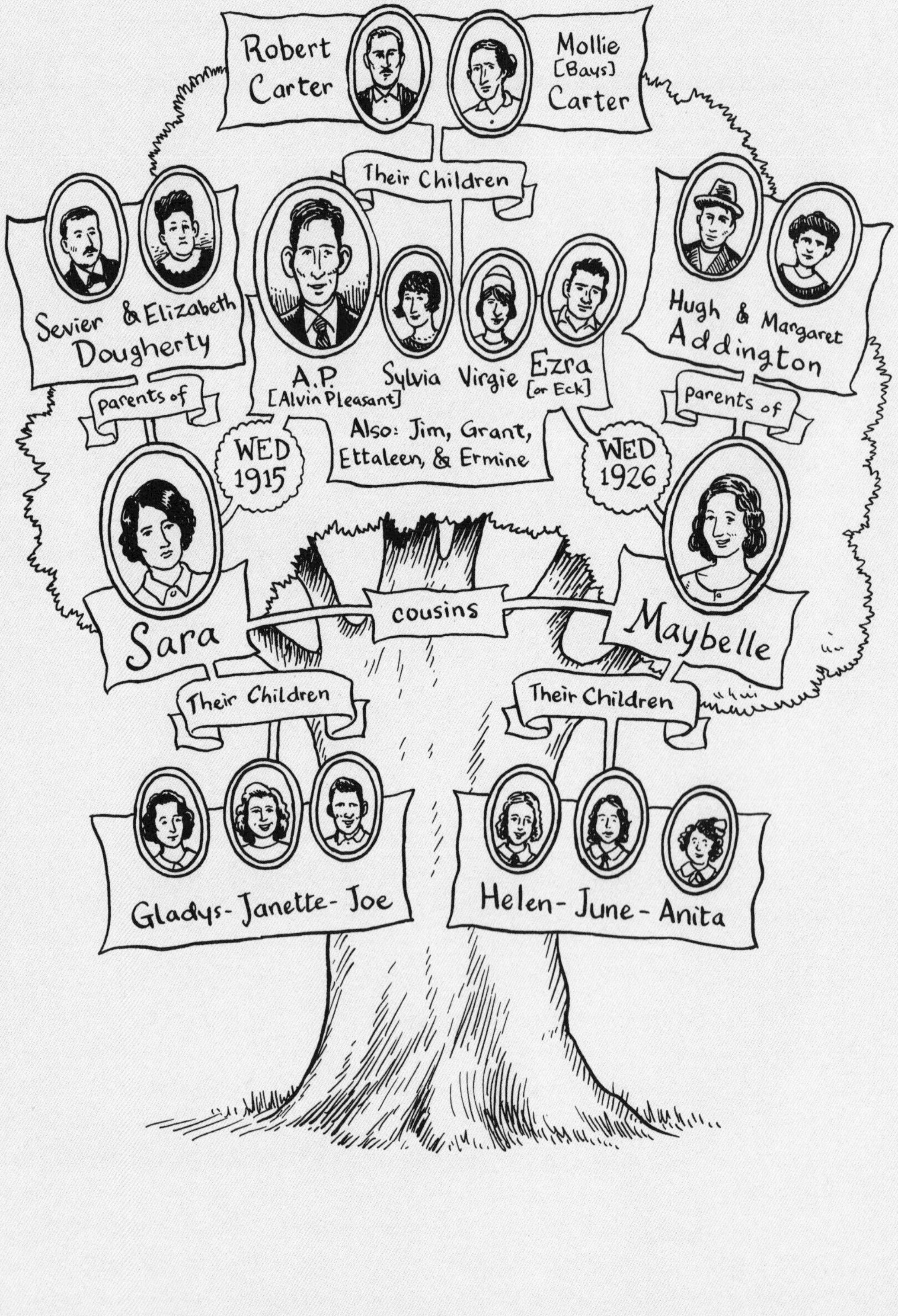
Robert Carter
Mollie [Bays] Carter
Their Children
Sevier & Elizabeth Dougherty
A.P. [Alvin Pleasant]
Sylvia
Virgie
Ezra [or Eck]
Hugh & Margaret Addington
parents of
Also: Jim, Grant, Ettaleen, & Ermine
parents of
WED 1915
WED 1926
Sara
cousins
Maybelle
Their Children
Their Children
Gladys- Janette- Joe
Helen- June- Anita

Preface

Who were the Carter Family—and why is there a graphic novel about them?

We've answered this question hundreds of times over the decade-long course of this project. The best way is to work backward. You know Johnny Cash, right? His wife was June Carter Cash . . . She was one of three daughters of Maybelle Carter, who was the lead guitarist and a singer for the original Carter Family.

You may know her better as "Mother Maybelle," in her role as the grand matriarch of the country music scene in the 1960s and '70s. She occupied that role with grace and humility, and encouraged new generations of songwriters and performers to blossom in the musical hothouse of Nashville.

Usually, about the time I mention June Carter Cash, the person I'm talking with will nod his or her head and say, "Oh . . . Oh yeah! I know her! Cool!"

It's a valid point of reference—and it works as an elevator speech about the project. But the original Carter Family is much more than a distant footnote to the careers of Johnny and June. They are the foundation upon which all of commercial country music (and, by extension, rock 'n' roll) rests. They broke the ground that modern performers take for granted. They helped shape the popular song as we know it today. They kindled the flames of interest in the vast, rich Anglo-Saxon body of ballads, love songs, and narratives that might have otherwise vanished on the horizon of the twentieth century.

The Carter Family and their music never quite went away. Songs like "Wildwood Flower," "I'm Thinking Tonight of My Blue Eyes," and "Can the Circle Be Unbroken?" remain standards of the American country-folk songbook. These are three of the nearly three hundred songs that A.P. Carter arranged, usually from existing material. Though he did write several songs for the Carter Family, Alvin Pleasant Carter is, in Charles Wolfe's words, the "master chef" of country music.

From his youth, A.P. Carter was fascinated by the old songs that floated around the hills of his native Virginia. He was exquisitely aware that these tunes, carried by emigrant farmers and gray-haired settlers, were in danger of dying. He felt it was his job to save them from extinction.

A.P.'s future bride, Sara Dougherty, lived in neighboring Copper Creek. She, too, embraced music from childhood on.

SUMMER 1910

Son, that's good! I usta be a pretty good fiddler—'til y'r maw made me give it up...
You're like me. Y'take after them old songs, too...
After supper t'night, c'd ya teach me some?
Mandy Groves learnt me this'n—"Gypsy Davey..."
Sing it to me, Pa!

Gifted with a resonant, haunting voice, Sara could sing a song and make you believe it came from her personal experience. Self-accompanied on the jangly autoharp, a zitherlike instrument developed in the late nineteenth century, Sara's singing was incomparable. The moment A.P. heard that voice, he was hooked.

Sara's cousin, Maybelle Addington, joined the team in the mid-1920s. Her husky, melancholy voice blended beautifully with Sara's yearning leads—and with A.P.'s intermittent, tremulous backup. Most important, Maybelle was a genius of the guitar. On her own, she developed a manner of playing that combined the strum of the rhythm guitar with the single-note picking of the lead. This technique was dubbed "the Carter scratch," and has influenced enough guitarists to fill the Grand Canyon.

This trio invested each song they sang with the breadth of their hearts and souls. Their repertoire leaned heavily toward spirituals (they were devout Christians), but also embraced love songs, ballads, narrative songs, blues, humorous novelties, and the occasional song of social commentary.

In 1927, the Carter Family were a key player in an event historians call "the big bang of country music"—a week-long series of recording sessions held in Bristol, a town on the Tennessee-Virginia border, by Victor Records and its canny freelance A&R man Ralph Peer. The six recordings the Carters made in Bristol were the start of a fifteen-year career that brought them to the forefront of the burgeoning country music scene.

By the time they disbanded in early 1943, the Carter Family were veterans of live performance, radio broadcasts, and the recording studio. A.P. dabbled in recording and held the occasional reunion of the Carter Family, but preferred to keep a low profile in his Clinch Mountain home. Sara, always a reluctant star, came in and out of the limelight, but chose to spend most of her time with her second husband, Coy Bays, in California. Maybelle kept on performing with her three daughters as the Carter Sisters and Mother Maybelle. She remained in the spotlight until her death.

The Carter Family's music influenced many other greats: Woody Guthrie, Hank Williams Sr., Bob Dylan, Lucinda Williams, the alt-country scene, the folk revival of the 1960s . . . From Guthrie's rousing "This Land Is Your Land" to Dylan's "Blowin' in the Wind," the influence of A.P. Carter's song craft cuts a deep swath through all American music.

That answers the question, "Who were the Carter Family?"

Now, why is there a graphic novel about them? The story of their lives and career is a great American saga. Echoes of Shakespeare, Dickens, and Horatio Alger are here. A touch of Mark Twain and a pinch of Charles Portis can be seen in the sometimes funny, sometimes brutally sad narrative of the Carter Family.

Their rise to fame; their internal struggles; the triumphs, betrayals, and breakthroughs they experienced; the otherness of their rural world; and their religious beliefs made this a story we had to tell. The medium of comics, as uniquely American as the Carter Family's music, seems utterly apt for this narrative.

My grandmother, who worked as a schoolteacher in Appalachian mining towns in the early 1920s, used to sing a Carter Family song to me as a kind of lullaby. As an infant, the "too late . . . too late" refrain of the song "One Little Word" (adapted by A.P. from an 1899 pop song authored by Gussie Davis) made a great impression on me. I wouldn't find out what the song was, and where it came from, until the 1980s.

I'm grateful to be a part of this effort to tell the remarkable story of the Carter Family's life and music. It's funny, it's moving, and it's uniquely American. I hope it means as much to you as it does to us.

FRANK M. YOUNG
Seattle, Washington
February 2012

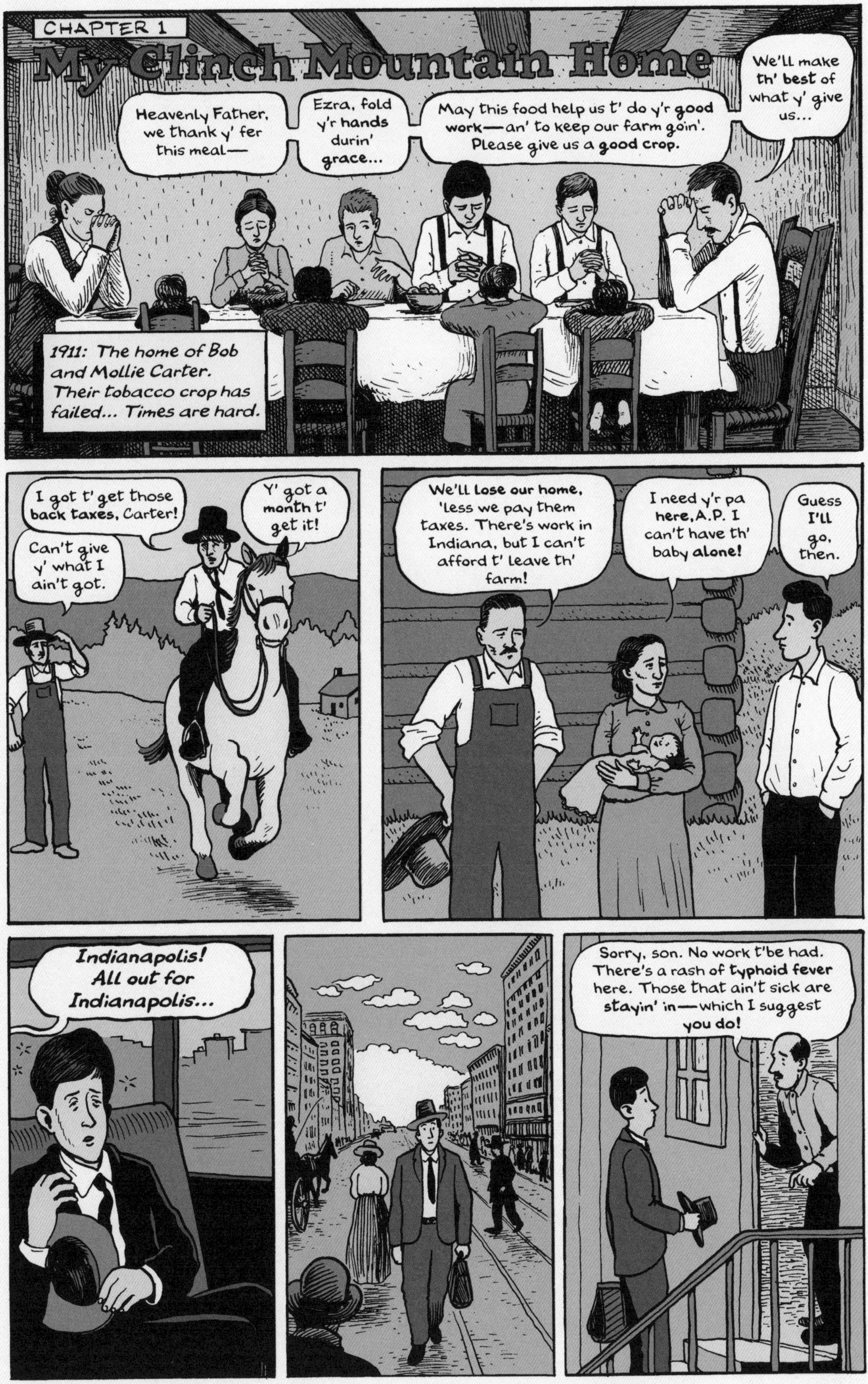
CHAPTER 1
My Clinch Mountain Home
Heavenly Father, we thank y' fer this meal—
Ezra, fold y'r hands durin' grace...
May this food help us t' do y'r good work—an' to keep our farm goin'. Please give us a good crop.
We'll make th' best of what y' give us...
1911: The home of Bob and Mollie Carter. Their tobacco crop has failed... Times are hard.
I got t' get those back taxes, Carter!
Y' got a month t' get it!
Can't give y' what I ain't got.
We'll lose our home, 'less we pay them taxes. There's work in Indiana, but I can't afford t' leave th' farm!
I need y'r pa here, A.P. I can't have th' baby alone!
Guess I'll go, then.
Indianapolis! All out for Indianapolis...
Sorry, son. No work t'be had. There's a rash of typhoid fever here. Those that ain't sick are stayin' in—which I suggest you do!

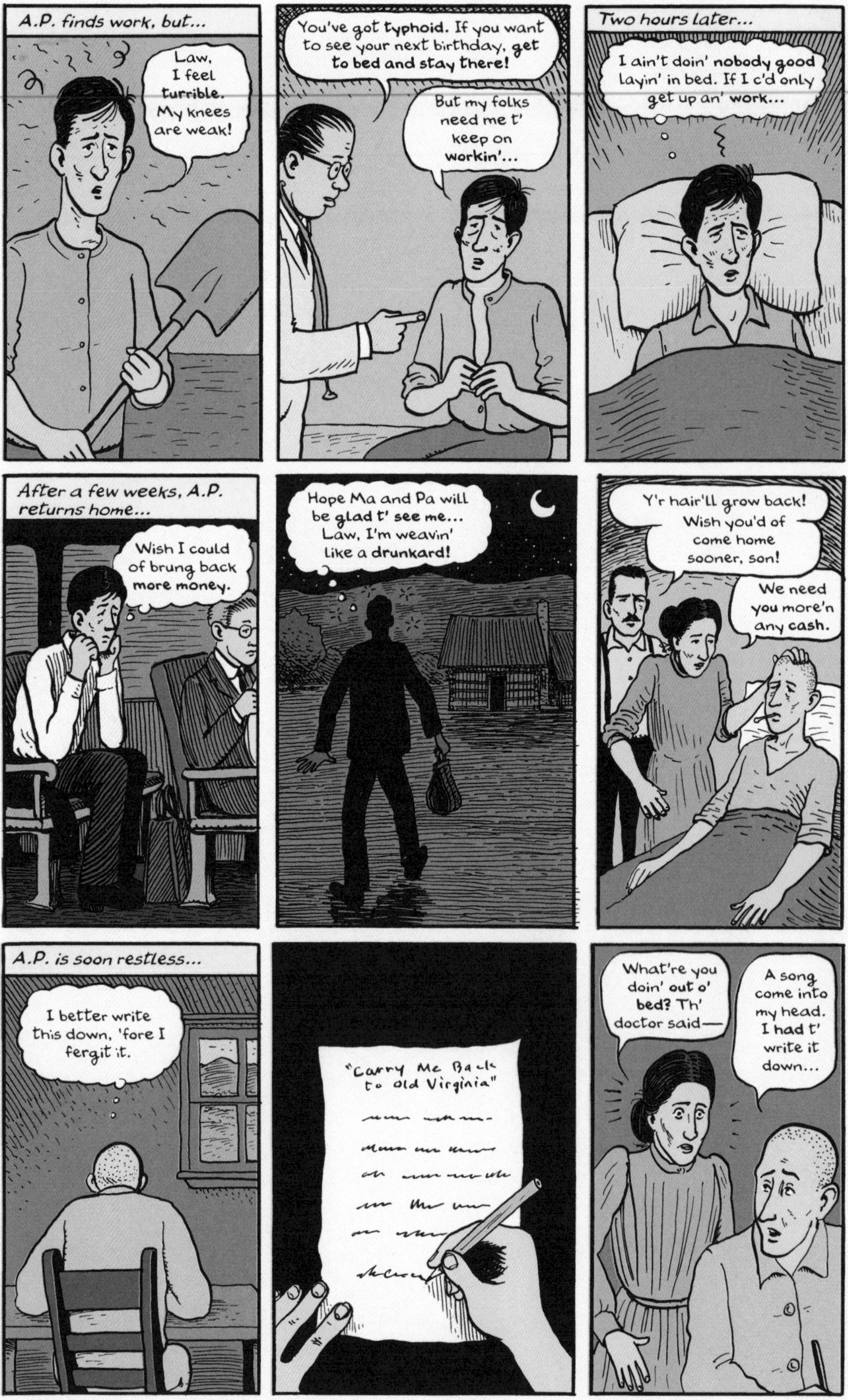
A.P. finds work, but...
Law, I feel turrible. My knees are weak!
You've got typhoid. If you want to see your next birthday, get to bed and stay there!
But my folks need me t' keep on workin'...
Two hours later...
I ain't doin' nobody good layin' in bed. If I c'd only get up an' work...
After a few weeks, A.P. returns home...
Wish I could of brung back more money.
Hope Ma and Pa will be glad t' see me... Law, I'm weavin' like a drunkard!
Y'r hair'll grow back! Wish you'd of come home sooner, son!
We need you more'n any cash.
A.P. is soon restless...
I better write this down, 'fore I fergit it.
"Carry Me Back to Old Virginia"
What're you doin' out o' bed? Th' doctor said—
A song come into my head. I had t' write it down...

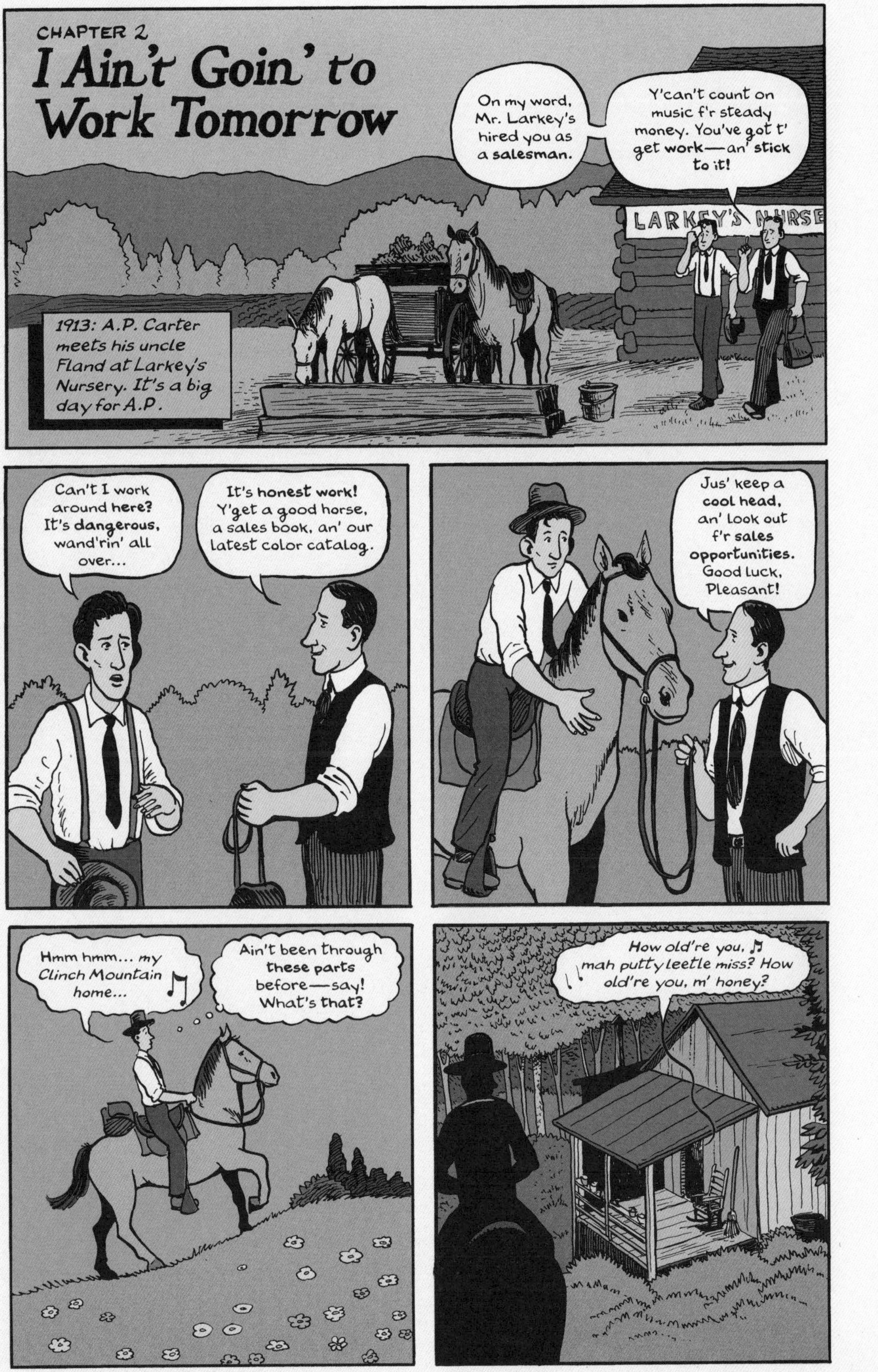
CHAPTER 2
I Ain't Goin' to Work Tomorrow
1913: A.P. Carter meets his uncle Fland at Larkey's Nursery. It's a big day for A.P.
On my word, Mr. Larkey's hired you as a salesman.
Y'can't count on music f'r steady money. You've got t' get work—an' stick to it!
LARKEY'S
Can't I work around here? It's dangerous, wand'rin' all over...
It's honest work! Y'get a good horse, a sales book, an' our latest color catalog.
Jus' keep a cool head, an' look out f'r sales opportunities. Good luck, Pleasant!
Hmm hmm... my Clinch Mountain home...
Ain't been through these parts before—say! What's that?
How old're you, mah putty leetle miss? How old're you, m' honey?

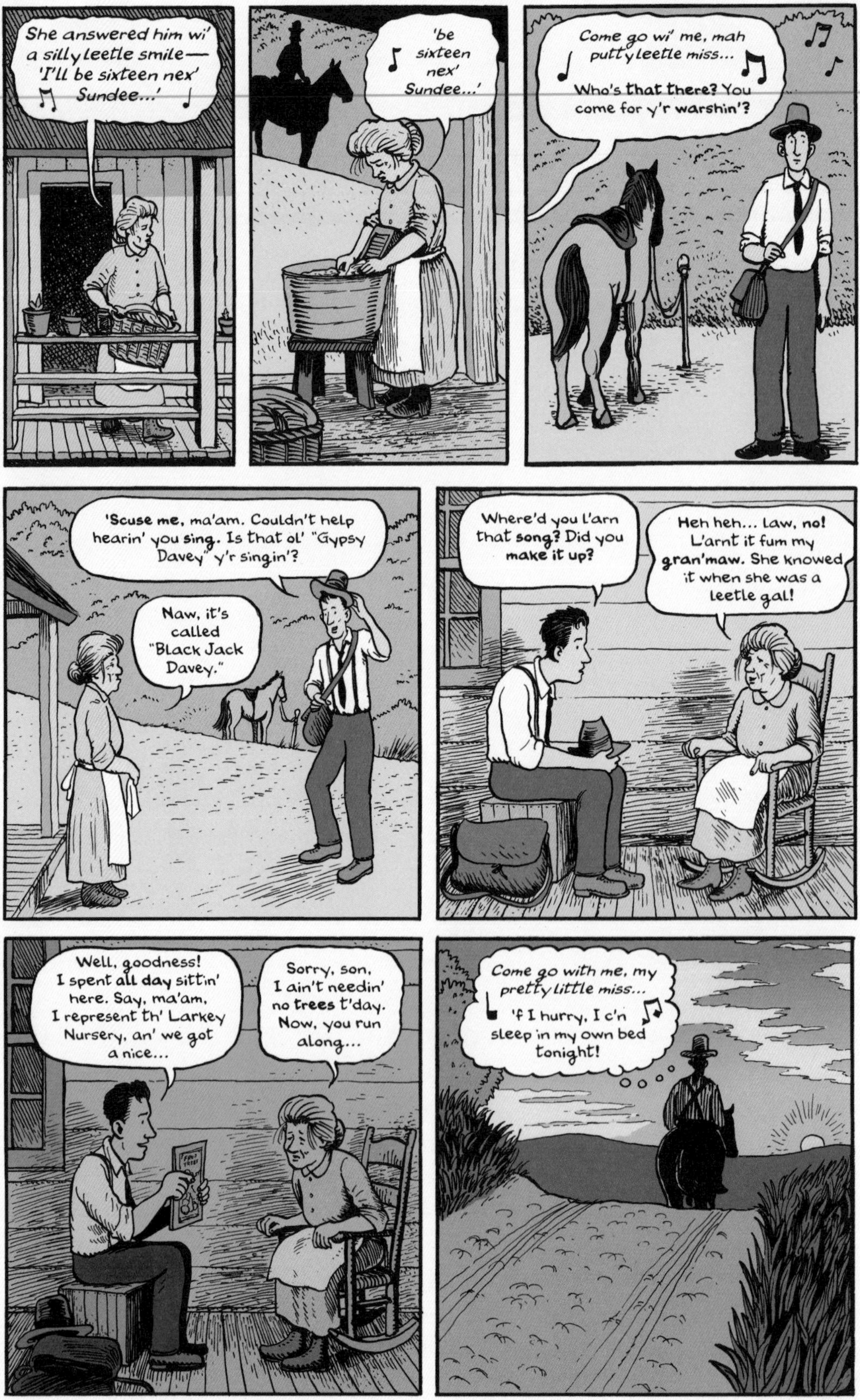
She answered him wi' a silly leetle smile— 'I'll be sixteen nex' Sundee...'
'be sixteen nex' Sundee...'
Come go wi' me, mah putty leetle miss...
Who's that there? You come for y'r warshin'?
'Scuse me, ma'am. Couldn't help hearin' you sing. Is that ol' "Gypsy Davey" y'r singin'?
Naw, it's called "Black Jack Davey."
Where'd you l'arn that song? Did you make it up?
Heh heh... law, no! L'arnt it fum my gran'maw. She knowed it when she was a leetle gal!
Well, goodness! I spent all day sittin' here. Say, ma'am, I represent th' Larkey Nursery, an' we got a nice...
Sorry, son, I ain't needin' no trees t'day. Now, you run along...
Come go with me, my pretty little miss...
'f I hurry, I c'n sleep in my own bed tonight!

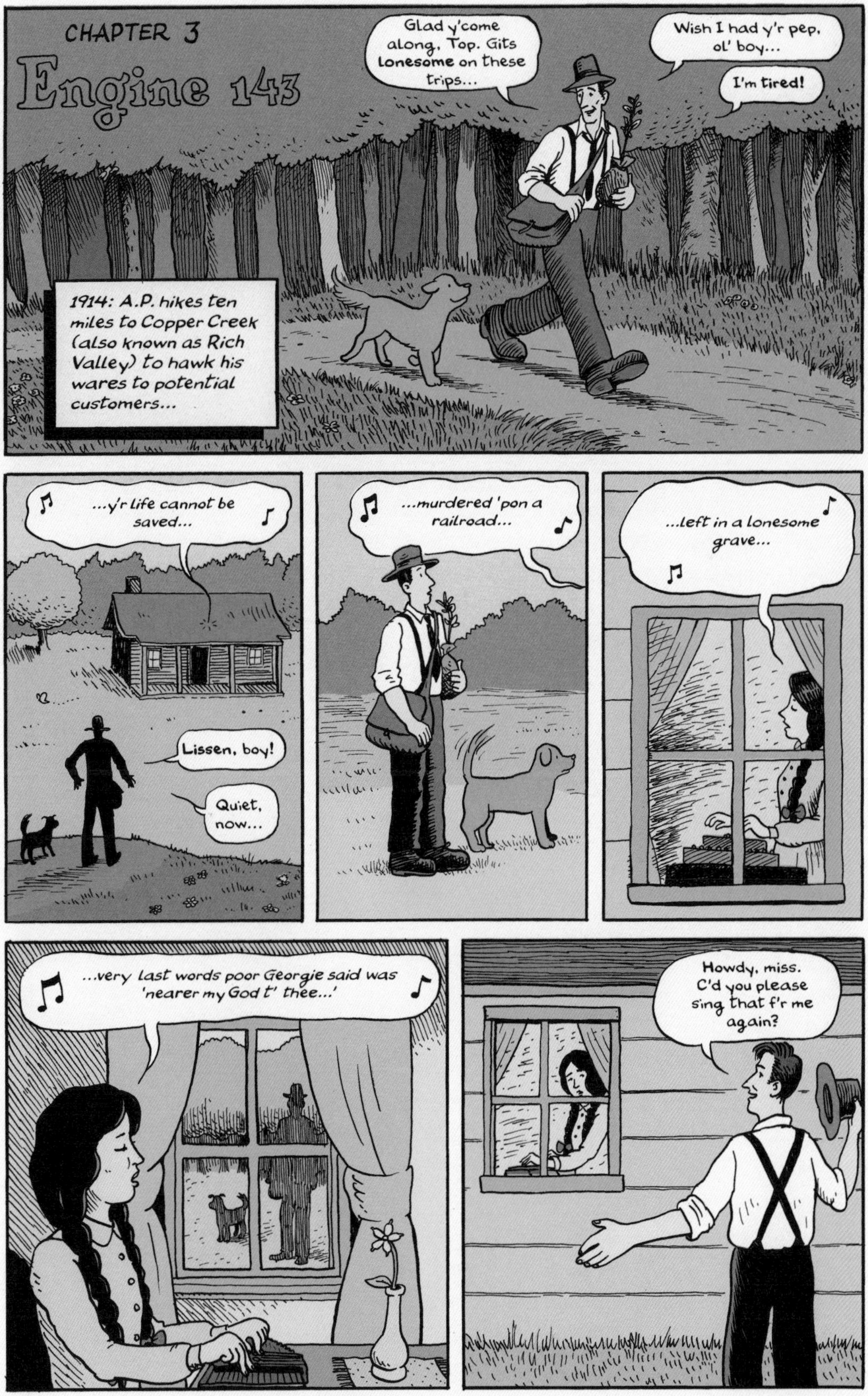
CHAPTER 3
Engine 143
Glad y'come along, Top. Gits lonesome on these trips...
Wish I had y'r pep, ol' boy...
I'm tired!
1914: A.P. hikes ten miles to Copper Creek (also known as Rich Valley) to hawk his wares to potential customers...
...y'r life cannot be saved...
Lissen, boy!
Quiet, now...
...murdered 'pon a railroad...
...left in a lonesome grave...
...very last words poor Georgie said was 'nearer my God t' thee...'
Howdy, miss. C'd you please sing that f'r me again?

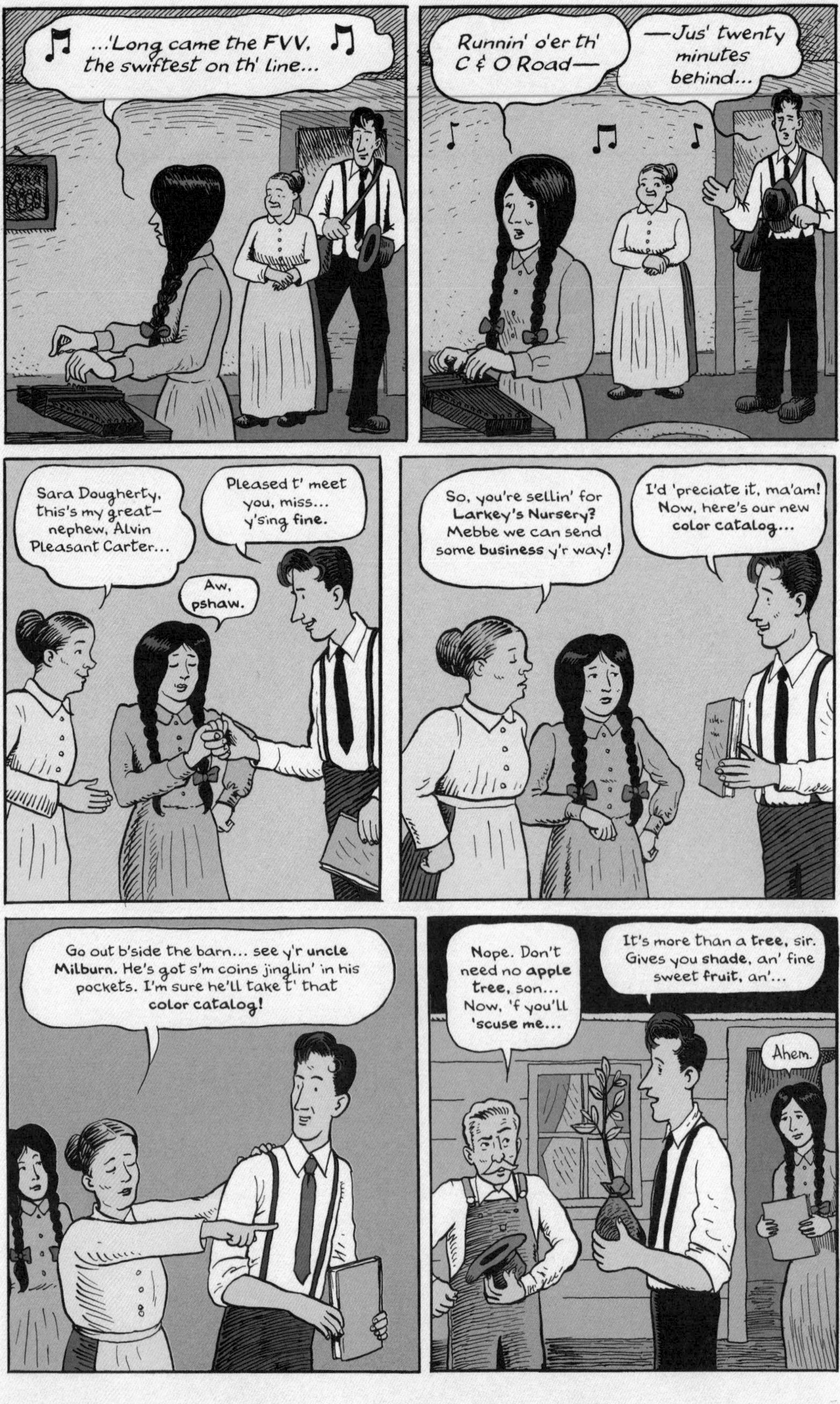
...'Long came the FVV, the swiftest on th' line...
Runnin' o'er th' C & O Road—
—Jus' twenty minutes behind...
Sara Dougherty, this's my great-nephew, Alvin Pleasant Carter...
Pleased t' meet you, miss... y'sing fine.
Aw, pshaw.
So, you're sellin' for Larkey's Nursery? Mebbe we can send some business y'r way!
I'd 'preciate it, ma'am! Now, here's our new color catalog...
Go out b'side the barn... see y'r uncle Milburn. He's got s'm coins jinglin' in his pockets. I'm sure he'll take t' that color catalog!
Nope. Don't need no apple tree, son... Now, 'f you'll 'scuse me...
It's more than a tree, sir. Gives you shade, an' fine sweet fruit, an'...
Ahem.

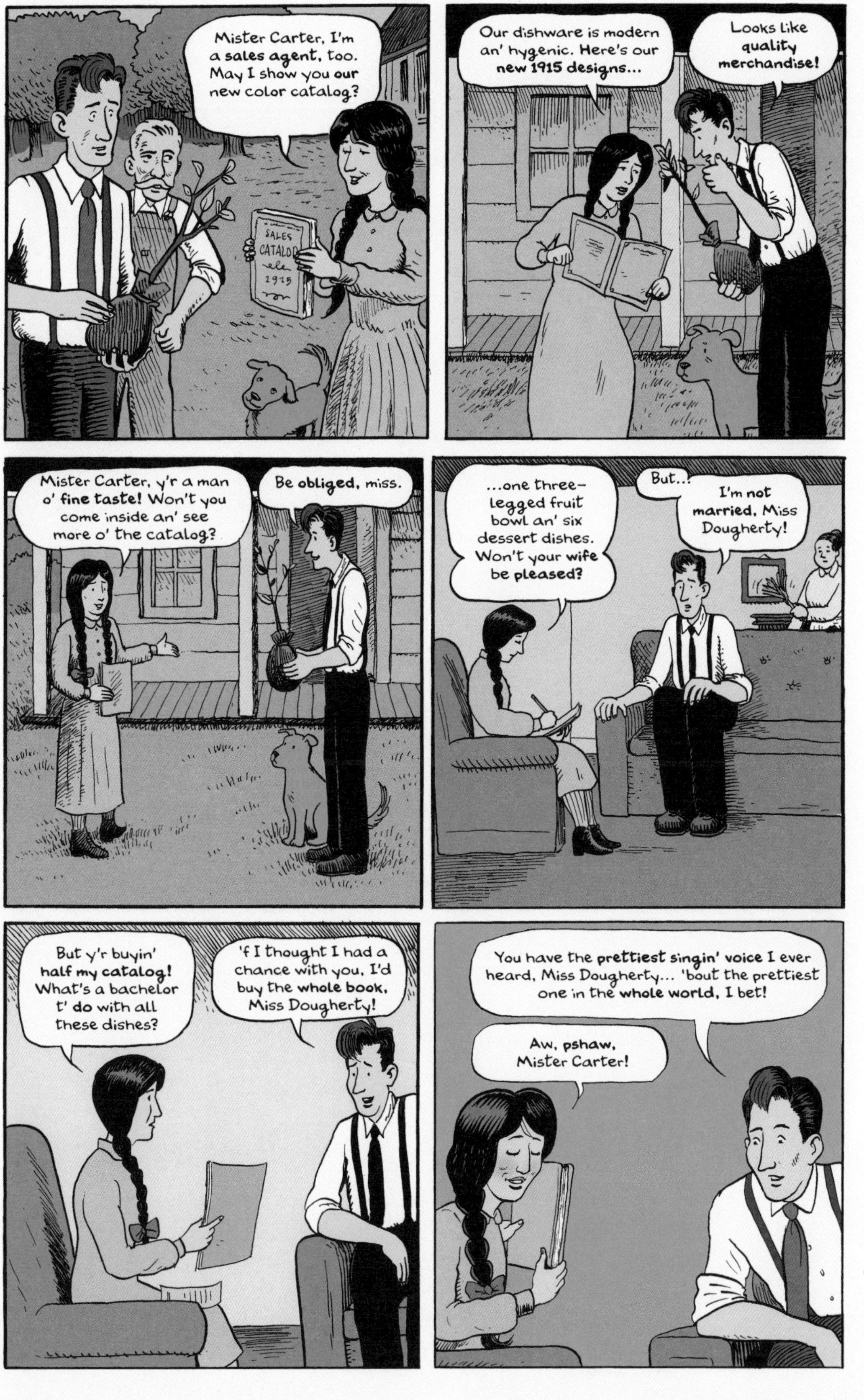
Mister Carter, I'm a sales agent, too. May I show you our new color catalog?
SALES CATALOG 1915
Our dishware is modern an' hygenic. Here's our new 1915 designs...
Looks like quality merchandise!
Mister Carter, y'r a man o' fine taste! Won't you come inside an' see more o' the catalog?
Be obliged, miss.
...one three-legged fruit bowl an' six dessert dishes. Won't your wife be pleased?
But...
I'm not married, Miss Dougherty!
But y'r buyin' half my catalog! What's a bachelor t' do with all these dishes?
'f I thought I had a chance with you, I'd buy the whole book, Miss Dougherty!
You have the prettiest singin' voice I ever heard, Miss Dougherty... 'bout the prettiest one in the whole world, I bet!
Aw, pshaw, Mister Carter!

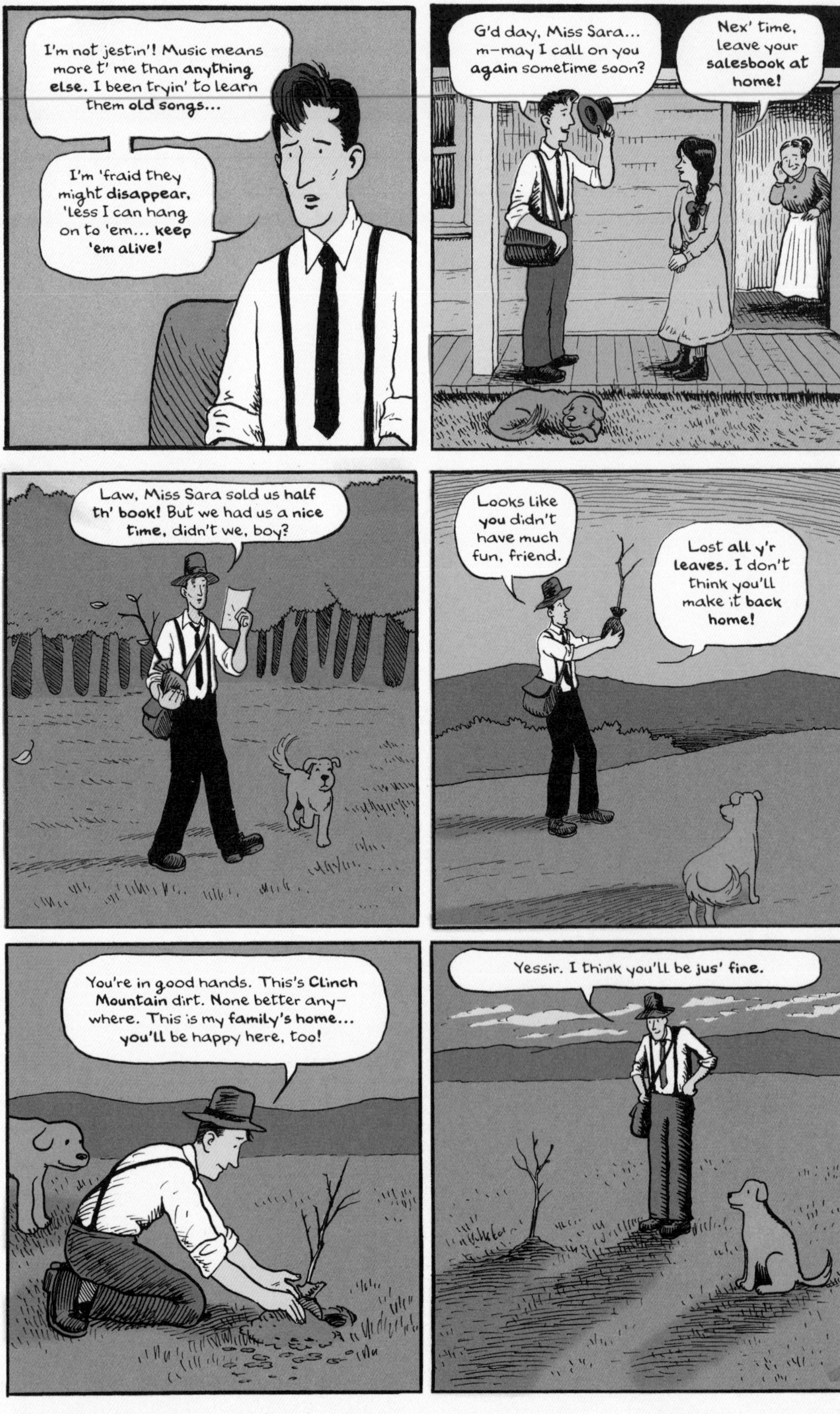
I'm not jestin'! Music means more t' me than **anything else.** I been tryin' to learn them **old songs...**
I'm 'fraid they might **disappear,** 'less I can hang on to 'em... **keep 'em alive!**
G'd day, Miss Sara... m-may I call on you **again** sometime soon?
Nex' time, leave your **salesbook at home!**
Law, Miss Sara sold us **half th' book!** But we had us a **nice time,** didn't we, boy?
Looks like **you** didn't have much fun, friend.
Lost **all** y'r **leaves.** I don't think you'll make it **back home!**
You're in good hands. This's **Clinch Mountain** dirt. None better anywhere. This is my **family's home... you'll** be happy here, too!
Yessir. I think you'll be **jus' fine.**

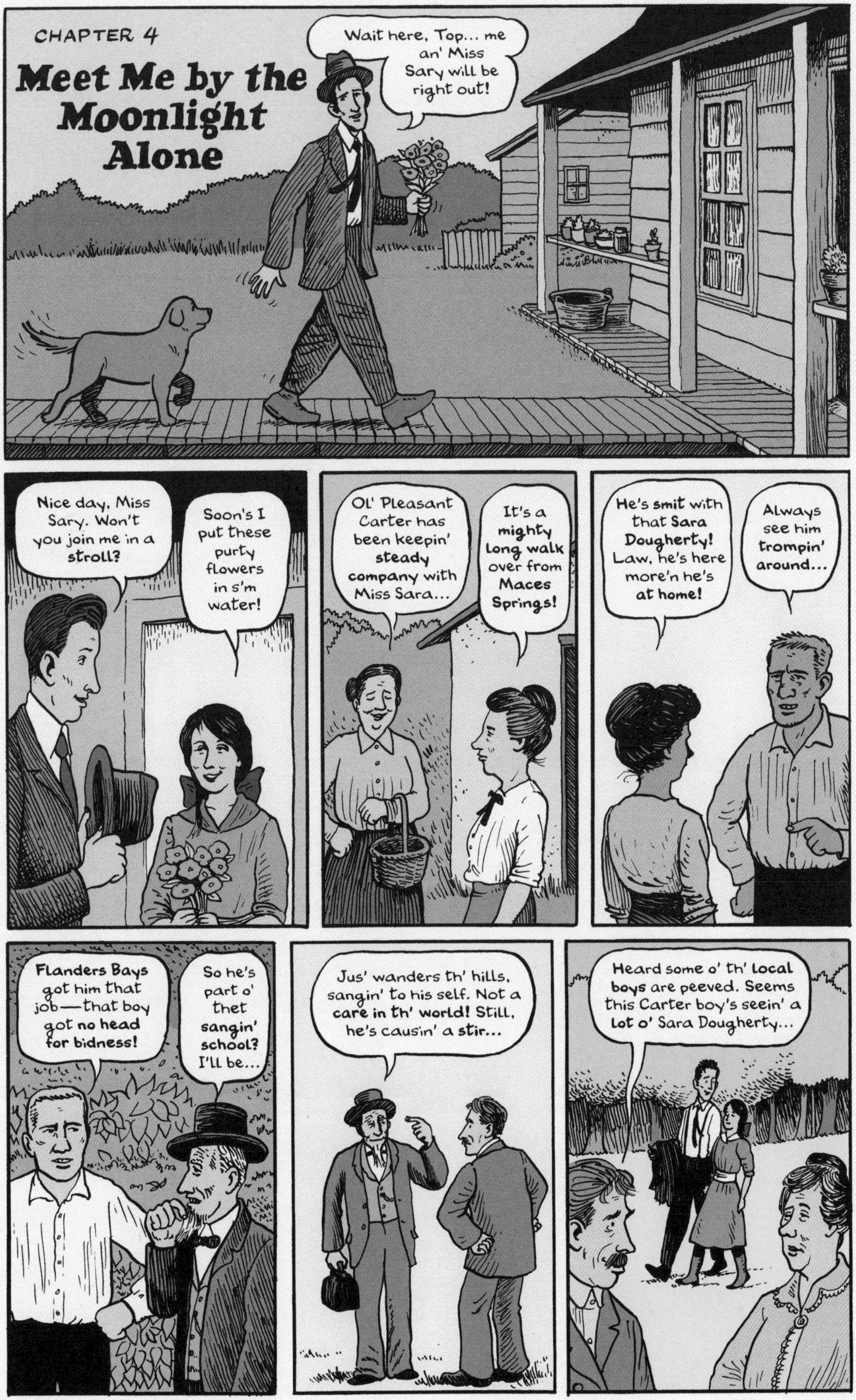
CHAPTER 4
Meet Me by the Moonlight Alone
Wait here, Top... me an' Miss Sary will be right out!
Nice day, Miss Sary. Won't you join me in a stroll?
Soon's I put these purty flowers in s'm water!
Ol' Pleasant Carter has been keepin' steady company with Miss Sara...
It's a mighty long walk over from Maces Springs!
He's smit with that Sara Dougherty! Law, he's here more'n he's at home!
Always see him trompin' around...
Flanders Bays got him that job—that boy got no head for bidness!
So he's part o' thet sangin' school? I'll be...
Jus' wanders th' hills, sangin' to his self. Not a care in th' world! Still, he's causin' a stir...
Heard some o' th' local boys are peeved. Seems this Carter boy's seein' a lot o' Sara Dougherty...

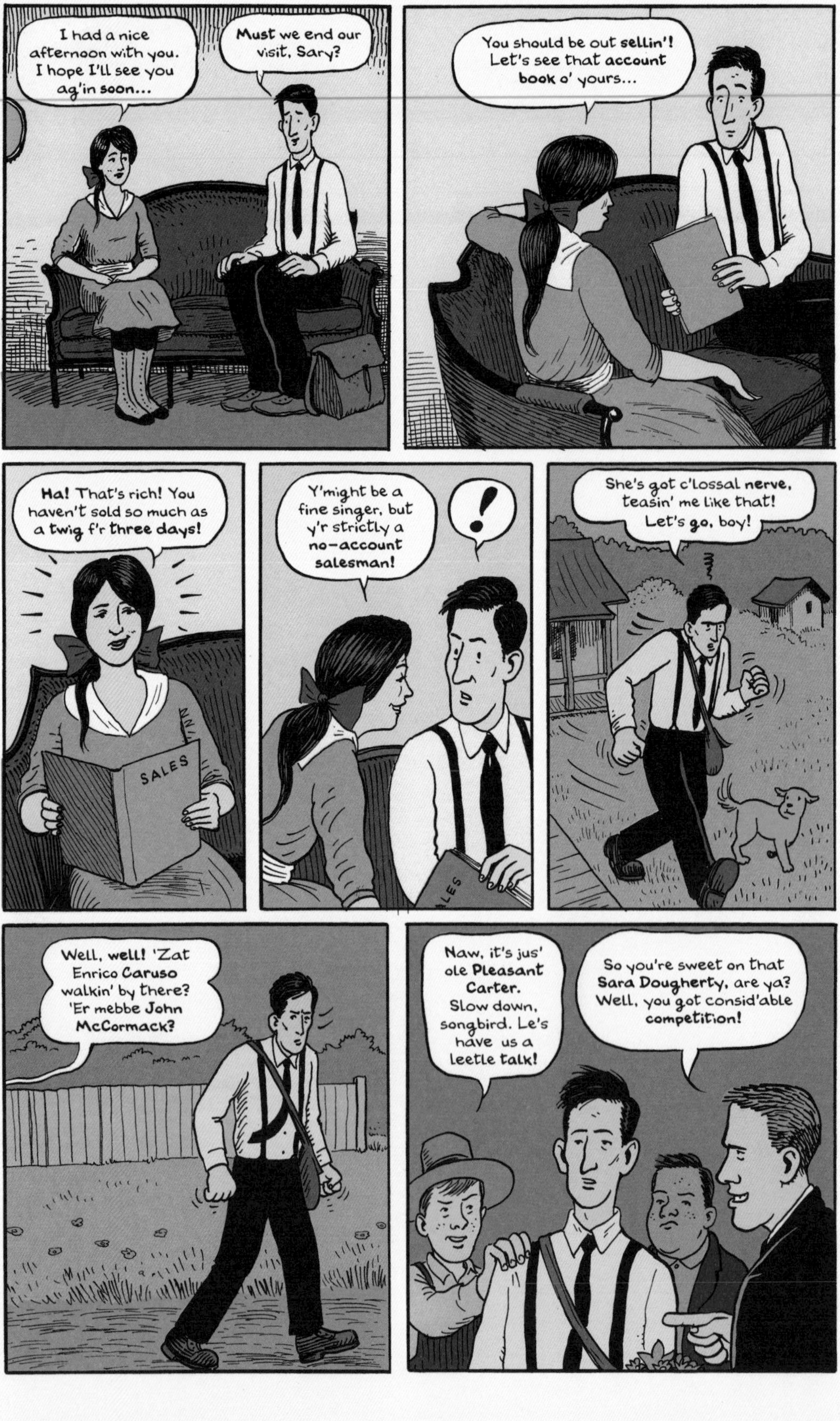

I had a nice afternoon with you. I hope I'll see you ag'in soon...
Must we end our visit, Sary?
You should be out sellin'! Let's see that account book o' yours...
Ha! That's rich! You haven't sold so much as a twig f'r three days!
SALES
Y'might be a fine singer, but y'r strictly a no-account salesman!
!
She's got c'lossal nerve, teasin' me like that! Let's go, boy!
Well, well! 'Zat Enrico Caruso walkin' by there? 'Er mebbe John McCormack?
Naw, it's jus' ole Pleasant Carter. Slow down, songbird. Le's have us a leetle talk!
So you're sweet on that Sara Dougherty, are ya? Well, you got consid'able competition!

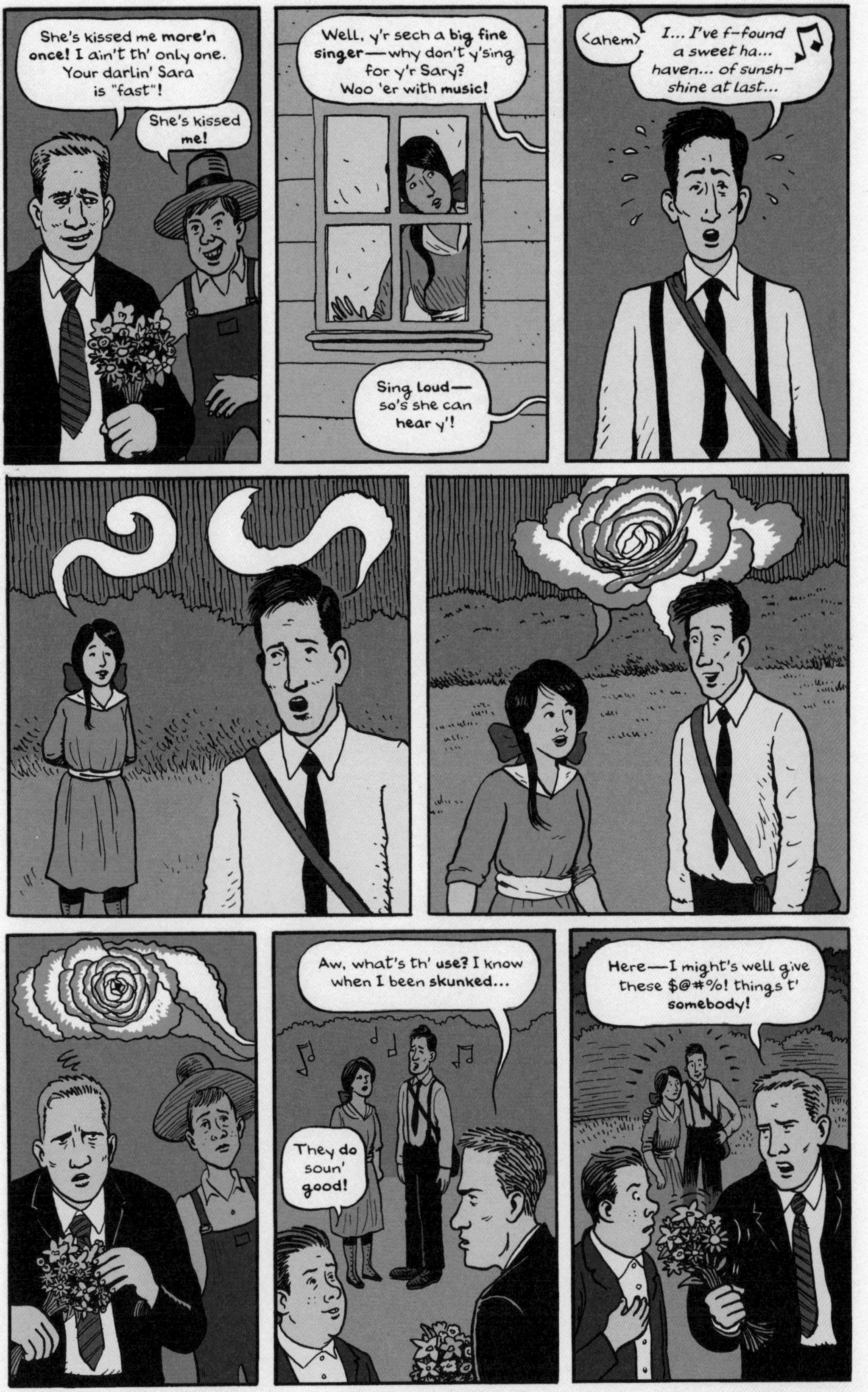
She's kissed me more'n once! I ain't th' only one. Your darlin' Sara is "fast"!
She's kissed me!
Well, y'r sech a big fine singer—why don't y'sing for y'r Sary? Woo 'er with music!
Sing loud—so's she can hear y'!
<ahem>
I... I've f-found a sweet ha... haven... of sunsh-shine at last...
Aw, what's th' use? I know when I been skunked...
They do soun' good!
Here—I might's well give these $@#%! things t' somebody!

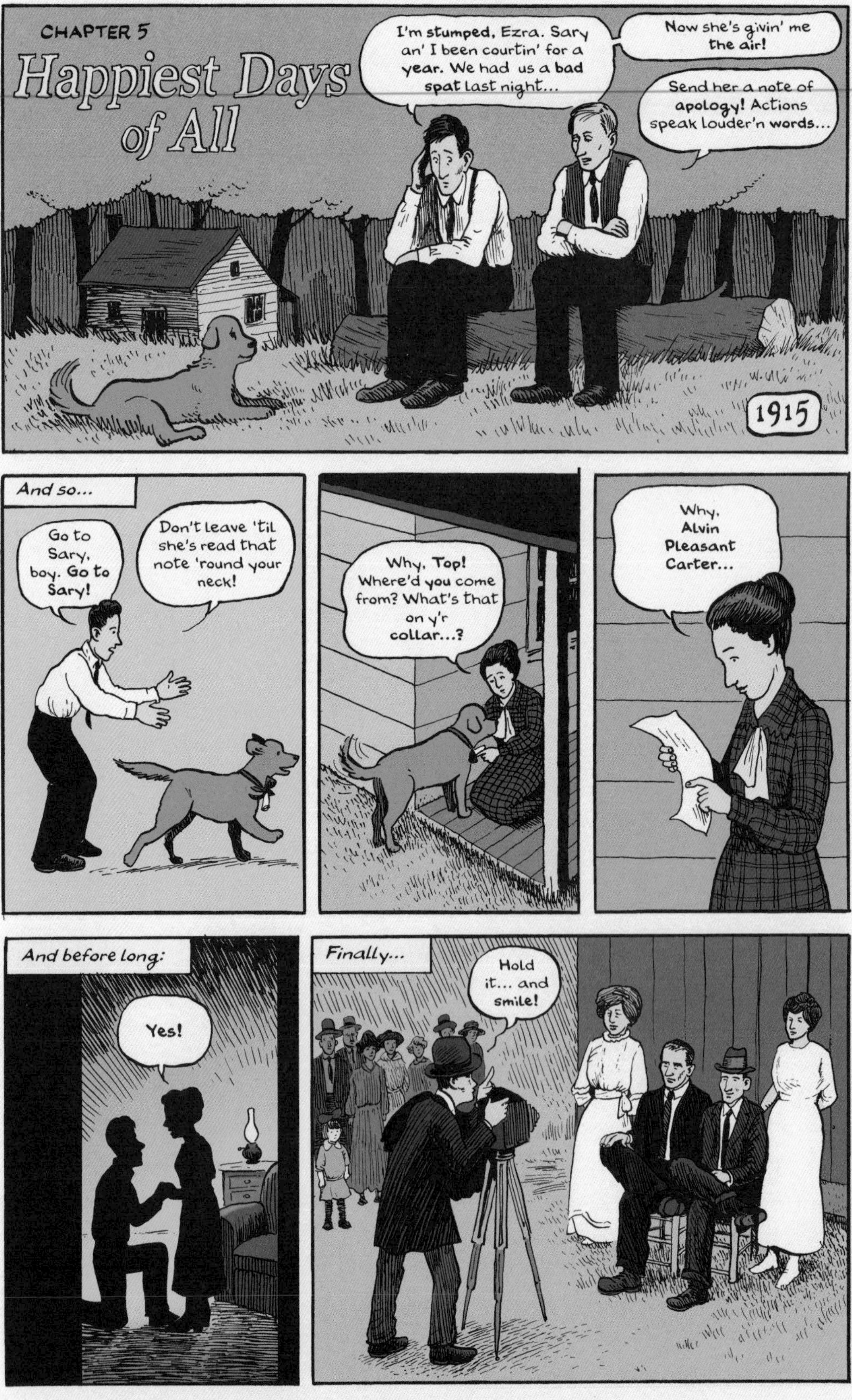
CHAPTER 5
Happiest Days of All
I'm stumped, Ezra. Sary an' I been courtin' for a year. We had us a bad spat last night...
Now she's givin' me the air!
Send her a note of apology! Actions speak louder'n words...
1915
And so...
Go to Sary, boy. Go to Sary!
Don't leave 'til she's read that note 'round your neck!
Why, Top! Where'd you come from? What's that on y'r collar...?
Why, Alvin Pleasant Carter...
And before long:
Yes!
Finally...
Hold it... and smile!

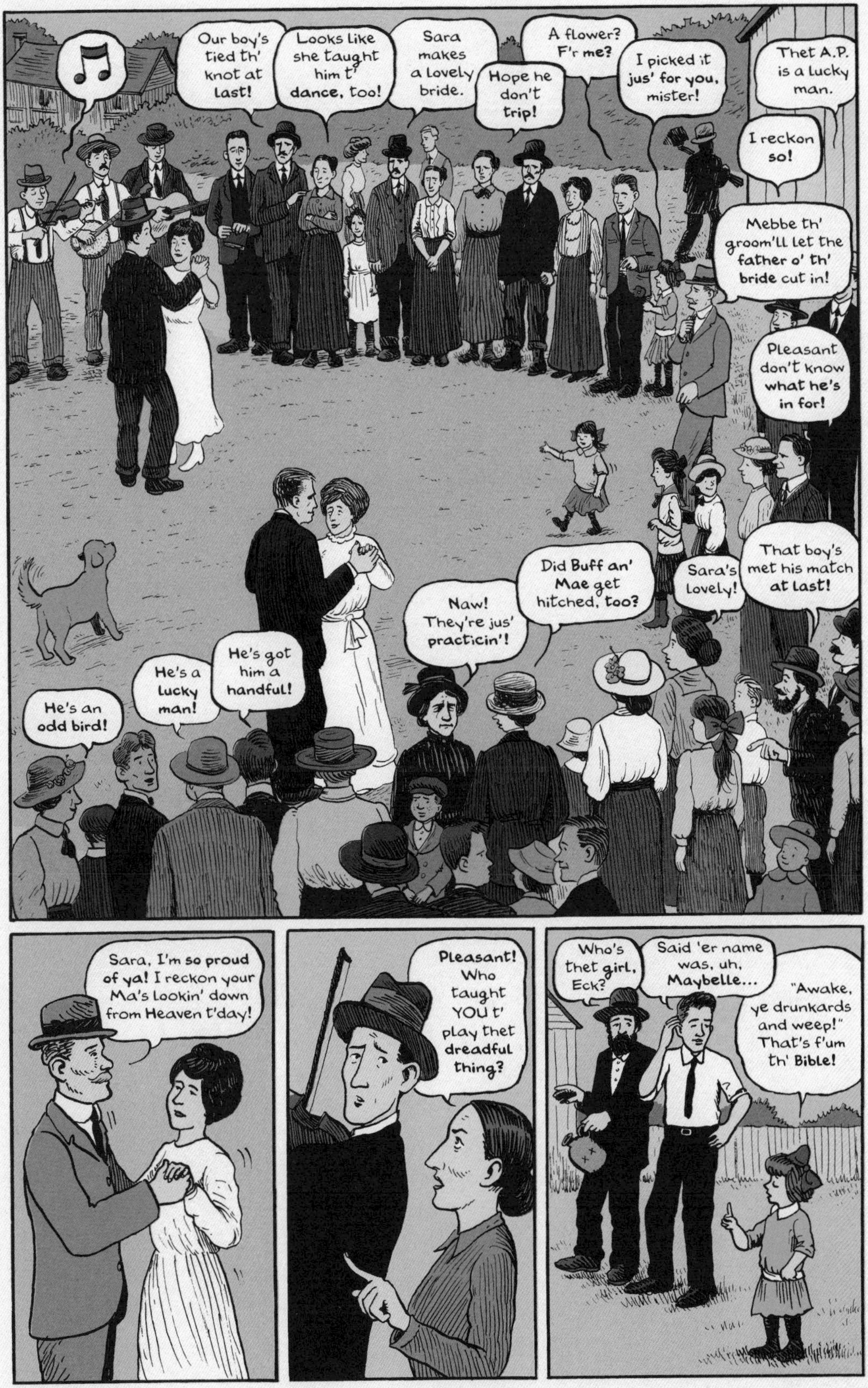
Our boy's tied th' knot at last!
Looks like she taught him t' dance, too!
Sara makes a lovely bride.
Hope he don't trip!
A flower? F'r me?
I picked it jus' for you, mister!
Thet A.P. is a lucky man.
I reckon so!
Mebbe th' groom'll let the father o' th' bride cut in!
Pleasant don't know what he's in for!
That boy's met his match at last!
Sara's lovely!
Did Buff an' Mae get hitched, too?
Naw! They're jus' practicin'!
He's got him a handful!
He's a lucky man!
He's an odd bird!
Sara, I'm so proud of ya! I reckon your Ma's lookin' down from Heaven t'day!
Pleasant! Who taught YOU t' play thet dreadful thing?
Who's thet girl, Eck?
Said 'er name was, uh, Maybelle...
"Awake, ye drunkards and weep!" That's f'um th' Bible!

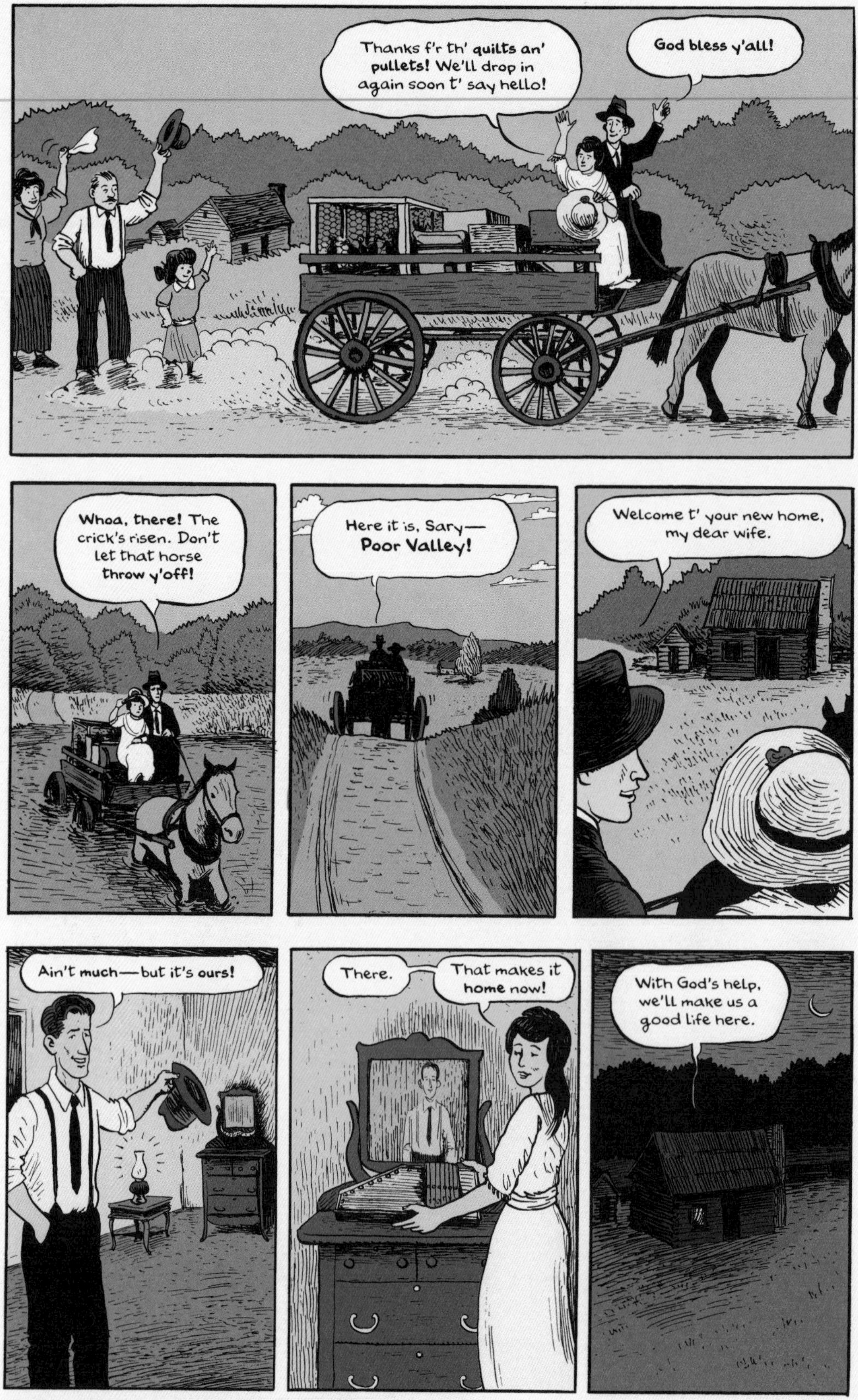
Thanks f'r th' quilts an' pullets! We'll drop in again soon t' say hello!
God bless y'all!
Whoa, there! The crick's risen. Don't let that horse throw y'off!
Here it is, Sary— Poor Valley!
Welcome t' your new home, my dear wife.
Ain't much—but it's ours!
There.
That makes it home now!
With God's help, we'll make us a good life here.

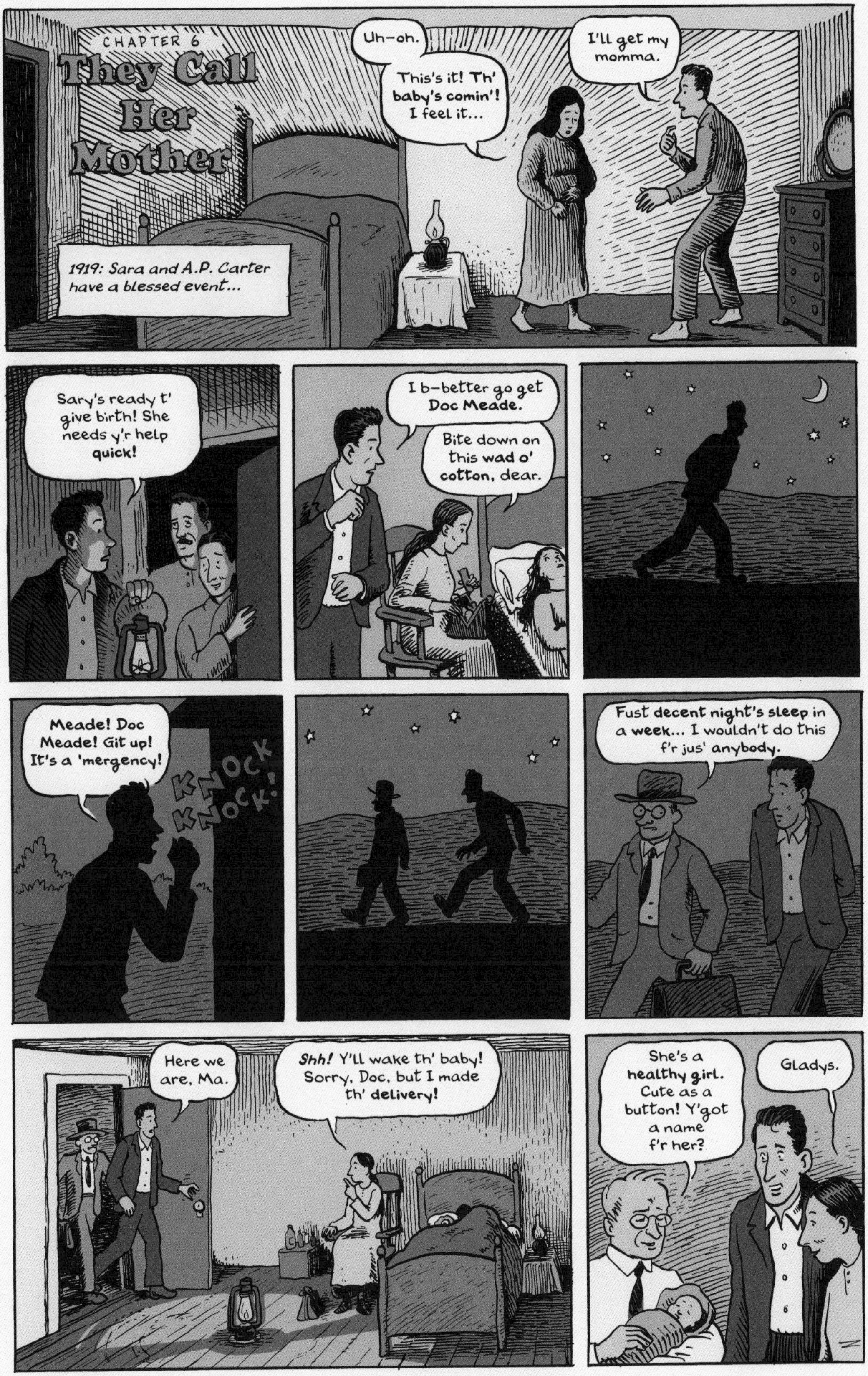
CHAPTER 6
They Call Her Mother
1919: Sara and A.P. Carter have a blessed event...
Uh-oh.
This's it! Th' baby's comin'! I feel it...
I'll get my momma.
Sary's ready t' give birth! She needs y'r help quick!
I b-better go get Doc Meade.
Bite down on this wad o' cotton, dear.
Meade! Doc Meade! Git up! It's a 'mergency!
KNOCK KNOCK!
Fust decent night's sleep in a week... I wouldn't do this f'r jus' anybody.
Here we are, Ma.
Shh! Y'll wake th' baby! Sorry, Doc, but I made th' delivery!
She's a healthy girl. Cute as a button! Y'got a name f'r her?
Gladys.

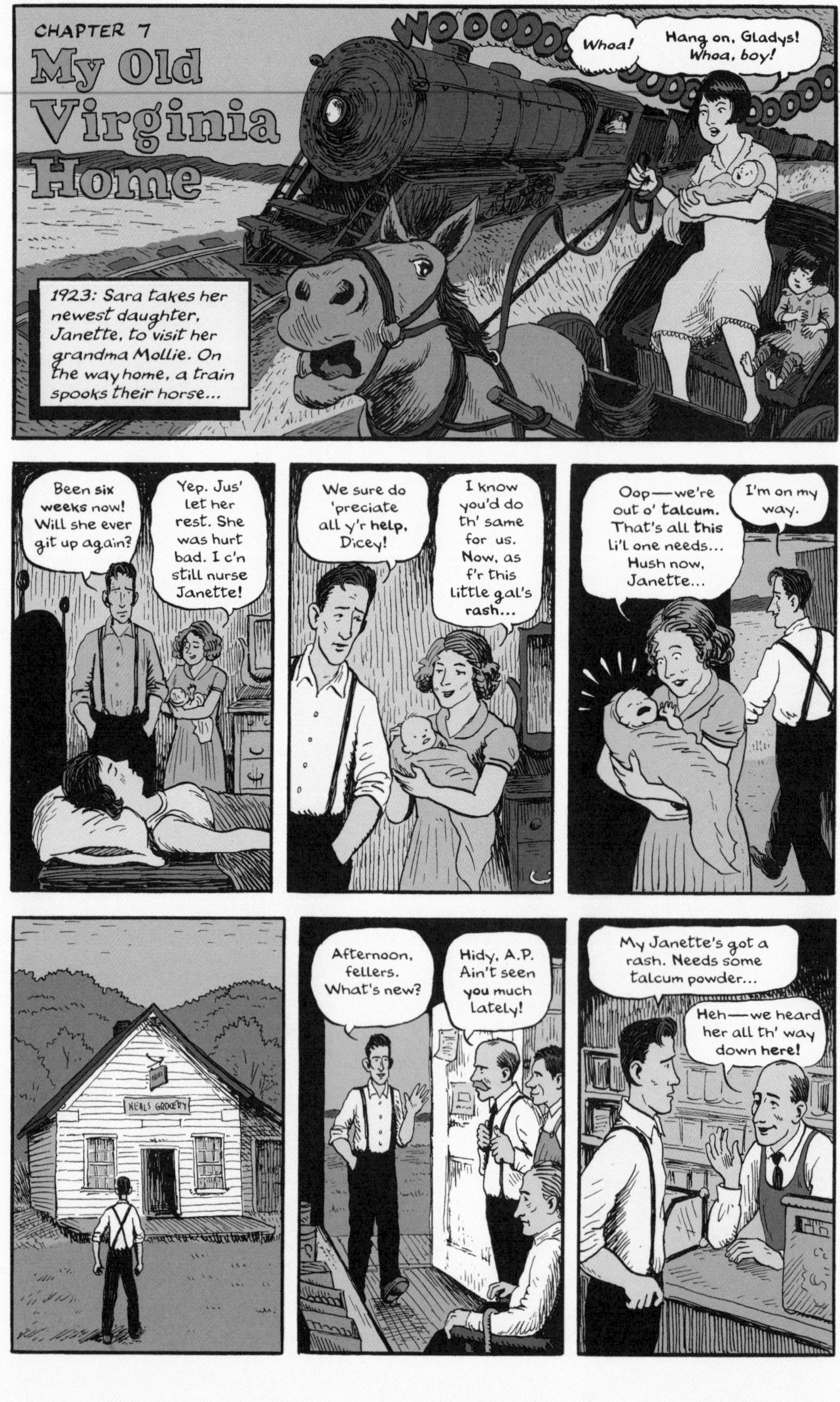
CHAPTER 7
My Old Virginia Home
WOOOOOOO
Whoa!
Hang on, Gladys! Whoa, boy!
1923: Sara takes her newest daughter, Janette, to visit her grandma Mollie. On the way home, a train spooks their horse...
Been six weeks now! Will she ever git up again?
Yep. Jus' let her rest. She was hurt bad. I c'n still nurse Janette!
We sure do 'preciate all y'r help, Dicey!
I know you'd do th' same for us. Now, as f'r this little gal's rash...
Oop—we're out o' talcum. That's all this li'l one needs... Hush now, Janette...
I'm on my way.
NEALS GROCERY
Afternoon, fellers. What's new?
Hidy, A.P. Ain't seen you much lately!
My Janette's got a rash. Needs some talcum powder...
Heh—we heard her all th' way down here!

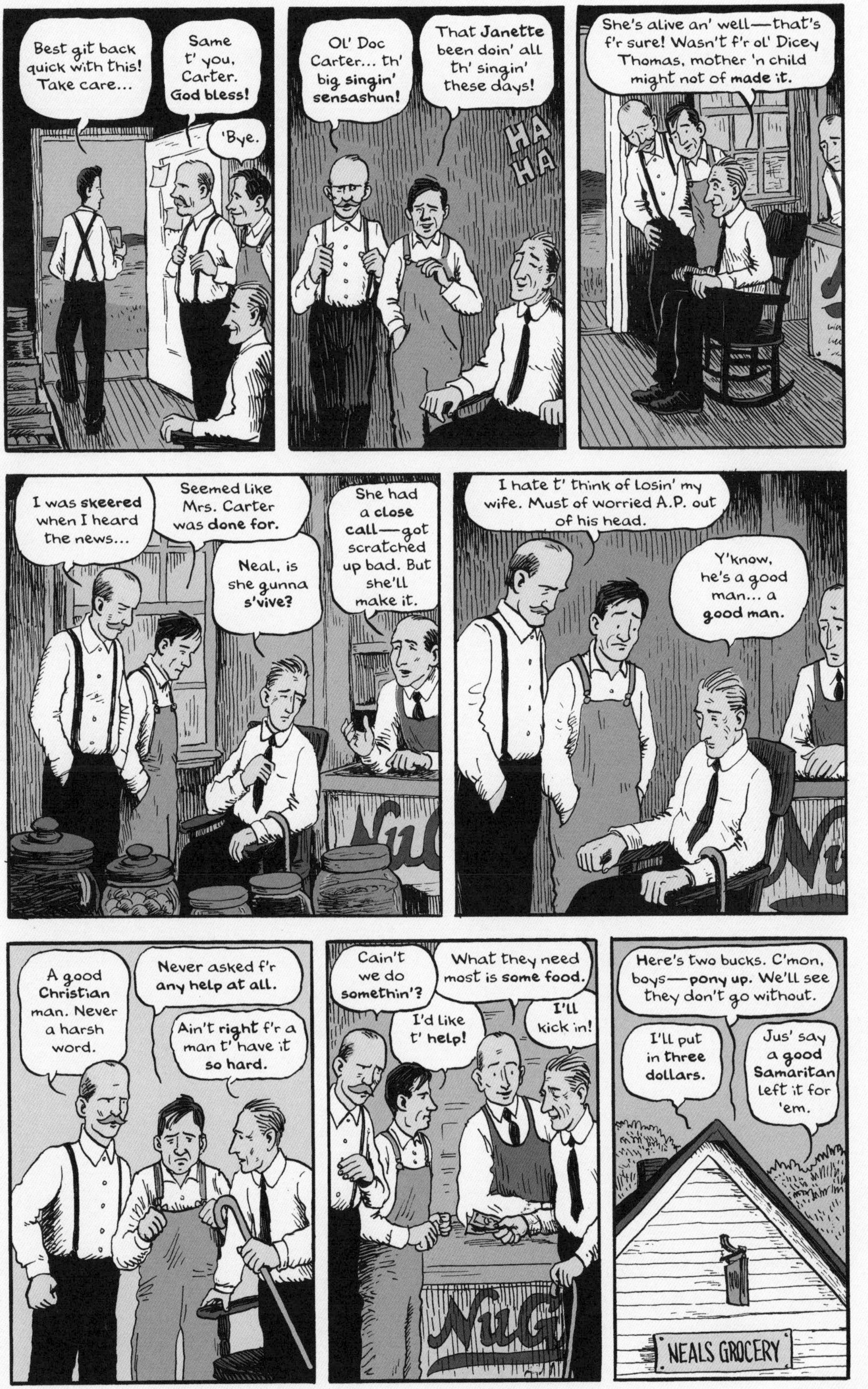
Best git back quick with this! Take care...
Same t' you, Carter. God bless!
'Bye.
Ol' Doc Carter... th' big singin' sensashun!
That Janette been doin' all th' singin' these days!
HA HA
She's alive an' well—that's f'r sure! Wasn't f'r ol' Dicey Thomas, mother 'n child might not of made it.
I was skeered when I heard the news...
Seemed like Mrs. Carter was done for.
Neal, is she gunna s'vive?
She had a close call—got scratched up bad. But she'll make it.
I hate t' think of losin' my wife. Must of worried A.P. out of his head.
Y'know, he's a good man... a good man.
A good Christian man. Never a harsh word.
Never asked f'r any help at all.
Ain't right f'r a man t' have it so hard.
Cain't we do somethin'?
What they need most is some food.
I'd like t' help!
I'll kick in!
Here's two bucks. C'mon, boys—pony up. We'll see they don't go without.
I'll put in three dollars.
Jus' say a good Samaritan left it for 'em.
NEALS GROCERY

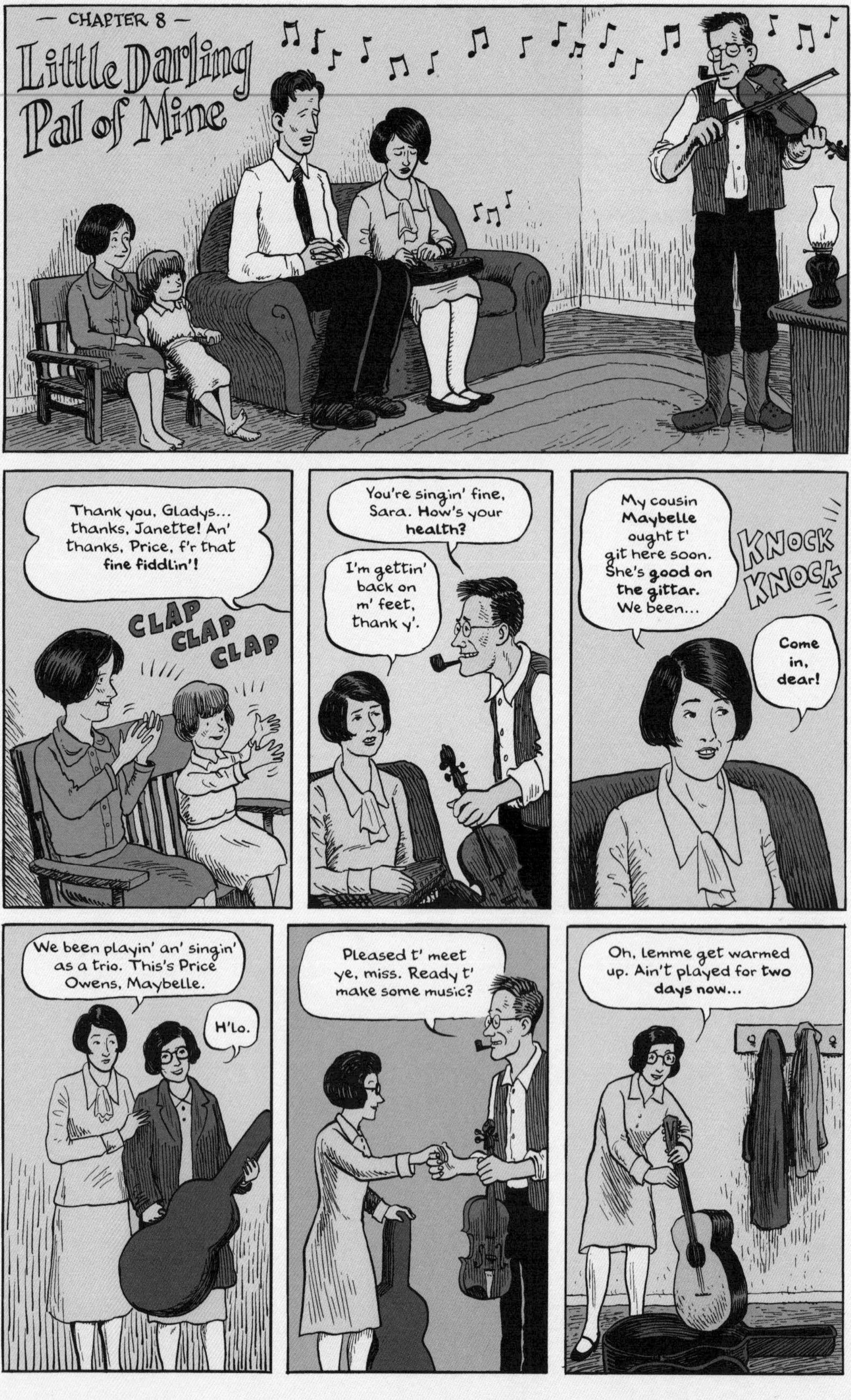
— CHAPTER 8 —
Little Darling Pal of Mine
Thank you, Gladys... thanks, Janette! An' thanks, Price, f'r that fine fiddlin'!
CLAP CLAP CLAP
You're singin' fine, Sara. How's your health?
I'm gettin' back on m' feet, thank y'.
My cousin Maybelle ought t' git here soon. She's good on the gittar. We been...
KNOCK KNOCK
Come in, dear!
We been playin' an' singin' as a trio. This's Price Owens, Maybelle.
H'lo.
Pleased t' meet ye, miss. Ready t' make some music?
Oh, lemme get warmed up. Ain't played for two days now...

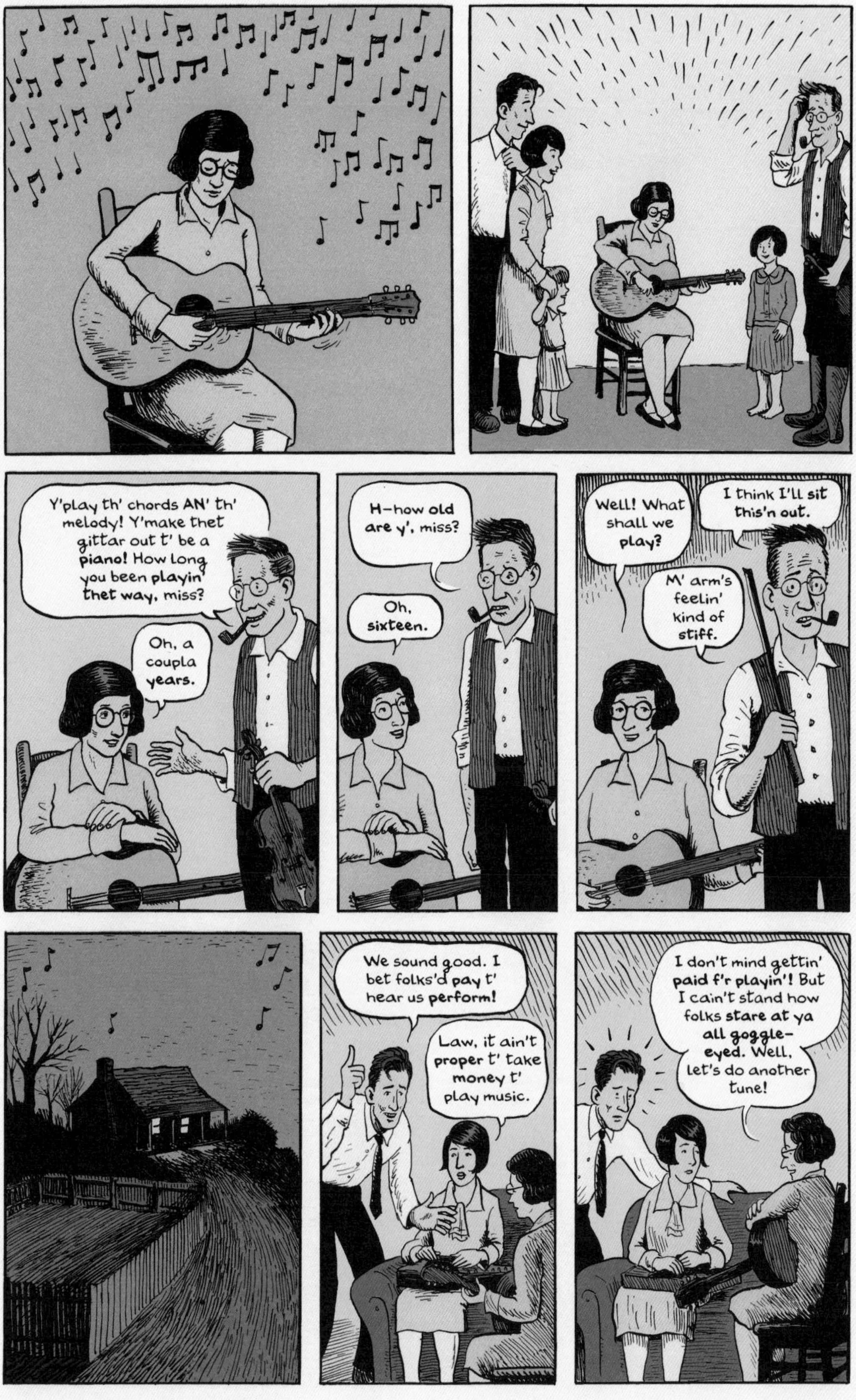
Y'play th' chords AN' th' melody! Y'make thet gittar out t' be a piano! How long you been playin thet way, miss?
Oh, a coupla years.
H—how old are y', miss?
Oh, sixteen.
Well! What shall we play?
I think I'll sit this'n out.
M' arm's feelin' kind of stiff.
We sound good. I bet folks'd pay t' hear us perform!
Law, it ain't proper t' take money t' play music.
I don't mind gettin' paid f'r playin'! But I cain't stand how folks stare at ya all goggle-eyed. Well, let's do another tune!

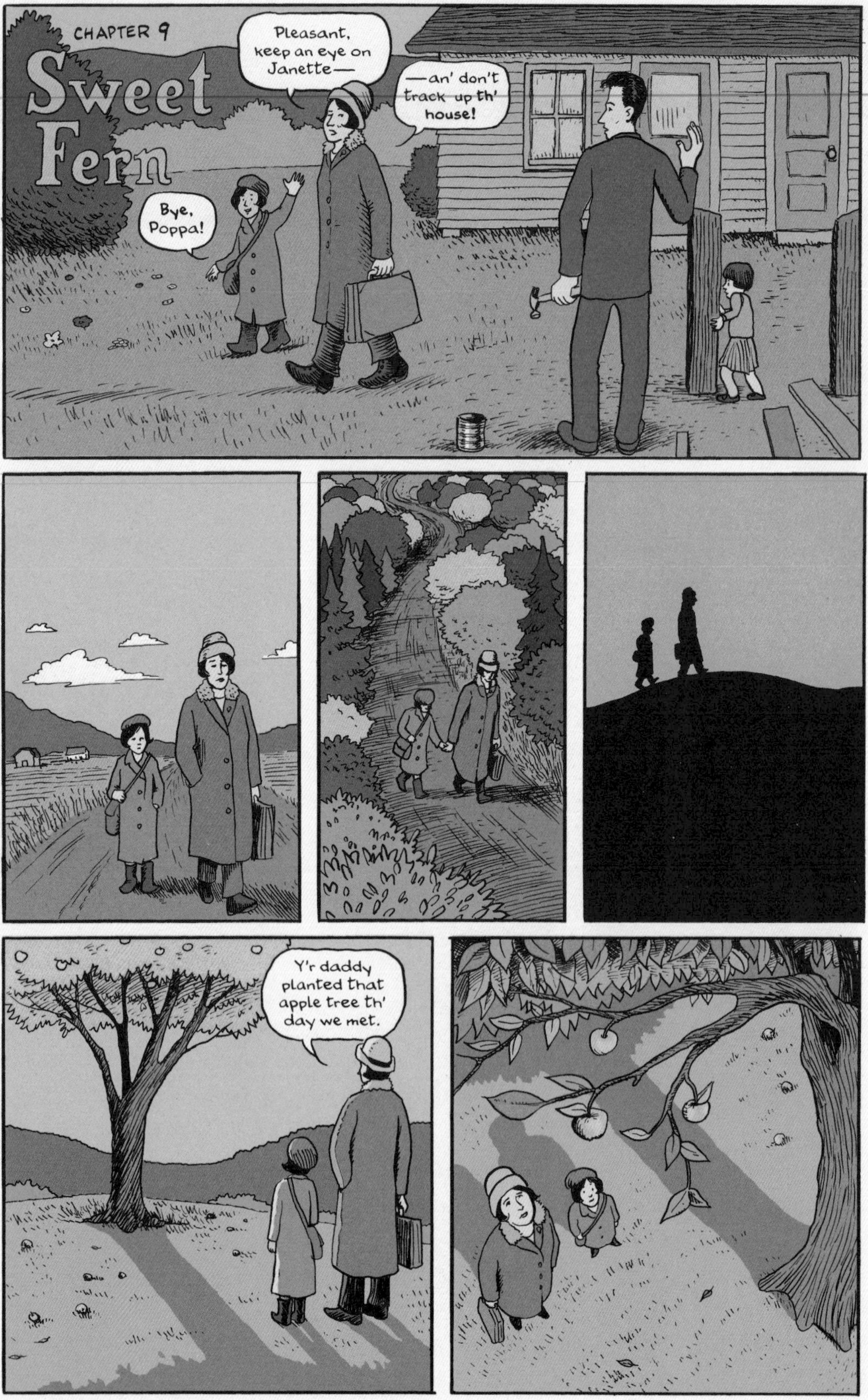
CHAPTER 9
Sweet Fern
Pleasant, keep an eye on Janette—
—an' don't track up th' house!
Bye, Poppa!
Y'r daddy planted that apple tree th' day we met.

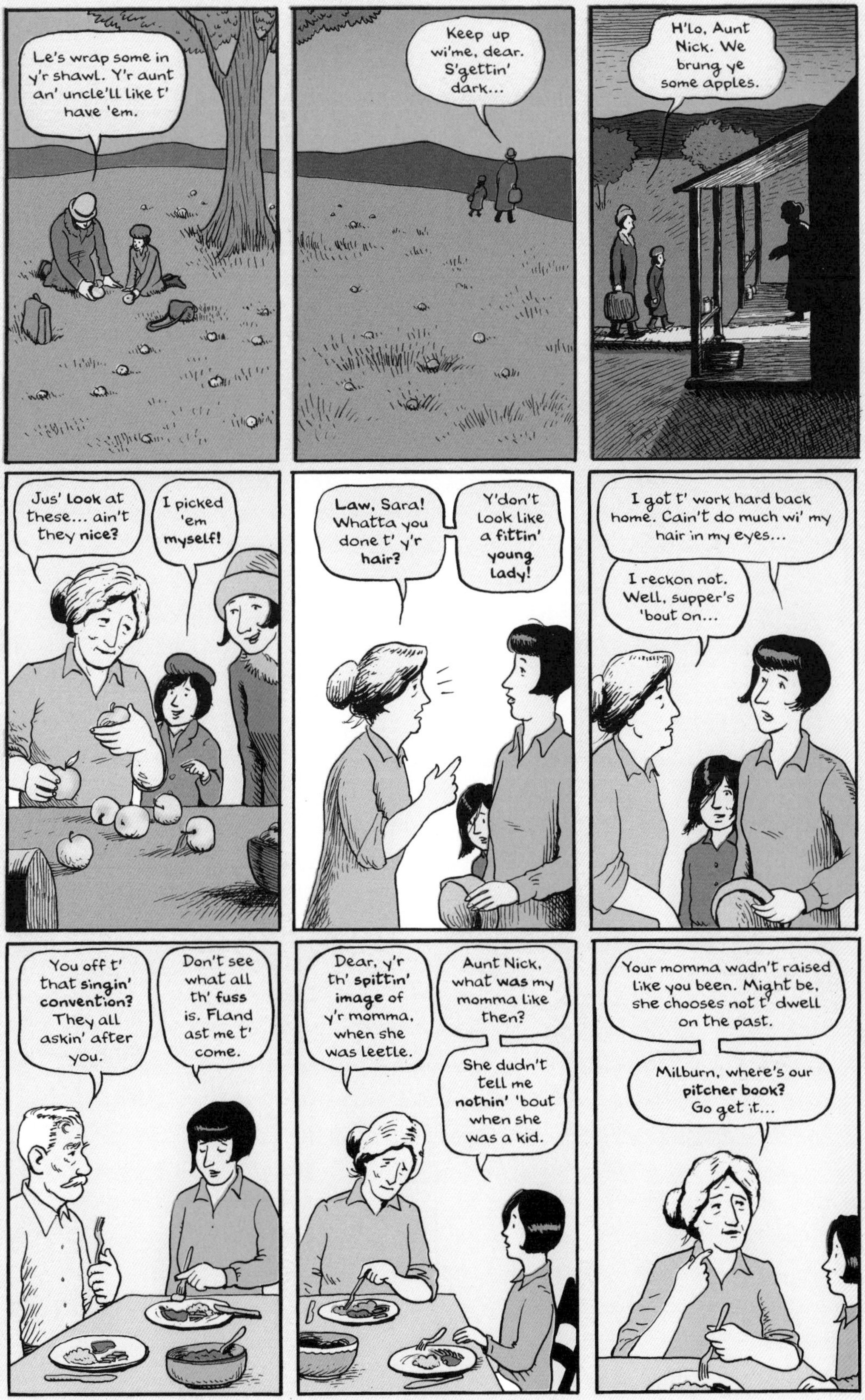
Le's wrap some in y'r shawl. Y'r aunt an' uncle'll like t' have 'em.
Keep up wi'me, dear. S'gettin' dark...
H'lo, Aunt Nick. We brung ye some apples.
Jus' look at these... ain't they nice?
I picked 'em myself!
Law, Sara! Whatta you done t' y'r hair?
Y'don't look like a fittin' young lady!
I got t' work hard back home. Cain't do much wi' my hair in my eyes...
I reckon not. Well, supper's 'bout on...
You off t' that singin' convention? They all askin' after you.
Don't see what all th' fuss is. Fland ast me t' come.
Dear, y'r th' spittin' image of y'r momma, when she was leetle.
Aunt Nick, what was my momma like then?
She dudn't tell me nothin' 'bout when she was a kid.
Your momma wadn't raised like you been. Might be, she chooses not t' dwell on the past.
Milburn, where's our pitcher book? Go get it...

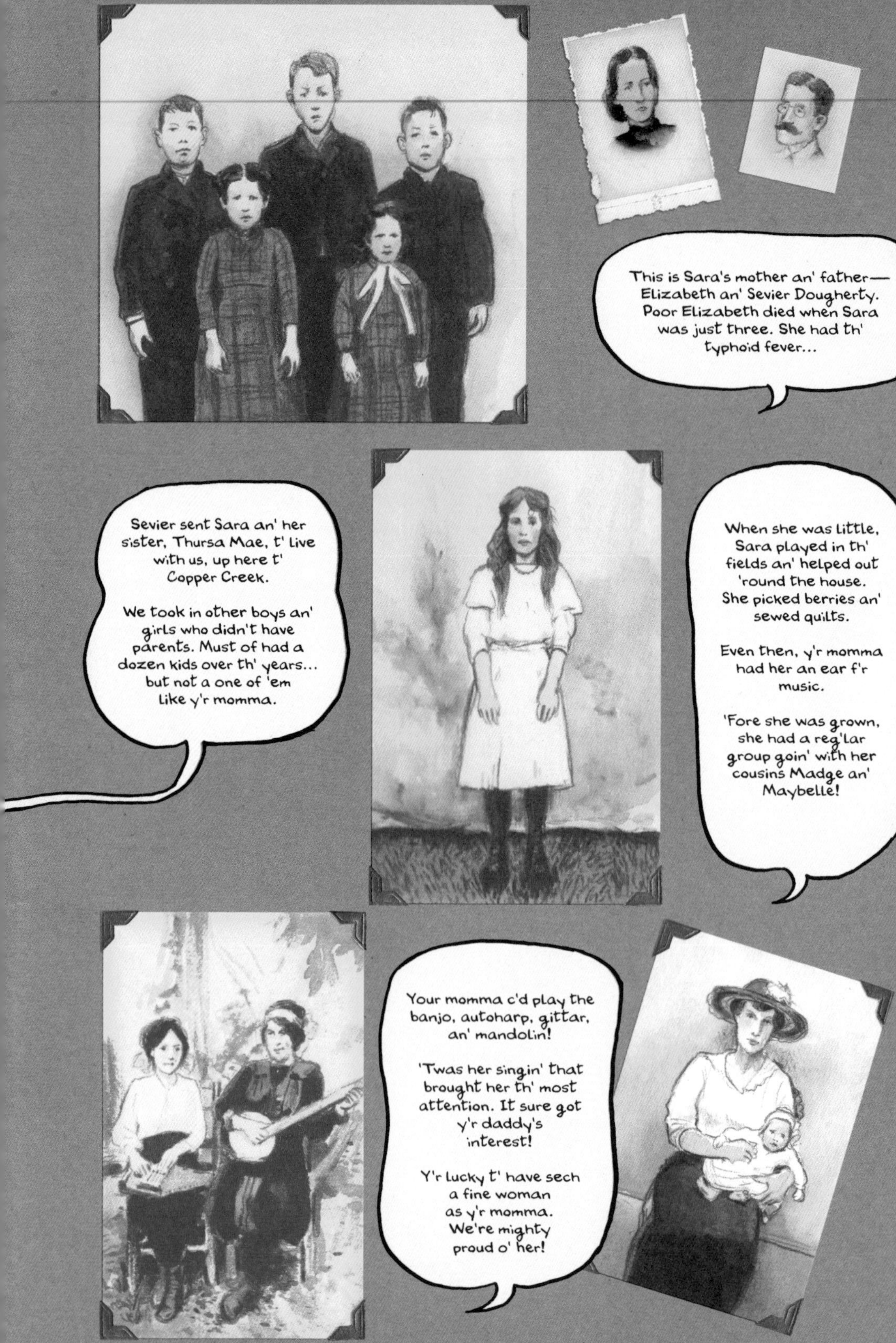
This is Sara's mother an' father— Elizabeth an' Sevier Dougherty. Poor Elizabeth died when Sara was just three. She had th' typhoid fever...
Sevier sent Sara an' her sister, Thursa Mae, t' live with us, up here t' Copper Creek.
We took in other boys an' girls who didn't have parents. Must of had a dozen kids over th' years... but not a one of 'em like y'r momma.
When she was little, Sara played in th' fields an' helped out 'round the house. She picked berries an' sewed quilts.
Even then, y'r momma had her an ear f'r music.
'Fore she was grown, she had a reg'lar group goin' with her cousins Madge an' Maybelle!
Your momma c'd play the banjo, autoharp, gittar, an' mandolin!
'Twas her singin' that brought her th' most attention. It sure got y'r daddy's interest!
Y'r lucky t' have sech a fine woman as y'r momma. We're mighty proud o' her!

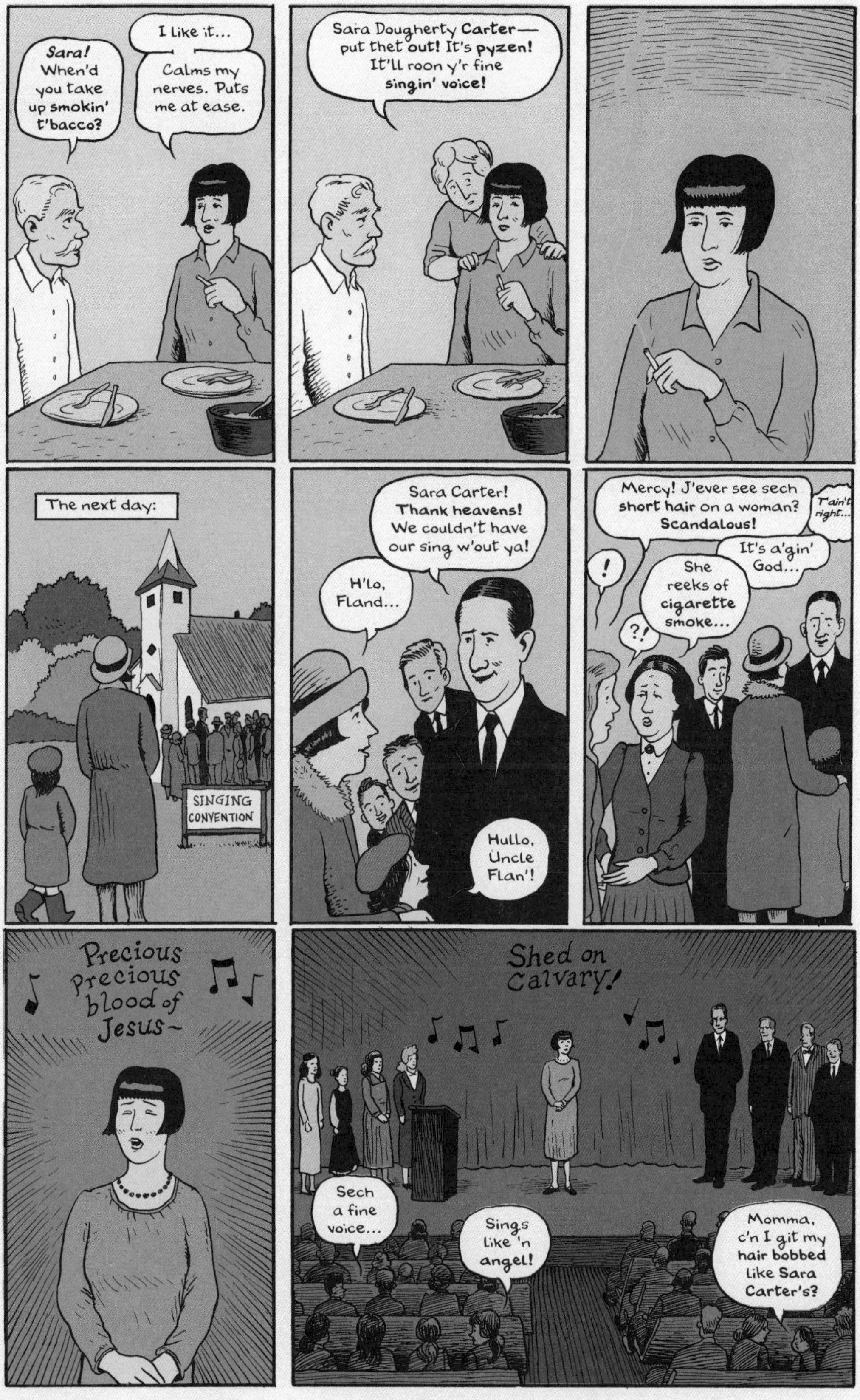
Sara! When'd you take up smokin' t'bacco?
I like it...
Calms my nerves. Puts me at ease.
Sara Dougherty Carter— put thet out! It's pyzen! It'll roon y'r fine singin' voice!
The next day:
SINGING CONVENTION
Sara Carter! Thank heavens! We couldn't have our sing w'out ya!
H'lo, Fland...
Hullo, Uncle Flan'!
Mercy! J'ever see sech short hair on a woman? Scandalous!
T'ain't right...
It's a'gin' God...
!
She reeks of cigarette smoke...
?!
Precious precious blood of Jesus~
Shed on Calvary!
Sech a fine voice...
Sings like 'n angel!
Momma, c'n I git my hair bobbed like Sara Carter's?

CHAPTER 10

The Birds Were Singing of You

We're in f'r it **now**! Eck's car is **busted**, an' so are we! We gotta raise some cash, **quick**! What c'n we do?

All I know t'do is sing, Pleasant. Sing an' raise our children...

Outside of Charlottesville, A.P. and Sara have car trouble...

...Rev'rind, we're good Christians. We sing th' ol' hymns an' spirituals. C'n we get y'r blessin' t' do a singin' show t'night?

Tell Miss Higgins it's fine with me.

...we put on a clean show. We're in a jam, an' we need t' raise some cash...

You're welcome to use th' school-house, sech as it is...

C'd you tell y'r customers? Th' show's in th' school-house. It starts at 7 P.M.

Doubt y'll draw a crowd on sech short notice... but good luck.

DRINK NuGra

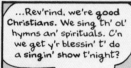 

♪ *Anchored in love divine...*

Sary! We got enough money t' fix th' car—an' money t' spare!

An' the hand you got at th' end—y' went over like wildfire!

Law! They was just bein' polite.

No, ma'am! Ain't no one else sings like you, Sary! Y'r one in a million!

Aw, pshaw!

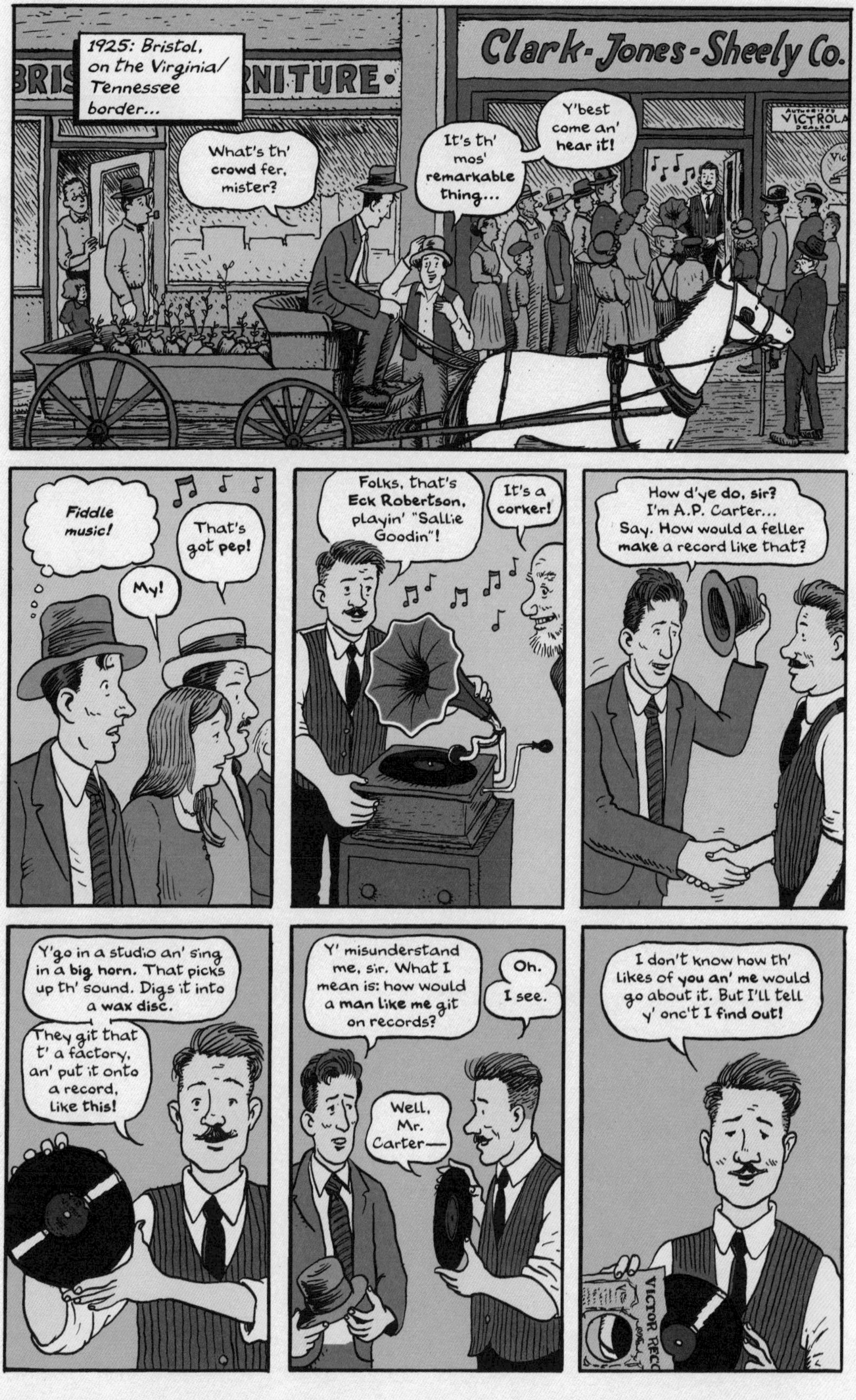
1925: Bristol, on the Virginia/ Tennessee border...
BRIS NITURE
Clark-Jones-Sheely Co.
VICTROLA
What's th' crowd fer, mister?
It's th' mos' remarkable thing...
Y'best come an' hear it!
Fiddle music!
My!
That's got pep!
Folks, that's Eck Robertson, playin' "Sallie Goodin"!
It's a corker!
How d'ye do, sir? I'm A.P. Carter... Say. How would a feller make a record like that?
Y'go in a studio an' sing in a big horn. That picks up th' sound. Digs it into a wax disc.
They git that t' a factory, an' put it onto a record, like this!
Y' misunderstand me, sir. What I mean is: how would a man like me git on records?
Oh. I see.
Well, Mr. Carter—
I don't know how th' likes of you an' me would go about it. But I'll tell y' onc't I find out!

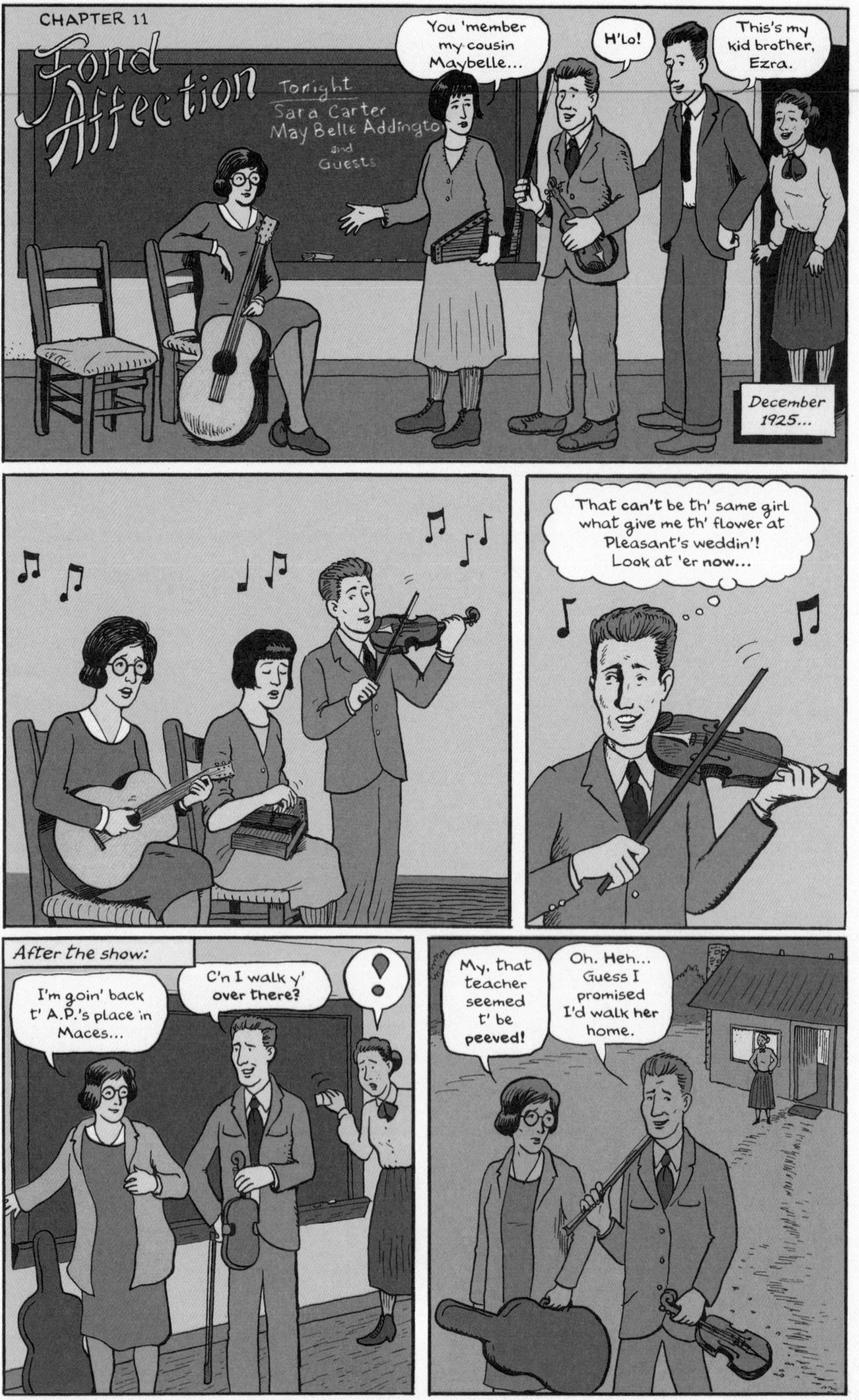
CHAPTER 11
Fond Affection
Tonight
Sara Carter
May Belle Addington
and
Guests
You 'member my cousin Maybelle...
H'lo!
This's my kid brother, Ezra.
December 1925...
That can't be th' same girl what give me th' flower at Pleasant's weddin'! Look at 'er now...
After the show:
I'm goin' back t' A.P.'s place in Maces...
C'n I walk y' over there?
My, that teacher seemed t' be peeved!
Oh. Heh... Guess I promised I'd walk her home.

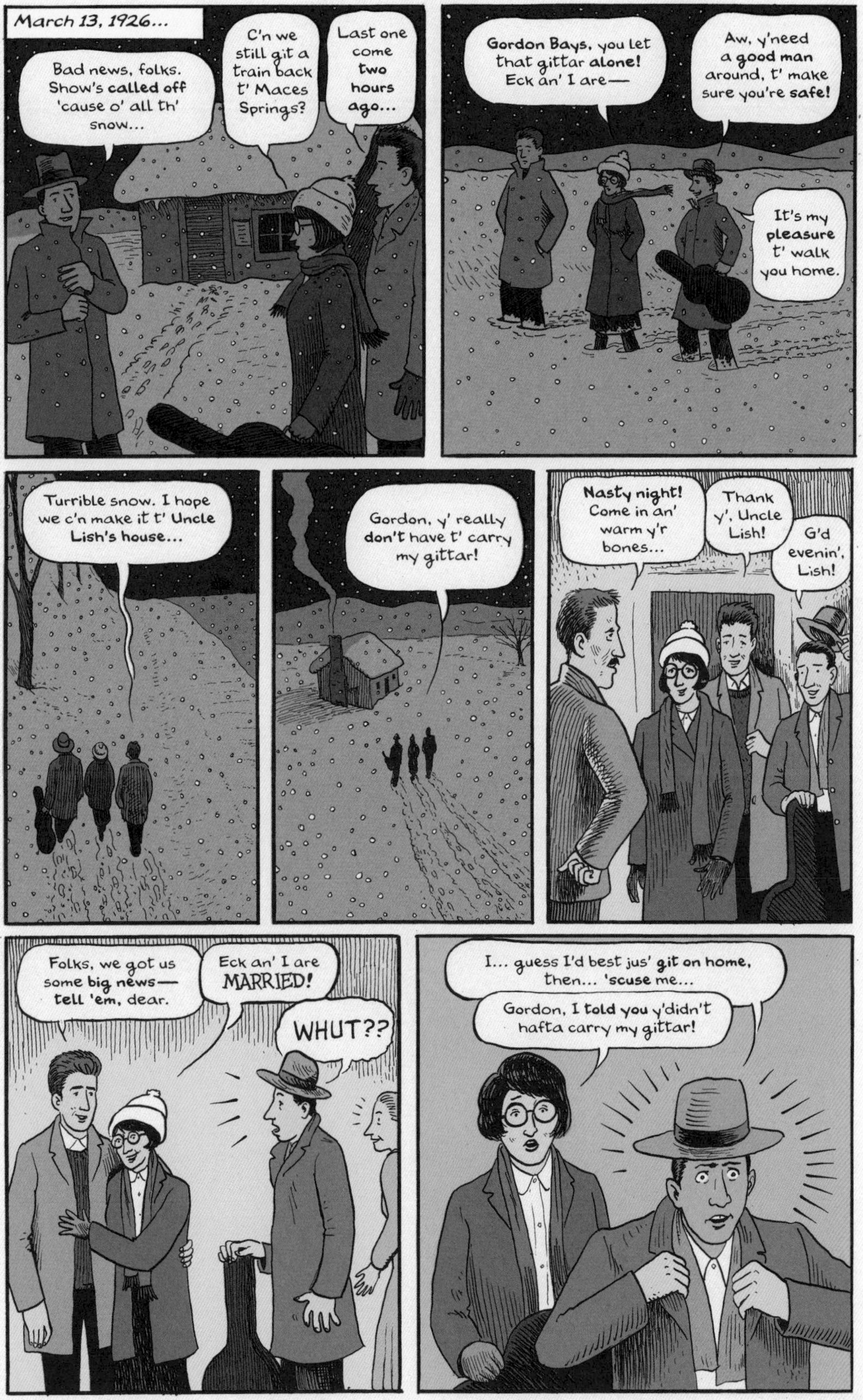
March 13, 1926...
Bad news, folks. Show's called off 'cause o' all th' snow...
C'n we still git a train back t' Maces Springs?
Last one come two hours ago...
Gordon Bays, you let that gittar alone! Eck an' I are—
Aw, y'need a good man around, t' make sure you're safe!
It's my pleasure t' walk you home.
Turrible snow. I hope we c'n make it t' Uncle Lish's house...
Gordon, y' really don't have t' carry my gittar!
Nasty night! Come in an' warm y'r bones...
Thank y', Uncle Lish!
G'd evenin', Lish!
Folks, we got us some big news— tell 'em, dear.
Eck an' I are MARRIED!
WHUT??
I... guess I'd best jus' git on home, then... 'scuse me...
Gordon, I told you y'didn't hafta carry my gittar!

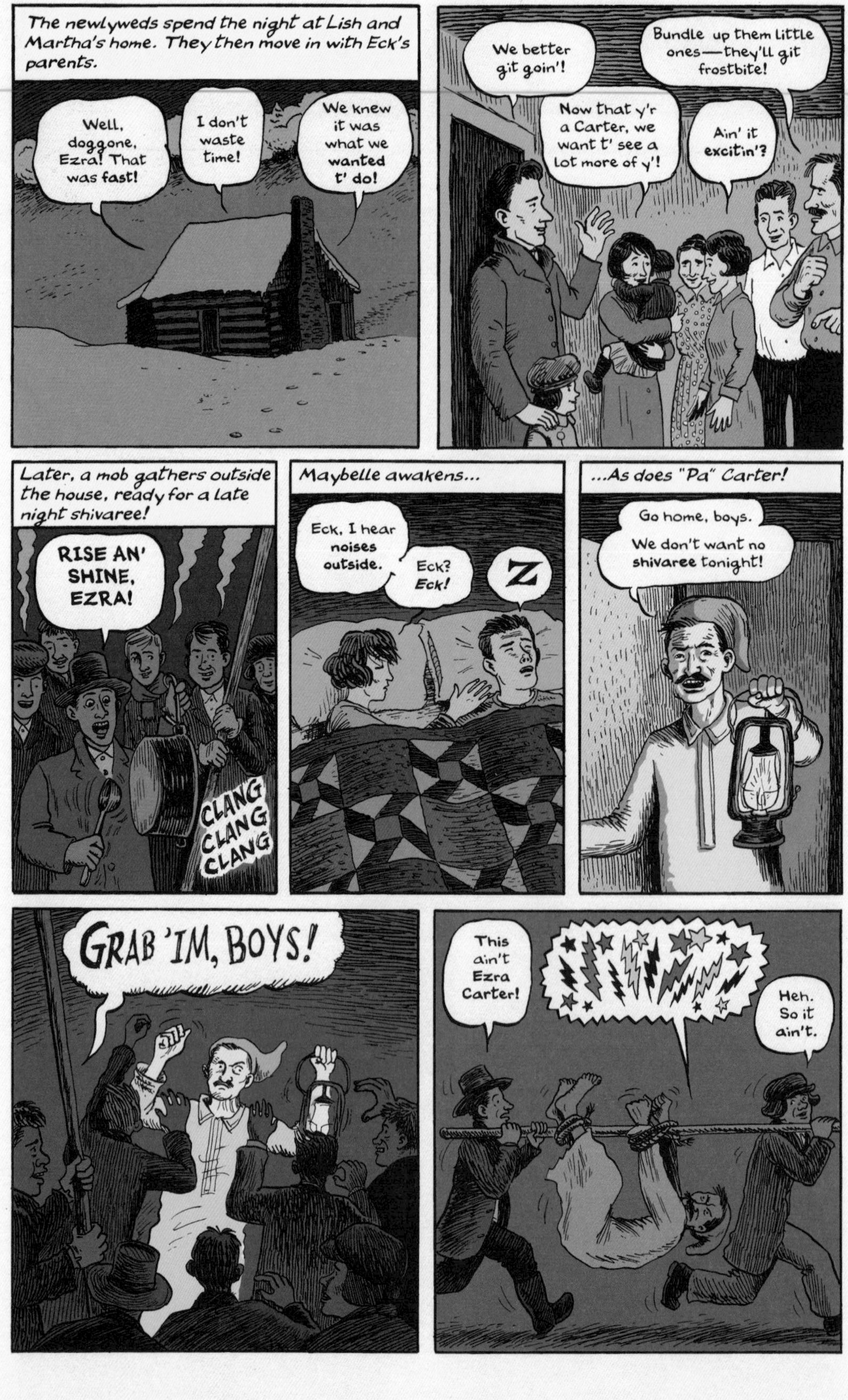
The newlyweds spend the night at Lish and Martha's home. They then move in with Eck's parents.
Well, doggone, Ezra! That was fast!
I don't waste time!
We knew it was what we wanted t' do!
We better git goin'!
Bundle up them little ones—they'll git frostbite!
Now that y'r a Carter, we want t' see a lot more of y'!
Ain' it excitin'?
Later, a mob gathers outside the house, ready for a late night shivaree!
RISE AN' SHINE, EZRA!
CLANG CLANG CLANG
Maybelle awakens...
Eck, I hear noises outside.
Eck? Eck!
Z
...As does "Pa" Carter!
Go home, boys.
We don't want no shivaree tonight!
GRAB 'IM, BOYS!
This ain't Ezra Carter!
Heh. So it ain't.

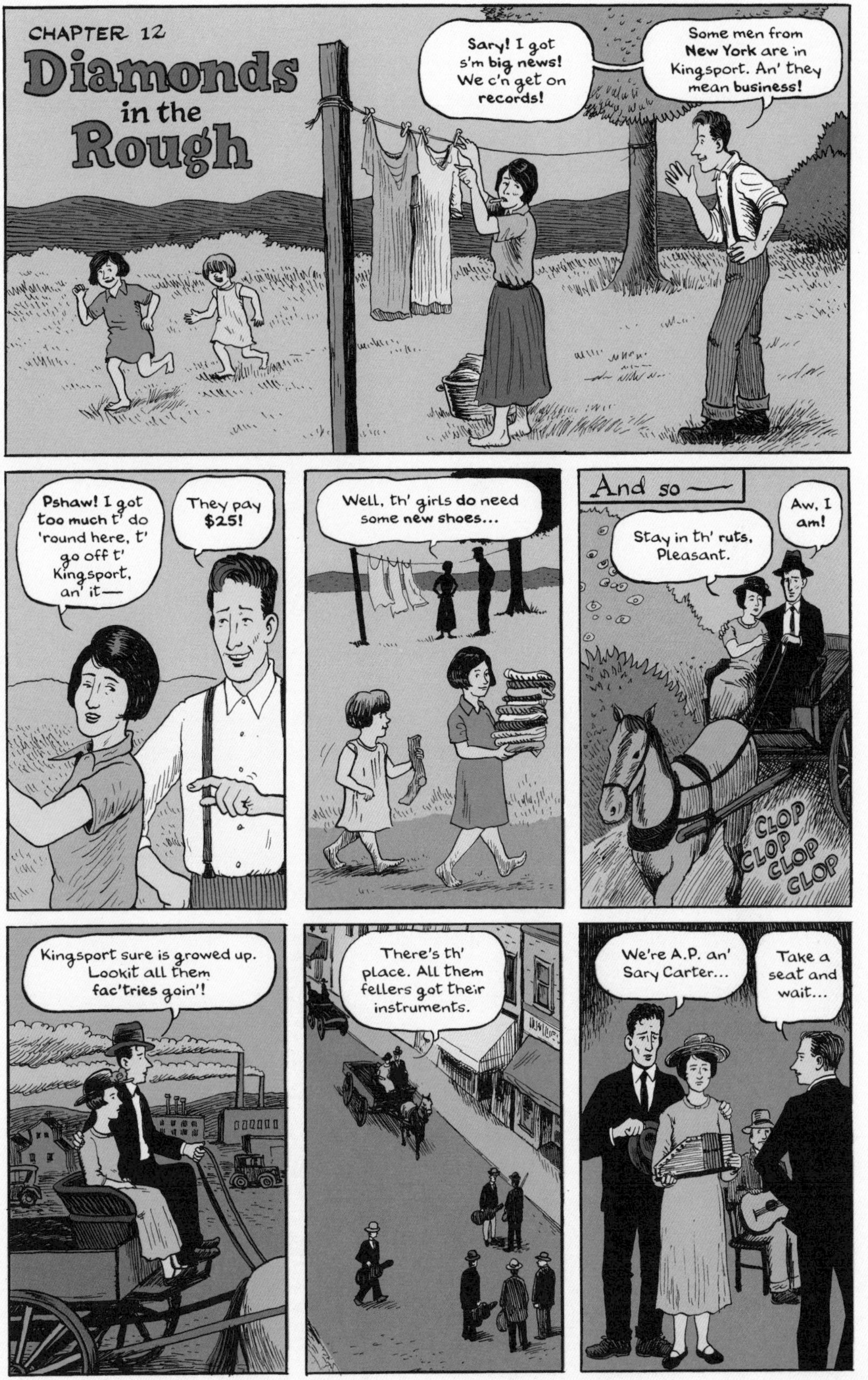
CHAPTER 12
Diamonds in the Rough
Sary! I got s'm big news! We c'n get on records!
Some men from New York are in Kingsport. An' they mean business!
Pshaw! I got too much t' do 'round here, t' go off t' Kingsport, an' it—
They pay $25!
Well, th' girls do need some new shoes...
And so—
Stay in th' ruts, Pleasant.
Aw, I am!
CLOP CLOP CLOP CLOP
Kingsport sure is growed up. Lookit all them fac'tries goin'!
There's th' place. All them fellers got their instruments.
We're A.P. an' Sary Carter...
Take a seat and wait...

That's Doc Carter. He's a **talented** fiddler. He's kinda shy, but...

Hmm... "Fiddlin' Doc Carter"! That'd look good on a record label. We can **sell** that!

Jenkins! Is Jenkins here?

Ri' cheer, mister!

Right this way, Mister Jenkins.

Wonder what's behind them curtains?

More curtains. An' some kinda horn s'posed t' take your voice.

Finally...

Carter! A.P. and Sara Carter!

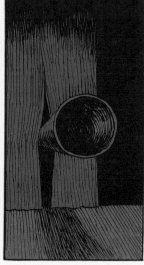

Right this way, folks. Don't be shy!

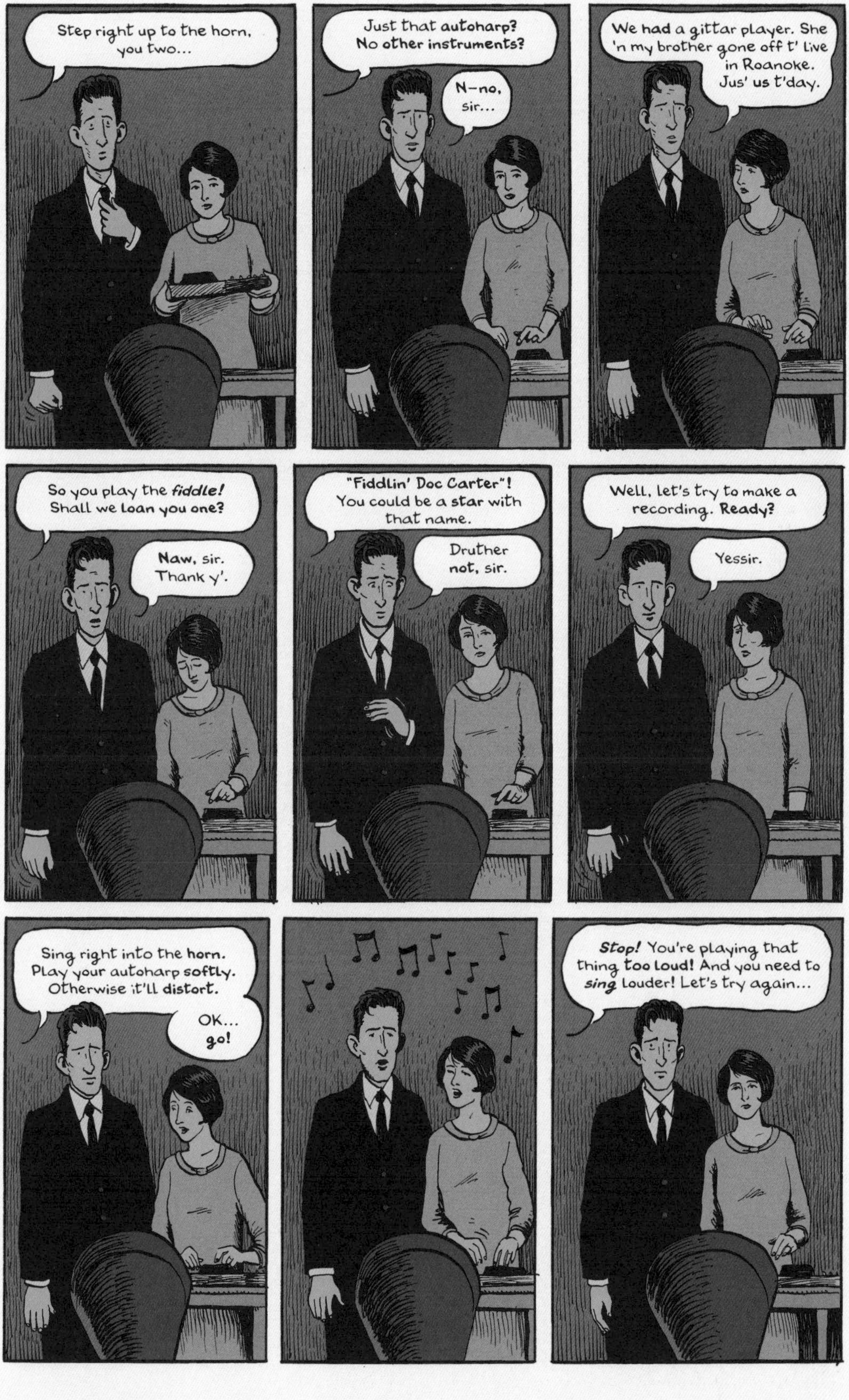
Step right up to the horn, you two...
Just that autoharp? No other instruments?
N–no, sir...
We had a gittar player. She 'n my brother gone off t' live in Roanoke. Jus' us t'day.
So you play the fiddle! Shall we loan you one?
Naw, sir. Thank y'.
"Fiddlin' Doc Carter"! You could be a star with that name.
Druther not, sir.
Well, let's try to make a recording. Ready?
Yessir.
Sing right into the horn. Play your autoharp softly. Otherwise it'll distort.
OK... go!
Stop! You're playing that thing too loud! And you need to sing louder! Let's try again...

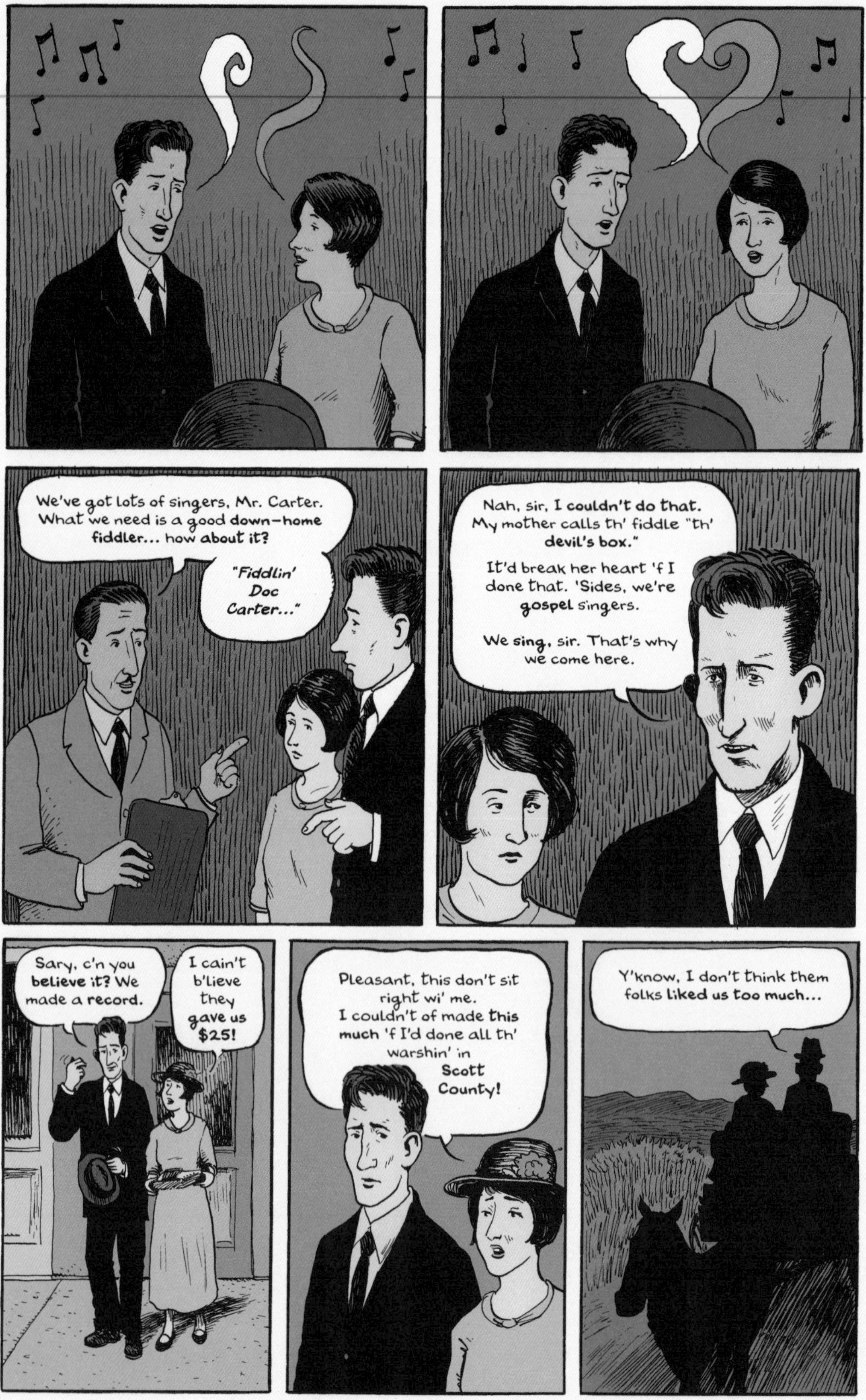
We've got lots of singers, Mr. Carter. What we need is a good down-home fiddler... how about it?
"Fiddlin' Doc Carter..."
Nah, sir, I couldn't do that. My mother calls th' fiddle "th' devil's box."
It'd break her heart 'f I done that. 'Sides, we're gospel singers.
We sing, sir. That's why we come here.
Sary, c'n you believe it? We made a record.
I cain't b'lieve they gave us $25!
Pleasant, this don't sit right wi' me. I couldn't of made this much 'f I'd done all th' warshin' in Scott County!
Y'know, I don't think them folks liked us too much...

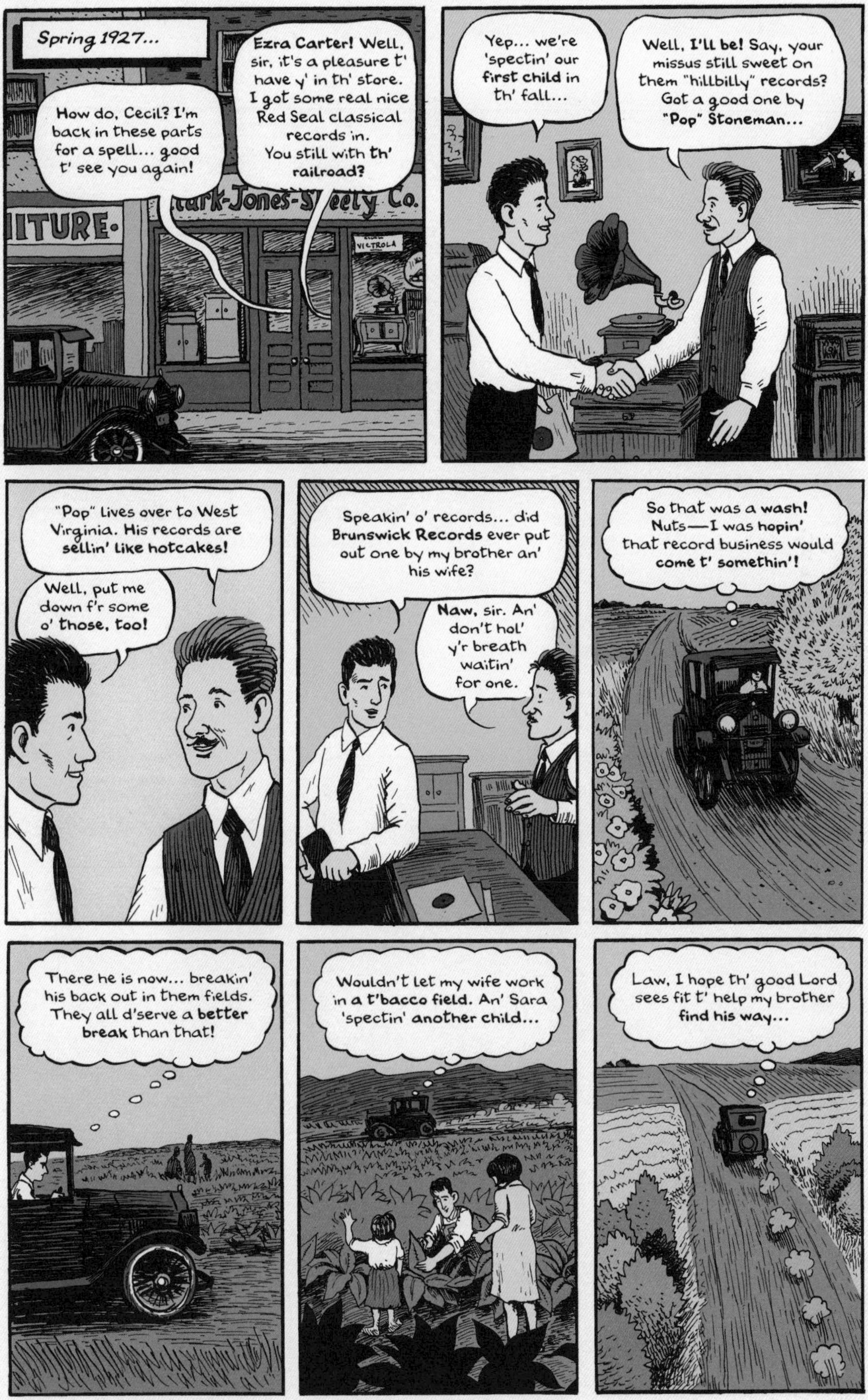
Spring 1927...
How do, Cecil? I'm back in these parts for a spell... good t' see you again!
Ezra Carter! Well, sir, it's a pleasure t' have y' in th' store. I got some real nice Red Seal classical records in. You still with th' railroad?
VICTROLA
Yep... we're 'spectin' our first child in th' fall...
Well, I'll be! Say, your missus still sweet on them "hillbilly" records? Got a good one by "Pop" Stoneman...
"Pop" lives over to West Virginia. His records are sellin' like hotcakes!
Well, put me down f'r some o' those, too!
Speakin' o' records... did Brunswick Records ever put out one by my brother an' his wife?
Naw, sir. An' don't hol' y'r breath waitin' for one.
So that was a wash! Nuts—I was hopin' that record business would come t' somethin'!
There he is now... breakin' his back out in them fields. They all d'serve a better break than that!
Wouldn't let my wife work in a t'bacco field. An' Sara 'spectin' another child...
Law, I hope th' good Lord sees fit t' help my brother find his way...

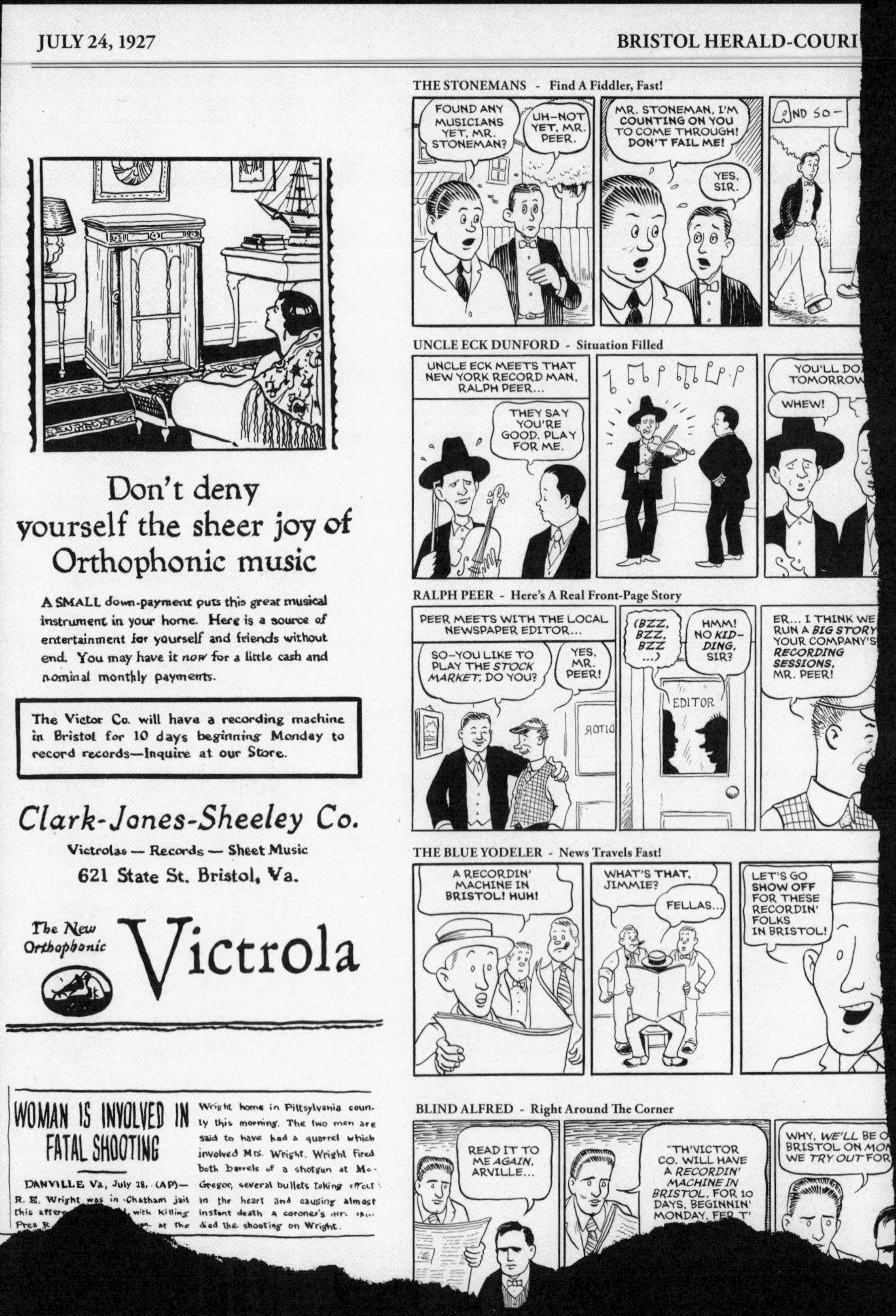
JULY 24, 1927
BRISTOL HERALD-COURI
Don't deny yourself the sheer joy of Orthophonic music
A SMALL down-payment puts this great musical instrument in your home. Here is a source of entertainment for yourself and friends without end. You may have it now for a little cash and nominal monthly payments.
The Victor Co. will have a recording machine in Bristol for 10 days beginning Monday to record records—Inquire at our Store.
Clark-Jones-Sheeley Co.
Victrolas — Records — Sheet Music
621 State St. Bristol, Va.
The New Orthophonic Victrola
WOMAN IS INVOLVED IN FATAL SHOOTING
DANVILLE Va, July 28, (AP)— R. E. Wright was in Chatham jail this after
with Killing
Pres R
at the
Wright home in Pittsylvania county this morning. The two men are said to have had a quarrel which involved Mrs. Wright. Wright fired both barrels of a shotgun at McGregor, several bullets taking effect in the heart and causing almost instant death a coroner's
died the shooting on Wright.
THE STONEMANS - Find A Fiddler, Fast!
FOUND ANY MUSICIANS YET, MR. STONEMAN?
UH—NOT YET, MR. PEER.
MR. STONEMAN, I'M COUNTING ON YOU TO COME THROUGH! DON'T FAIL ME!
YES, SIR.
AND SO—
UNCLE ECK DUNFORD - Situation Filled
UNCLE ECK MEETS THAT NEW YORK RECORD MAN, RALPH PEER...
THEY SAY YOU'RE GOOD. PLAY FOR ME.
YOU'LL DO TOMORROW
WHEW!
RALPH PEER - Here's A Real Front-Page Story
PEER MEETS WITH THE LOCAL NEWSPAPER EDITOR...
SO—YOU LIKE TO PLAY THE STOCK MARKET, DO YOU?
YES, MR. PEER!
(BZZ, BZZ, BZZ ...)
HMM! NO KIDDING, SIR?
EDITOR
ER... I THINK WE RUN A BIG STORY YOUR COMPANY'S RECORDING SESSIONS, MR. PEER!
THE BLUE YODELER - News Travels Fast!
A RECORDIN' MACHINE IN BRISTOL! HUH!
WHAT'S THAT, JIMMIE?
FELLAS...
LET'S GO SHOW OFF FOR THESE RECORDIN' FOLKS IN BRISTOL!
BLIND ALFRED - Right Around The Corner
READ IT TO ME AGAIN, ARVILLE...
"TH'VICTOR CO. WILL HAVE A RECORDIN' MACHINE IN BRISTOL, FOR 10 DAYS, BEGINNIN' MONDAY, FER T'
WHY, WE'LL BE O BRISTOL ON MON WE TRY OUT FOR

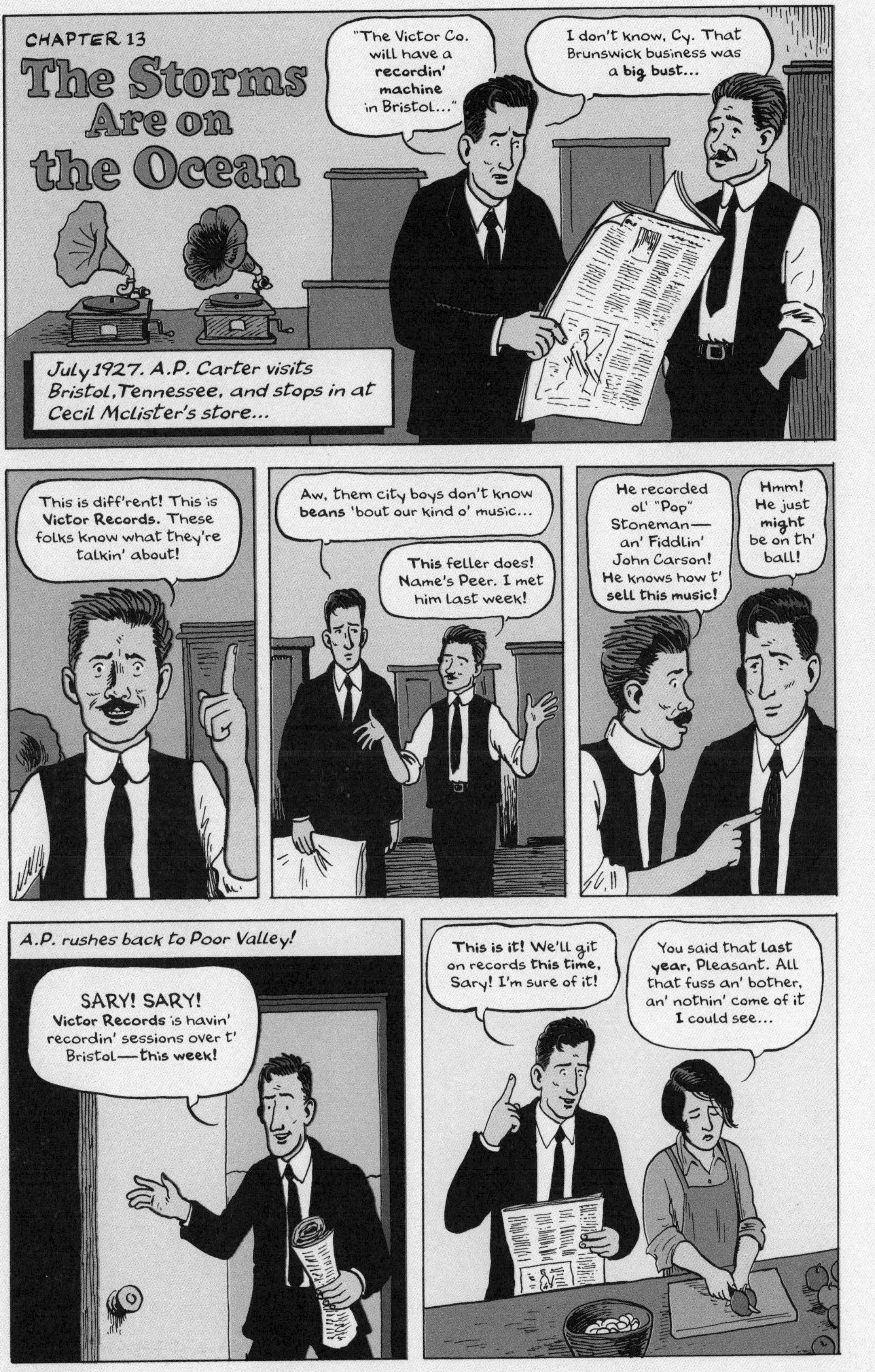
CHAPTER 13
The Storms Are on the Ocean
"The Victor Co. will have a recordin' machine in Bristol..."
I don't know, Cy. That Brunswick business was a big bust...
July 1927. A.P. Carter visits Bristol, Tennessee, and stops in at Cecil Mclister's store...
This is diff'rent! This is Victor Records. These folks know what they're talkin' about!
Aw, them city boys don't know beans 'bout our kind o' music...
This feller does! Name's Peer. I met him last week!
He recorded ol' "Pop" Stoneman— an' Fiddlin' John Carson! He knows how t' sell this music!
Hmm! He just might be on th' ball!
A.P. rushes back to Poor Valley!
SARY! SARY! Victor Records is havin' recordin' sessions over t' Bristol—this week!
This is it! We'll git on records this time, Sary! I'm sure of it!
You said that last year, Pleasant. All that fuss an' bother, an' nothin' come of it I could see...

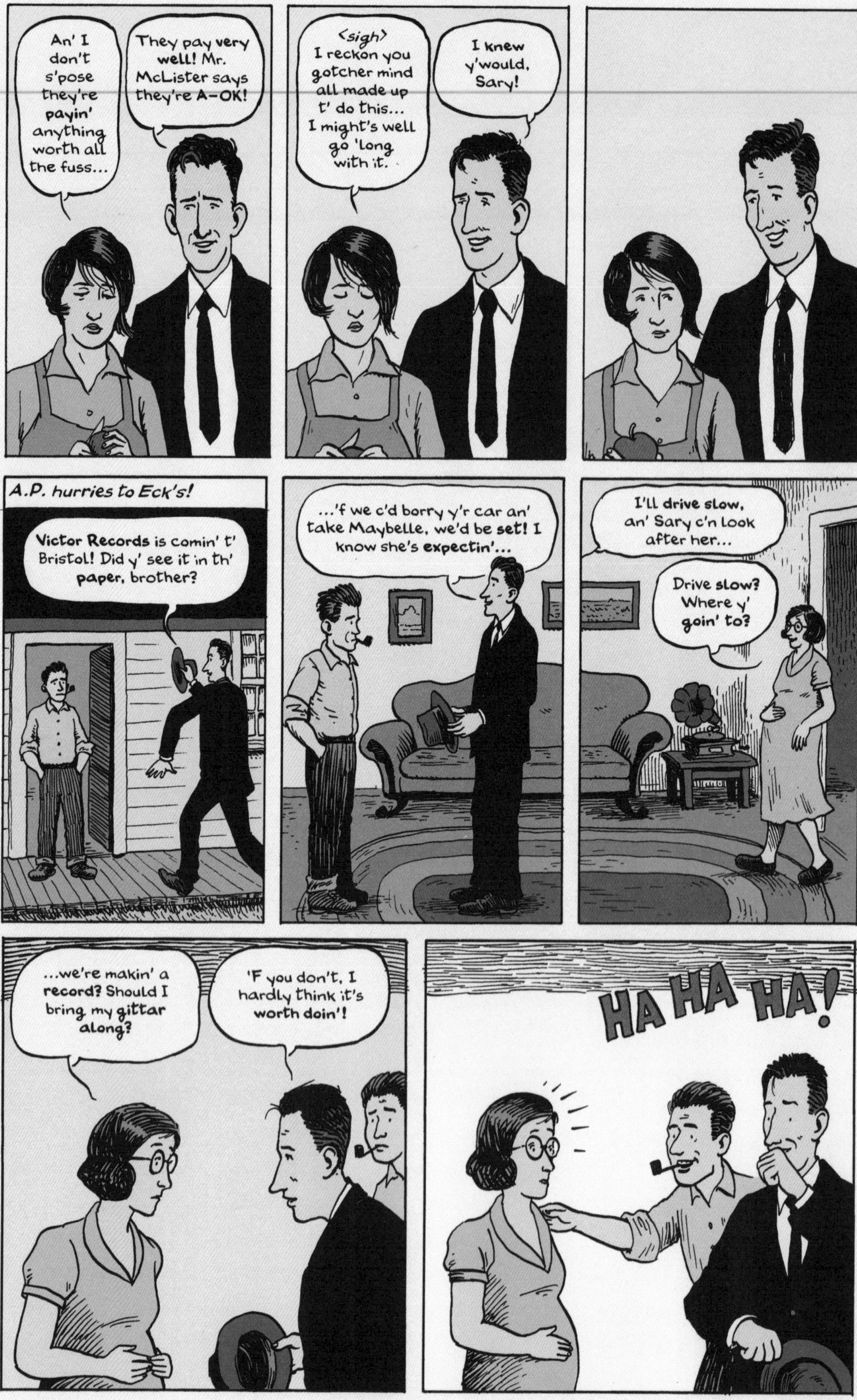
An' I don't s'pose they're payin' anything worth all the fuss...
They pay very well! Mr. McLister says they're A-OK!
<sigh> I reckon you gotcher mind all made up t' do this... I might's well go 'long with it.
I knew y'would, Sary!
A.P. hurries to Eck's!
Victor Records is comin' t' Bristol! Did y' see it in th' paper, brother?
...'f we c'd borry y'r car an' take Maybelle, we'd be set! I know she's expectin'...
I'll drive slow, an' Sary c'n look after her...
Drive slow? Where y' goin' to?
...we're makin' a record? Should I bring my gittar along?
'F you don't, I hardly think it's worth doin'!
HA HA HA!

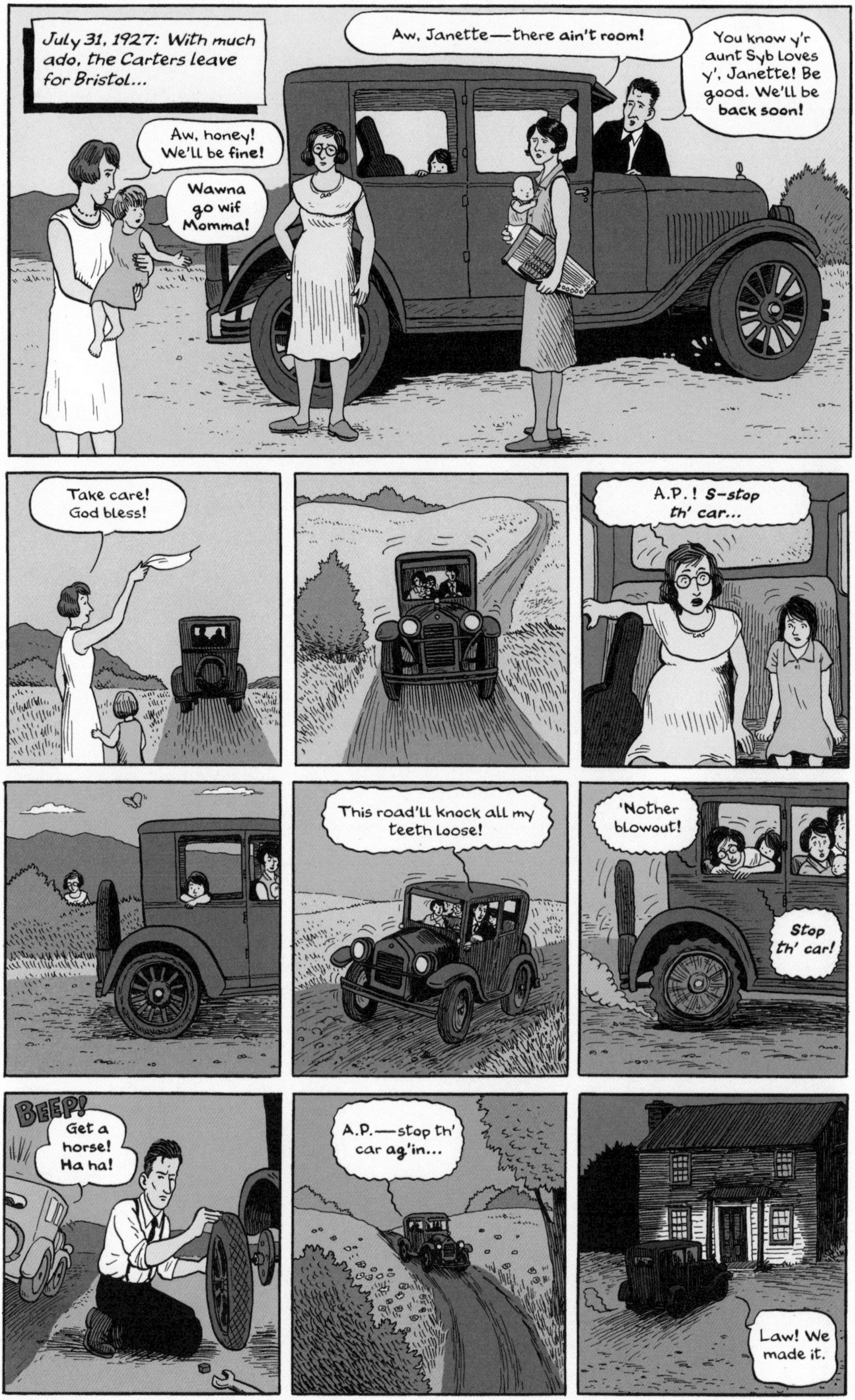
July 31, 1927: With much ado, the Carters leave for Bristol...
Aw, Janette—there ain't room!
You know y'r aunt Syb loves y', Janette! Be good. We'll be back soon!
Aw, honey! We'll be fine!
Wawna go wif Momma!
Take care! God bless!
A.P.! S-stop th' car...
This road'll knock all my teeth loose!
'Nother blowout!
Stop th' car!
BEEP!
Get a horse! Ha ha!
A.P.—stop th' car ag'in...
Law! We made it.

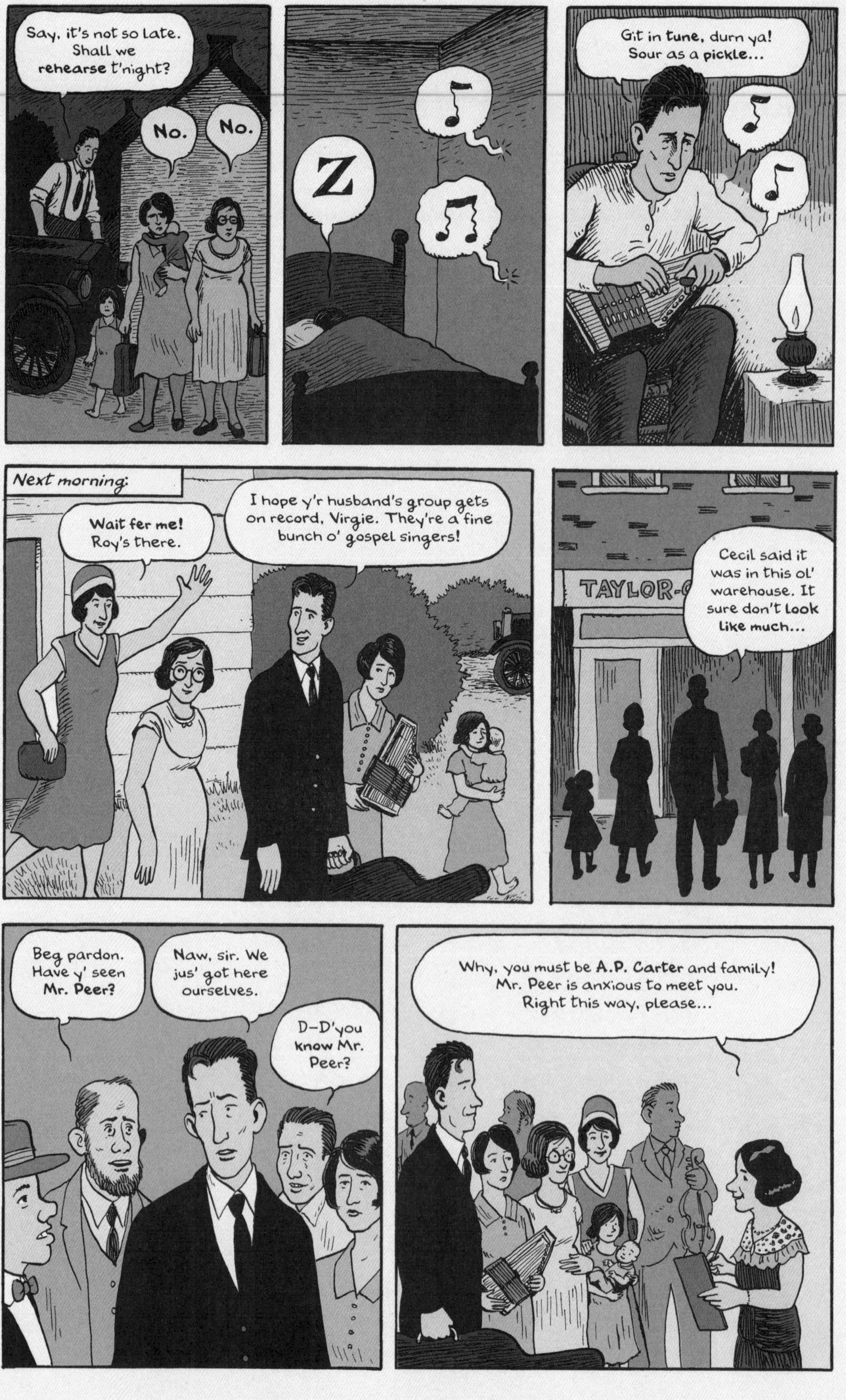
Say, it's not so late. Shall we rehearse t'night?
No.
No.
Z
Git in tune, durn ya! Sour as a pickle...
Next morning:
Wait fer me! Roy's there.
I hope y'r husband's group gets on record, Virgie. They're a fine bunch o' gospel singers!
TAYLOR-C
Cecil said it was in this ol' warehouse. It sure don't look like much...
Beg pardon. Have y' seen Mr. Peer?
Naw, sir. We jus' got here ourselves.
D-D'you know Mr. Peer?
Why, you must be A.P. Carter and family! Mr. Peer is anxious to meet you. Right this way, please...

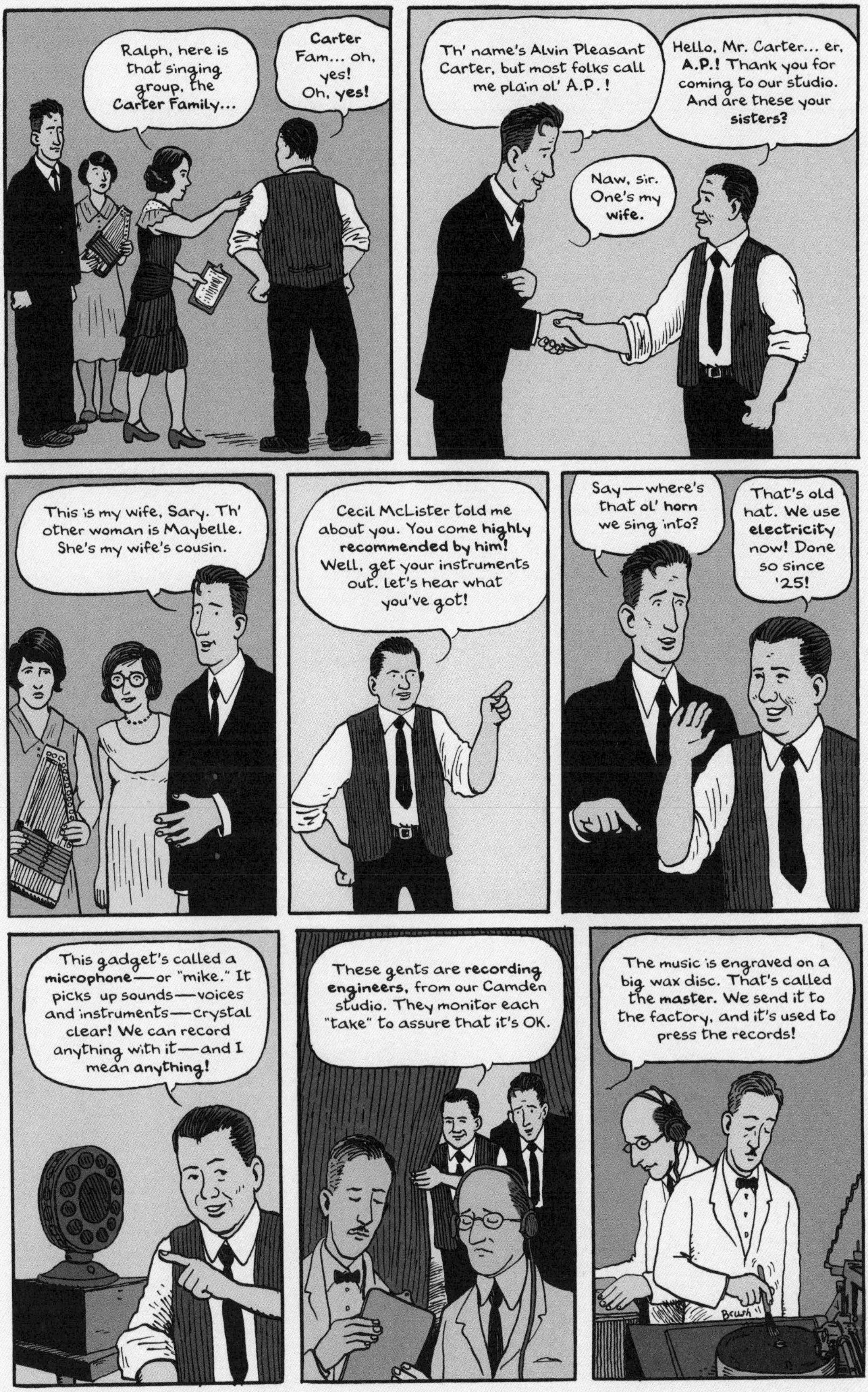
Ralph, here is that singing group, the Carter Family...
Carter Fam... oh, yes! Oh, yes!
Th' name's Alvin Pleasant Carter, but most folks call me plain ol' A.P.!
Hello, Mr. Carter... er, A.P.! Thank you for coming to our studio. And are these your sisters?
Naw, sir. One's my wife.
This is my wife, Sary. Th' other woman is Maybelle. She's my wife's cousin.
Cecil McLister told me about you. You come highly recommended by him! Well, get your instruments out. let's hear what you've got!
Say—where's that ol' horn we sing into?
That's old hat. We use electricity now! Done so since '25!
This gadget's called a microphone—or "mike." It picks up sounds—voices and instruments—crystal clear! We can record anything with it—and I mean anything!
These gents are recording engineers, from our Camden studio. They monitor each "take" to assure that it's OK.
The music is engraved on a big wax disc. That's called the master. We send it to the factory, and it's used to press the records!
Brush

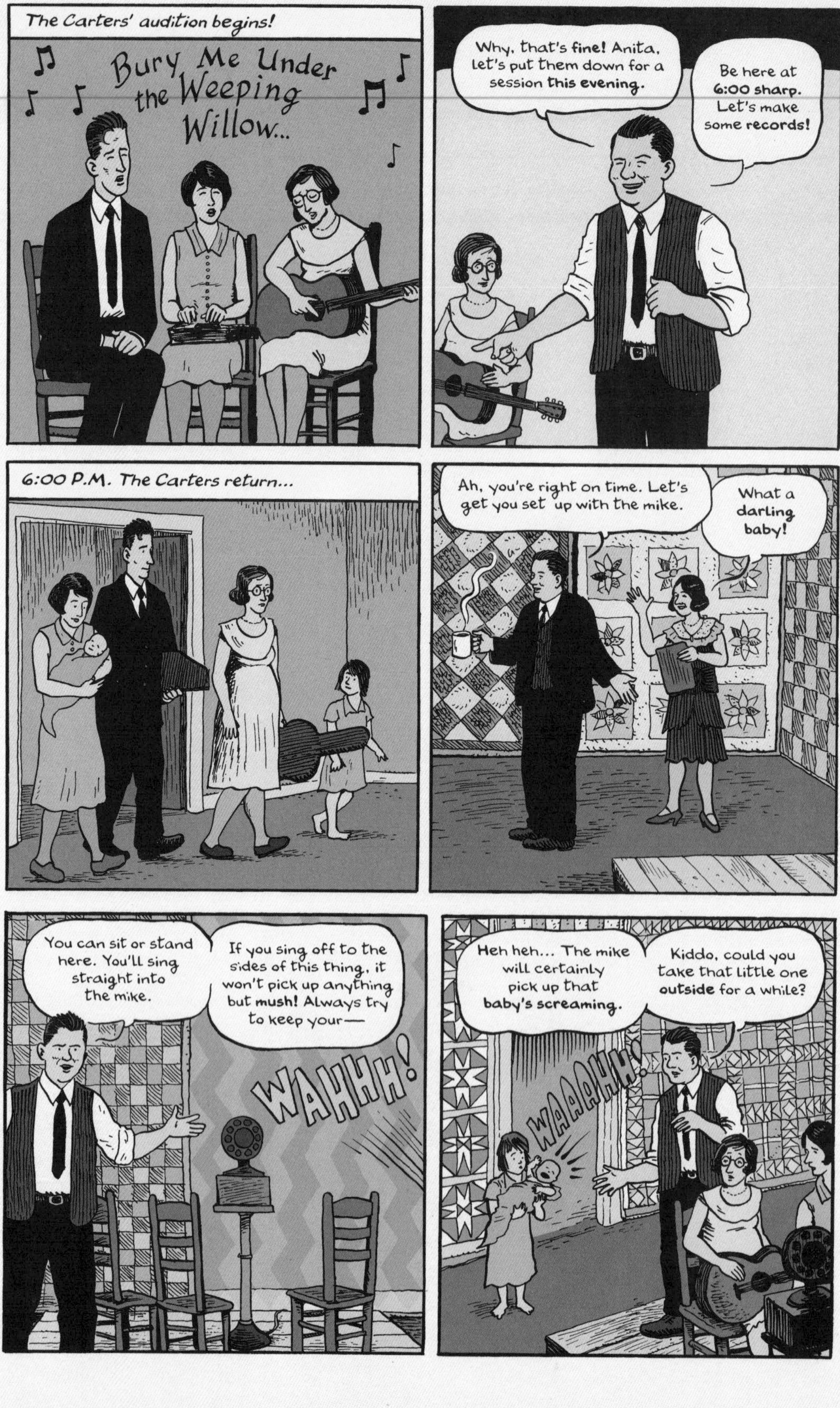
The Carters' audition begins!
Bury Me Under the Weeping Willow...
Why, that's fine! Anita, let's put them down for a session this evening.
Be here at 6:00 sharp. Let's make some records!
6:00 P.M. The Carters return...
Ah, you're right on time. Let's get you set up with the mike.
What a darling baby!
You can sit or stand here. You'll sing straight into the mike.
If you sing off to the sides of this thing, it won't pick up anything but mush! Always try to keep your—
WAHHH!
Heh heh... The mike will certainly pick up that baby's screaming.
Kiddo, could you take that little one outside for a while?
WAAAHH!

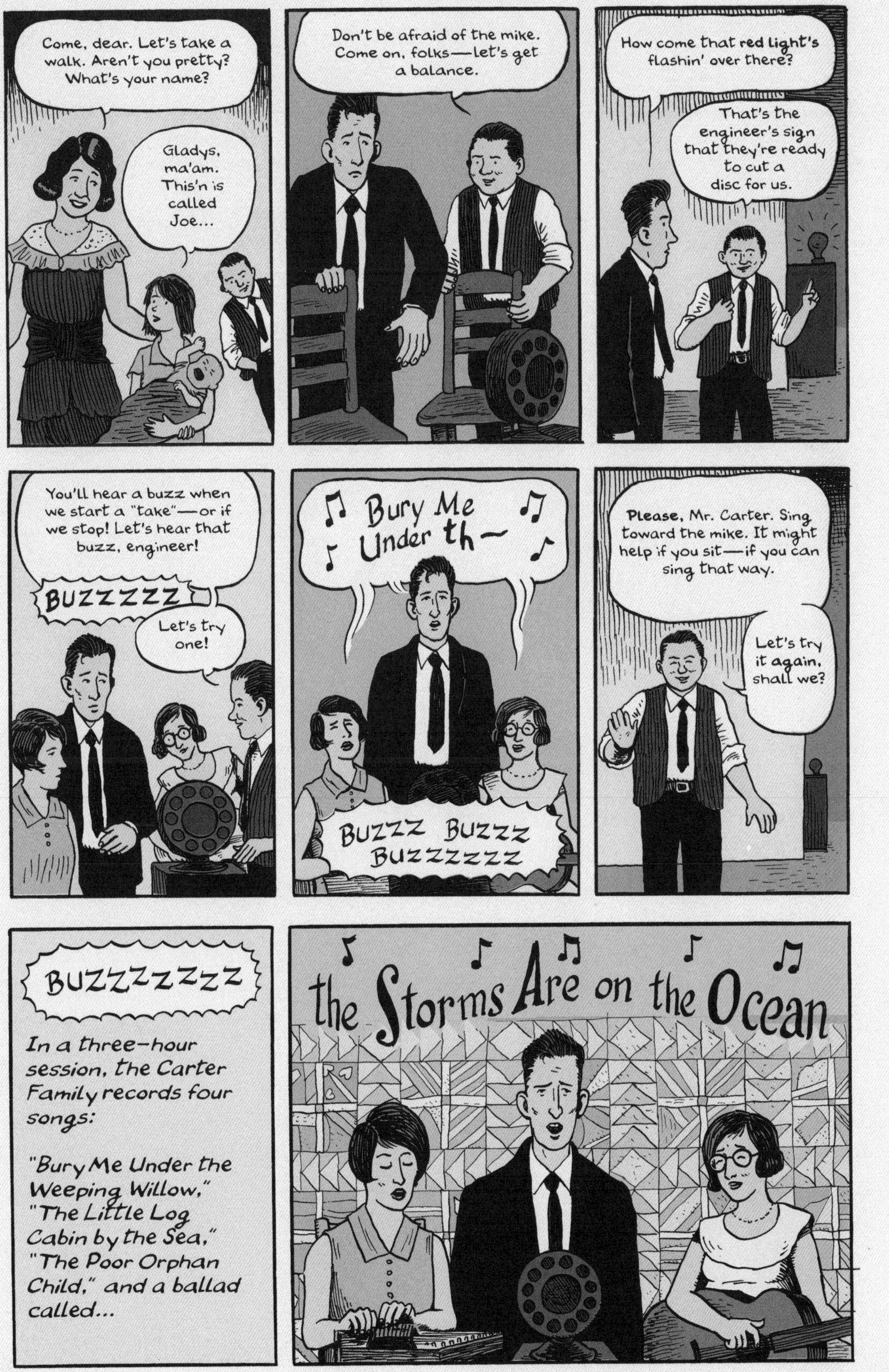
Come, dear. Let's take a walk. Aren't you pretty? What's your name?
Gladys, ma'am. This'n is called Joe...
Don't be afraid of the mike. Come on, folks—let's get a balance.
How come that red light's flashin' over there?
That's the engineer's sign that they're ready to cut a disc for us.
You'll hear a buzz when we start a "take"—or if we stop! Let's hear that buzz, engineer!
BUZZZZZ
Let's try one!
Bury Me Under th—
BUZZZ BUZZZ BUZZZZZZ
Please, Mr. Carter. Sing toward the mike. It might help if you sit—if you can sing that way.
Let's try it again, shall we?
BUZZZZZZZ
In a three-hour session, the Carter Family records four songs:
"Bury Me Under the Weeping Willow," "The Little Log Cabin by the Sea," "The Poor Orphan Child," and a ballad called...
the Storms Are on the Ocean

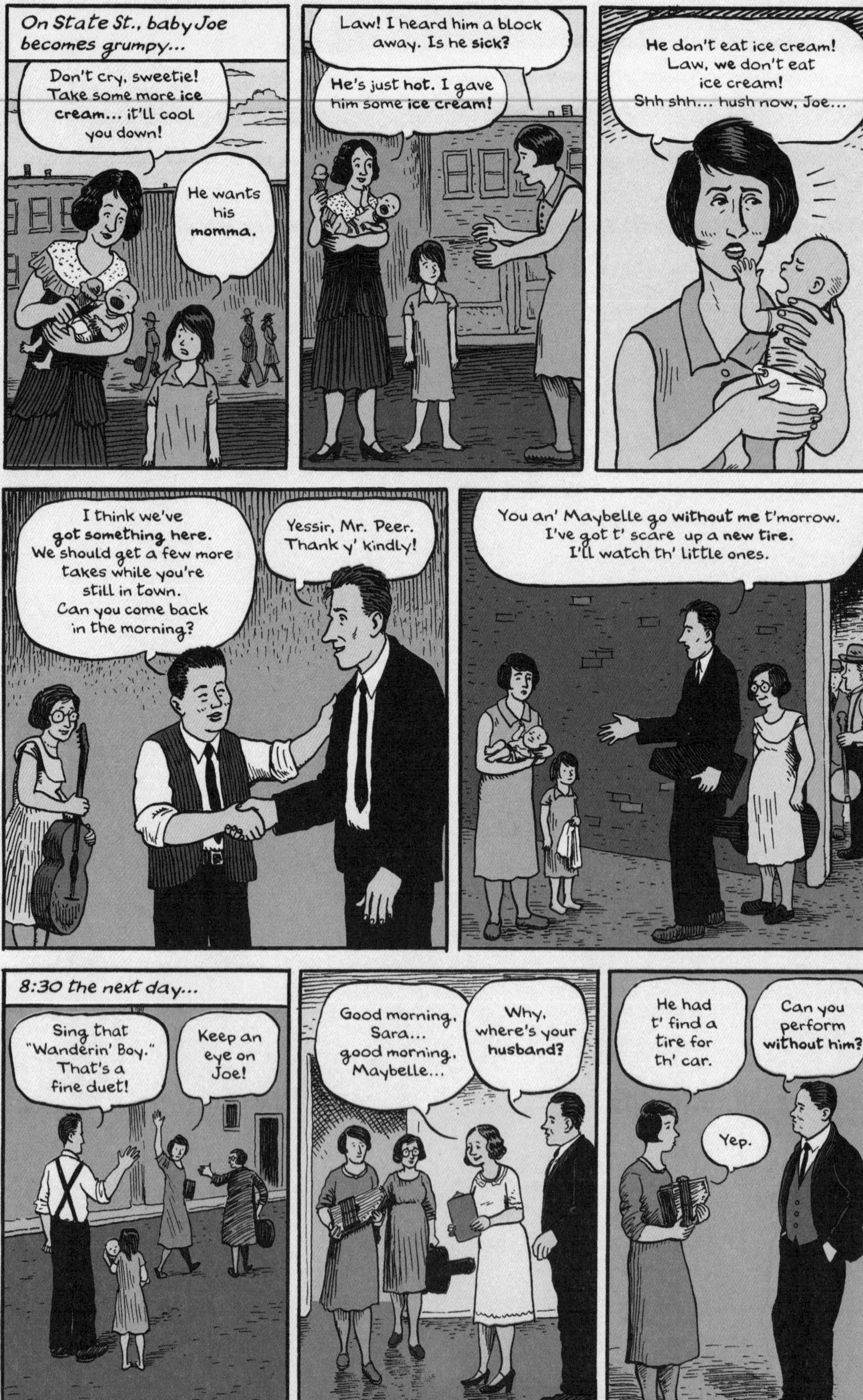
On State St., baby Joe becomes grumpy...
Don't cry, sweetie! Take some more ice cream... it'll cool you down!
He wants his momma.
Law! I heard him a block away. Is he sick?
He's just hot. I gave him some ice cream!
He don't eat ice cream! Law, we don't eat ice cream! Shh shh... hush now, Joe...
I think we've got something here. We should get a few more takes while you're still in town. Can you come back in the morning?
Yessir, Mr. Peer. Thank y' kindly!
You an' Maybelle go without me t'morrow. I've got t' scare up a new tire. I'll watch th' little ones.
8:30 the next day...
Sing that "Wanderin' Boy." That's a fine duet!
Keep an eye on Joe!
Good morning, Sara... good morning, Maybelle...
Why, where's your husband?
He had t' find a tire for th' car.
Can you perform without him?
Yep.

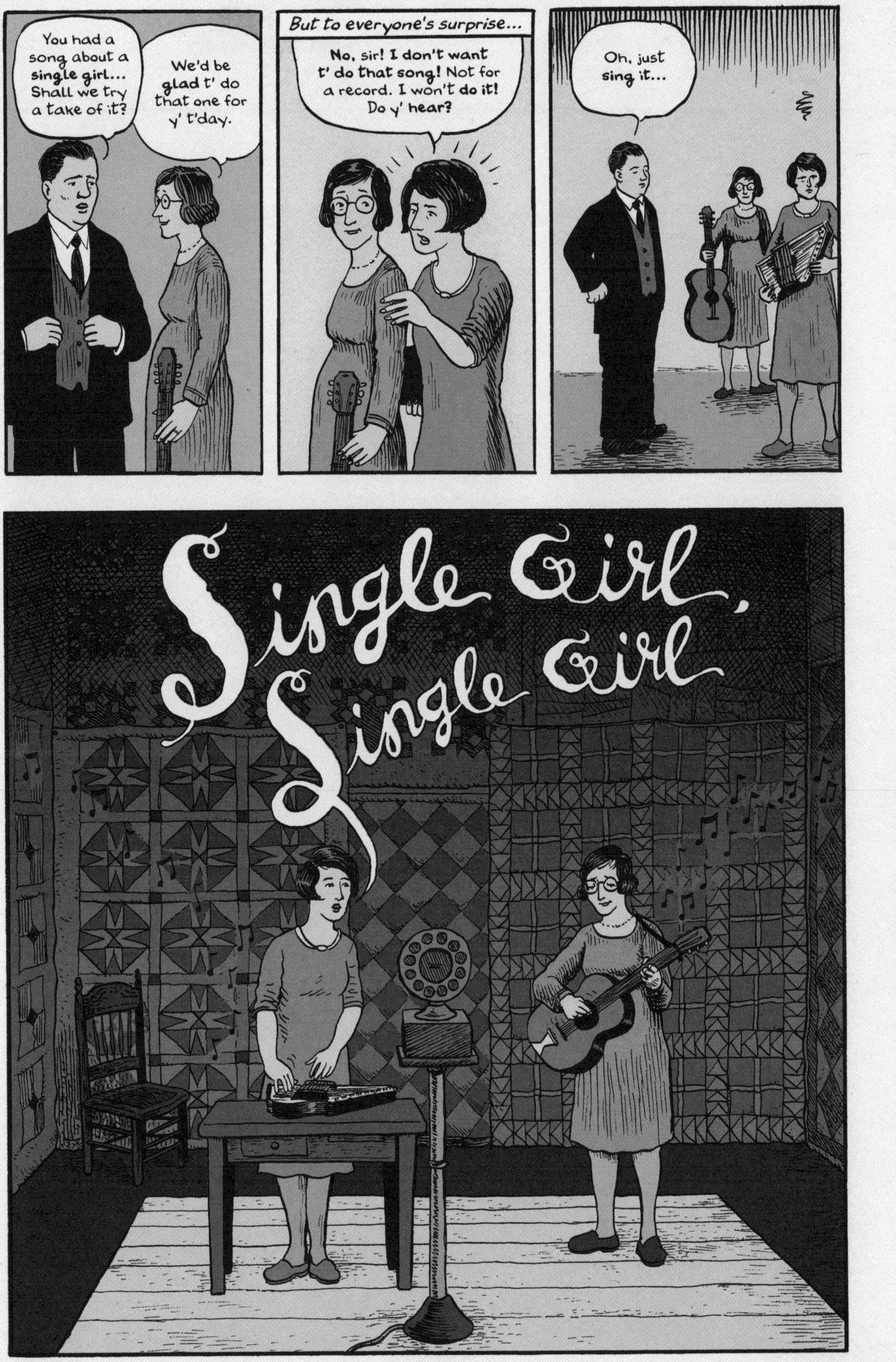
You had a song about a single girl... Shall we try a take of it?
We'd be glad t' do that one for y' t'day.
But to everyone's surprise...
No, sir! I don't want t' do that song! Not for a record. I won't do it! Do y' hear?
Oh, just sing it...
Single Girl, Single Girl

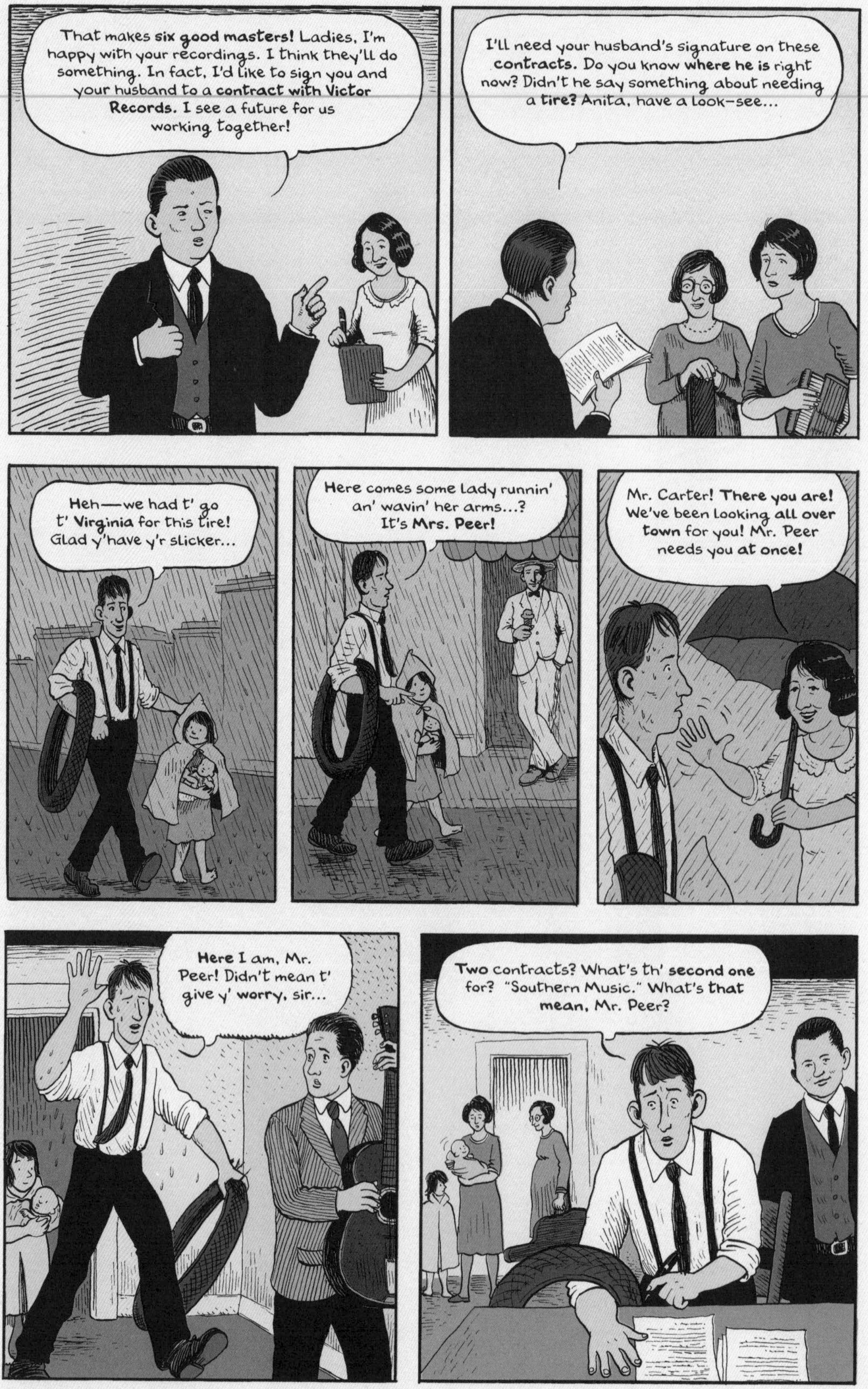
That makes six good masters! Ladies, I'm happy with your recordings. I think they'll do something. In fact, I'd like to sign you and your husband to a contract with Victor Records. I see a future for us working together!
I'll need your husband's signature on these contracts. Do you know where he is right now? Didn't he say something about needing a tire? Anita, have a look-see...
Heh—we had t' go t' Virginia for this tire! Glad y'have y'r slicker...
Here comes some lady runnin' an' wavin' her arms...? It's Mrs. Peer!
Mr. Carter! There you are! We've been looking all over town for you! Mr. Peer needs you at once!
Here I am, Mr. Peer! Didn't mean t' give y' worry, sir...
Two contracts? What's th' second one for? "Southern Music." What's that mean, Mr. Peer?

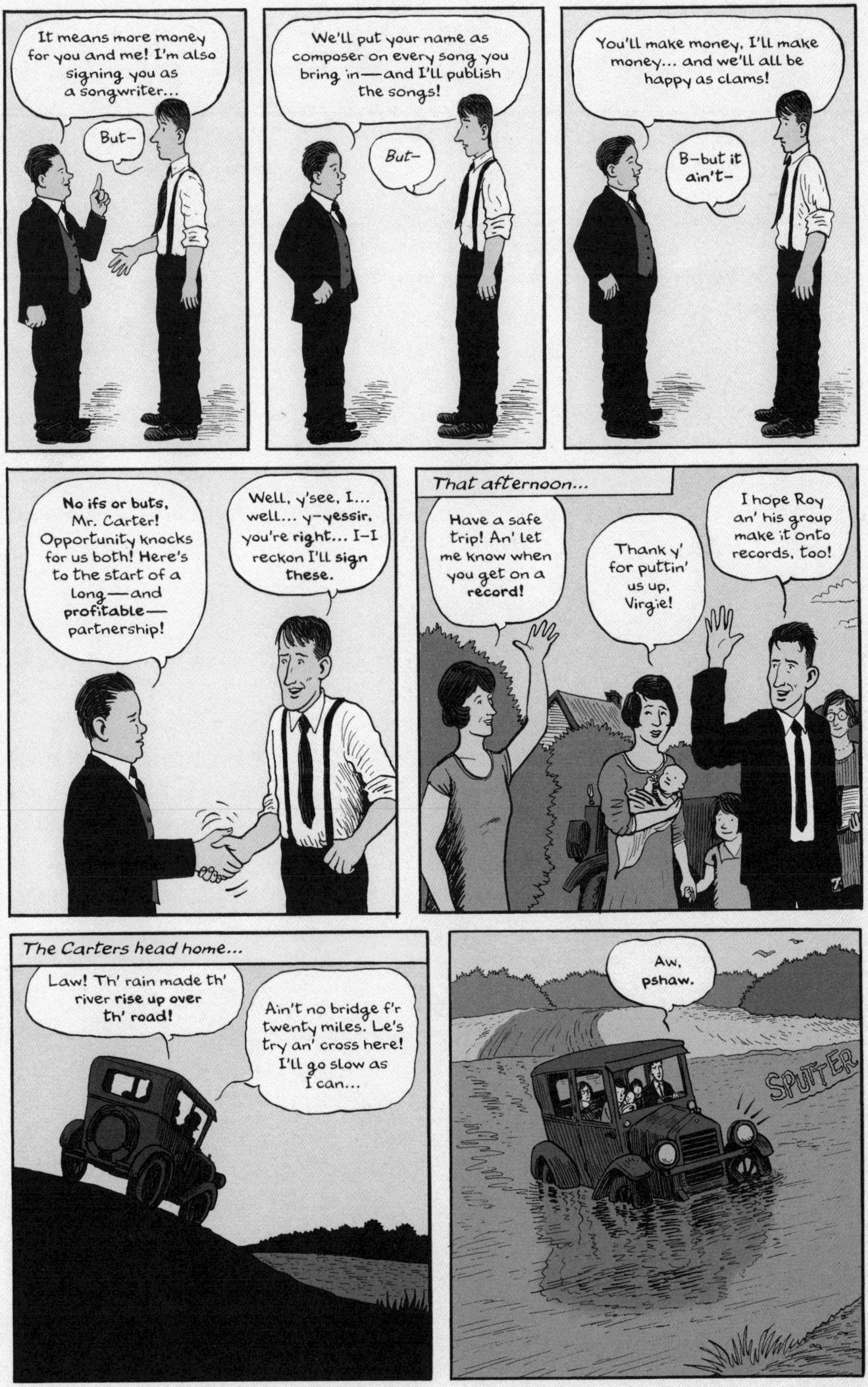
It means more money for you and me! I'm also signing you as a songwriter...
But-
We'll put your name as composer on every song you bring in—and I'll publish the songs!
But-
You'll make money, I'll make money... and we'll all be happy as clams!
B-but it ain't-
No ifs or buts, Mr. Carter! Opportunity knocks for us both! Here's to the start of a long—and profitable—partnership!
Well, y'see, I... well... y-yessir, you're right... I-I reckon I'll sign these.
That afternoon...
Have a safe trip! An' let me know when you get on a record!
Thank y' for puttin' us up, Virgie!
I hope Roy an' his group make it onto records, too!
The Carters head home...
Law! Th' rain made th' river rise up over th' road!
Ain't no bridge f'r twenty miles. Le's try an' cross here! I'll go slow as I can...
Aw, pshaw.
SPUTTER

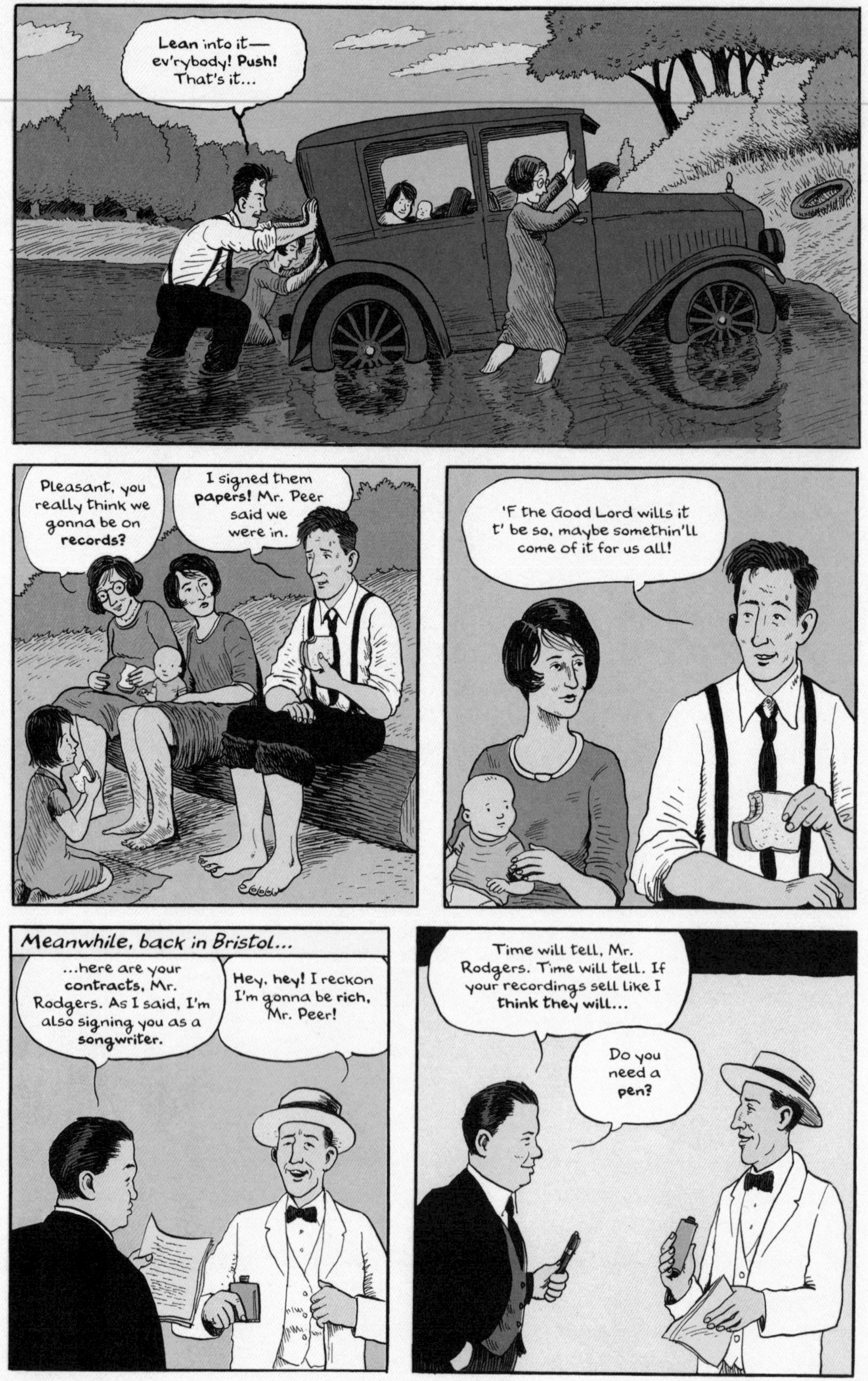
Lean into it—
ev'rybody! Push!
That's it...
Pleasant, you really think we gonna be on records?
I signed them papers! Mr. Peer said we were in.
'F the Good Lord wills it t' be so, maybe somethin'll come of it for us all!
Meanwhile, back in Bristol...
...here are your contracts, Mr. Rodgers. As I said, I'm also signing you as a songwriter.
Hey, hey! I reckon I'm gonna be rich, Mr. Peer!
Time will tell, Mr. Rodgers. Time will tell. If your recordings sell like I think they will...
Do you need a pen?

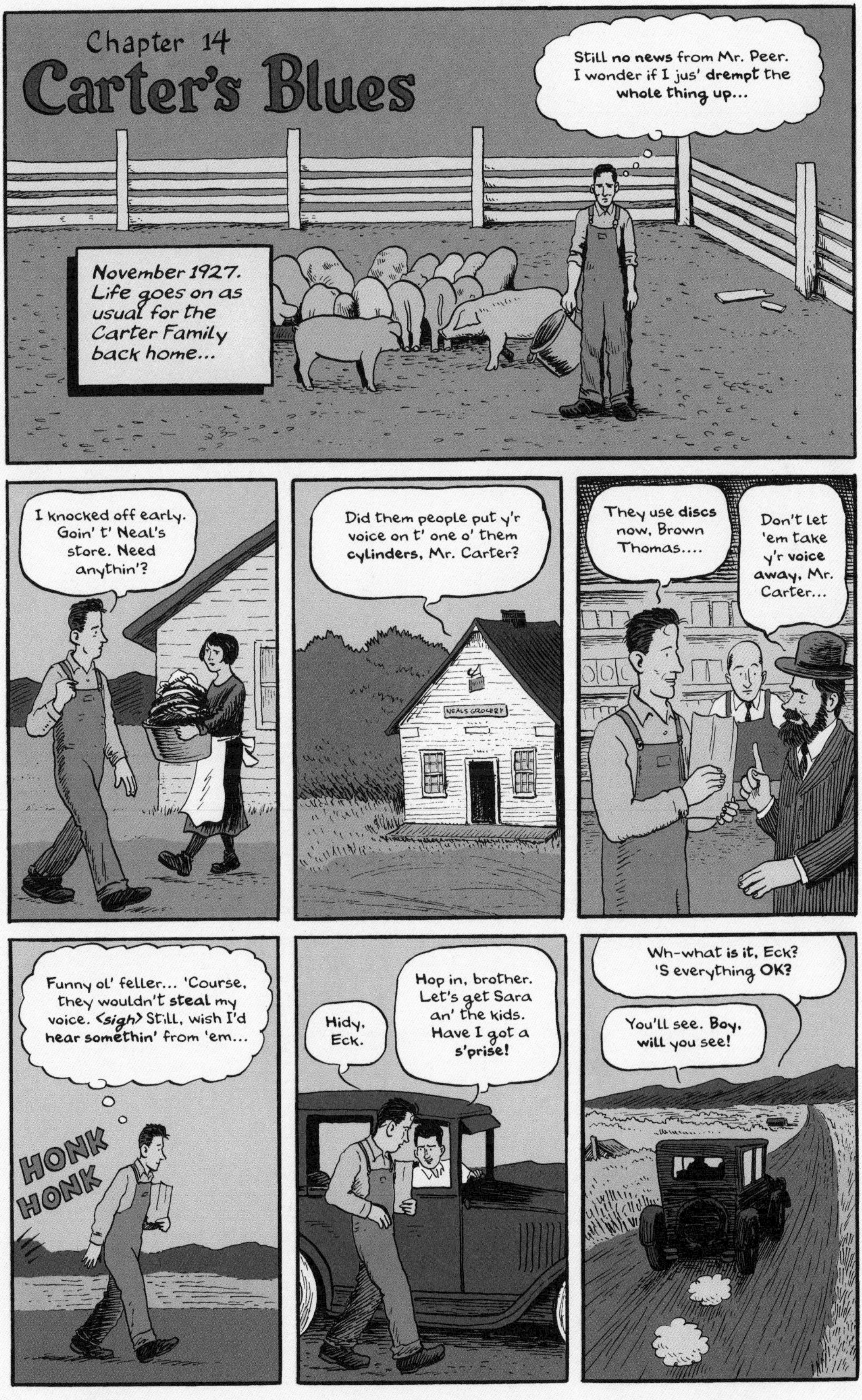
Chapter 14
Carter's Blues
Still no news from Mr. Peer. I wonder if I jus' drempt the whole thing up...
November 1927. Life goes on as usual for the Carter Family back home...
I knocked off early. Goin' t' Neal's store. Need anythin'?
Did them people put y'r voice on t' one o' them cylinders, Mr. Carter?
NEALS GROCERY
They use discs now, Brown Thomas....
Don't let 'em take y'r voice away, Mr. Carter...
Funny ol' feller... 'Course, they wouldn't steal my voice. <sigh> Still, wish I'd hear somethin' from 'em...
HONK HONK
Hidy, Eck.
Hop in, brother. Let's get Sara an' the kids. Have I got a s'prise!
Wh-what is it, Eck? 'S everything OK?
You'll see. Boy, will you see!

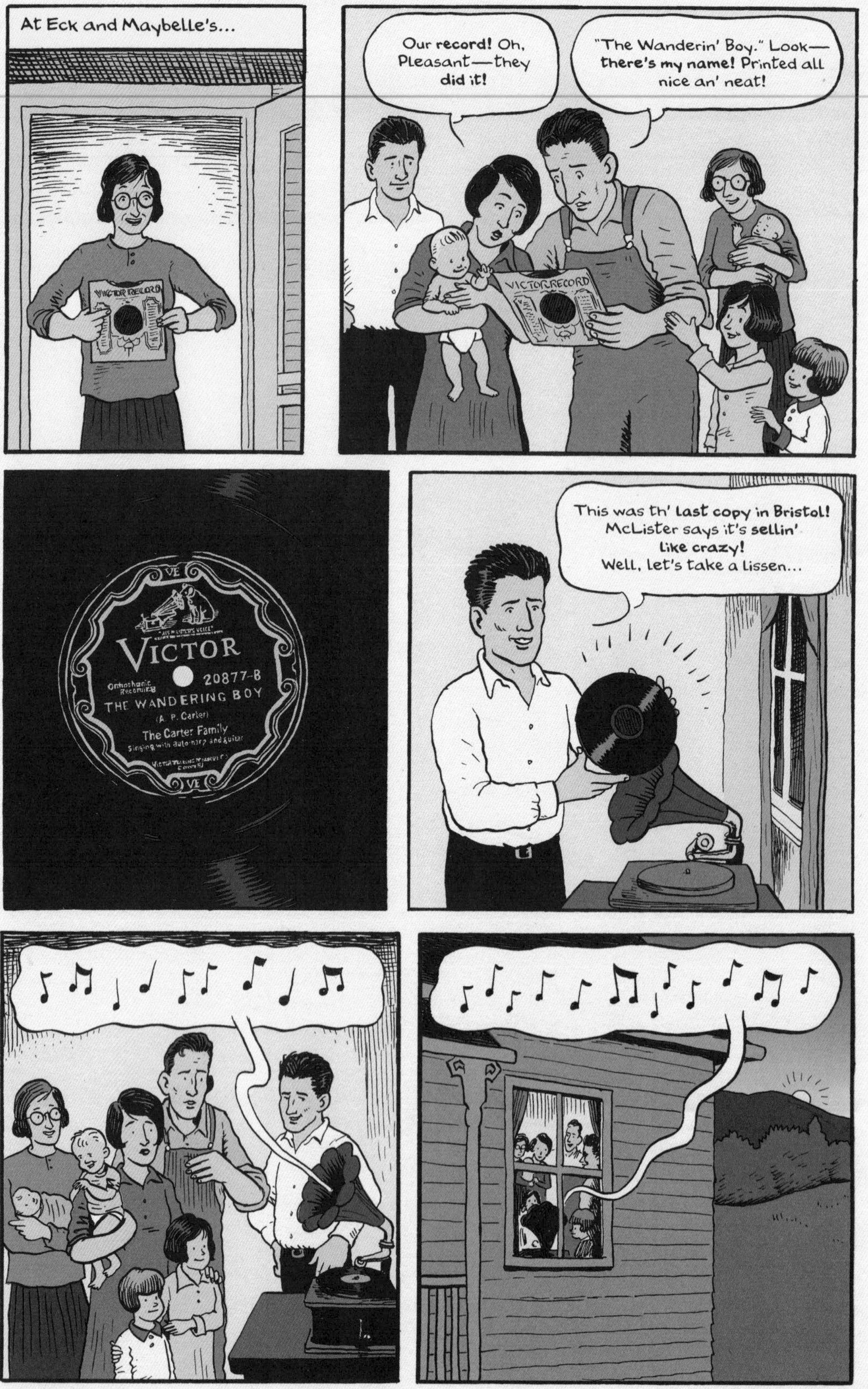
At Eck and Maybelle's...
Our record! Oh, Pleasant—they did it!
"The Wanderin' Boy." Look—there's my name! Printed all nice an' neat!
VICTOR RECORD
VICTOR
20877-B
THE WANDERING BOY
(A. P. Carter)
The Carter Family
This was th' last copy in Bristol! McLister says it's sellin' like crazy! Well, let's take a lissen...

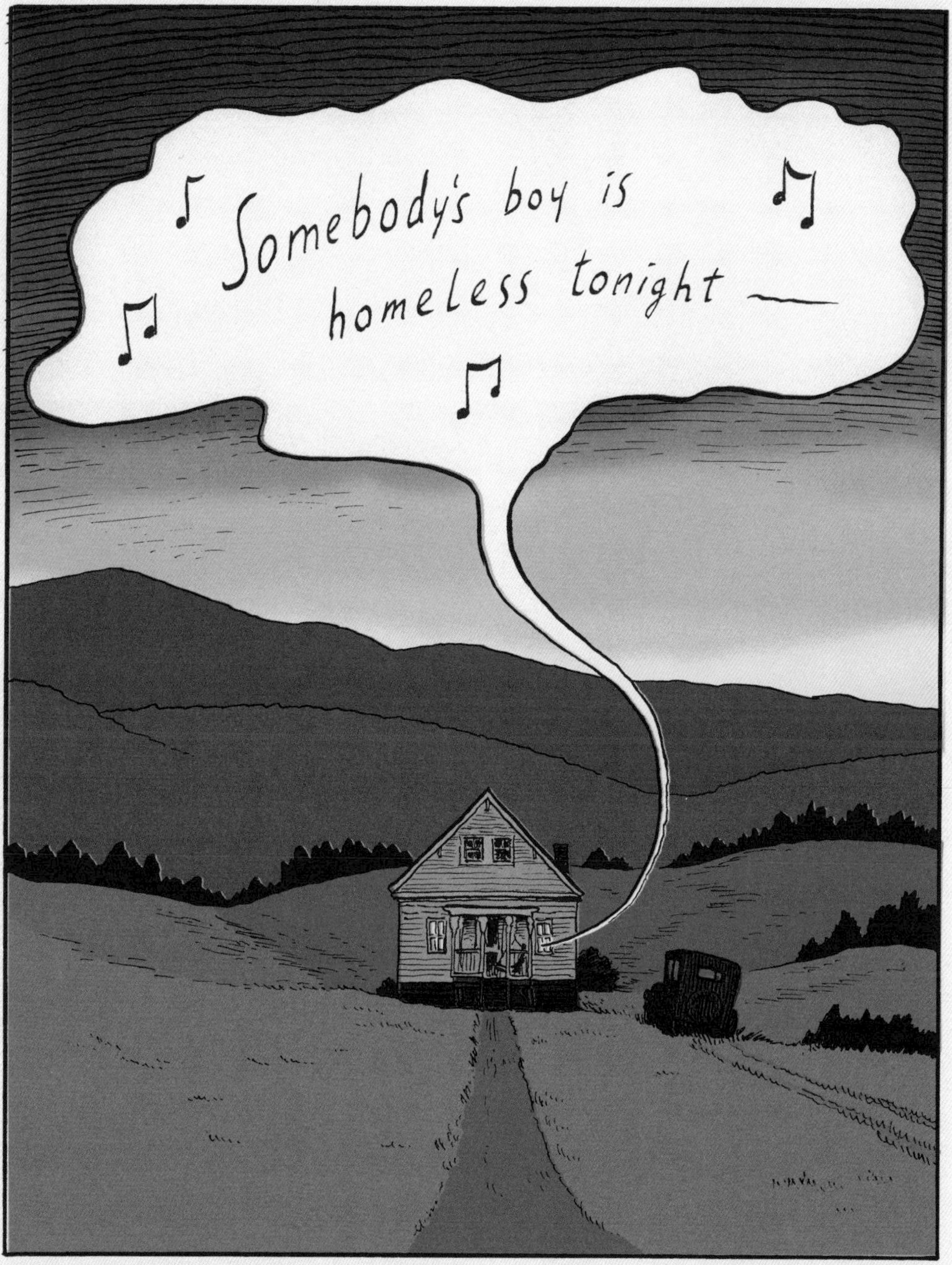
Somebody's boy is
homeless tonight —

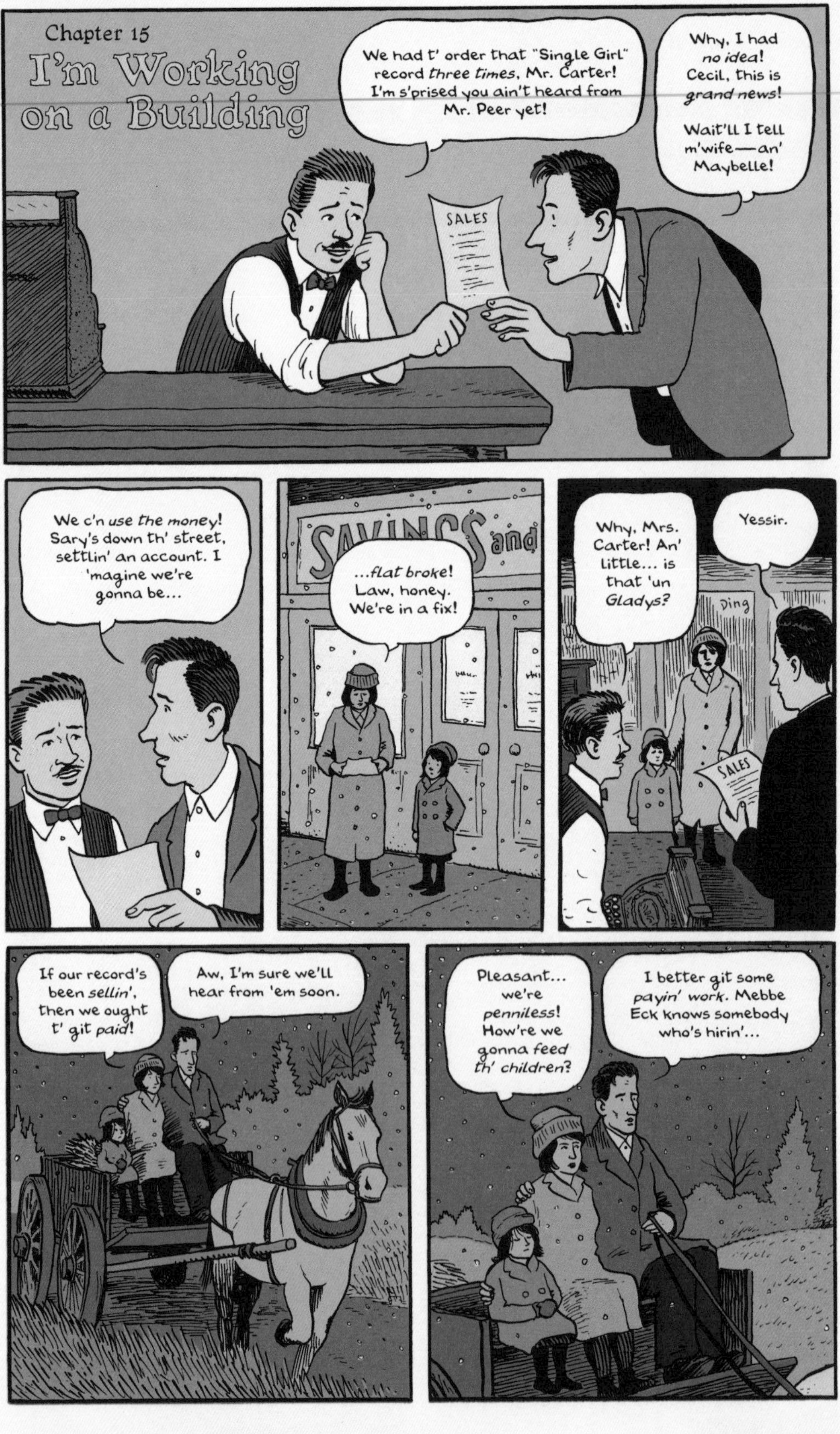
Chapter 15
I'm Working on a Building
We had t' order that "Single Girl" record *three times*, Mr. Carter! I'm s'prised you ain't heard from Mr. Peer yet!
SALES
Why, I had *no idea*! Cecil, this is *grand news*!
Wait'll I tell m'wife—an' Maybelle!
We c'n *use the money*! Sary's down th' street, settlin' an account. I 'magine we're gonna be...
SAVINGS and
...*flat broke*! Law, honey. We're in a fix!
Why, Mrs. Carter! An' little... is that 'un *Gladys*?
Yessir.
Ding
SALES
If our record's been *sellin'*, then we ought t' git *paid*!
Aw, I'm sure we'll hear from 'em soon.
Pleasant... we're *penniless*! How're we gonna feed th' children?
I better git some *payin'* work. Mebbe Eck knows somebody who's hirin'...

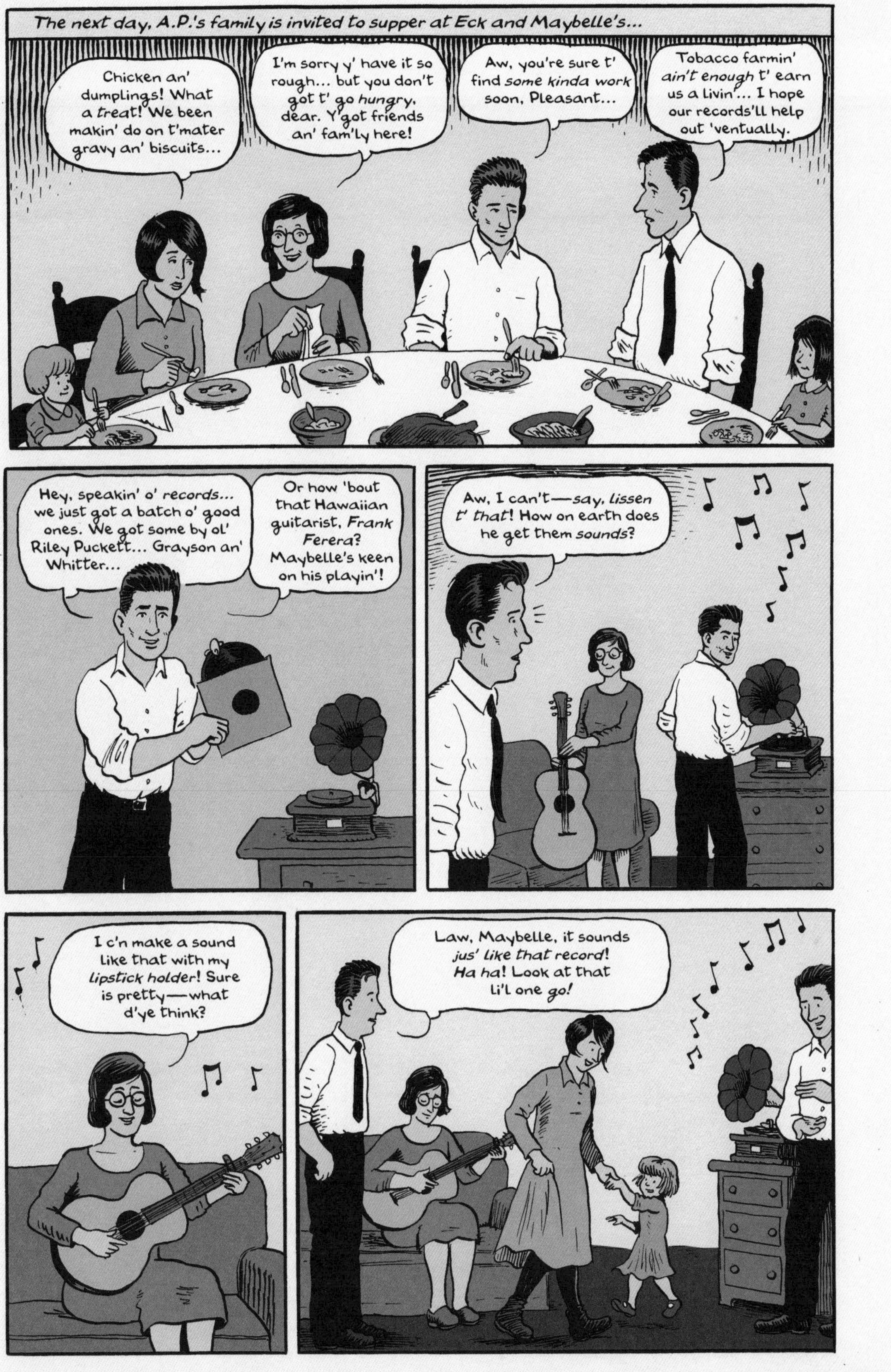
The next day, A.P.'s family is invited to supper at Eck and Maybelle's...
Chicken an' dumplings! What a *treat*! We been makin' do on t'mater gravy an' biscuits...
I'm sorry y' have it so rough... but you don't got t' go *hungry*, dear. Y'got friends an' fam'ly here!
Aw, you're sure t' find *some kinda work* soon, Pleasant...
Tobacco farmin' *ain't enough* t' earn us a livin'... I hope our records'll help out 'ventually.
Hey, speakin' o' *records*... we just got a batch o' good ones. We got some by ol' Riley Puckett... Grayson an' Whitter...
Or how 'bout that Hawaiian guitarist, *Frank Ferera*? Maybelle's keen on his playin'!
Aw, I can't—*say, lissen t' that*! How on earth does he get them *sounds*?
I c'n make a sound like that with my *lipstick holder*! Sure is pretty—what d'ye think?
Law, Maybelle, it sounds *jus' like that record*! *Ha ha*! Look at that li'l one *go*!

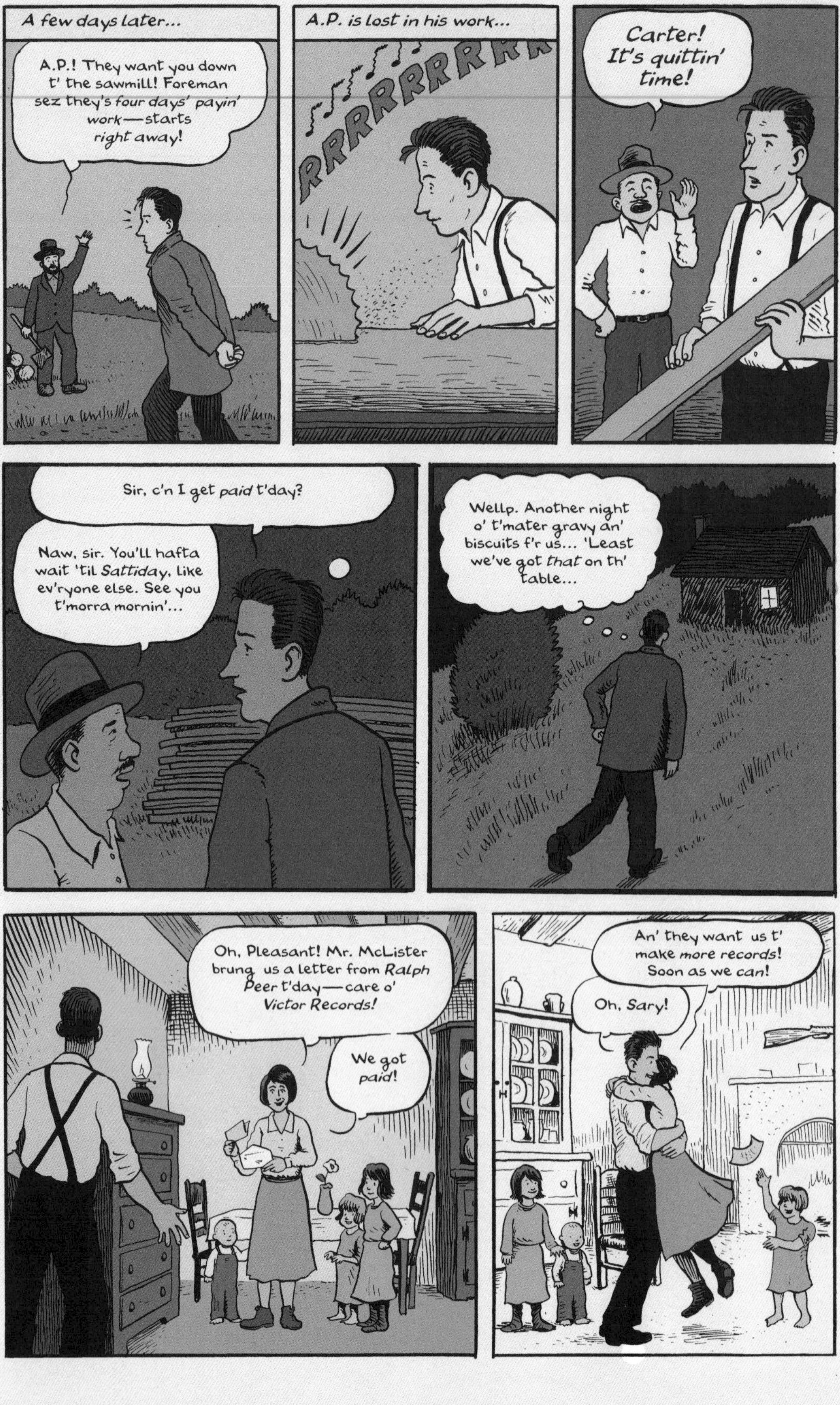
A few days later...
A.P.! They want you down t' the sawmill! Foreman sez they's *four days' payin'* work—starts *right* away!
A.P. is lost in his work...
RRRRRRRRRR
Carter! It's quittin' time!
Sir, c'n I get *paid* t'day?
Naw, sir. You'll hafta wait 'til *Sattiday*, like ev'ryone else. See you t'morra mornin'...
Wellp. Another night o' t'mater gravy an' biscuits f'r us... 'Least we've got *that* on th' table...
Oh, Pleasant! Mr. McLister brung us a letter from *Ralph Peer* t'day—care o' *Victor Records*!
We got *paid*!
An' they want us t' make *more* records! Soon as we *can*!
Oh, *Sary*!

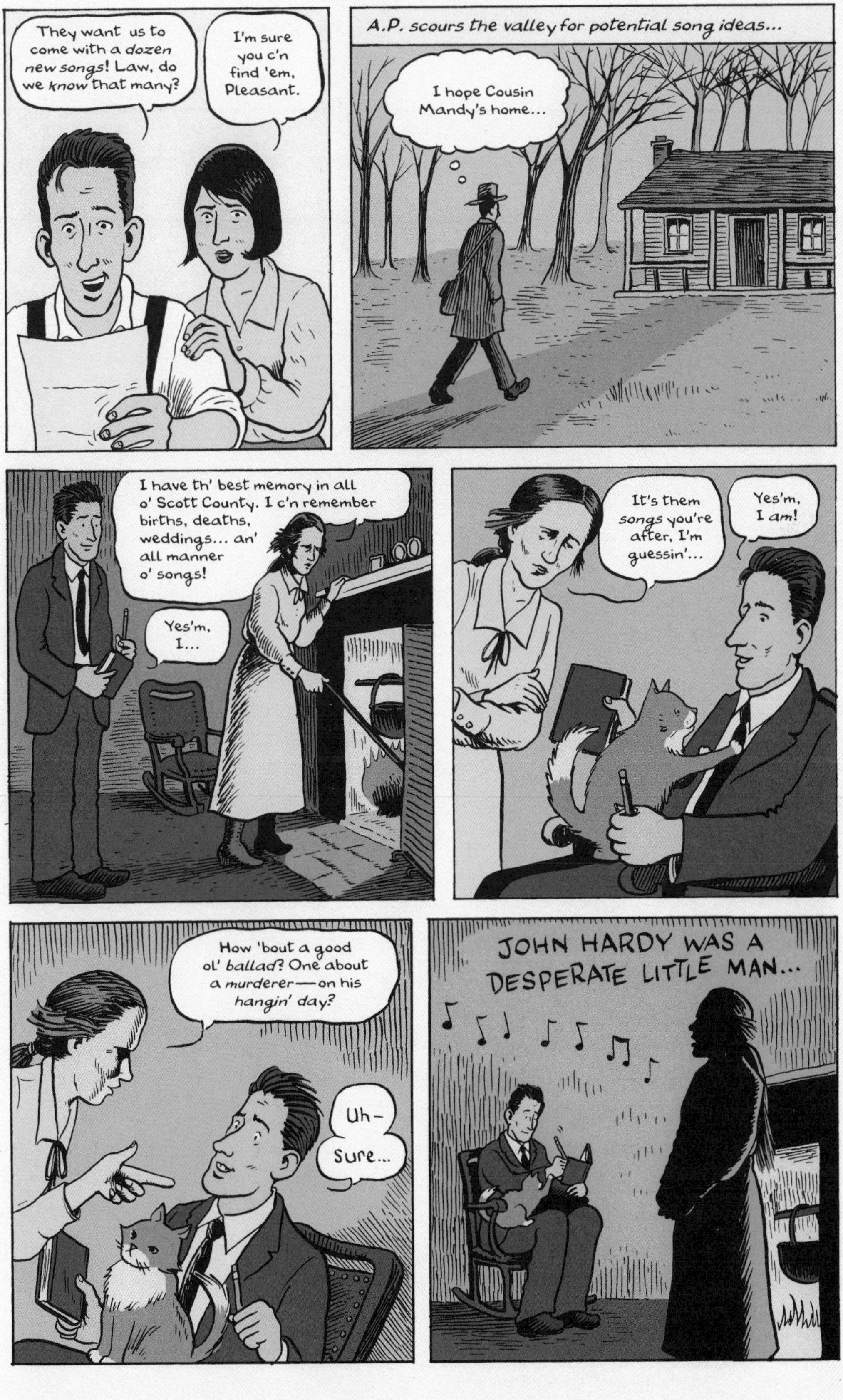
They want us to come with a *dozen new songs*! Law, do we *know* that many?
I'm sure you c'n find 'em, Pleasant.
A.P. scours the valley for potential song ideas...
I hope Cousin Mandy's home...
I have th' best memory in all o' Scott County. I c'n remember births, deaths, weddings... an' all manner o' songs!
Yes'm, I...
It's them *songs* you're after, I'm guessin'...
Yes'm, I *am*!
How 'bout a good ol' *ballad*? One about a *murderer*—on his *hangin'* day?
Uh- sure...
JOHN HARDY WAS A DESPERATE LITTLE MAN...

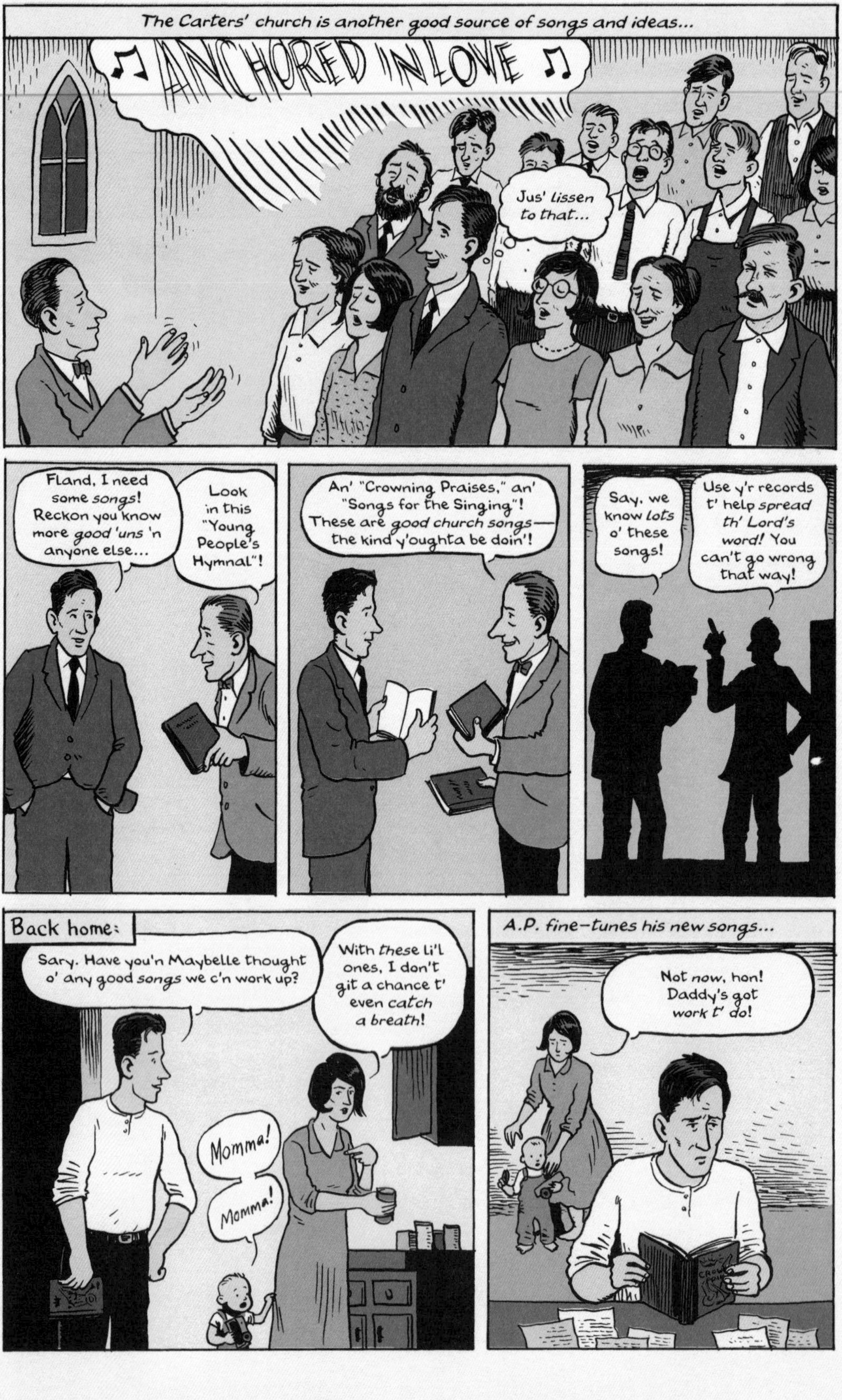
The Carters' church is another good source of songs and ideas...
ANCHORED IN LOVE
Jus' lissen to that...
Fland, I need some songs! Reckon you know more good 'uns 'n anyone else...
Look in this "Young People's Hymnal"!
An' "Crowning Praises," an' "Songs for the Singing"! These are good church songs— the kind y'oughta be doin'!
Say, we know lots o' these songs!
Use y'r records t' help spread th' Lord's word! You can't go wrong that way!
Back home:
Sary. Have you'n Maybelle thought o' any good songs we c'n work up?
With these li'l ones, I don't git a chance t' even catch a breath!
Momma!
Momma!
A.P. fine-tunes his new songs...
Not now, hon! Daddy's got work t' do!

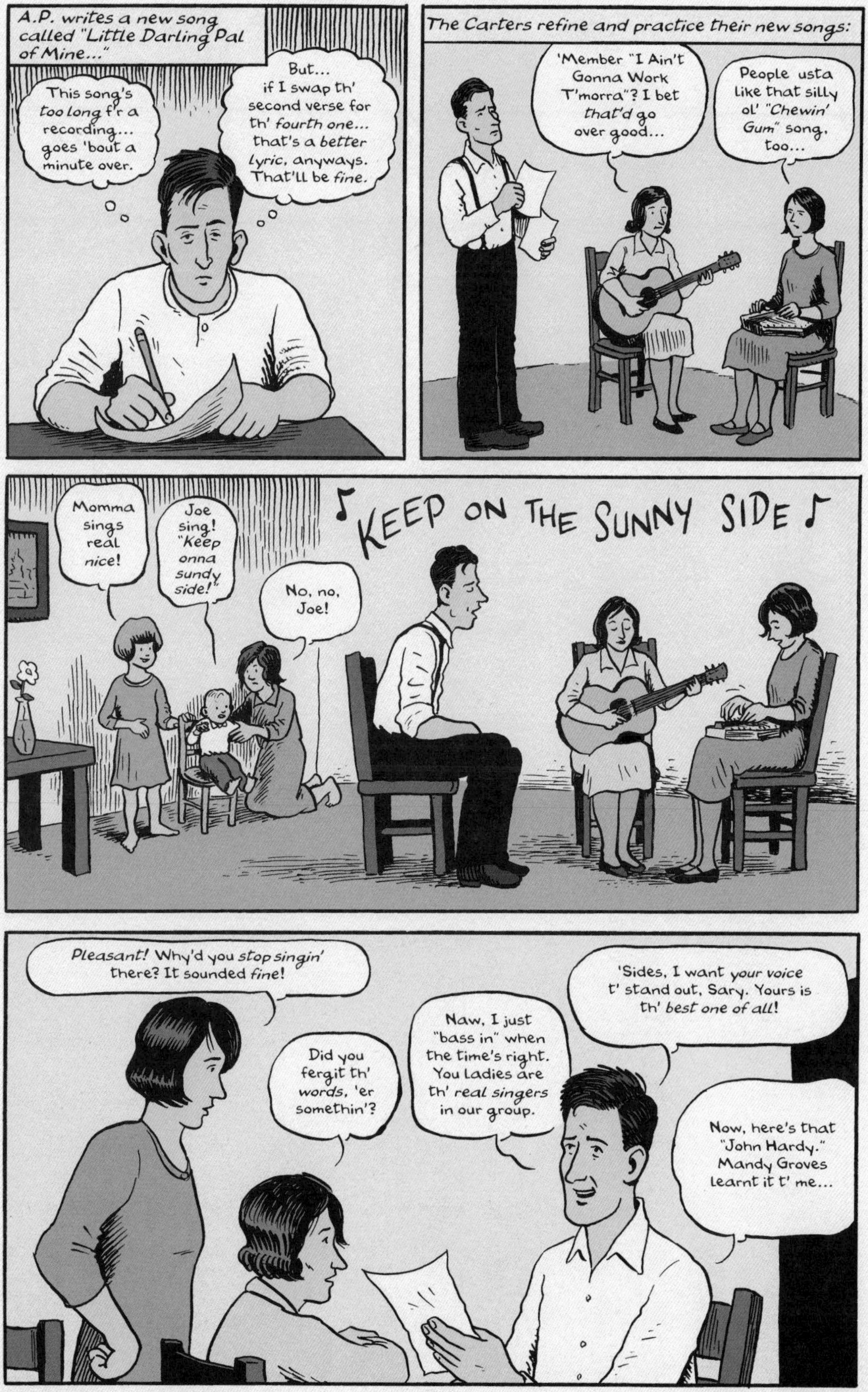
A.P. writes a new song called "Little Darling Pal of Mine..."
This song's too long f'r a recording... goes 'bout a minute over.
But... if I swap th' second verse for th' fourth one... that's a better lyric, anyways. That'll be fine.
The Carters refine and practice their new songs:
'Member "I Ain't Gonna Work T'morra"? I bet that'd go over good...
People usta like that silly ol' "Chewin' Gum" song, too...
Momma sings real nice!
Joe sing! "Keep onna sundy side!"
No, no, Joe!
KEEP ON THE SUNNY SIDE
Pleasant! Why'd you stop singin' there? It sounded fine!
Did you fergit th' words, 'er somethin'?
Naw, I just "bass in" when the time's right. You ladies are th' real singers in our group.
'Sides, I want your voice t' stand out, Sary. Yours is th' best one of all!
Now, here's that "John Hardy." Mandy Groves learnt it t' me...

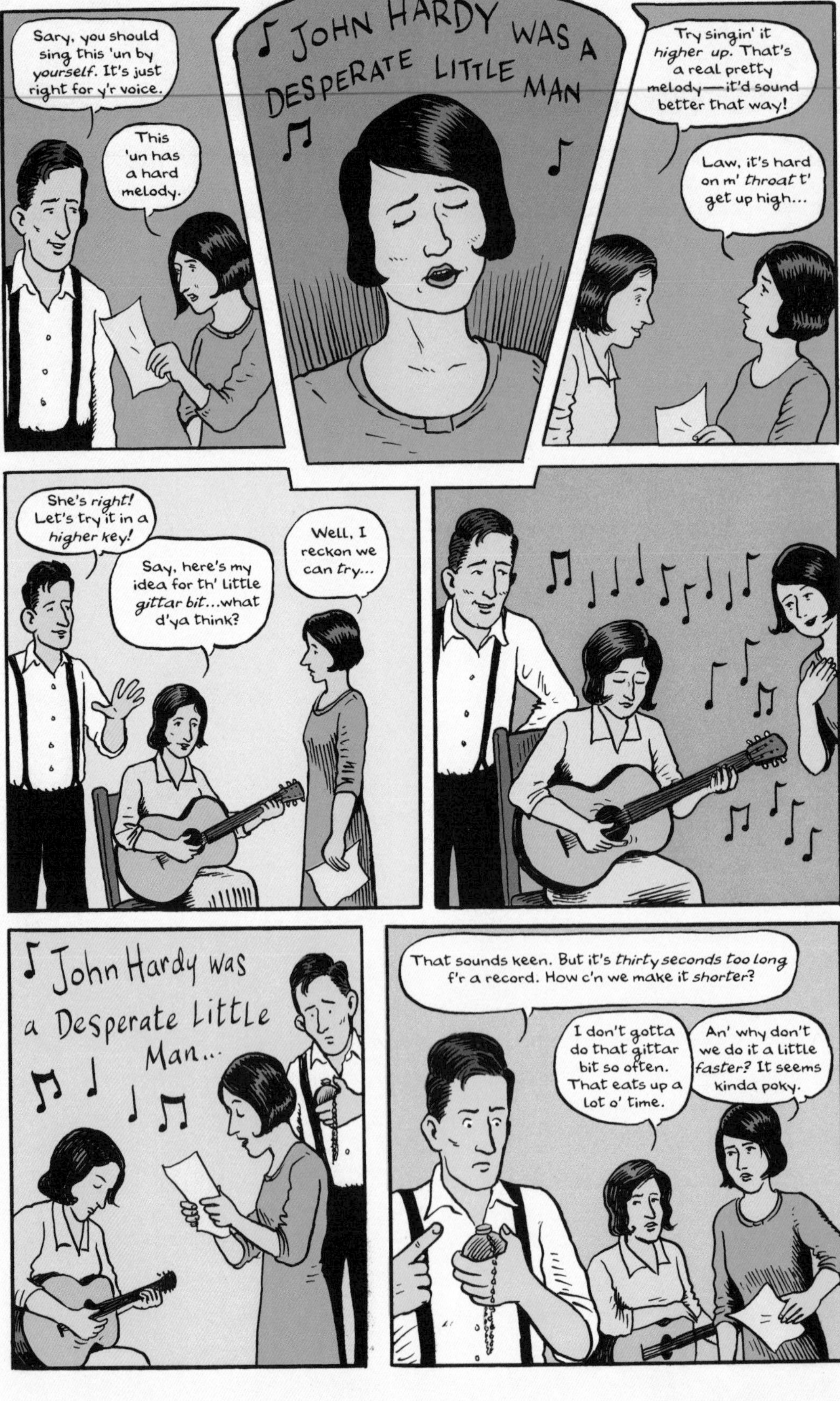
Sary, you should sing this 'un by *yourself*. It's just right for y'r voice.
This 'un has a hard melody.
JOHN HARDY WAS A DESPERATE LITTLE MAN
Try singin' it *higher up*. That's a real pretty melody—it'd sound better that way!
Law, it's hard on m' *throat* t' get up high...
She's *right!* Let's try it in a *higher key!*
Say, here's my idea for th' little *gittar bit*...what d'ya think?
Well, I reckon we can *try*...
John Hardy was a Desperate Little Man...
That sounds keen. But it's *thirty seconds too long* f'r a record. How c'n we make it *shorter*?
I don't gotta do that gittar bit so often. That eats up a lot o' time.
An' why don't we do it a little *faster*? It seems kinda poky.

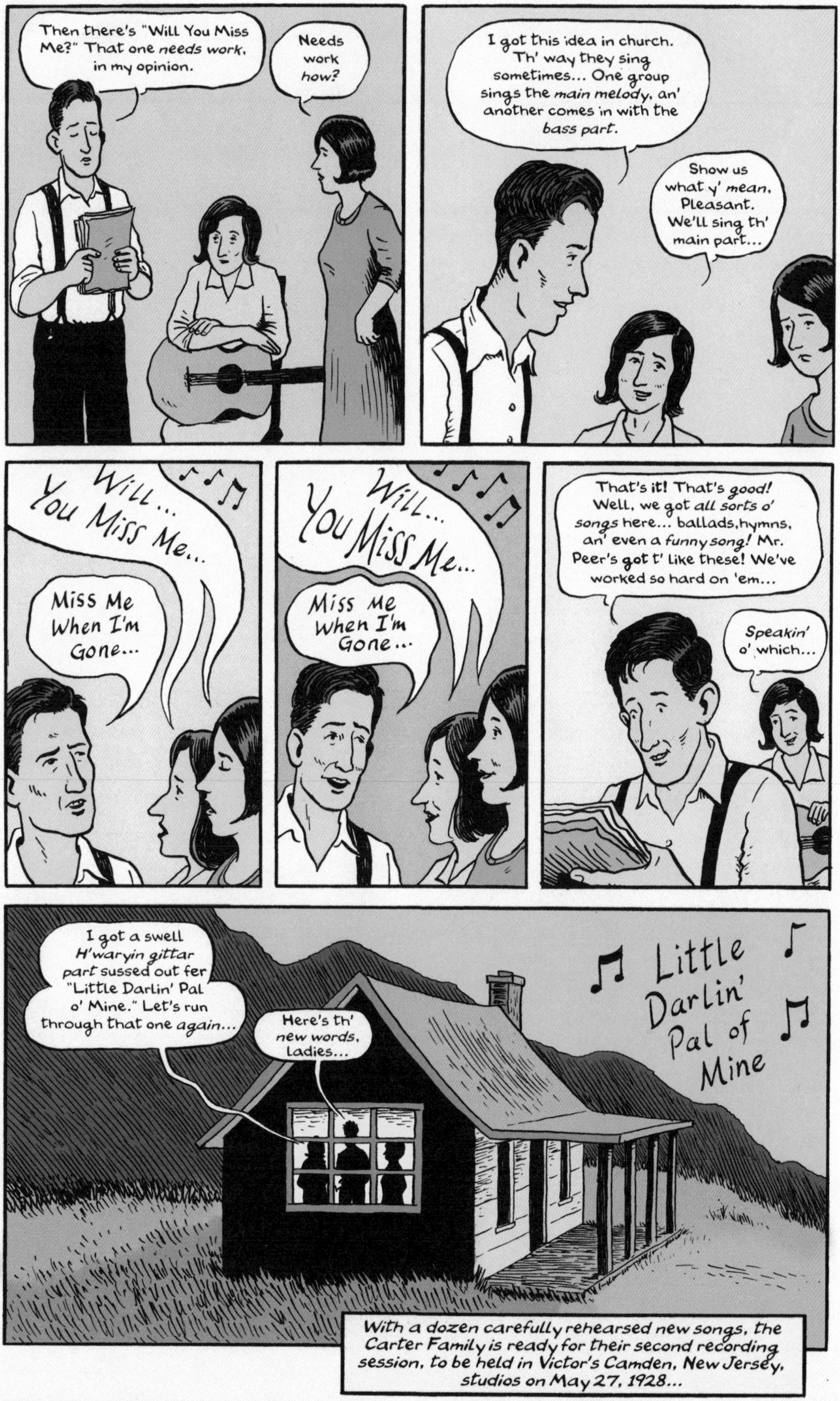
Then there's "Will You Miss Me?" That one *needs work*, in my opinion.
Needs work *how?*
I got this idea in church. Th' way they sing sometimes... One group sings the *main melody*, an' another comes in with the *bass part*.
Show us what y' *mean*, Pleasant. We'll sing th' main part...
Will... You Miss Me...
Miss Me When I'm Gone...
Will... You Miss Me...
Miss Me When I'm Gone...
That's **it!** That's *good!* Well, we got *all sorts o' songs* here... ballads, hymns, an' even a *funny song!* Mr. Peer's **got** t' like these! We've worked so hard on 'em...
Speakin' o' which...
I got a swell *H'waryin gittar part* sussed out fer "Little Darlin' Pal o' Mine." Let's run through that one *again*...
Here's th' *new words*, ladies...
Little Darlin' Pal of Mine
With a dozen carefully rehearsed new songs, the Carter Family is ready for their second recording session, to be held in Victor's Camden, New Jersey, studios on May 27, 1928...

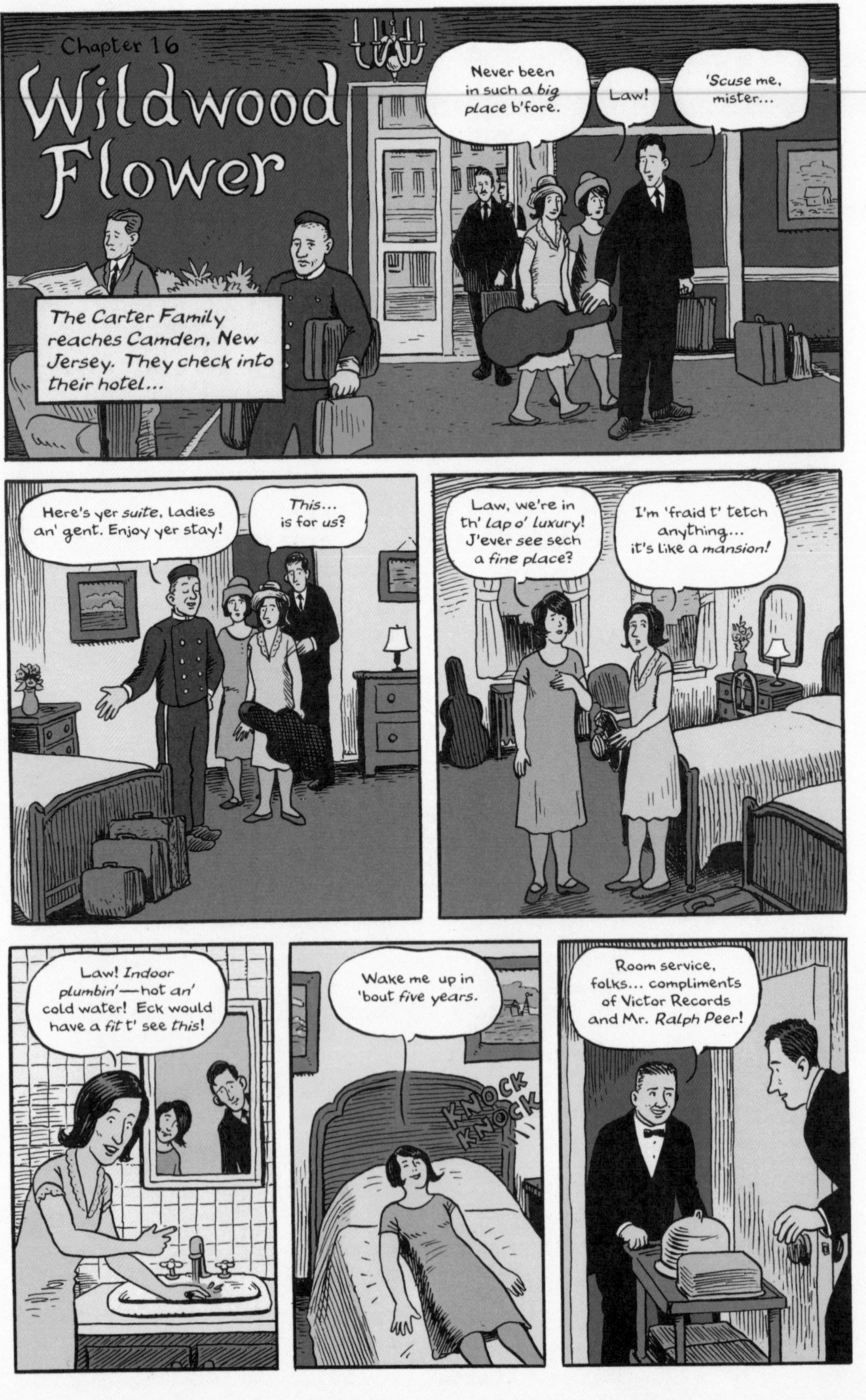
Chapter 16
Wildwood Flower
The Carter Family reaches Camden, New Jersey. They check into their hotel...
Never been in such a *big* place b'fore.
Law!
'Scuse me, mister...
Here's yer *suite*, ladies an' gent. Enjoy yer stay!
This... is for *us*?
Law, we're in th' *lap o' luxury*! J'ever see sech a *fine place*?
I'm 'fraid t' tetch anything... it's like a *mansion*!
Law! *Indoor plumbin'*—hot *an'* cold water! Eck would have a *fit* t' see *this*!
Wake me up in 'bout *five* years.
KNOCK KNOCK
Room service, folks... compliments of Victor Records and Mr. *Ralph Peer*!

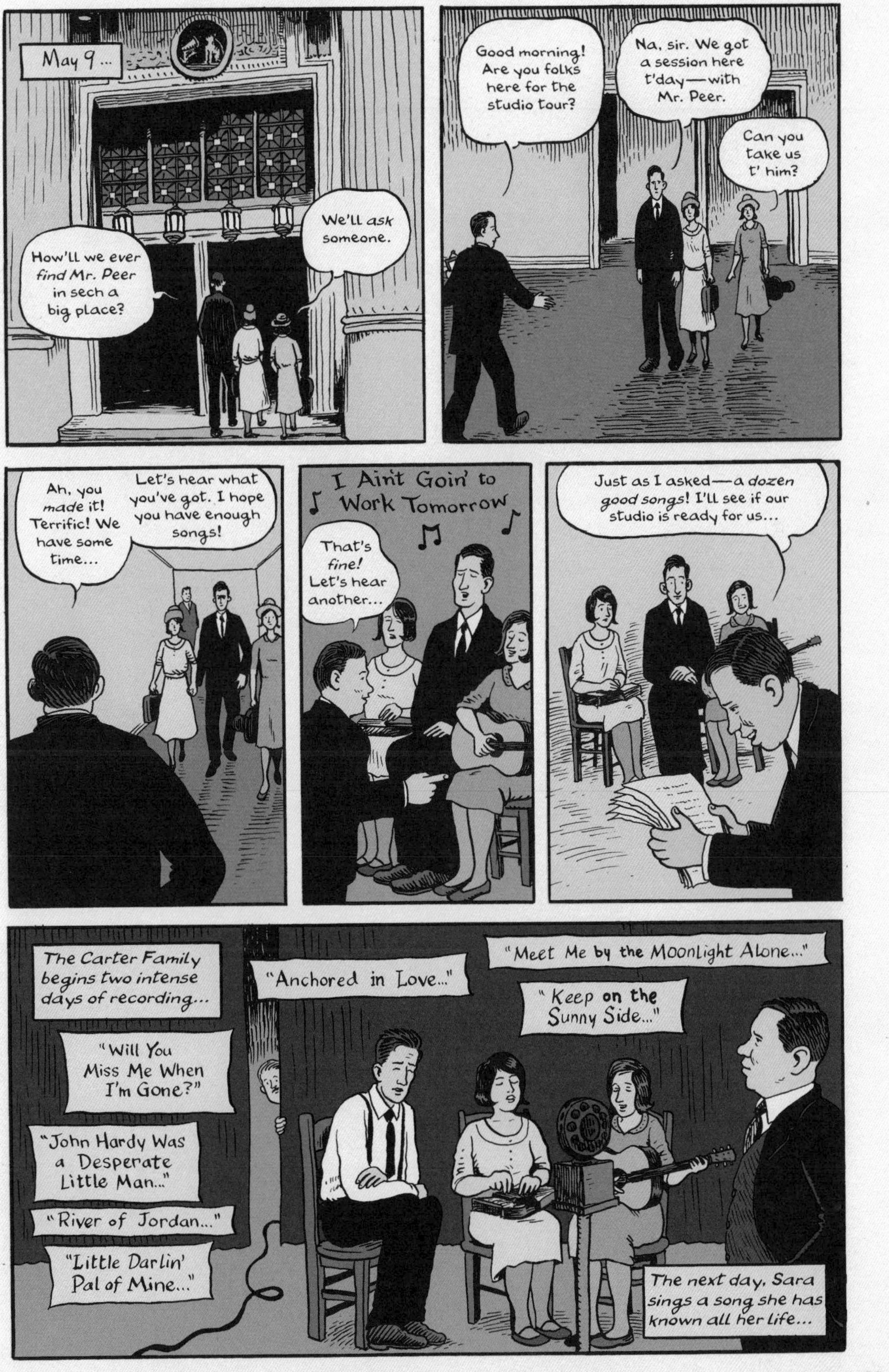
May 9...
How'll we ever find Mr. Peer in sech a big place?
We'll ask someone.
Good morning! Are you folks here for the studio tour?
Na, sir. We got a session here t'day—with Mr. Peer.
Can you take us t' him?
Ah, you made it! Terrific! We have some time...
Let's hear what you've got. I hope you have enough songs!
I Ain't Goin' to Work Tomorrow
That's fine! Let's hear another...
Just as I asked—a dozen good songs! I'll see if our studio is ready for us...
The Carter Family begins two intense days of recording...
"Anchored in Love..."
"Meet Me by the Moonlight Alone..."
"Keep on the Sunny Side..."
"Will You Miss Me When I'm Gone?"
"John Hardy Was a Desperate Little Man..."
"River of Jordan..."
"Little Darlin' Pal of Mine..."
The next day, Sara sings a song she has known all her life...

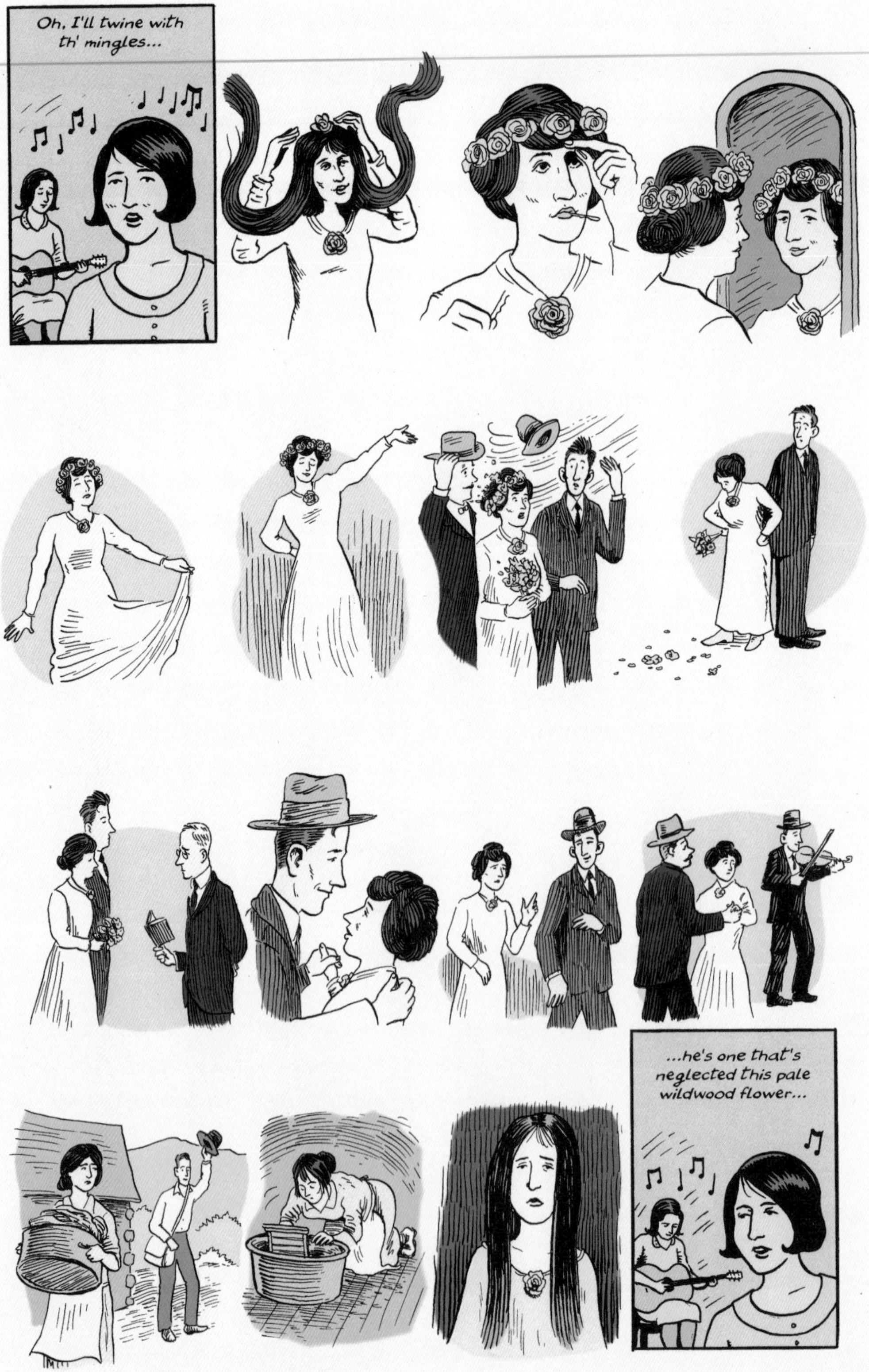
Oh, I'll twine with
th' mingles...
...he's one that's
neglected this pale
wildwood flower...

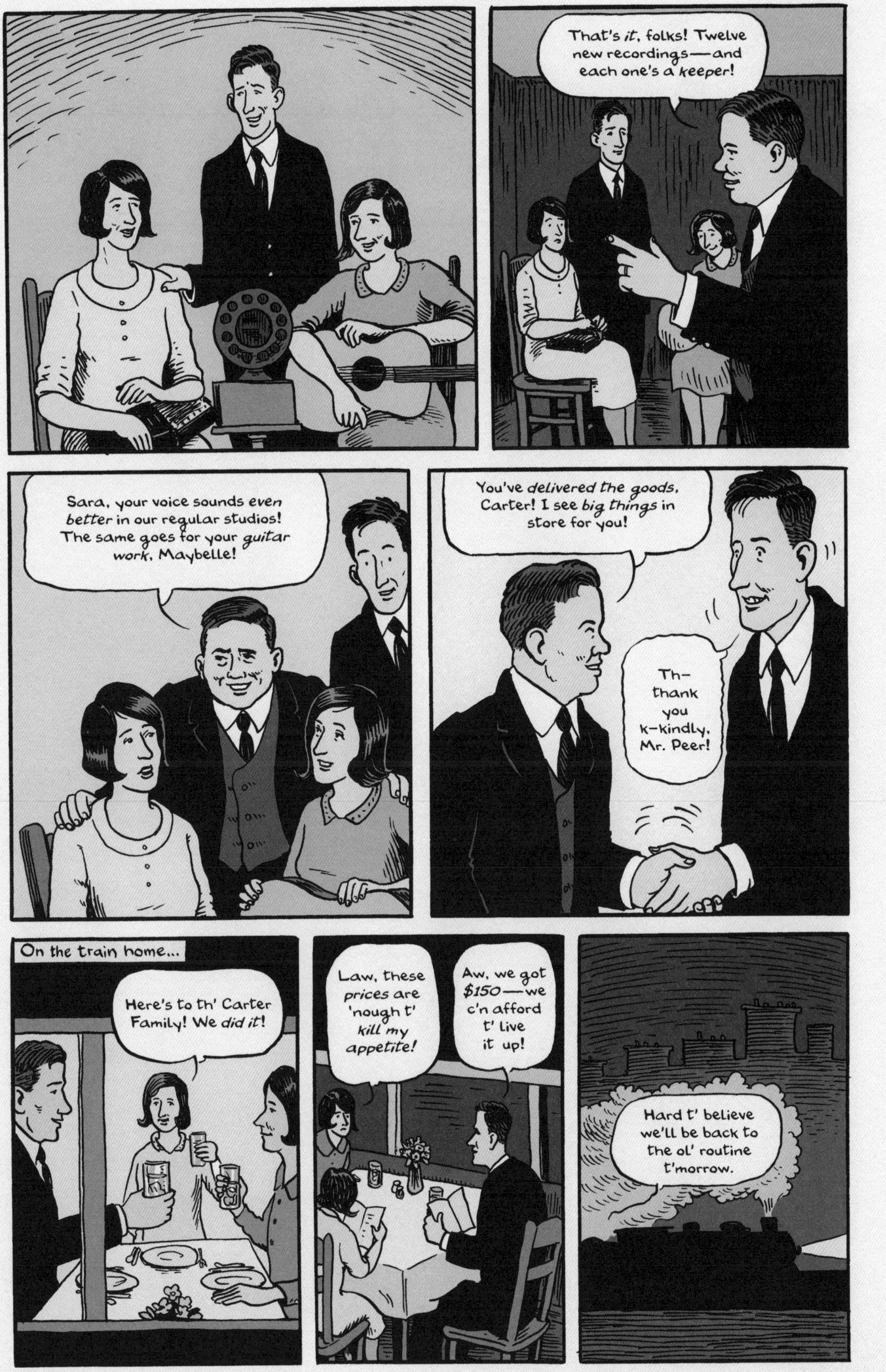
That's *it*, folks! Twelve new recordings—and each one's a *keeper*!
Sara, your voice sounds *even better* in our regular studios! The same goes for your *guitar* work, Maybelle!
You've *delivered the goods*, Carter! I see *big things* in store for you!
Th-thank you k-kindly, Mr. Peer!
On the train home...
Here's to th' Carter Family! We *did it*!
Law, these *prices* are 'nough t' *kill my appetite*!
Aw, we got *$150*—we c'n afford t' live it up!
Hard t' believe we'll be back to the ol' routine t'morrow.

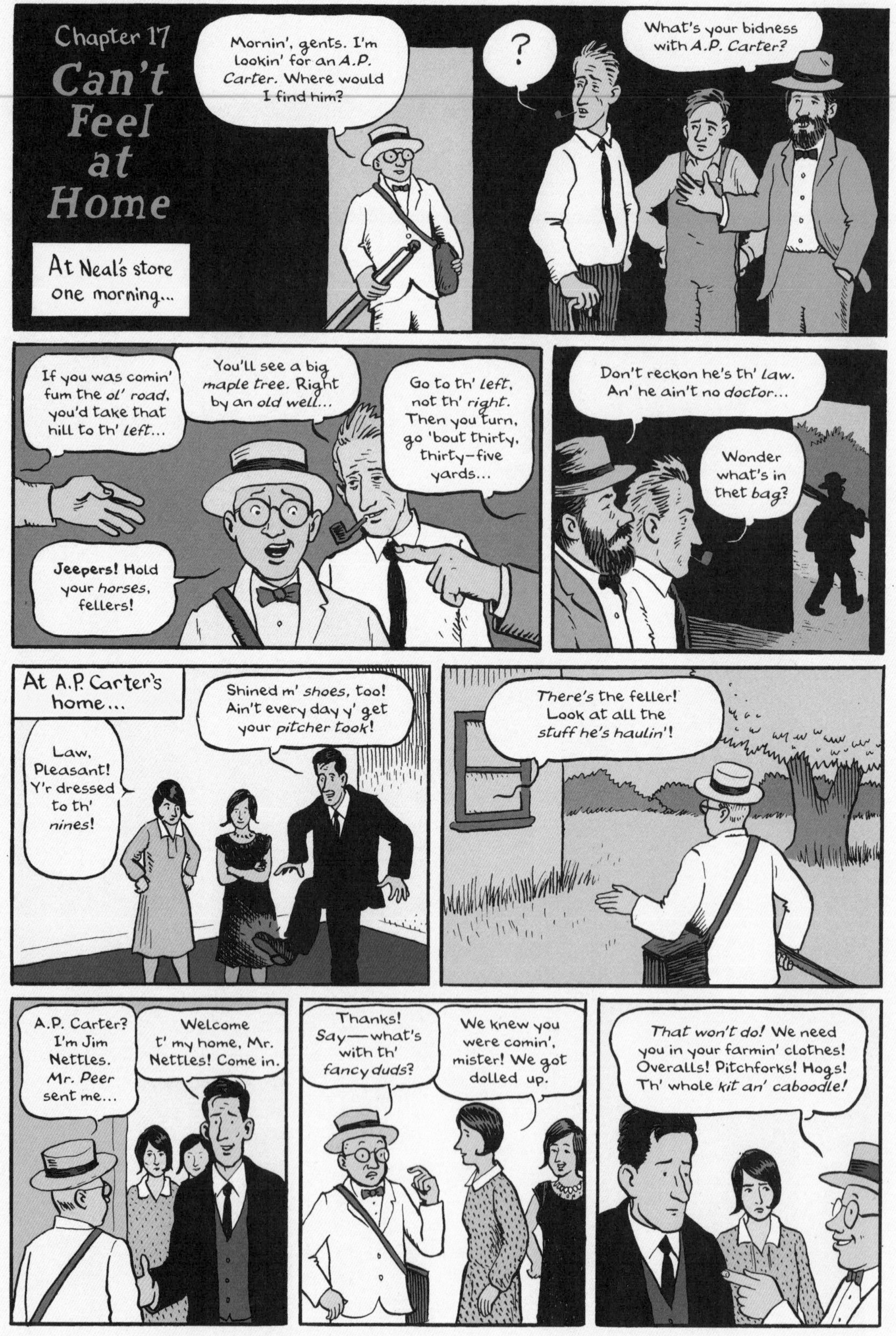
Chapter 17
Can't Feel at Home
At Neal's store one morning...
Mornin', gents. I'm lookin' for an A.P. Carter. Where would I find him?
?
What's your bidness with A.P. Carter?
If you was comin' fum the ol' road, you'd take that hill to th' left...
You'll see a big maple tree. Right by an old well...
Go to th' left, not th' right. Then you turn, go 'bout thirty, thirty-five yards...
Jeepers! Hold your horses, fellers!
Don't reckon he's th' law. An' he ain't no doctor...
Wonder what's in thet bag?
At A.P. Carter's home...
Law, Pleasant! Y'r dressed to th' nines!
Shined m' shoes, too! Ain't every day y' get your pitcher took!
There's the feller! Look at all the stuff he's haulin'!
A.P. Carter? I'm Jim Nettles. Mr. Peer sent me...
Welcome t' my home, Mr. Nettles! Come in.
Thanks! Say—what's with th' fancy duds?
We knew you were comin', mister! We got dolled up.
That won't do! We need you in your farmin' clothes! Overalls! Pitchforks! Hogs! Th' whole kit an' caboodle!

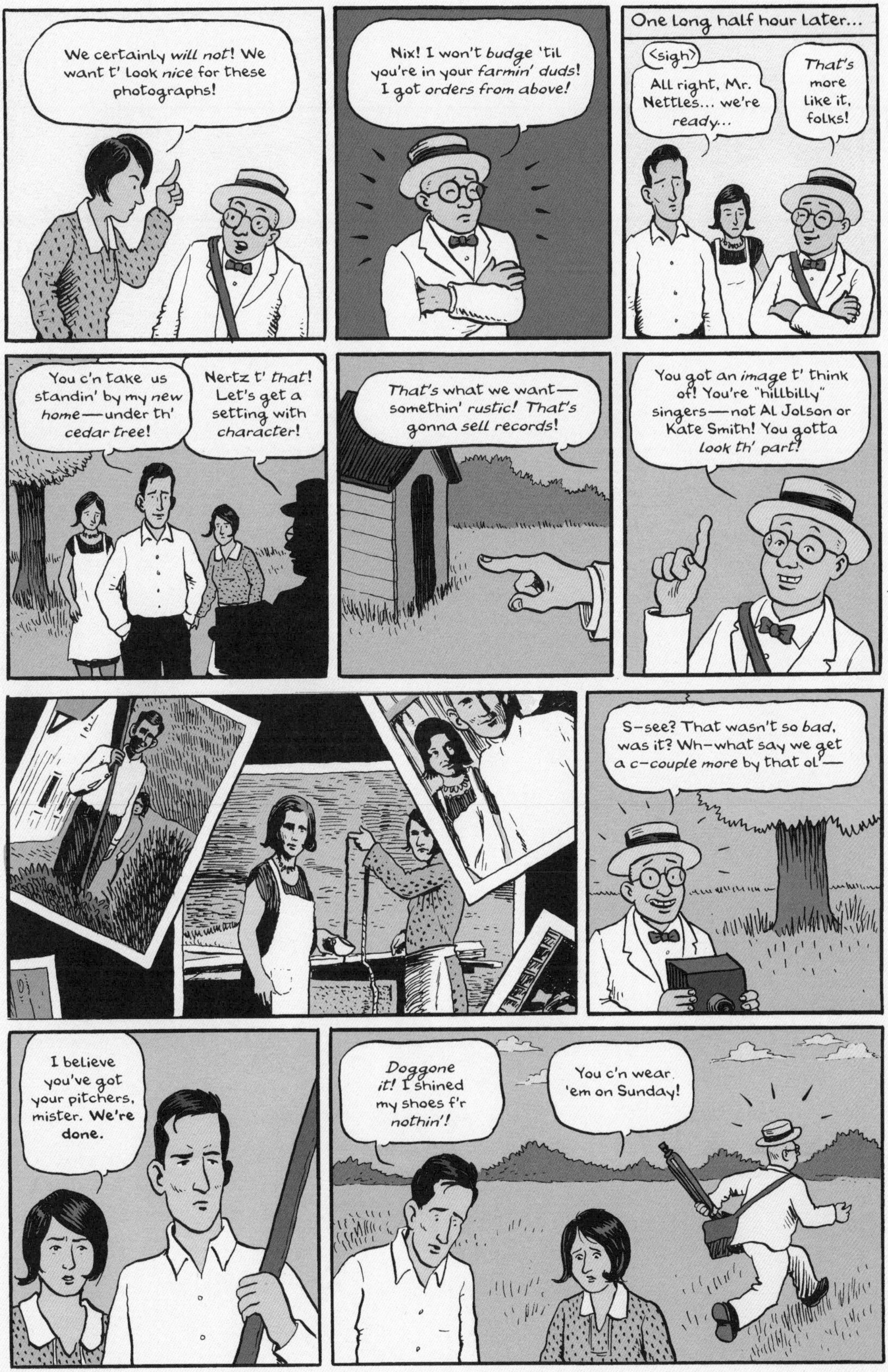
We certainly *will not*! We want t' look *nice* for these photographs!
Nix! I won't *budge* 'til you're in your *farmin' duds*! I got *orders from above*!
One long half hour later...
<sigh>
All right, Mr. Nettles... we're *ready*...
That's more like it, folks!
You c'n take us standin' by my *new home*—under th' *cedar tree*!
Nertz t' *that*! Let's get a setting with *character*!
That's what we want—somethin' *rustic*! *That's* gonna *sell records*!
You got an *image* t' think of! You're "hillbilly" singers—not Al Jolson or Kate Smith! You gotta *look th' part*!
S-see? That wasn't so *bad*, was it? Wh-what say we get a c-*couple more* by that ol'—
I believe you've got your pitchers, mister. **We're done.**
Doggone it! I shined my shoes f'r *nothin'*!
You c'n wear 'em on Sunday!

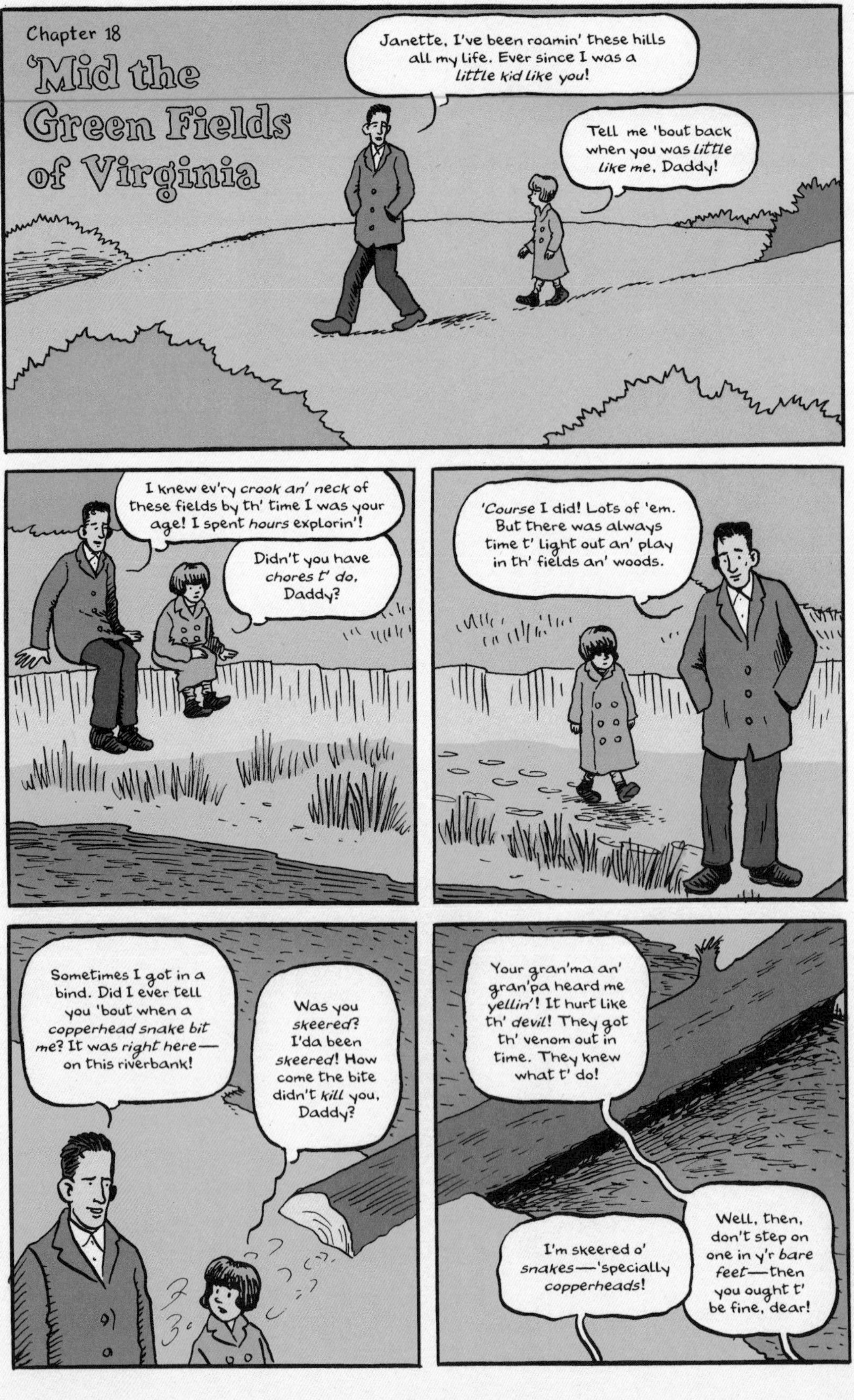
Chapter 18
'Mid the Green Fields of Virginia
Janette, I've been roamin' these hills all my life. Ever since I was a *little kid like you!*
Tell me 'bout back when you was *little like me*, Daddy!
I knew ev'ry *crook an' neck* of these fields by th' time I was your age! I spent *hours* explorin'!
Didn't you have *chores t' do*, Daddy?
'*Course* I did! Lots of 'em. But there was always time t' light out an' play in th' fields an' woods.
Sometimes I got in a bind. Did I ever tell you 'bout when a *copperhead snake bit me*? It was *right here*—on this riverbank!
Was you *skeered*? I'da been *skeered*! How come the bite didn't *kill* you, Daddy?
Your gran'ma an' gran'pa heard me *yellin'*! It hurt like th' *devil*! They got th' venom out in time. They knew what t' do!
I'm skeered o' *snakes*—'specially *copperheads*!
Well, then, don't step on one in y'r *bare feet*—then you ought t' be fine, dear!

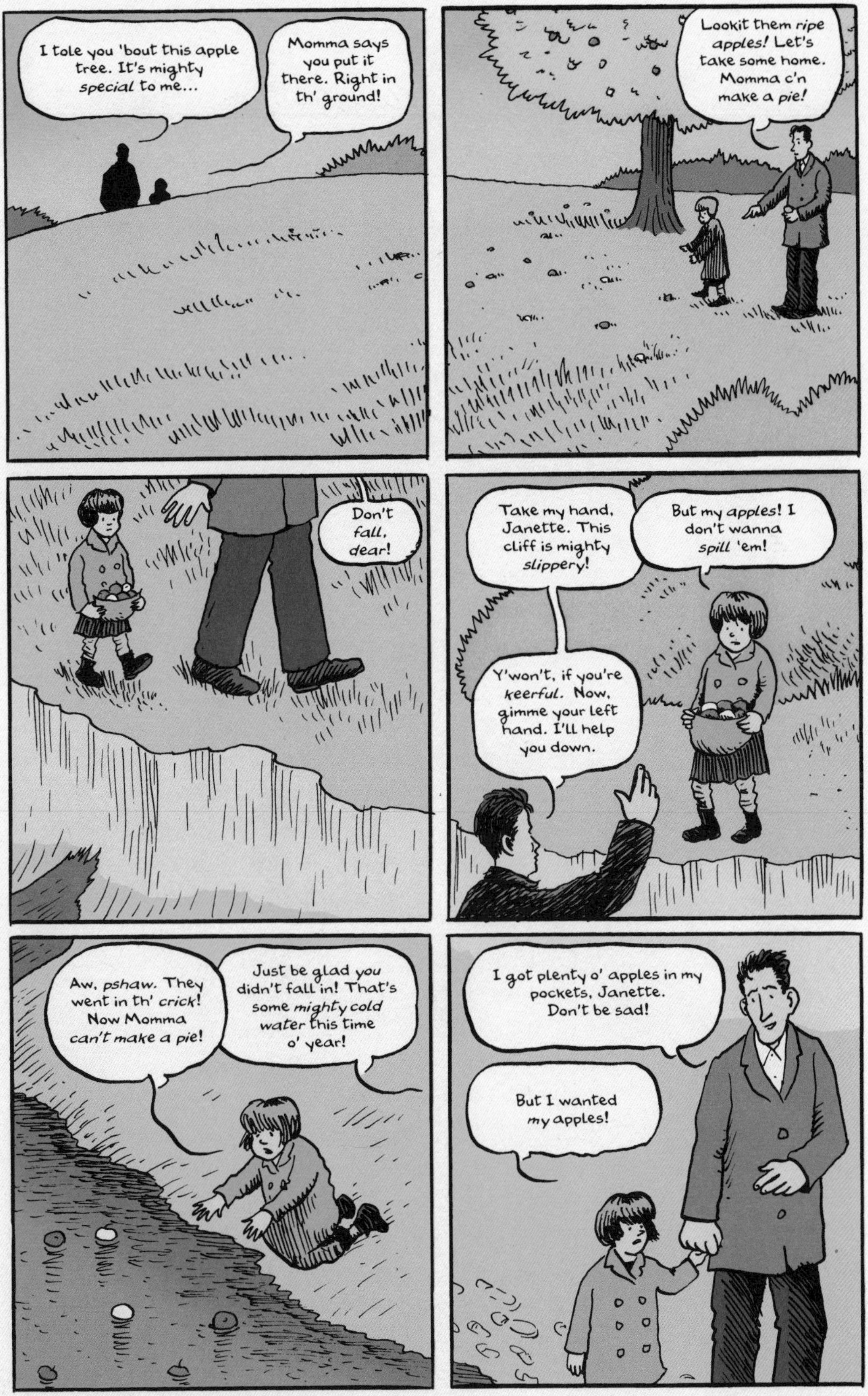
I tole you 'bout this apple tree. It's mighty *special* to me...
Momma says you put it there. Right in th' ground!
Lookit them *ripe apples!* Let's take some home. Momma c'n make a *pie!*
Don't *fall*, dear!
Take my hand, Janette. This cliff is mighty *slippery!*
But my *apples!* I don't wanna *spill* 'em!
Y'won't, if you're *keerful*. Now, gimme your left hand. I'll help you down.
Aw, *pshaw*. They went in th' *crick!* Now Momma *can't* make a *pie!*
Just be glad you didn't fall in! That's some *mighty* cold *water* this time o' year!
I got plenty o' apples in my pockets, Janette. Don't be sad!
But I wanted *my* apples!

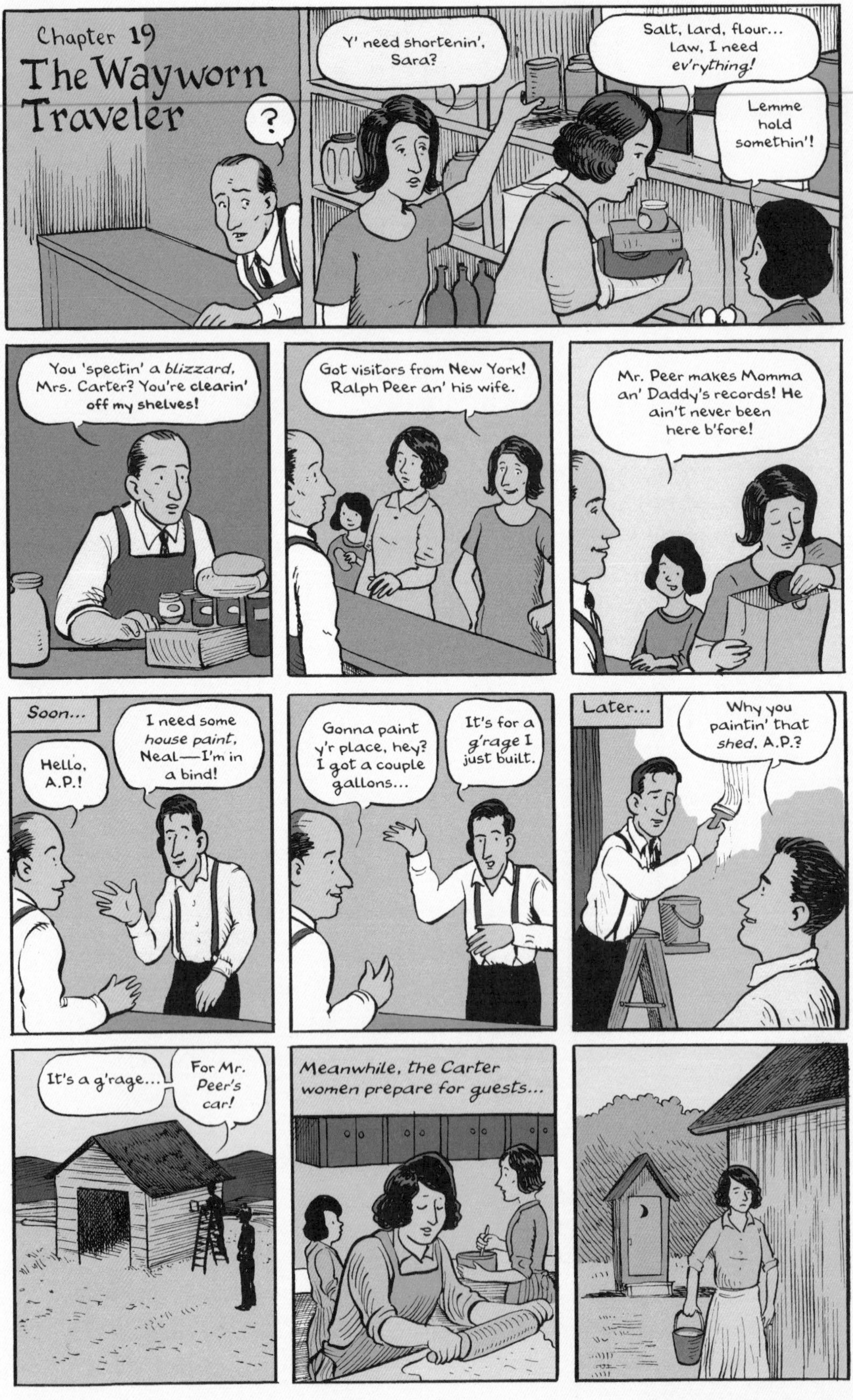
Chapter 19
The Wayworn Traveler
?
Y' need shortenin', Sara?
Salt, lard, flour... Law, I need ev'rything!
Lemme hold somethin'!
You 'spectin' a blizzard, Mrs. Carter? You're clearin' off my shelves!
Got visitors from New York! Ralph Peer an' his wife.
Mr. Peer makes Momma an' Daddy's records! He ain't never been here b'fore!
Soon...
Hello, A.P.!
I need some house paint, Neal—I'm in a bind!
Gonna paint y'r place, hey? I got a couple gallons...
It's for a g'rage I just built.
Later...
Why you paintin' that shed, A.P.?
It's a g'rage...
For Mr. Peer's car!
Meanwhile, the Carter women prepare for guests...

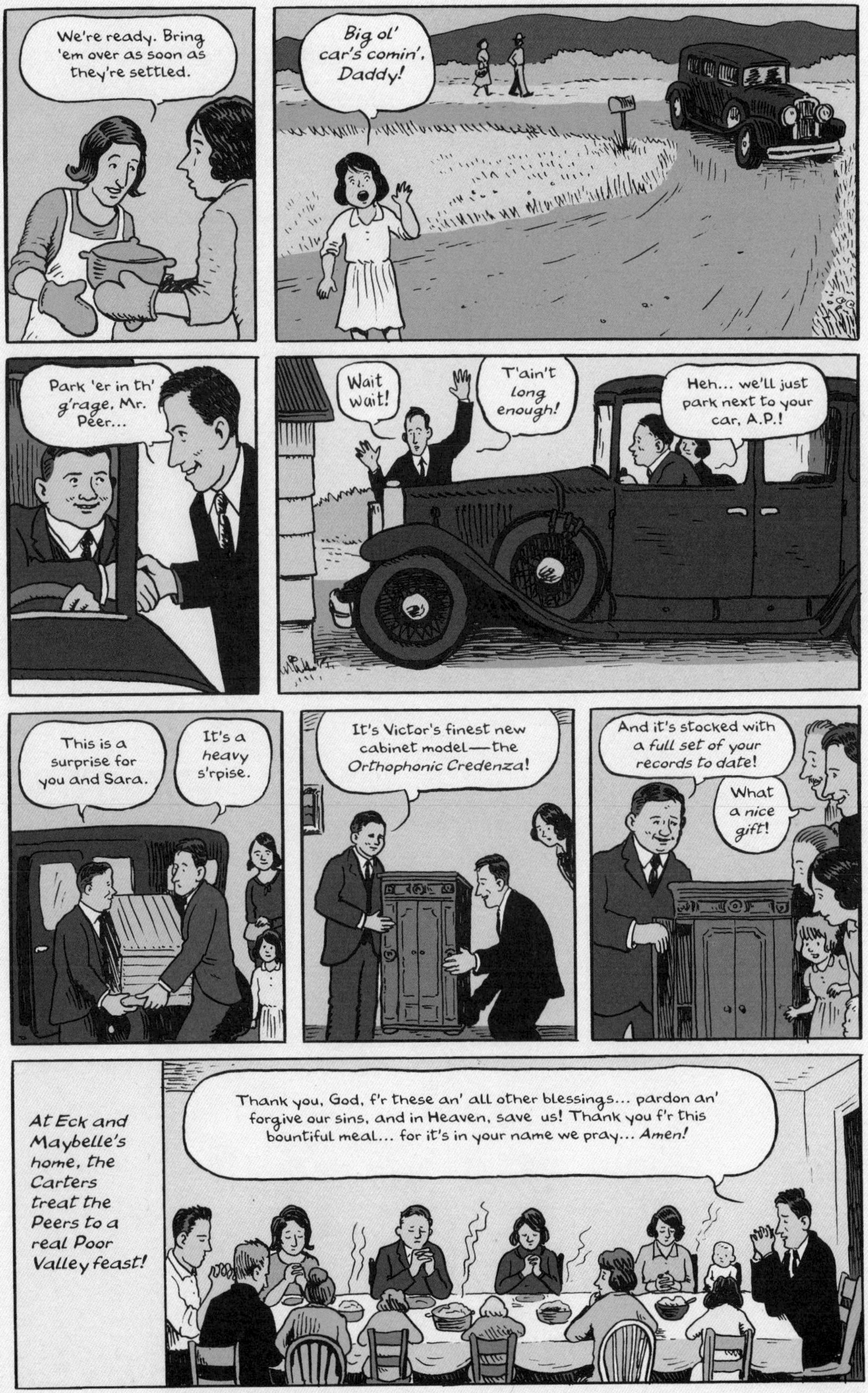
We're ready. Bring 'em over as soon as they're settled.
Big ol' car's comin', Daddy!
Park 'er in th' g'rage, Mr. Peer...
Wait wait!
T'ain't long enough!
Heh... we'll just park next to your car, A.P.!
This is a surprise for you and Sara.
It's a heavy s'rpise.
It's Victor's finest new cabinet model—the Orthophonic Credenza!
And it's stocked with a full set of your records to date!
What a nice gift!
At Eck and Maybelle's home, the Carters treat the Peers to a real Poor Valley feast!
Thank you, God, f'r these an' all other blessings... pardon an' forgive our sins, and in Heaven, save us! Thank you f'r this bountiful meal... for it's in your name we pray... Amen!

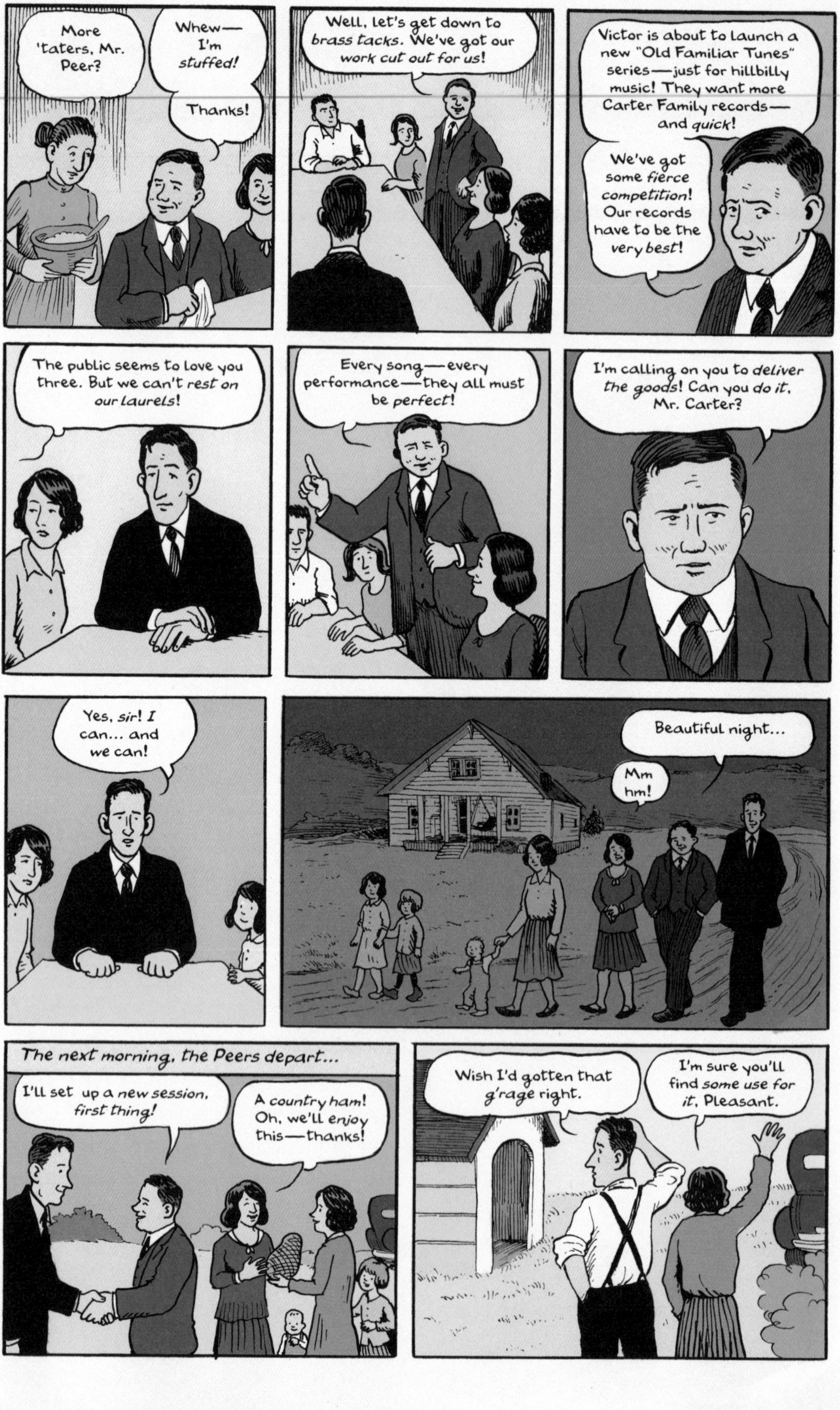
More 'taters, Mr. Peer?
Whew— I'm *stuffed!*
Thanks!
Well, let's get down to *brass tacks.* We've got our *work cut out for us!*
Victor is about to launch a new "Old Familiar Tunes" series—just for hillbilly music! They want more Carter Family records—and *quick!*
We've got some *fierce competition!* Our records have to be the *very best!*
The public seems to love you three. But we can't *rest on our laurels!*
Every song—every performance—they all must be *perfect!*
I'm calling on you to *deliver the goods!* Can you *do it,* Mr. Carter?
Yes, *sir! I* can... and we can!
Beautiful night...
Mm hm!
The next morning, the Peers depart...
I'll set up a *new session, first thing!*
A *country ham!* Oh, we'll *enjoy* this—thanks!
Wish I'd gotten that g'rage right.
I'm sure you'll find *some use for it,* Pleasant.

Chapter 20

The Program Is Morally Good

Beg pardon, mister... c'd you put this paper in y'r winder?

S'pose so... what's it fer?

"Look... Victor... artist..."

Thank y' kindly!

LOOK!

Victor Artist

P. C. CARTER

and the

r Family

give a

PROGRAM

Theatre

y August t.

Morally Good

25 C

Law, it's th' Carter Fam'ly!

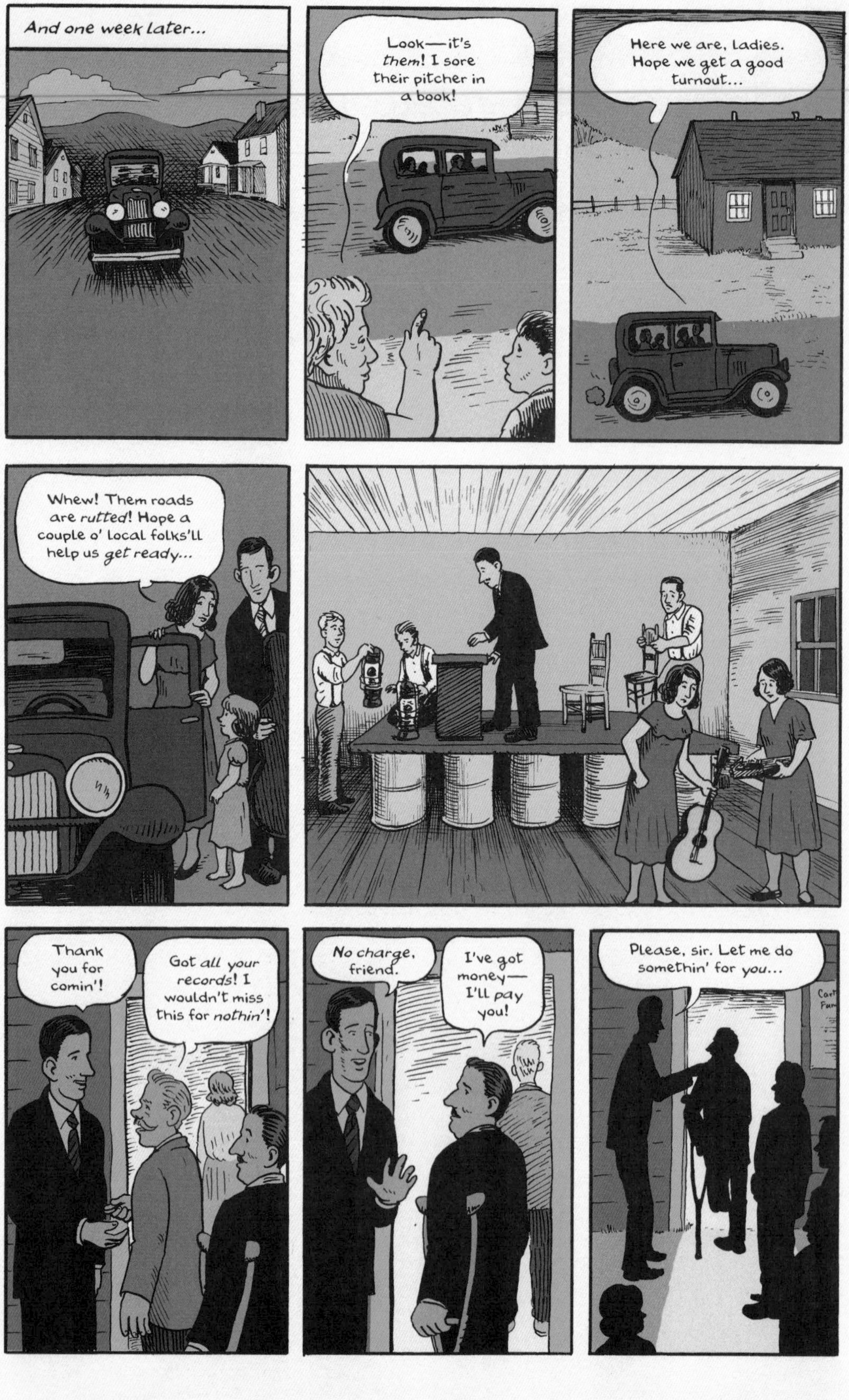
And one week later...
Look—it's *them*! I sore their pitcher in a book!
Here we are, ladies. Hope we get a good turnout...
Whew! Them roads are *rutted*! Hope a couple o' local folks'll help us *get* ready...
Thank you for comin'!
Got *all* your *records*! I wouldn't miss this for *nothin'*!
No charge, friend.
I've got money— I'll *pay* you!
Please, sir. Let me do somethin' for *you*...

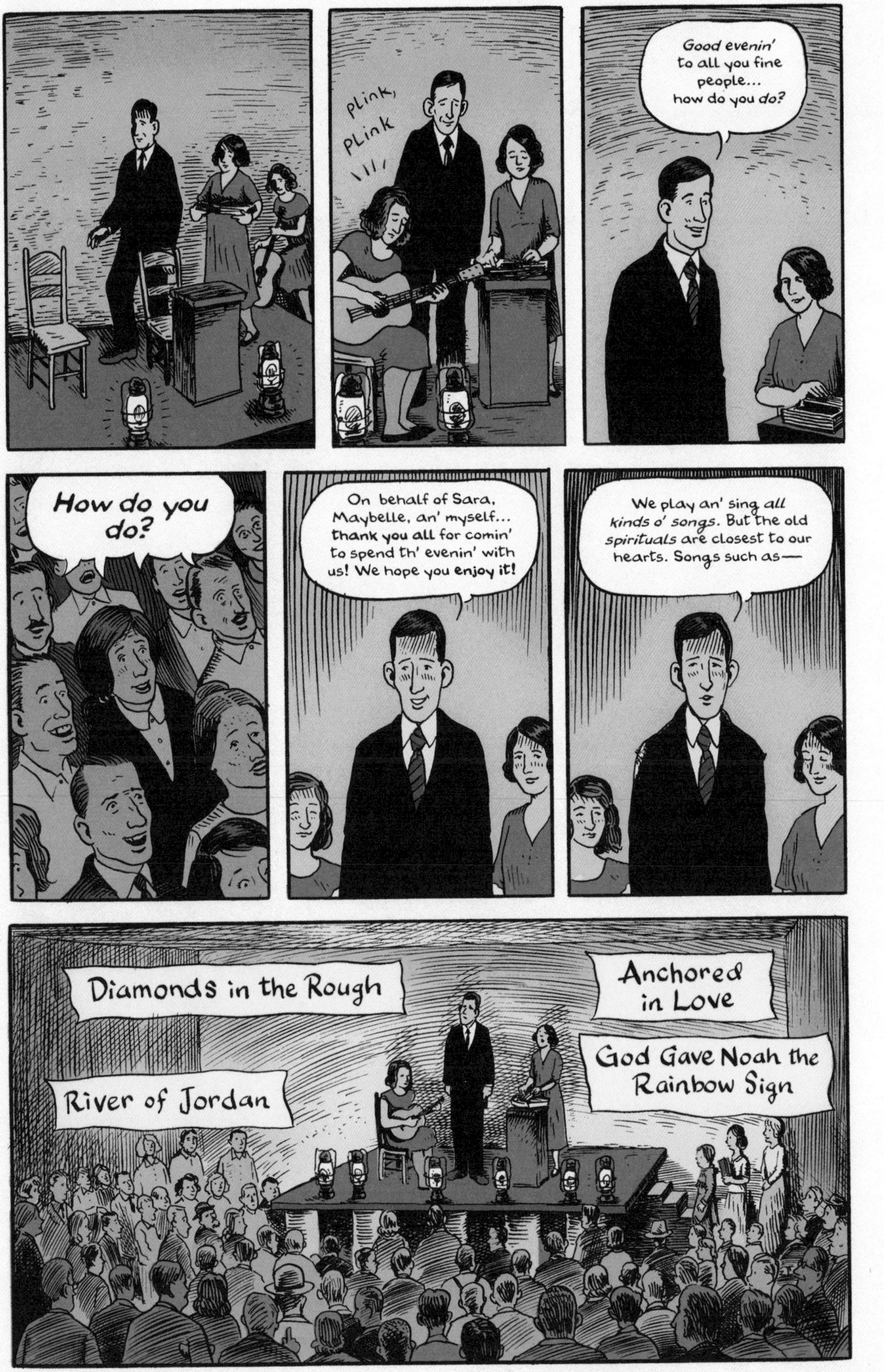
plink,
plink
Good evenin' to all you fine people... how do you *do?*
How do you do?
On behalf of Sara, Maybelle, an' myself... **thank you all** for comin' to spend th' evenin' with us! We hope you **enjoy it!**
We play an' sing *all kinds o' songs*. But the old *spirituals* are closest to our hearts. Songs such as—
Diamonds in the Rough
Anchored in Love
God Gave Noah the Rainbow Sign
River of Jordan

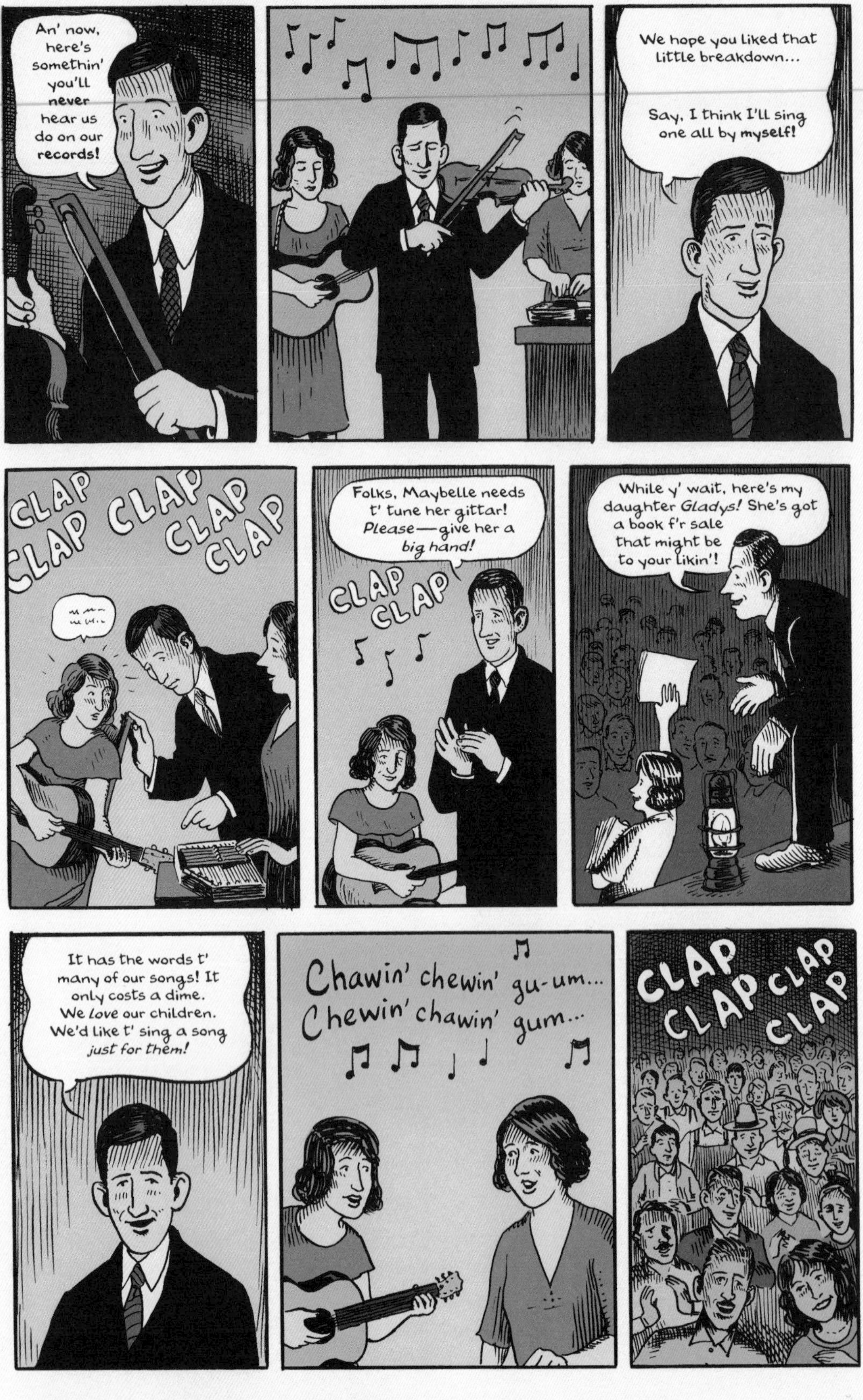
An' now, here's somethin' you'll never hear us do on our records!
We hope you liked that little breakdown...
Say, I think I'll sing one all by myself!
CLAP CLAP CLAP CLAP CLAP
Folks, Maybelle needs t' tune her gittar! Please—give her a big hand!
CLAP CLAP
While y' wait, here's my daughter Gladys! She's got a book f'r sale that might be to your likin'!
It has the words t' many of our songs! It only costs a dime. We love our children. We'd like t' sing a song just for them!
Chawin' chewin' gu-um...
Chewin' chawin' gum...
CLAP CLAP CLAP CLAP

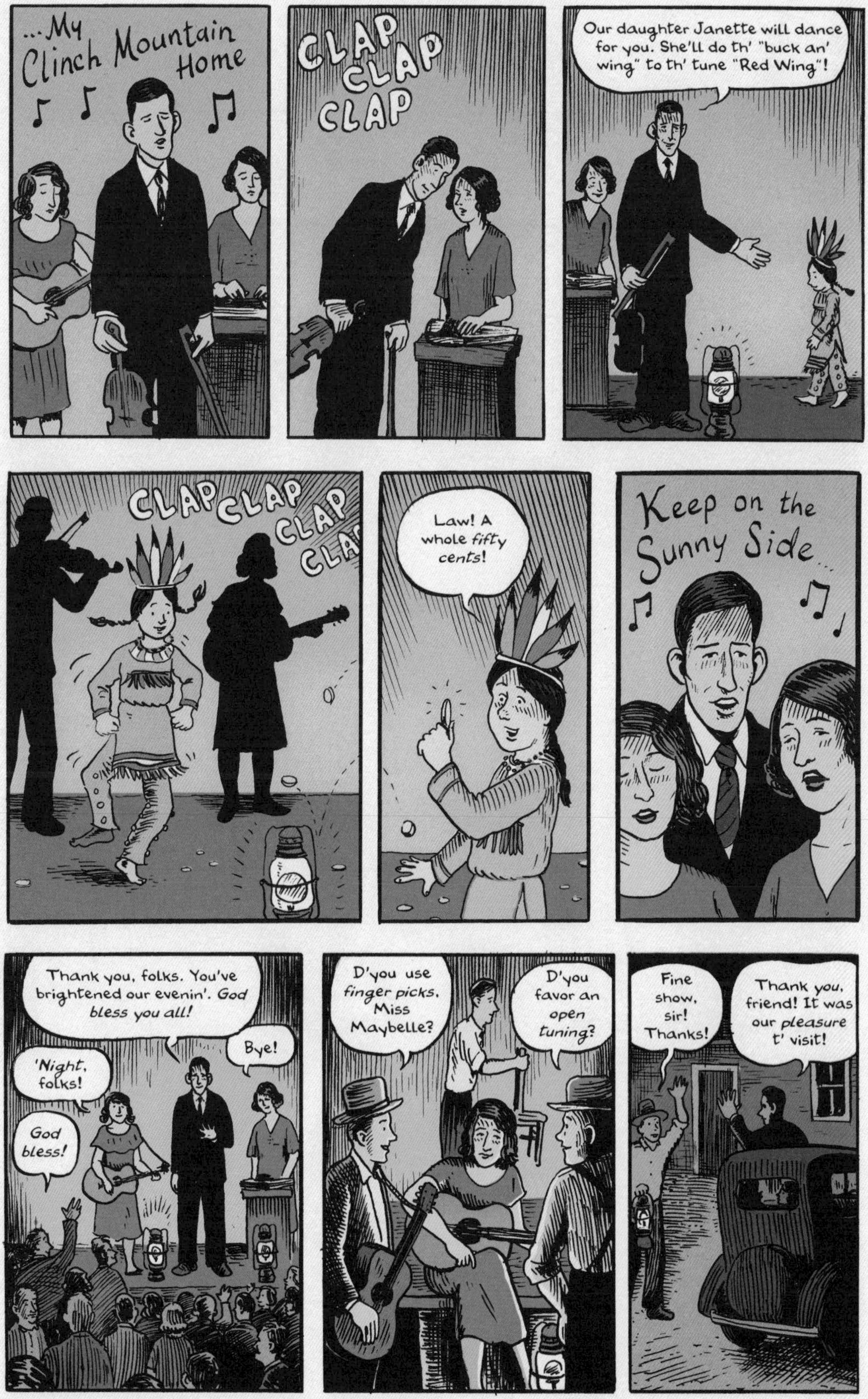
...My Clinch Mountain Home
CLAP CLAP CLAP
Our daughter Janette will dance for you. She'll do th' "buck an' wing" to th' tune "Red Wing"!
CLAP CLAP CLAP CLAP
Law! A whole *fifty* cents!
Keep on the Sunny Side...
Thank you, folks. You've brightened our evenin'. *God bless you all!*
'Night, folks!
Bye!
God bless!
D'you use *finger picks,* Miss Maybelle?
D'you favor an *open tuning*?
Fine show, sir! Thanks!
Thank you, friend! It was our *pleasure* t' visit!

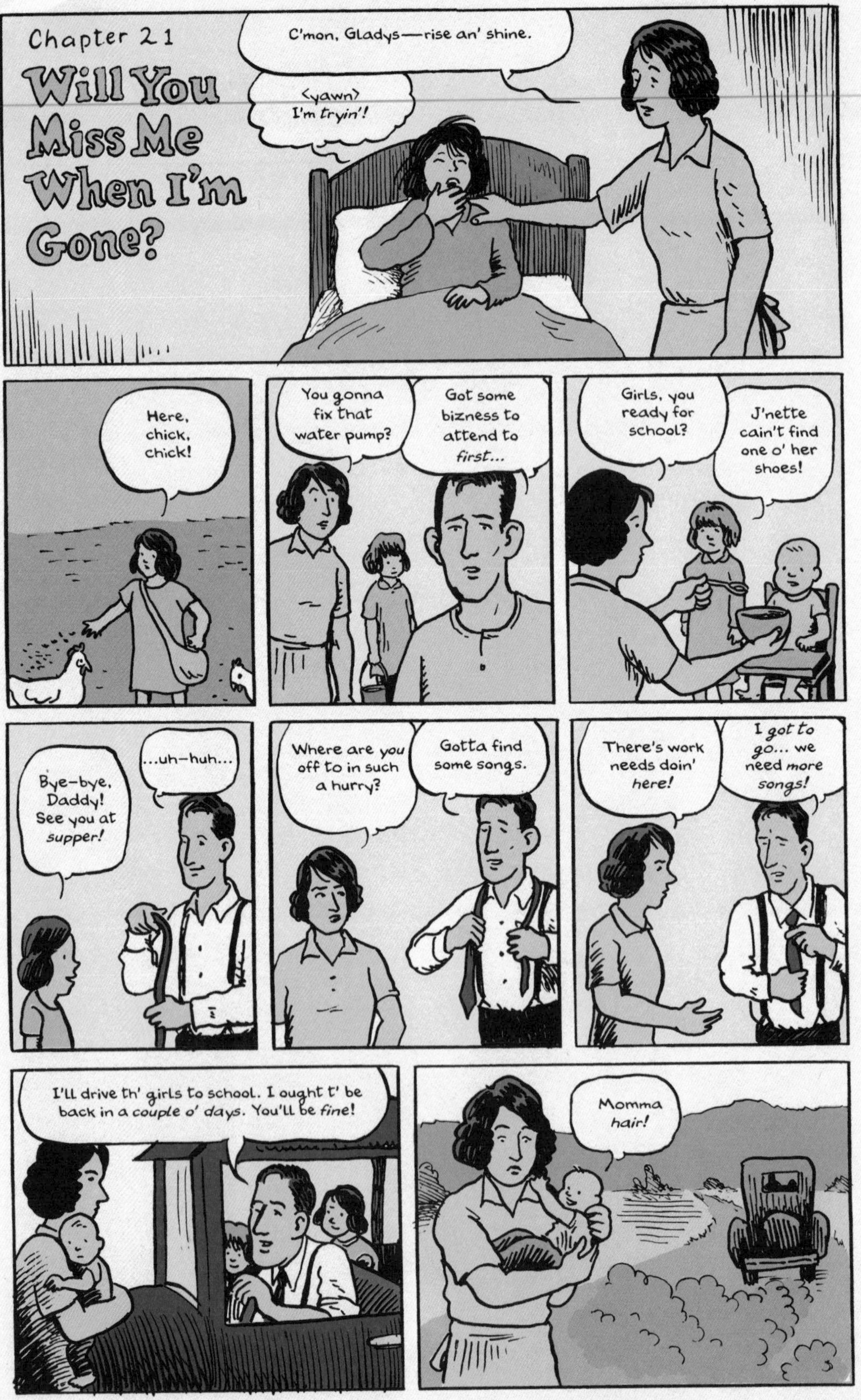
Chapter 21
Will You Miss Me When I'm Gone?
C'mon, Gladys—rise an' shine.
<yawn> I'm tryin'!
Here, chick, chick!
You gonna fix that water pump?
Got some bizness to attend to first...
Girls, you ready for school?
J'nette cain't find one o' her shoes!
Bye-bye, Daddy! See you at supper!
...uh-huh...
Where are you off to in such a hurry?
Gotta find some songs.
There's work needs doin' here!
I got to go... we need more songs!
I'll drive th' girls to school. I ought t' be back in a couple o' days. You'll be fine!
Momma hair!

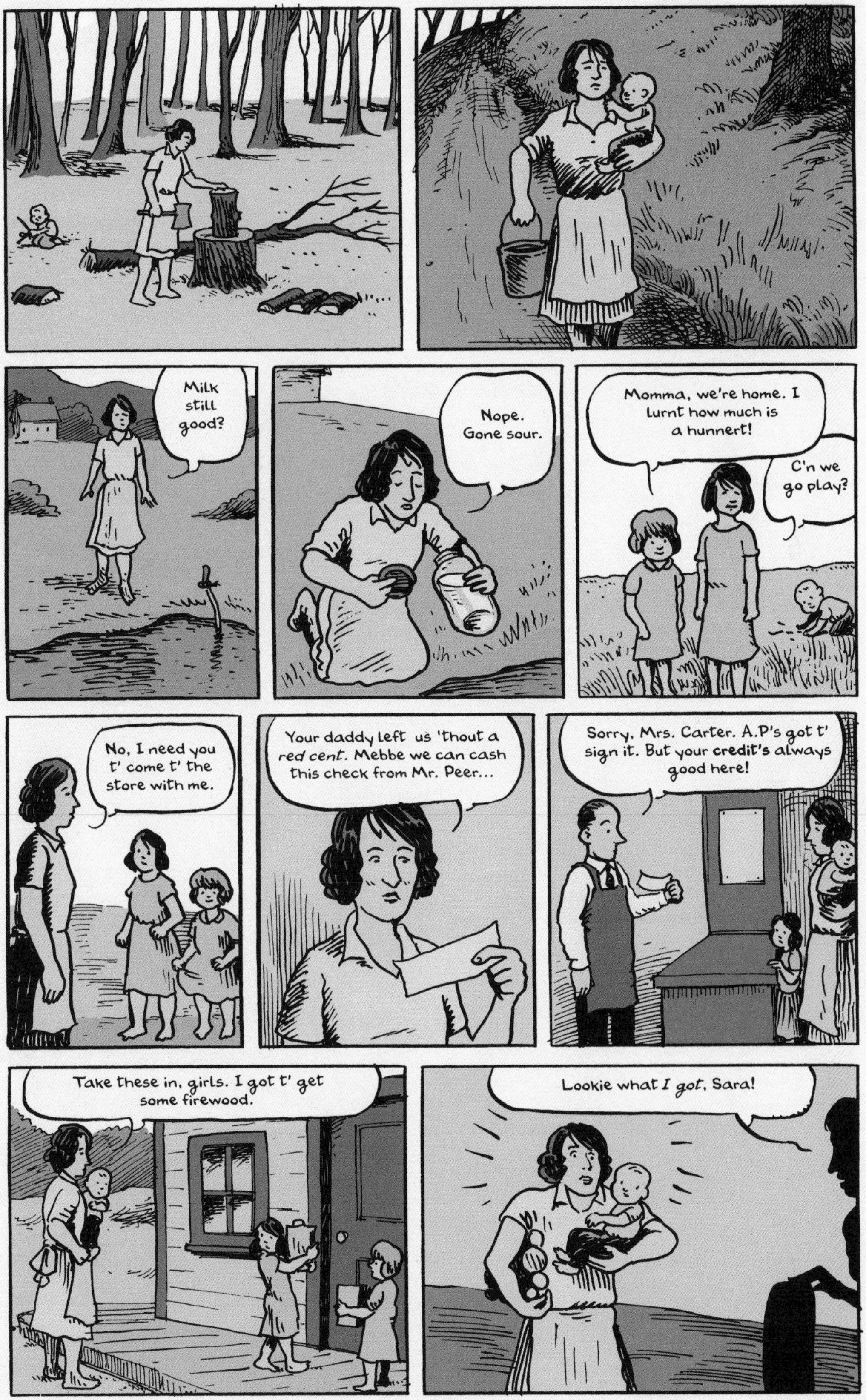
Milk still good?
Nope. Gone sour.
Momma, we're home. I lurnt how much is a hunnert!
C'n we go play?
No, I need you t' come t' the store with me.
Your daddy left us 'thout a *red cent*. Mebbe we can cash this check from Mr. Peer...
Sorry, Mrs. Carter. A.P's got t' sign it. But your **credit's** always good here!
Take these in, girls. I got t' get some firewood.
Lookie what *I got*, Sara!

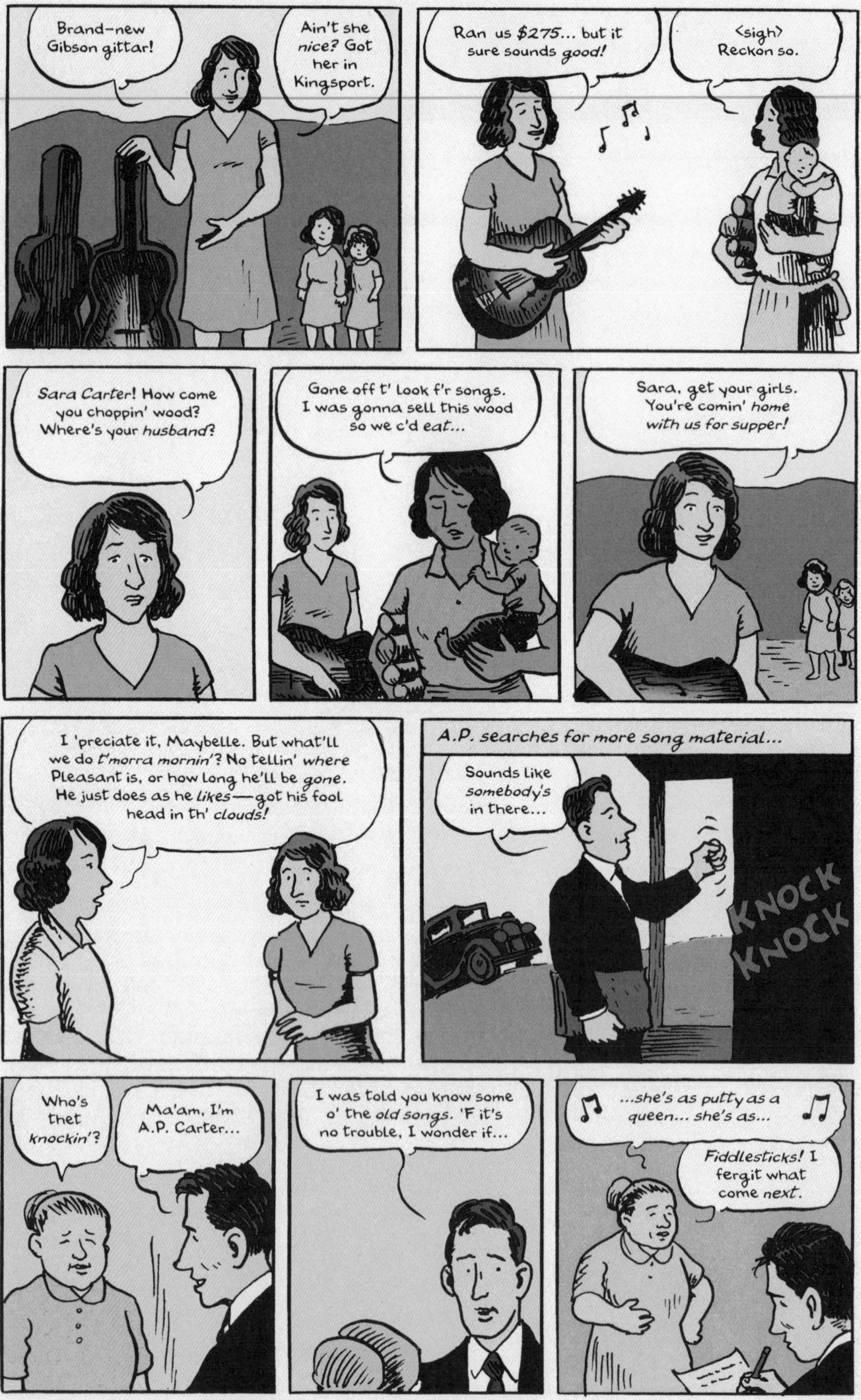
Brand-new Gibson gittar!
Ain't she nice? Got her in Kingsport.
Ran us $275... but it sure sounds good!
<sigh> Reckon so.
Sara Carter! How come you choppin' wood? Where's your husband?
Gone off t' look f'r songs. I was gonna sell this wood so we c'd eat...
Sara, get your girls. You're comin' home with us for supper!
I 'preciate it, Maybelle. But what'll we do t'morra mornin'? No tellin' where Pleasant is, or how long he'll be gone. He just does as he likes—got his fool head in th' clouds!
A.P. searches for more song material...
Sounds like somebody's in there...
KNOCK KNOCK
Who's thet knockin'?
Ma'am, I'm A.P. Carter...
I was told you know some o' the old songs. 'F it's no trouble, I wonder if...
...she's as putty as a queen... she's as...
Fiddlesticks! I fergit what come next.

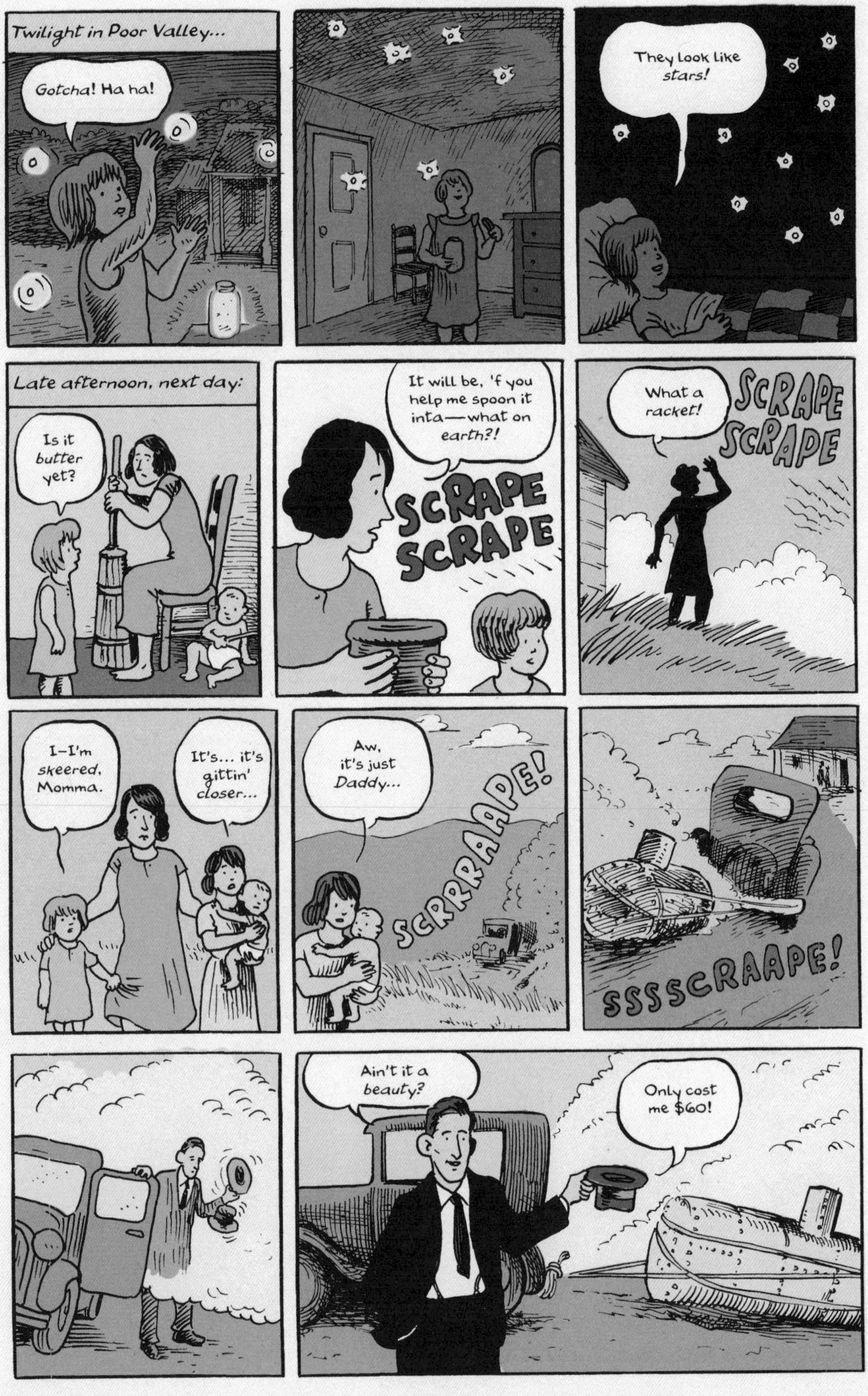
Twilight in Poor Valley...
Gotcha! Ha ha!
They look like stars!
Late afternoon, next day:
Is it butter yet?
It will be, 'f you help me spoon it inta—what on earth?!
SCRAPE SCRAPE
What a racket!
SCRAPE SCRAPE
I—I'm skeered, Momma.
It's... it's gittin' closer...
Aw, it's just Daddy...
SCRRAAPE!
SSSSCRAAPE!
Ain't it a beauty?
Only cost me $60!

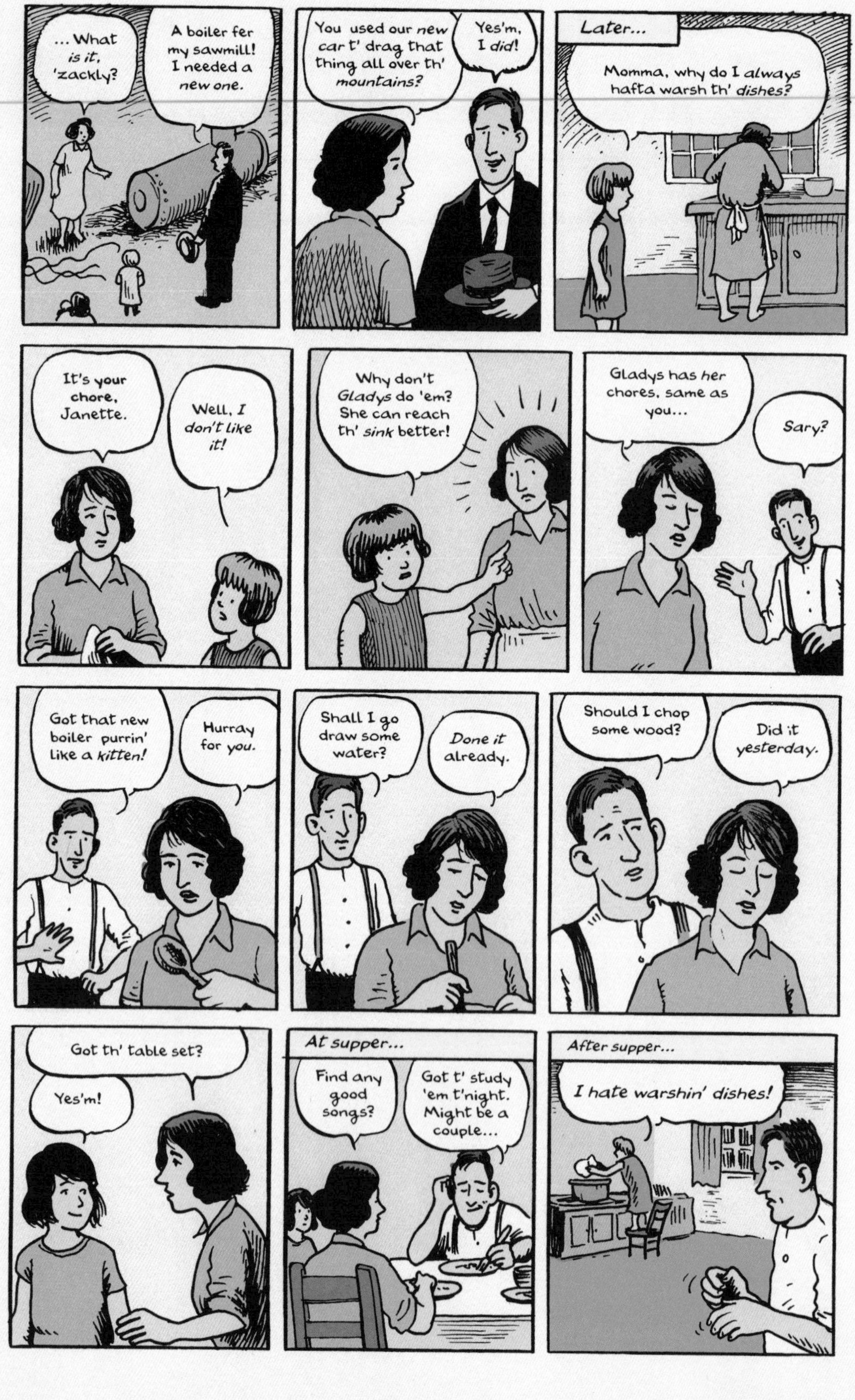
...What *is it*, 'zackly?
A boiler fer my sawmill! I needed a *new one*.
You used our *new* car t' drag that thing all over th' *mountains*?
Yes'm, I *did*!
Later...
Momma, why do I *always* hafta warsh th' *dishes*?
It's your chore, Janette.
Well, *I don't like it!*
Why don't *Gladys* do 'em? She can reach th' *sink* better!
Gladys has *her* chores, same as you...
Sary?
Got that new boiler purrin' like a *kitten!*
Hurray for you.
Shall I go draw some water?
Done it already.
Should I chop some wood?
Did it yesterday.
Got th' table set?
Yes'm!
At supper...
Find any good songs?
Got t' study 'em t'night. Might be a couple...
After supper...
I hate warshin' dishes!

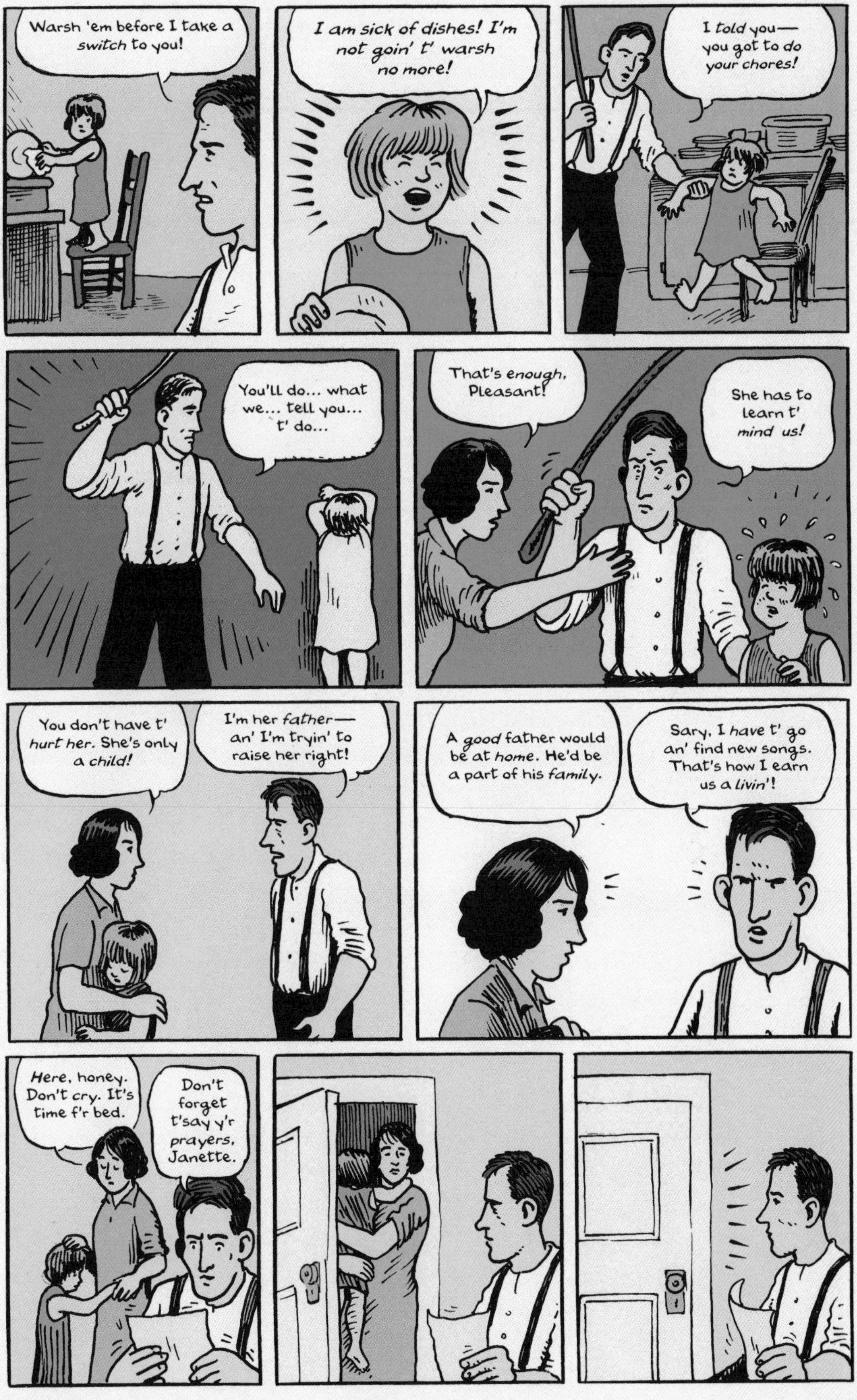
Warsh 'em before I take a *switch* to you!
I am sick of dishes! I'm not goin' t' warsh no more!
I *told* you— you got to do *your chores!*
You'll do... what we... tell you... t' do...
That's *enough*, Pleasant!
She has to learn t' *mind us!*
You don't have t' *hurt her*. She's only a *child!*
I'm her *father*— an' I'm tryin' to raise her right!
A *good* father would be at *home*. He'd be a part of his *family*.
Sary, I *have* t' go an' find new songs. That's how I earn us a *livin'*!
Here, honey. Don't cry. It's time f'r bed.
Don't forget t'say y'r prayers, Janette.

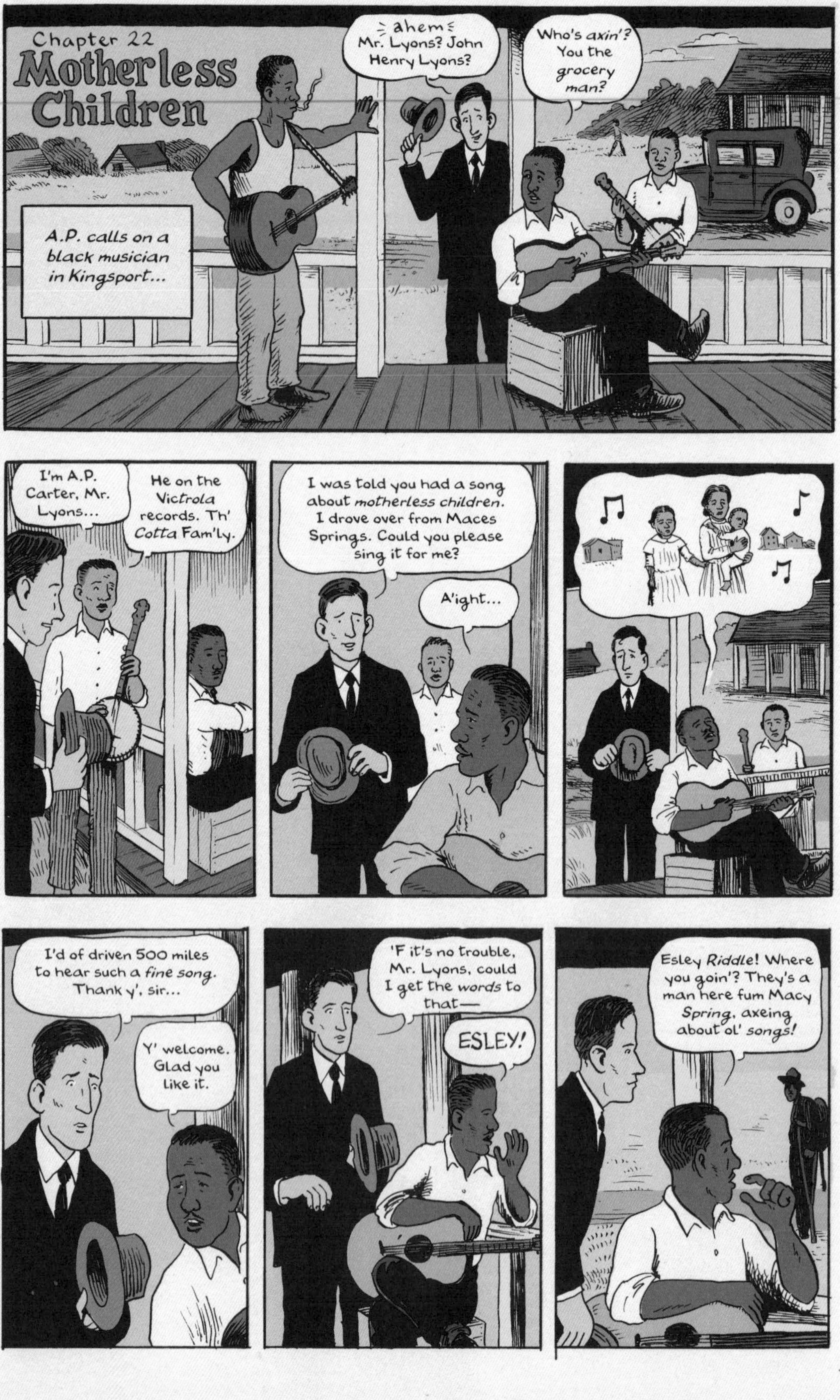
Chapter 22
Motherless Children
A.P. calls on a black musician in Kingsport...
ahem Mr. Lyons? John Henry Lyons?
Who's axin'? You the grocery man?
I'm A.P. Carter, Mr. Lyons...
He on the Victrola records. Th' Cotta Fam'ly.
I was told you had a song about motherless children. I drove over from Maces Springs. Could you please sing it for me?
A'ight...
I'd of driven 500 miles to hear such a fine song. Thank y', sir...
Y' welcome. Glad you like it.
'F it's no trouble, Mr. Lyons, could I get the words to that—
ESLEY!
Esley Riddle! Where you goin'? They's a man here fum Macy Spring, axeing about ol' songs!

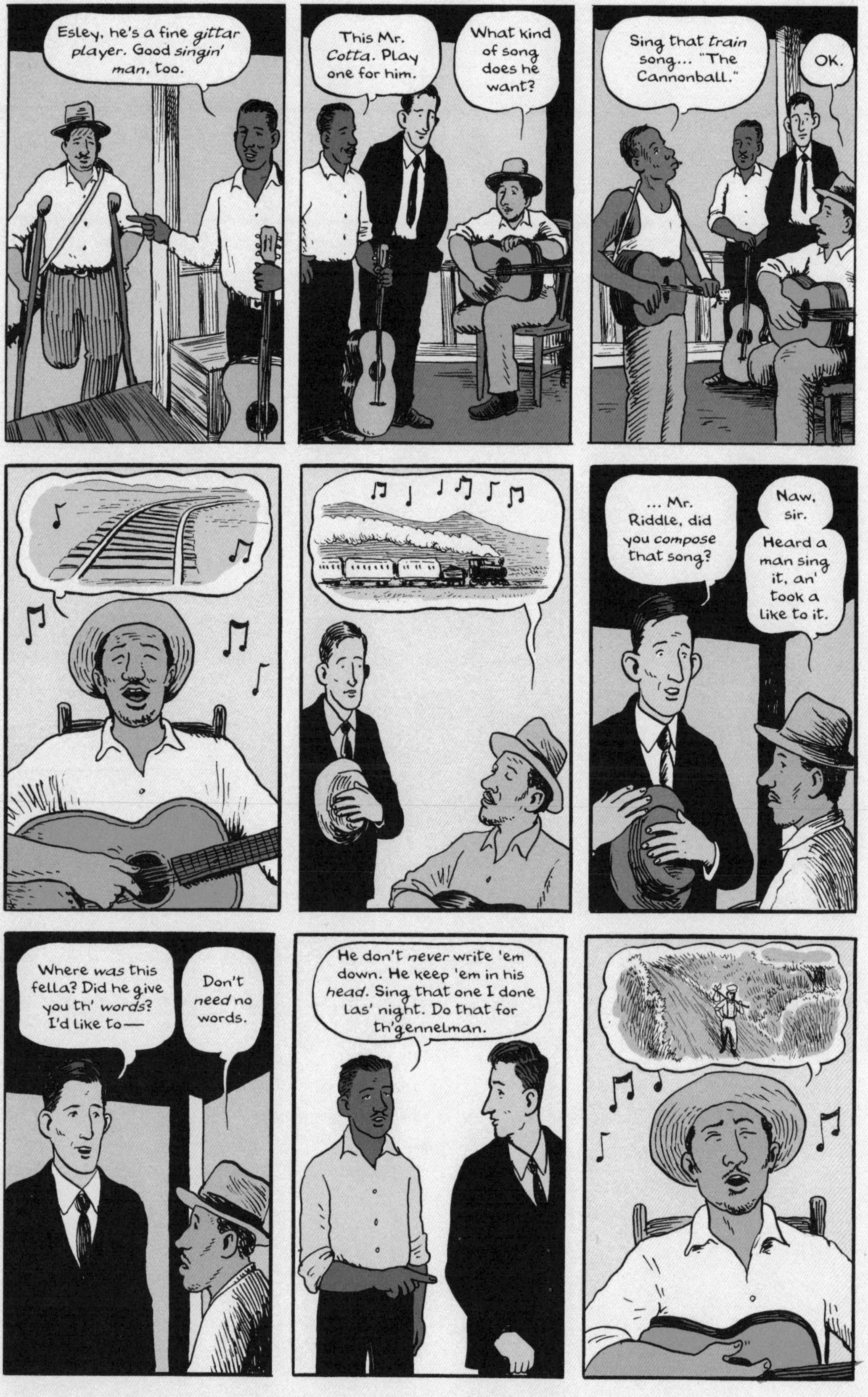
Esley, he's a fine *gittar* *player*. Good *singin'* *man*, too.
This Mr. *Cotta*. Play one for him.
What kind of song does he want?
Sing that *train* song... "The Cannonball."
OK.
... Mr. Riddle, did you *compose* that song?
Naw, sir.
Heard a man sing it, an' took a like to it.
Where *was* this fella? Did he give you th' *words*? I'd like to—
Don't *need* no words.
He don't *never* write 'em down. He keep 'em in his *head*. Sing that one I done las' night. Do that for th'gennelman.

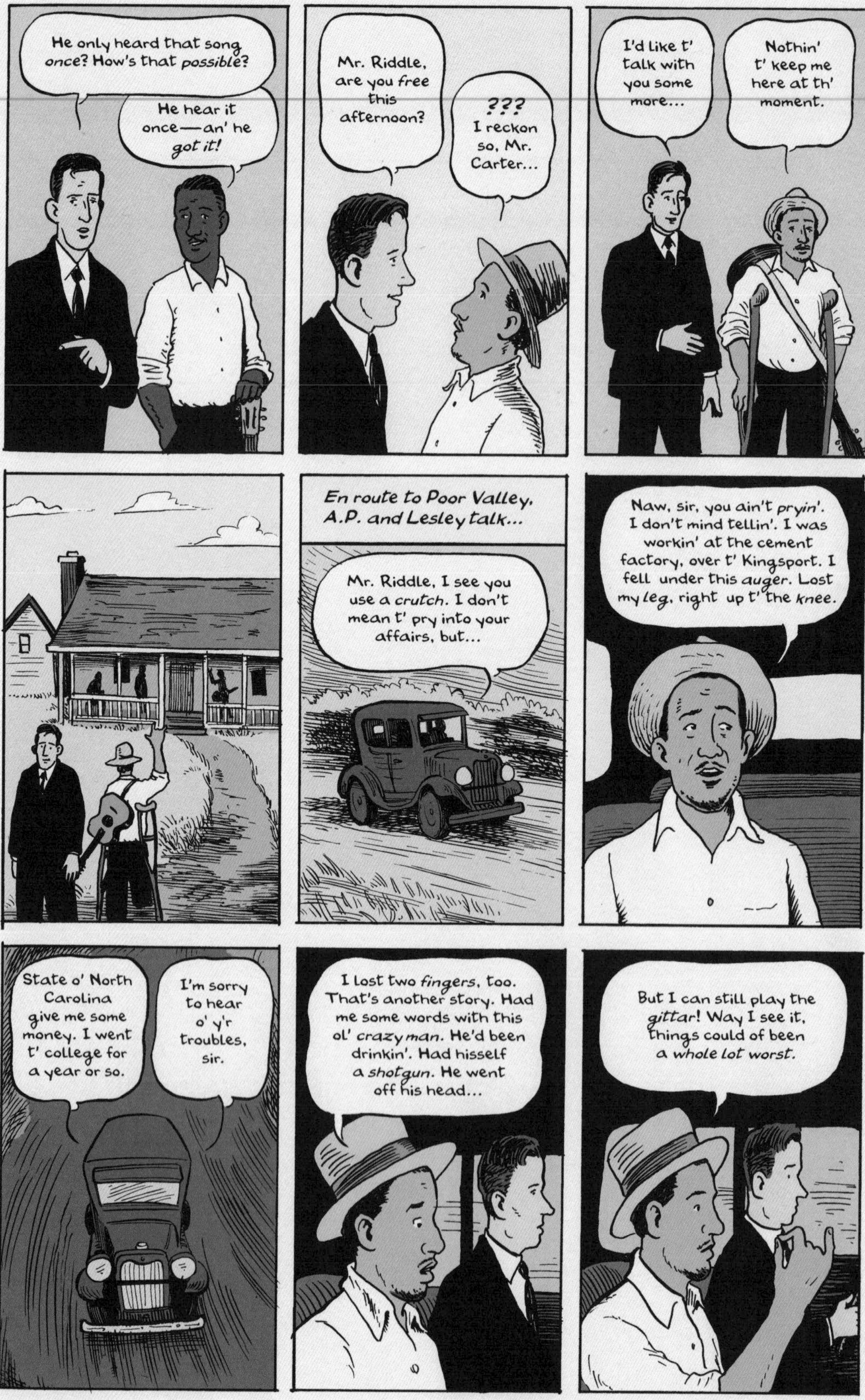
He only heard that song *once*? How's that *possible*?
He hear it once—an' he *got it!*
Mr. Riddle, are you free this afternoon?
??? I reckon so, Mr. Carter...
I'd like t' talk with you some more...
Nothin' t' keep me here at th' moment.
En route to Poor Valley, A.P. and Lesley talk...
Mr. Riddle, I see you use a *crutch*. I don't mean t' pry into your affairs, but...
Naw, sir, you ain't *pryin'*. I don't mind tellin'. I was workin' at the cement factory, over t' Kingsport. I fell under this *auger*. Lost my *leg*, right up t' the *knee*.
State o' North Carolina give me some money. I went t' college for a year or so.
I'm sorry to hear o' y'r troubles, sir.
I lost two *fingers*, too. That's another story. Had me some words with this ol' *crazy man*. He'd been drinkin'. Had hisself a *shotgun*. He went off his head...
But I can still play the *gittar*! Way I see it, things could of been a *whole lot worst*.

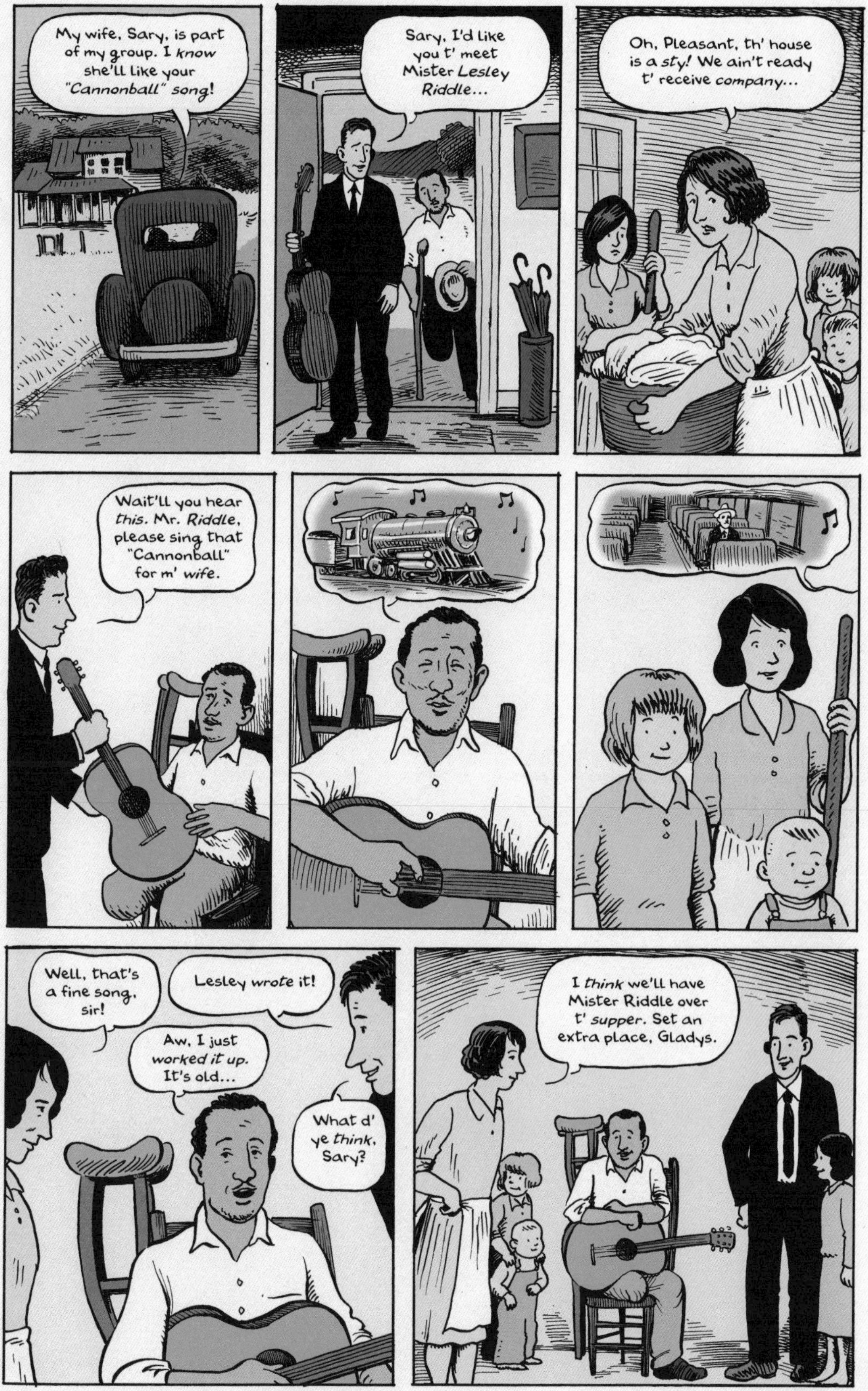
My wife, Sary, is part of my group. I *know* she'll like your "Cannonball" song!
Sary, I'd like you t' meet Mister *Lesley Riddle*...
Oh, Pleasant, th' house is a *sty!* We ain't ready t' receive *company*...
Wait'll you hear *this*. Mr. *Riddle*, please sing that "Cannonball" for m' *wife*.
Well, that's a fine song, sir!
Lesley *wrote* it!
Aw, I just *worked it up*. It's old...
What d' ye *think*, Sary?
I *think* we'll have Mister Riddle over t' *supper*. Set an extra place, Gladys.

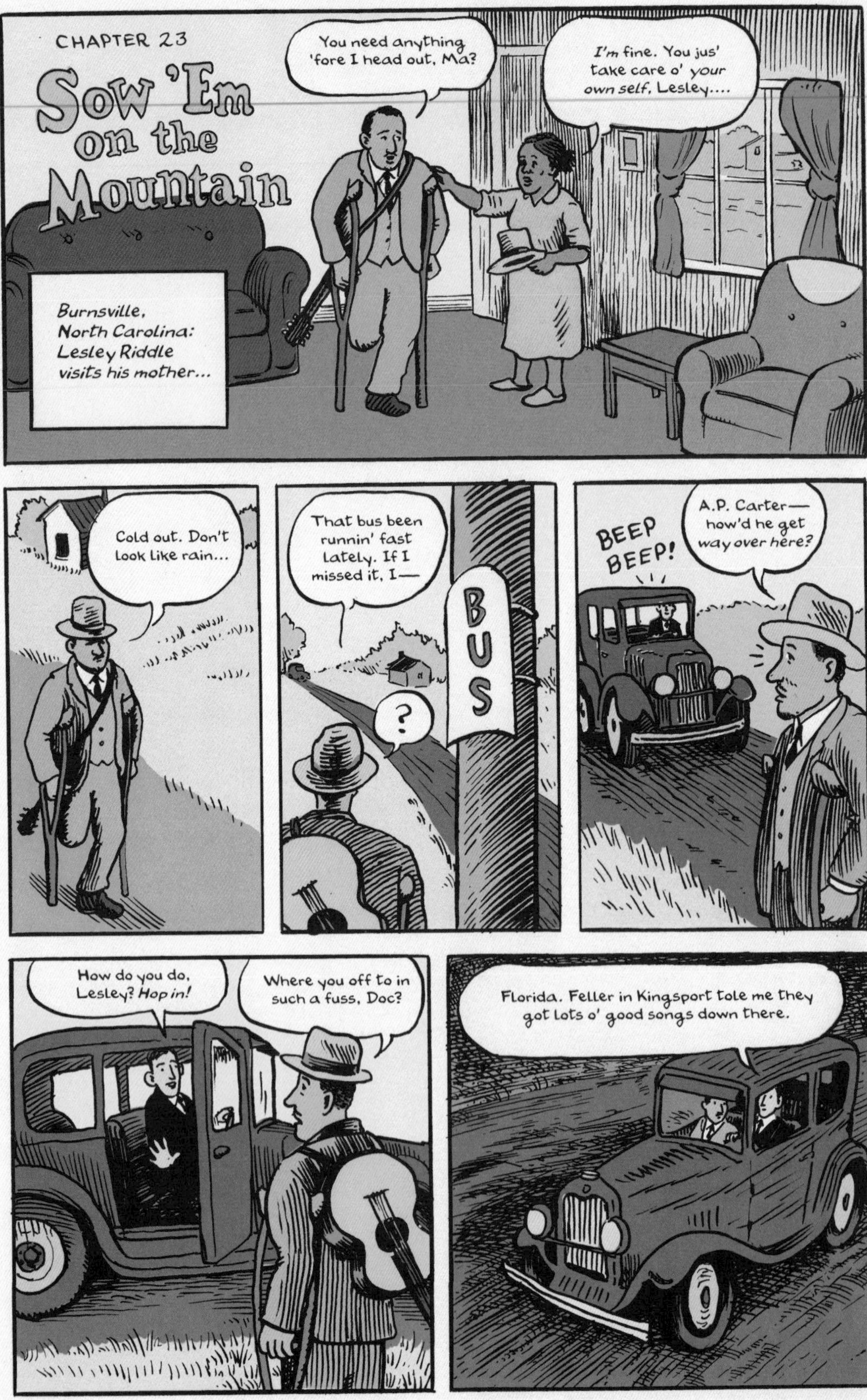
CHAPTER 23
Sow 'Em on the Mountain
You need anything 'fore I head out, Ma?
I'm fine. You jus' take care o' your own self, Lesley....
Burnsville, North Carolina: Lesley Riddle visits his mother...
Cold out. Don't look like rain...
That bus been runnin' fast lately. If I missed it, I—
BUS
?
BEEP BEEP!
A.P. Carter— how'd he get way over here?
How do you do, Lesley? Hop in!
Where you off to in such a fuss, Doc?
Florida. Feller in Kingsport tole me they got lots o' good songs down there.

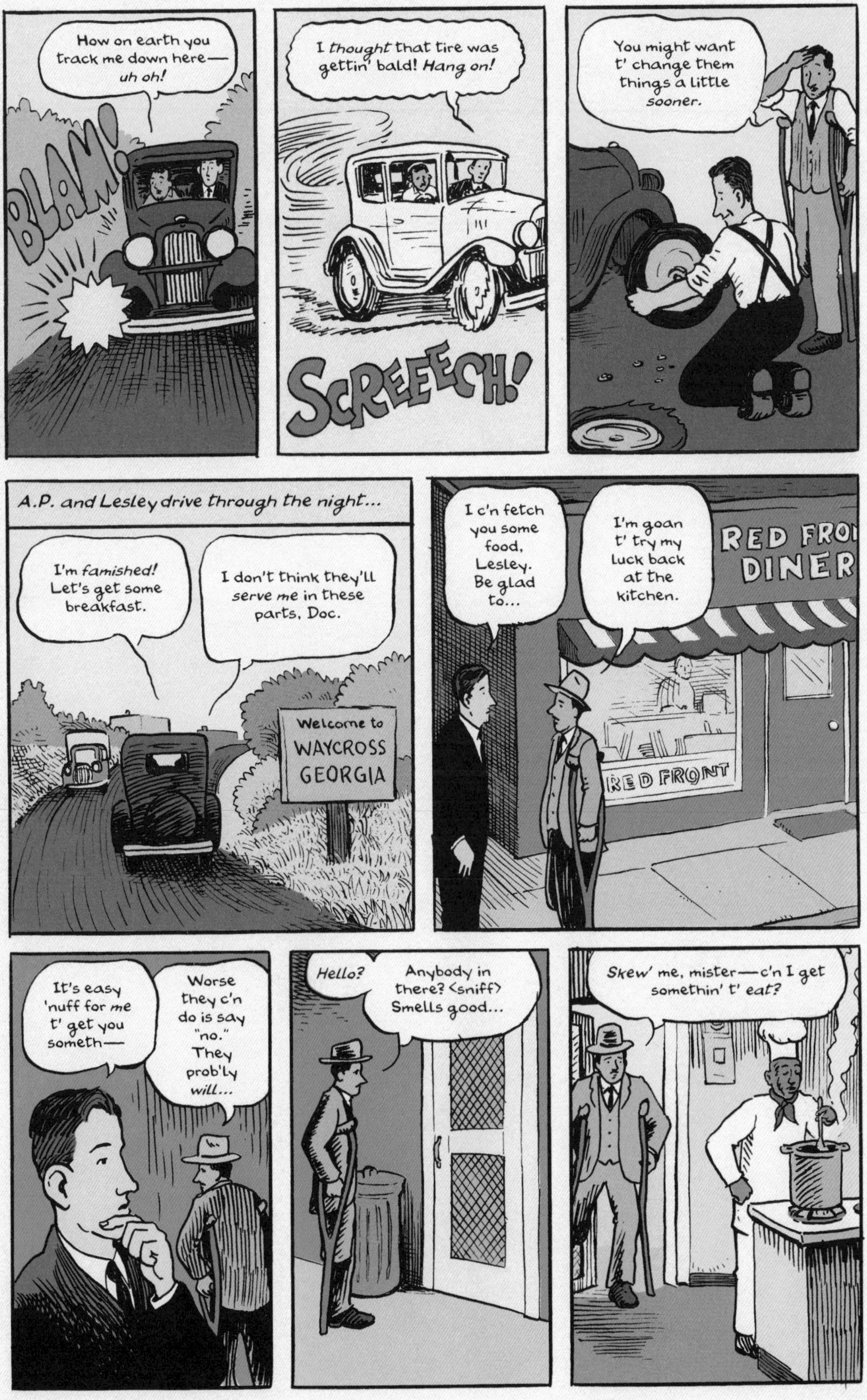
How on earth you track me down here— uh oh!
BLAM!
I thought that tire was gettin' bald! Hang on!
SCREEECH!
You might want t' change them things a little sooner.
A.P. and Lesley drive through the night...
I'm famished! Let's get some breakfast.
I don't think they'll serve me in these parts, Doc.
Welcome to WAYCROSS GEORGIA
I c'n fetch you some food, Lesley. Be glad to...
I'm goan t' try my luck back at the kitchen.
RED FRO
DINER
RED FRONT
It's easy 'nuff for me t' get you someth—
Worse they c'n do is say "no." They prob'ly will...
Hello?
Anybody in there? <sniff> Smells good...
Skew' me, mister—c'n I get somethin' t' eat?

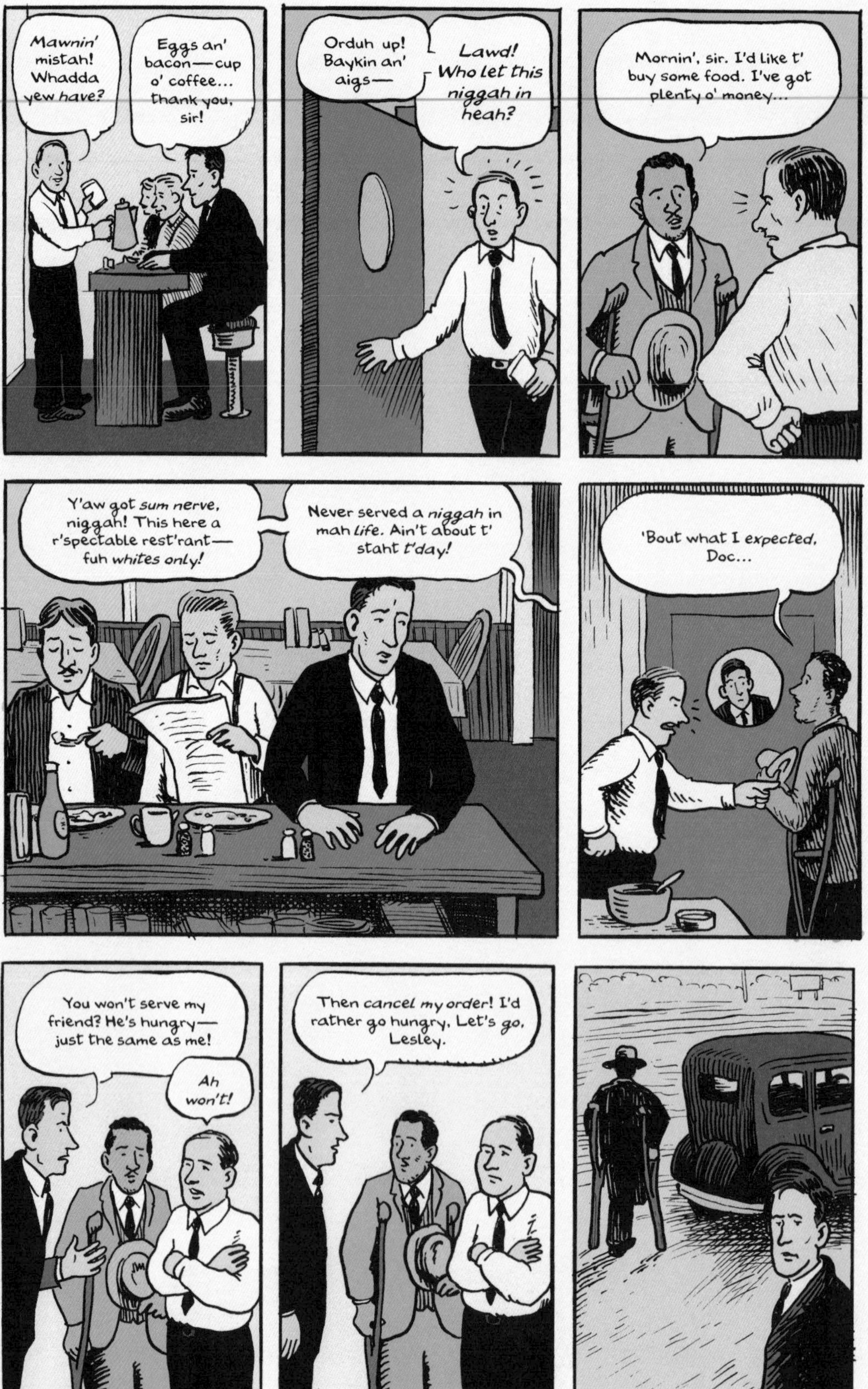
Mawnin' mistah! Whadda yew have?
Eggs an' bacon—cup o' coffee... thank you, sir!
Orduh up! Baykin an' aigs—
Lawd! Who let this niggah in heah?
Mornin', sir. I'd like t' buy some food. I've got plenty o' money...
Y'aw got sum nerve, niggah! This here a r'spectable rest'rant—fuh whites only!
Never served a niggah in mah life. Ain't about t' staht t'day!
'Bout what I expected, Doc...
You won't serve my friend? He's hungry—just the same as me!
Ah won't!
Then cancel my order! I'd rather go hungry. Let's go, Lesley.

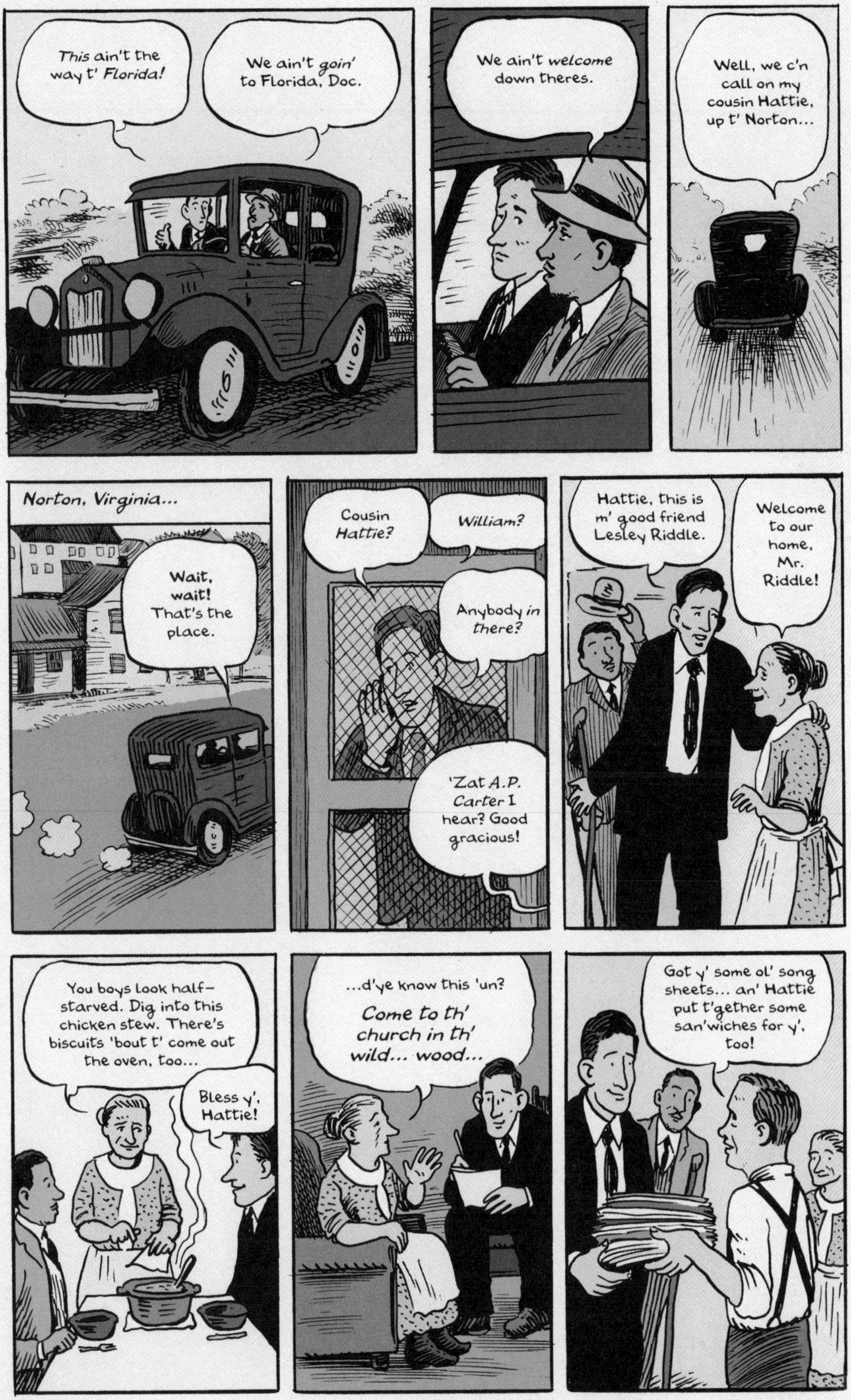
This ain't the way t' Florida!
We ain't goin' to Florida, Doc.
We ain't welcome down theres.
Well, we c'n call on my cousin Hattie, up t' Norton...
Norton, Virginia...
Wait, wait! That's the place.
Cousin Hattie?
William?
Anybody in there?
'Zat A.P. Carter I hear? Good gracious!
Hattie, this is m' good friend Lesley Riddle.
Welcome to our home, Mr. Riddle!
You boys look half-starved. Dig into this chicken stew. There's biscuits 'bout t' come out the oven, too...
Bless y', Hattie!
...d'ye know this 'un?
Come to th' church in th' wild... wood...
Got y' some ol' song sheets... an' Hattie put t'gether some san'wiches for y', too!

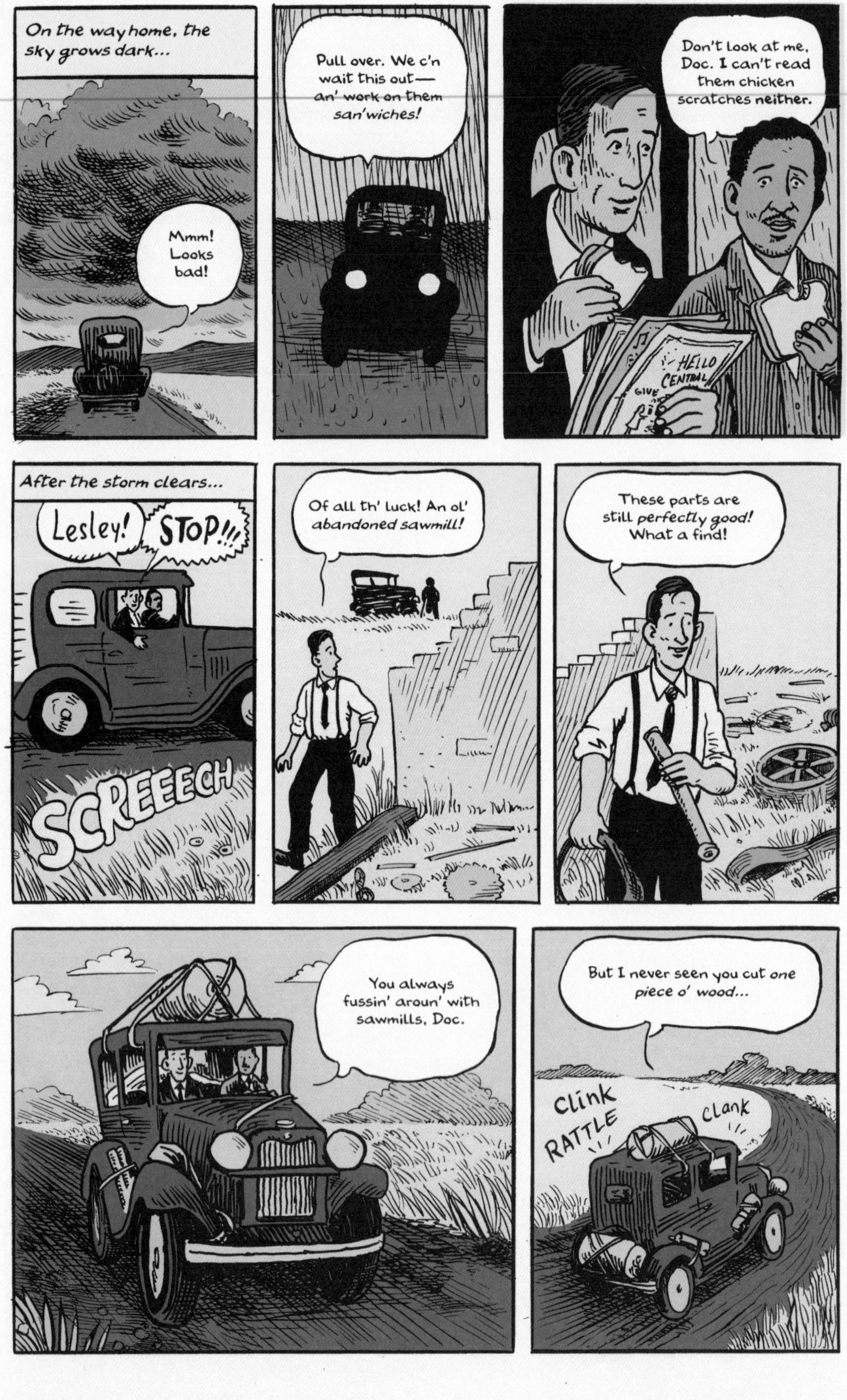
On the way home, the sky grows dark...
Mmm! Looks bad!
Pull over. We c'n wait this out— an' work on them san'wiches!
Don't look at me, Doc. I can't read them chicken scratches neither.
HELLO CENTRAL
GIVE
After the storm clears...
Lesley!
STOP!!!
SCREEECH
Of all th' luck! An ol' abandoned sawmill!
These parts are still perfectly good! What a find!
You always fussin' aroun' with sawmills, Doc.
But I never seen you cut one piece o' wood...
Clink
RATTLE
Clank

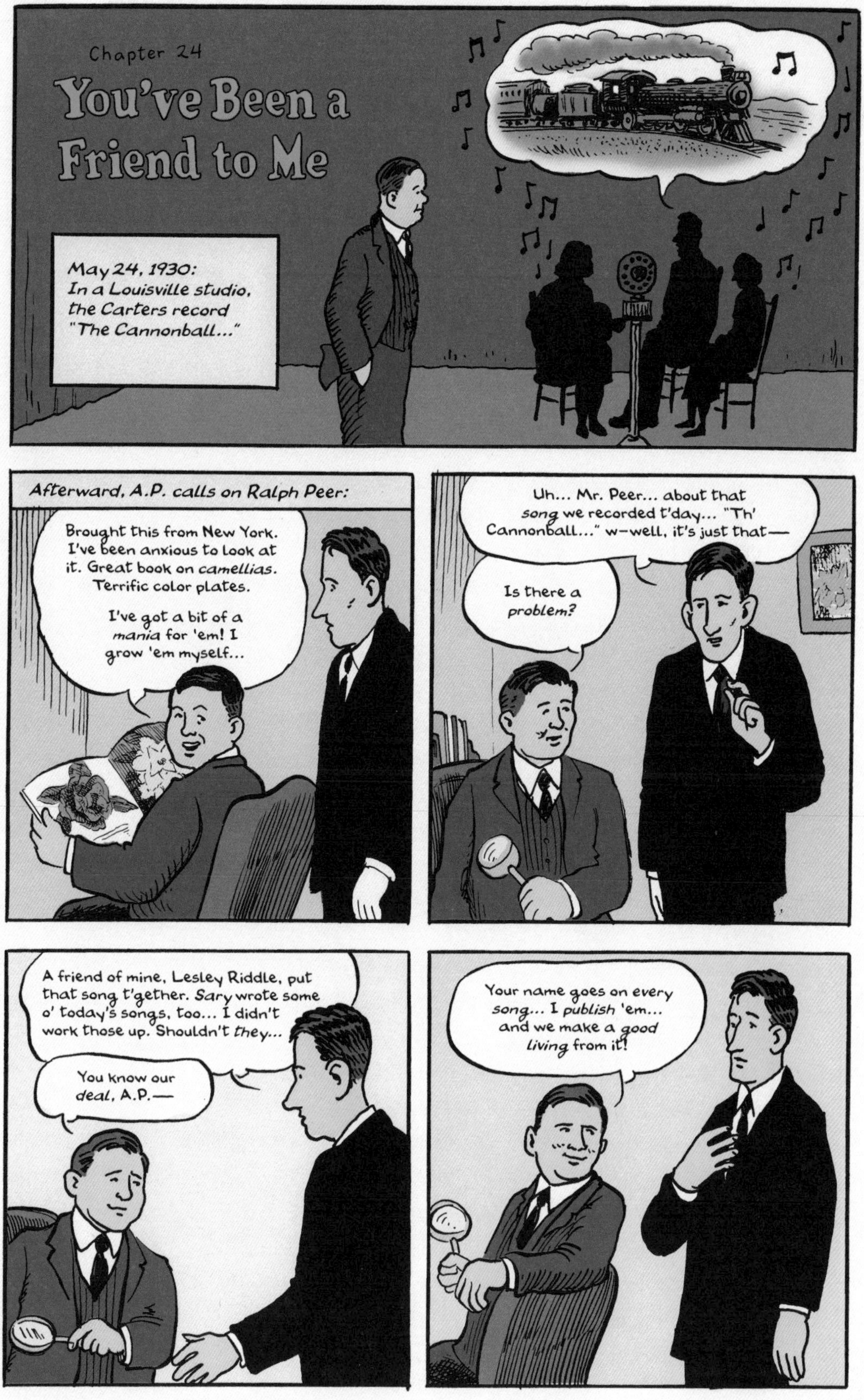
Chapter 24
You've Been a Friend to Me
May 24, 1930: In a Louisville studio, the Carters record "The Cannonball..."
Afterward, A.P. calls on Ralph Peer:
Brought this from New York. I've been anxious to look at it. Great book on *camellias*. Terrific color plates.
I've got a bit of a *mania* for 'em! I grow 'em myself...
Uh... Mr. Peer... about that *song* we recorded t'day... "Th' Cannonball..." w-well, it's just that—
Is there a *problem?*
A friend of mine, Lesley Riddle, put that song t'gether. *Sary* wrote some o' today's songs, too... I didn't work those up. Shouldn't *they*...
You know our *deal*, A.P.—
Your name goes on every *song*... I *publish* 'em... and we make a *good living* from it!

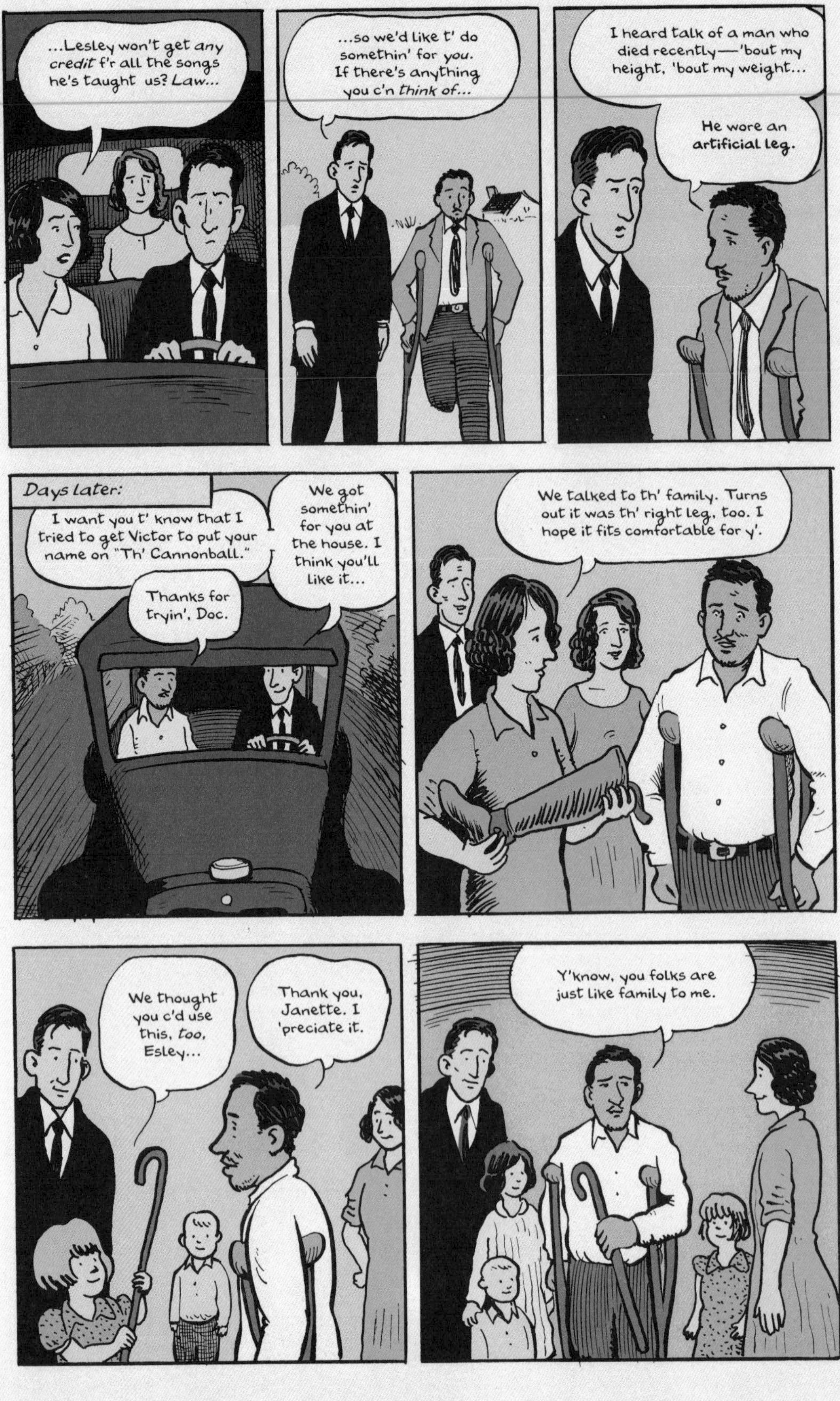
...Lesley won't get any credit f'r all the songs he's taught us? Law...
...so we'd like t' do somethin' for you. If there's anything you c'n think of...
I heard talk of a man who died recently—'bout my height, 'bout my weight...
He wore an artificial leg.
Days later:
I want you t' know that I tried to get Victor to put your name on "Th' Cannonball."
We got somethin' for you at the house. I think you'll like it...
Thanks for tryin', Doc.
We talked to th' family. Turns out it was th' right leg, too. I hope it fits comfortable for y'.
We thought you c'd use this, too, Esley...
Thank you, Janette. I 'preciate it.
Y'know, you folks are just like family to me.

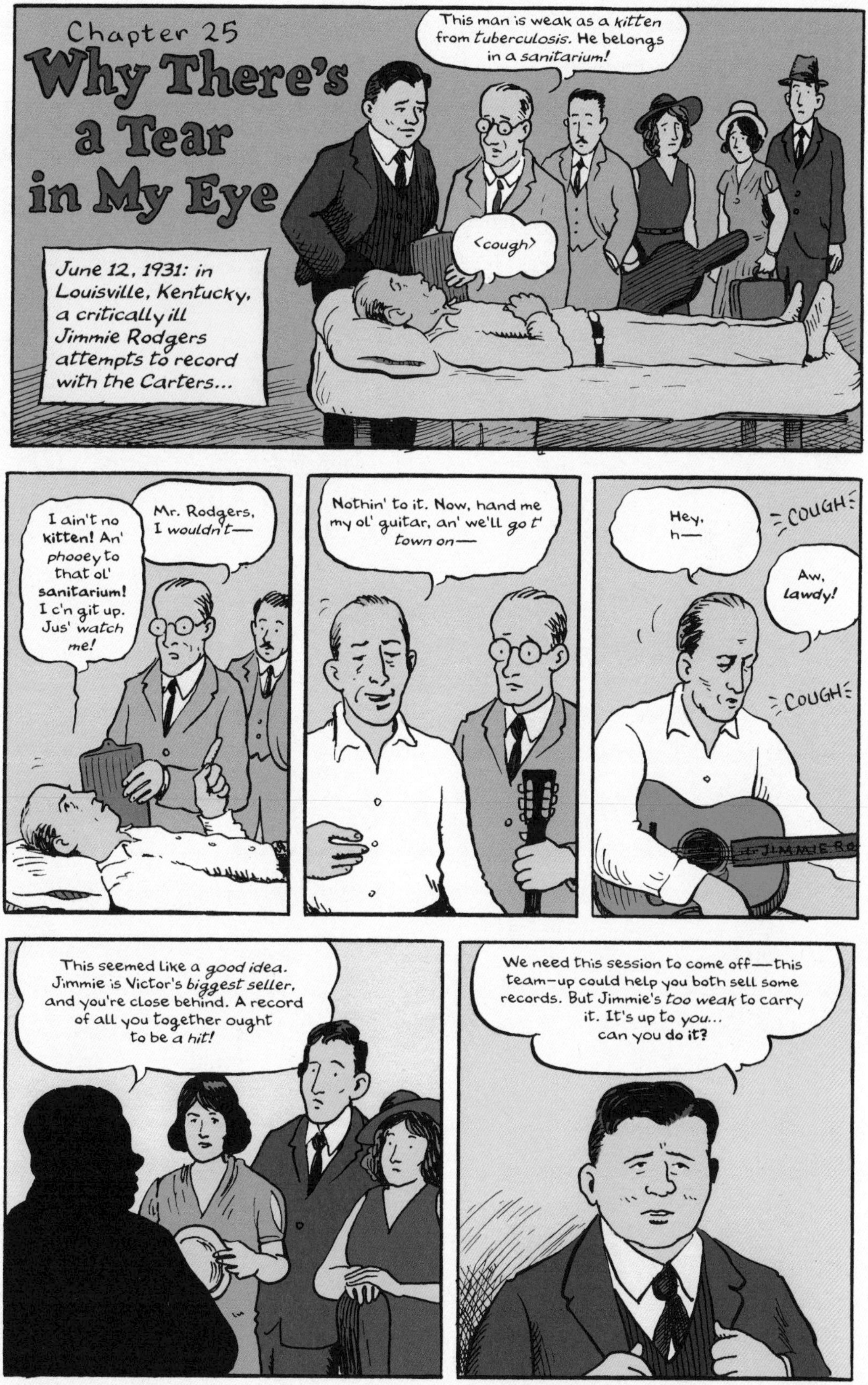
Chapter 25
Why There's a Tear in My Eye
This man is weak as a kitten from tuberculosis. He belongs in a sanitarium!
June 12, 1931: in Louisville, Kentucky, a critically ill Jimmie Rodgers attempts to record with the Carters...
<cough>
Mr. Rodgers, I wouldn't—
I ain't no kitten! An' phooey to that ol' sanitarium! I c'n git up. Jus' watch me!
Nothin' to it. Now, hand me my ol' guitar, an' we'll go t' town on—
Hey, h—
COUGH
Aw, lawdy!
COUGH
JIMMIE RO
This seemed like a good idea. Jimmie is Victor's biggest seller, and you're close behind. A record of all you together ought to be a hit!
We need this session to come off—this team-up could help you both sell some records. But Jimmie's too weak to carry it. It's up to you... can you do it?

Ulp! 〈gulp〉 Shore thing, Mr. Peer!

Jimmie hasn't the *strength* to play. Can you *ape* his style?

Yes'r. I know all his licks.

That'll do! Now, if we can just get Mr. Rodgers in front of the mike... and get some *usable* takes...

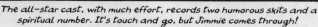

The all-star cast, with much effort, records two humorous skits and a spiritual number. It's touch and go, but Jimmie comes through!

COUGH COUGH!

After the session...

This'll go down in his'try! Hold that pose, folks!

(Say, Toots. Howzabout you 'n' me goin' out an' doin' th' town?)

(Oh... you'll hafta ask my husband 'bout that!)

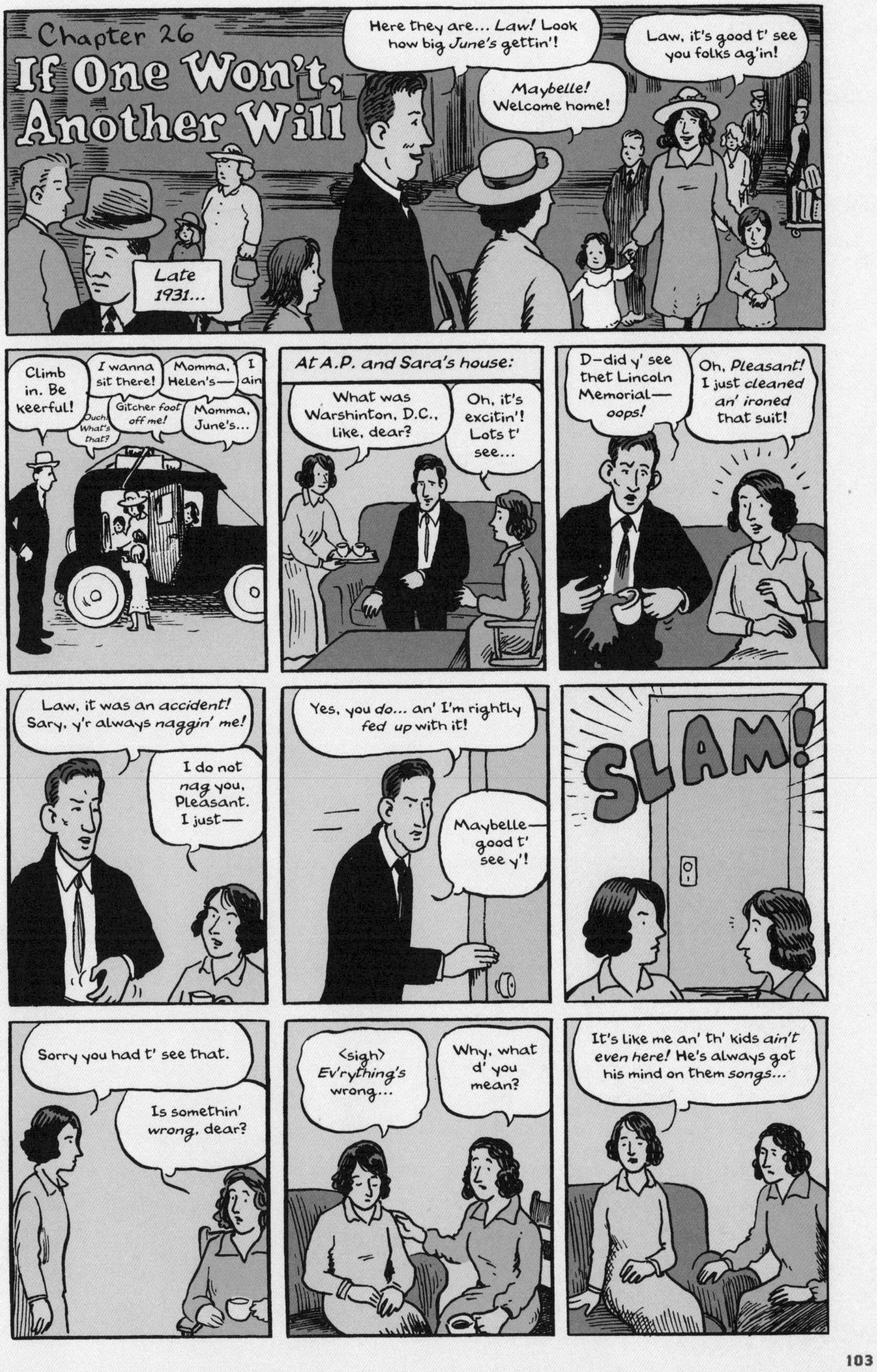
Chapter 26
If One Won't, Another Will
Late 1931...
Here they are... *Law!* Look how big *June's* gettin'!
Maybelle! Welcome home!
Law, it's good t' see you folks ag'in!
Climb in. Be keerful!
I wanna sit there!
Momma, Helen's—
I ain
Ouch! What's that?
Gitcher *foot* off me!
Momma, June's...
At A.P. and Sara's house:
What was Warshinton, D.C., like, dear?
Oh, it's excitin'! Lots t' see...
D-did y' see thet Lincoln Memorial— *oops!*
Oh, *Pleasant!* I just *cleaned an' ironed* that suit!
Law, it was an *accident!* Sary, y'r always *naggin' me!*
I do not *nag* you, Pleasant. I just—
Yes, you *do*... an' I'm rightly *fed up* with it!
Maybelle— good t' see y'!
SLAM!
Sorry you had t' see that.
Is somethin' *wrong*, dear?
<sigh> *Ev'rything's* wrong...
Why, what d' you mean?
It's like me an' th' kids *ain't even here!* He's always got his mind on them *songs*...

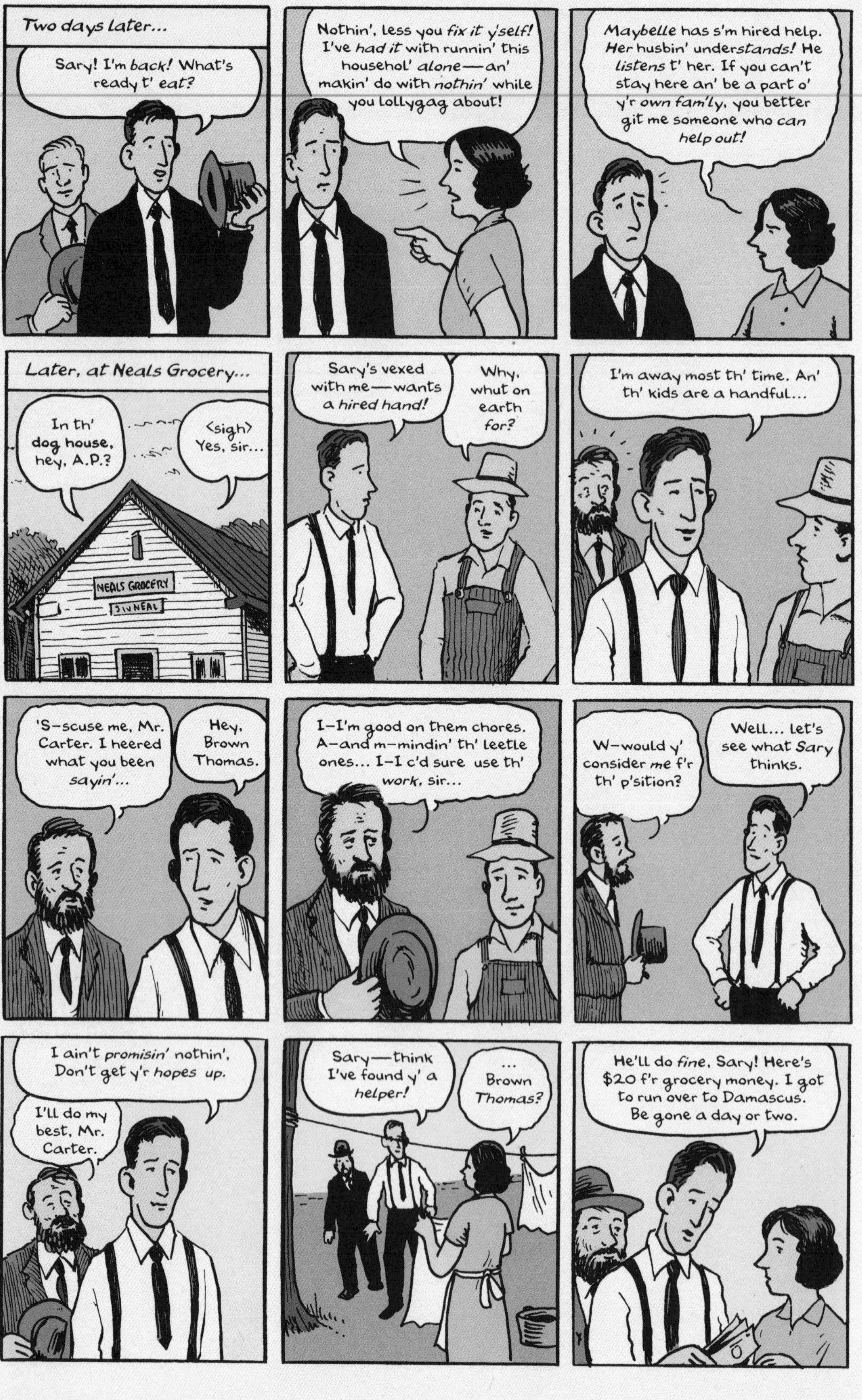
Two days later...
Sary! I'm back! What's ready t' eat?
Nothin', less you fix it y'self! I've had it with runnin' this househol' alone—an' makin' do with nothin' while you lollygag about!
Maybelle has s'm hired help. Her husbin' understands! He listens t' her. If you can't stay here an' be a part o' y'r own fam'ly, you better git me someone who can help out!
Later, at Neals Grocery...
In th' dog house, hey, A.P.?
<sigh> Yes, sir...
NEALS GROCERY
Sary's vexed with me—wants a hired hand!
Why, whut on earth for?
I'm away most th' time. An' th' kids are a handful...
'S-scuse me, Mr. Carter. I heered what you been sayin'...
Hey, Brown Thomas.
I-I'm good on them chores. A-and m-mindin' th' leetle ones... I-I c'd sure use th' work, sir...
W-would y' consider me f'r th' p'sition?
Well... let's see what Sary thinks.
I ain't promisin' nothin', Don't get y'r hopes up.
I'll do my best, Mr. Carter.
Sary—think I've found y' a helper!
... Brown Thomas?
He'll do fine, Sary! Here's $20 f'r grocery money. I got to run over to Damascus. Be gone a day or two.

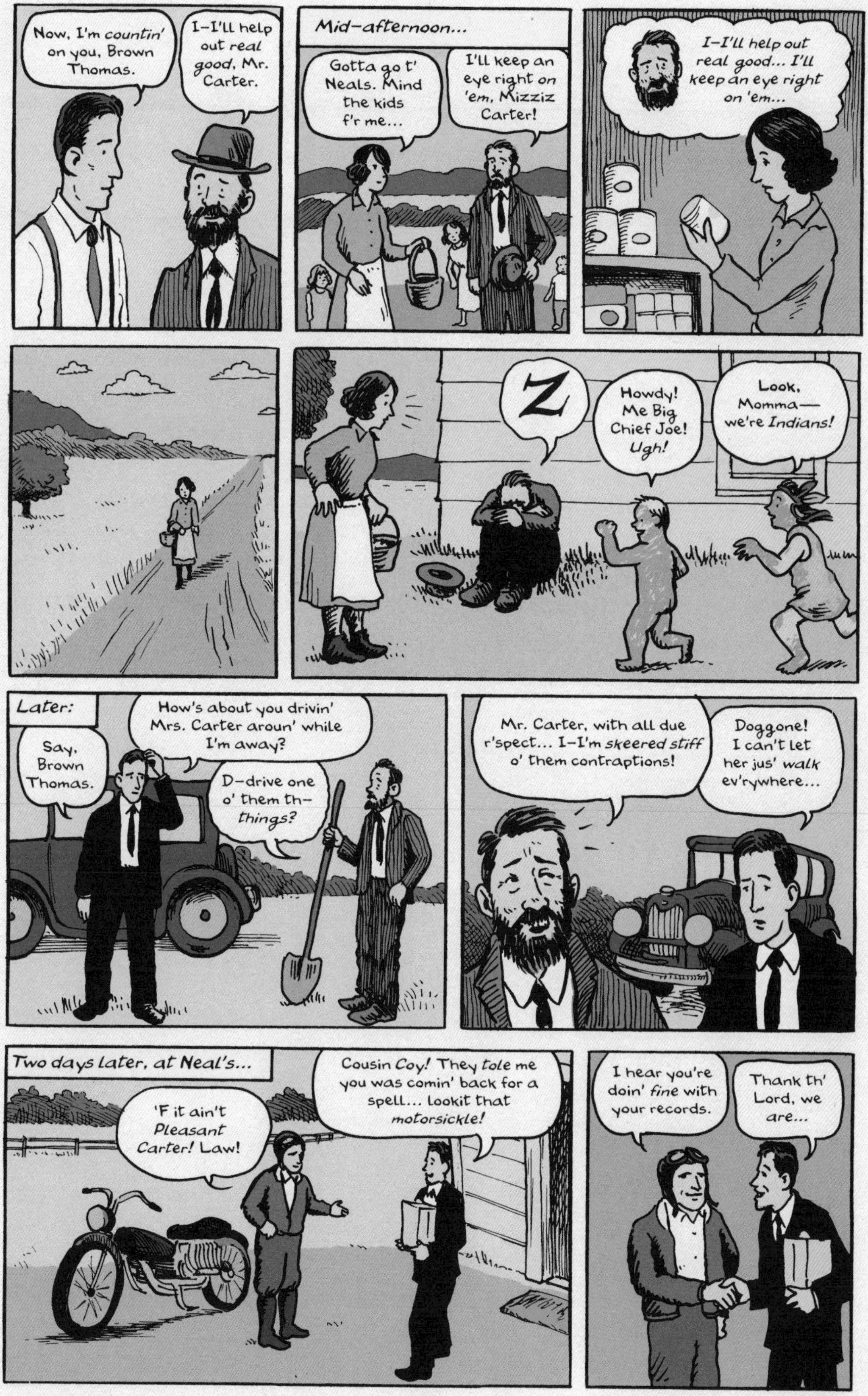
Now, I'm countin' on you, Brown Thomas.
I-I'll help out real good, Mr. Carter.
Mid-afternoon...
Gotta go t' Neals. Mind the kids f'r me...
I'll keep an eye right on 'em, Mizziz Carter!
I-I'll help out real good... I'll keep an eye right on 'em...
Z
Howdy! Me Big Chief Joe! Ugh!
Look, Momma— we're Indians!
Later:
Say, Brown Thomas.
How's about you drivin' Mrs. Carter aroun' while I'm away?
D-drive one o' them th-things?
Mr. Carter, with all due r'spect... I-I'm skeered stiff o' them contraptions!
Doggone! I can't let her jus' walk ev'rywhere...
Two days later, at Neal's...
'F it ain't Pleasant Carter! Law!
Cousin Coy! They tole me you was comin' back for a spell... lookit that motorsickle!
I hear you're doin' fine with your records.
Thank th' Lord, we are...

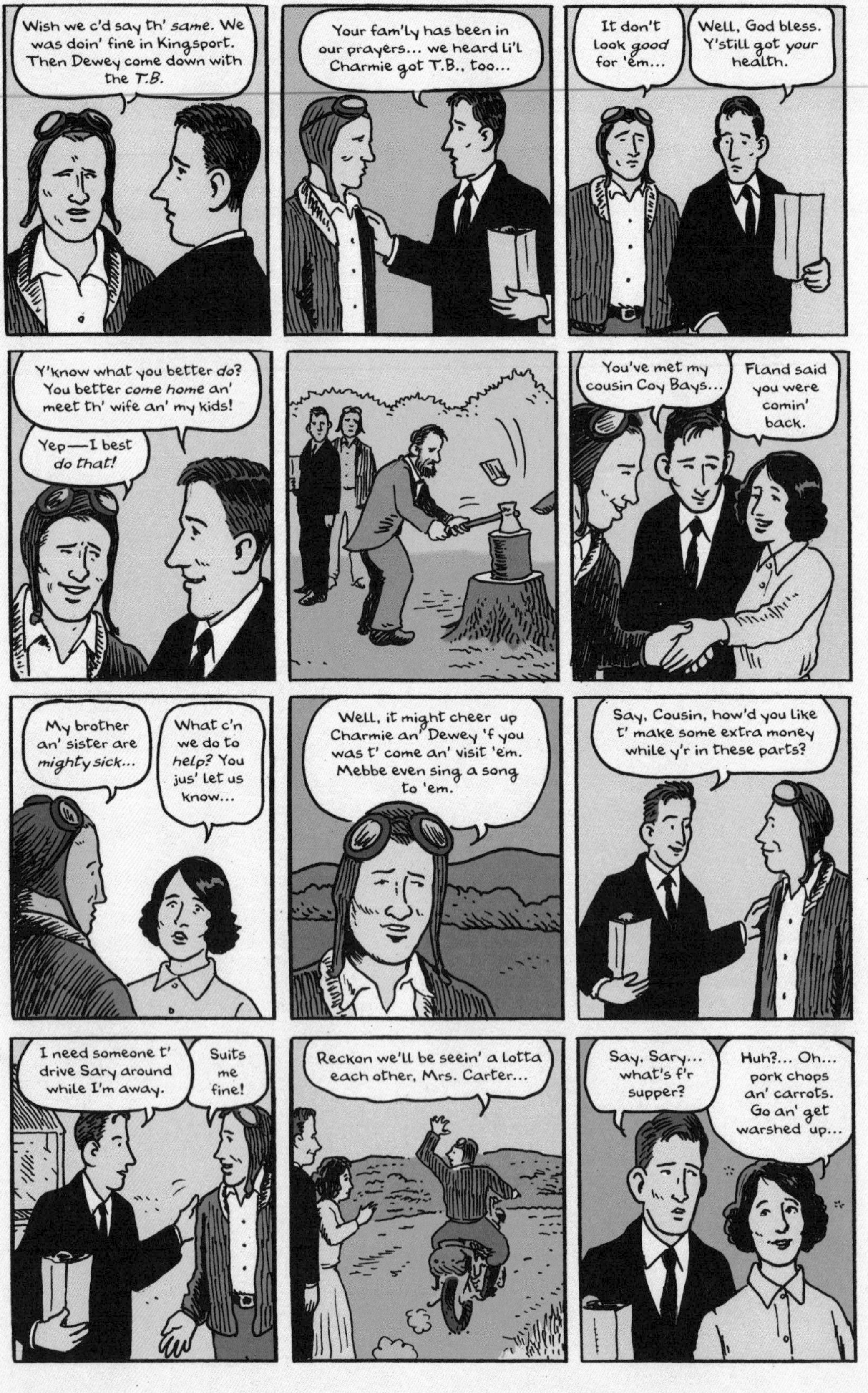
Wish we c'd say th' *same.* We was doin' fine in Kingsport. Then Dewey come down with the *T.B.*
Your fam'ly has been in our prayers... we heard li'l Charmie got T.B., too...
It don't look *good* for 'em...
Well, God bless. Y'still got *your* health.
Y'know what you better *do*? You better *come home* an' meet th' wife an' my kids!
Yep—I best *do that!*
You've met my cousin Coy Bays...
Fland said you were comin' back.
My brother an' sister are *mighty sick*...
What c'n we do to *help*? You jus' let us know...
Well, it might cheer up Charmie an' Dewey 'f you was t' come an' visit 'em. Mebbe even sing a song to 'em.
Say, Cousin, how'd you like t' make some extra money while y'r in these parts?
I need someone t' drive Sary around while I'm away.
Suits me fine!
Reckon we'll be seein' a lotta each other, Mrs. Carter...
Say, Sary... what's f'r supper?
Huh?... Oh... pork chops an' carrots. Go an' get warshed up...

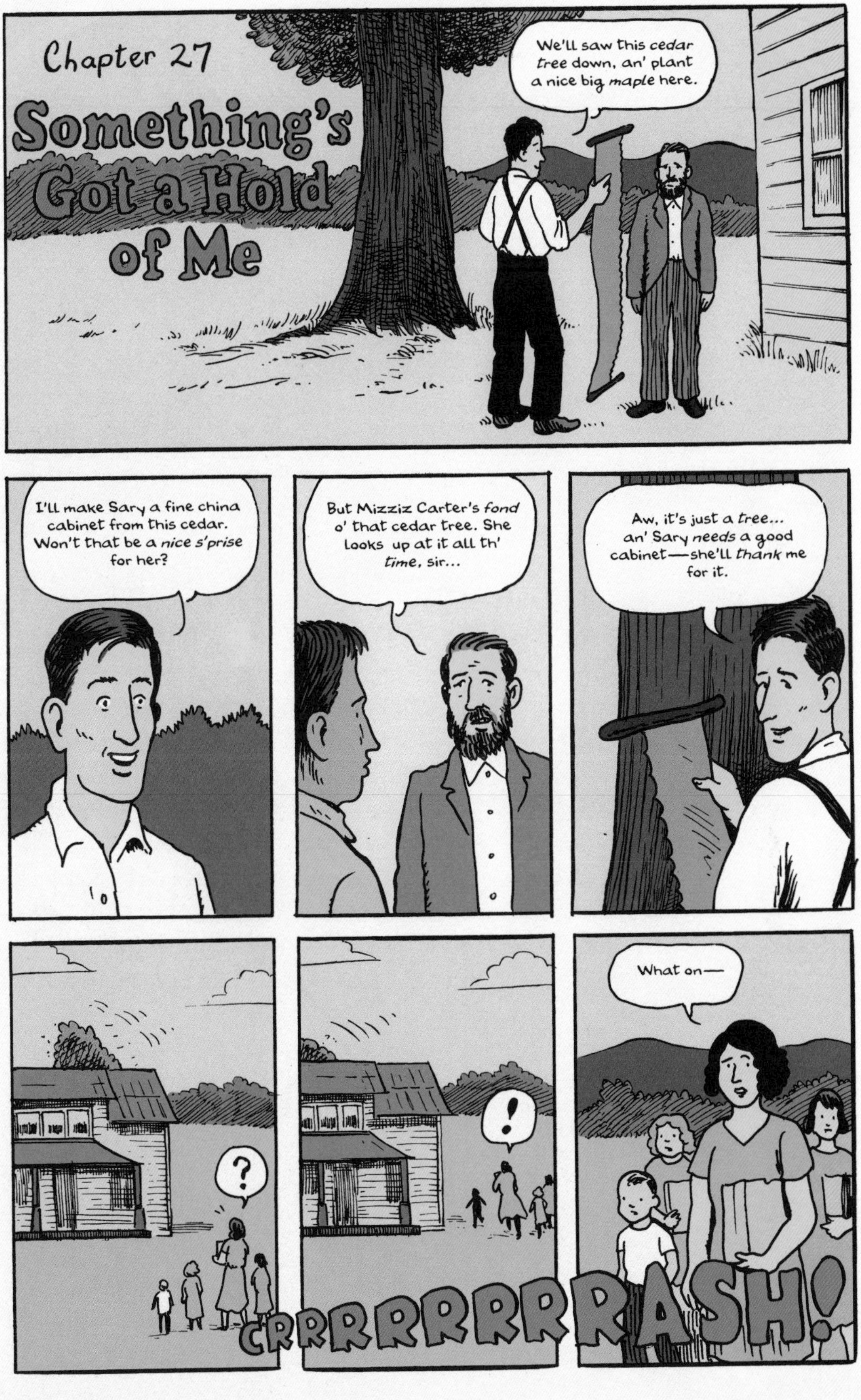
Chapter 27
Something's Got a Hold of Me
We'll saw this cedar tree down, an' plant a nice big maple here.
I'll make Sary a fine china cabinet from this cedar. Won't that be a nice s'prise for her?
But Mizziz Carter's fond o' that cedar tree. She looks up at it all th' time, sir...
Aw, it's just a tree... an' Sary needs a good cabinet—she'll thank me for it.
?
!
What on—
CRRRRRRRRASH!

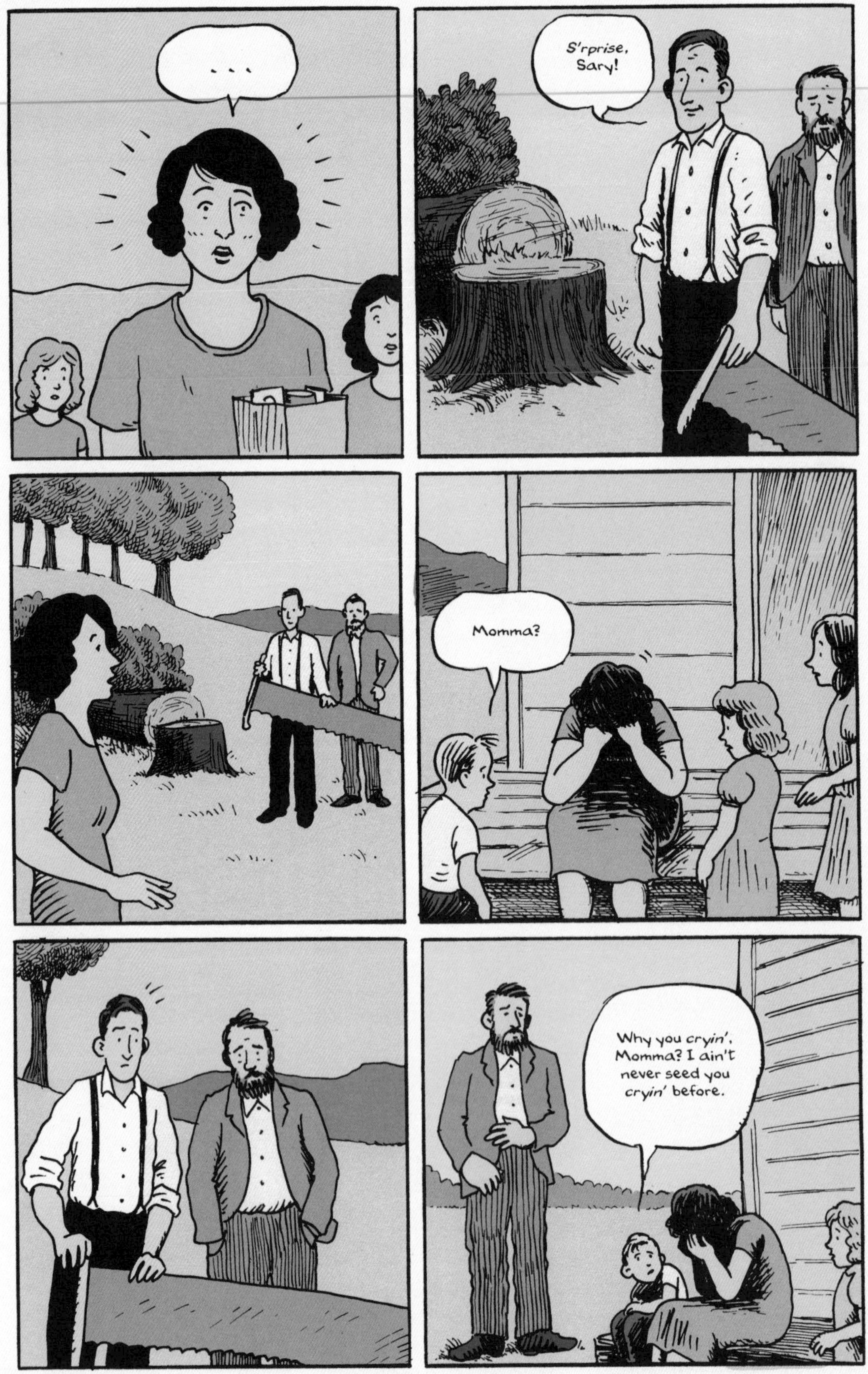
. . .
S'rprise, Sary!
Momma?
Why you cryin', Momma? I ain't never seed you cryin' before.

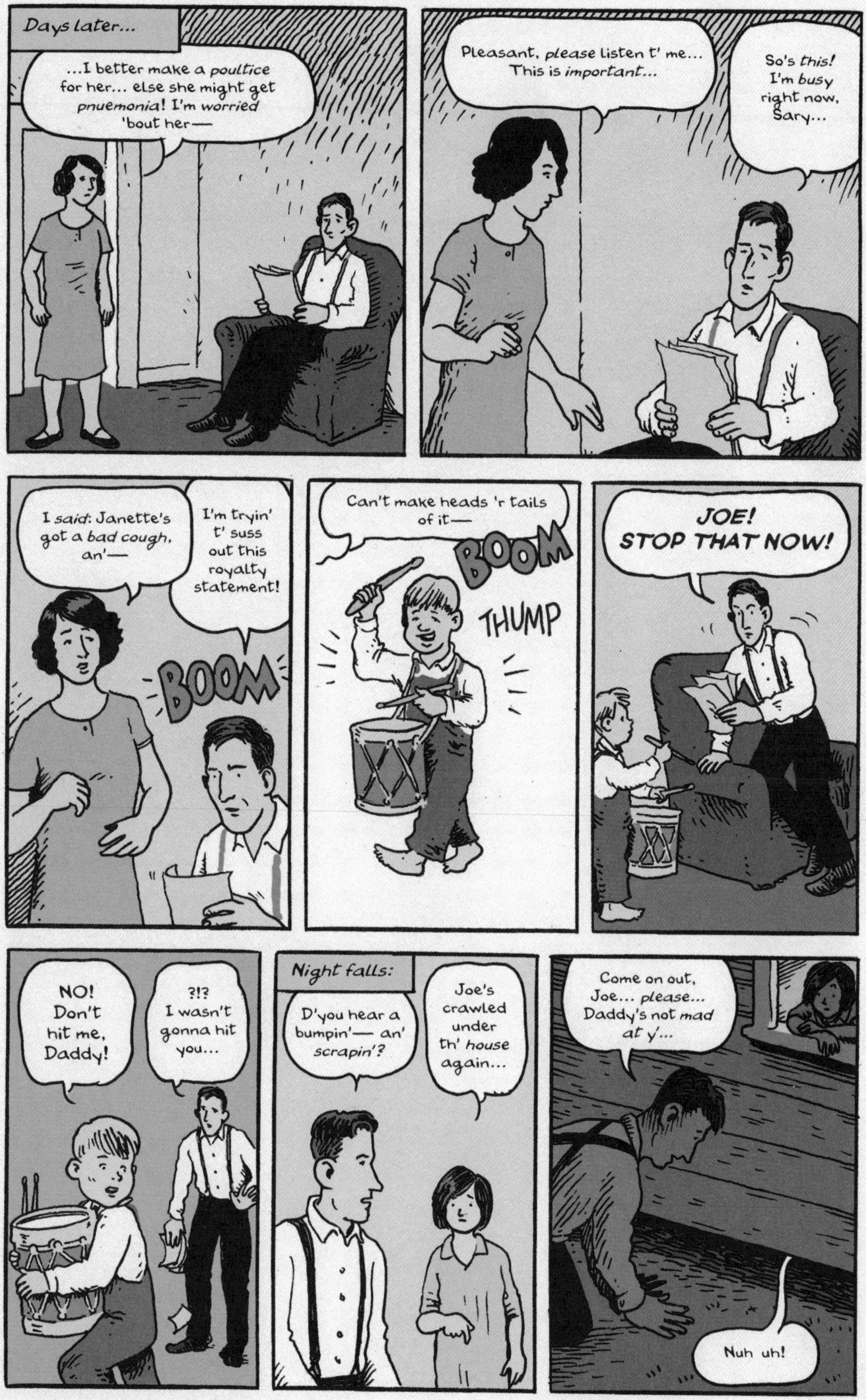
Days later...
...I better make a poultice for her... else she might get pnuemonia! I'm worried 'bout her—
Pleasant, please listen t' me... This is important...
So's this! I'm busy right now, Sary...
I said: Janette's got a bad cough, an'—
I'm tryin' t' suss out this royalty statement!
BOOM
Can't make heads 'r tails of it—
BOOM
THUMP
JOE! STOP THAT NOW!
NO! Don't hit me, Daddy!
?!? I wasn't gonna hit you...
Night falls:
D'you hear a bumpin'— an' scrapin'?
Joe's crawled under th' house again...
Come on out, Joe... please... Daddy's not mad at y'...
Nuh uh!

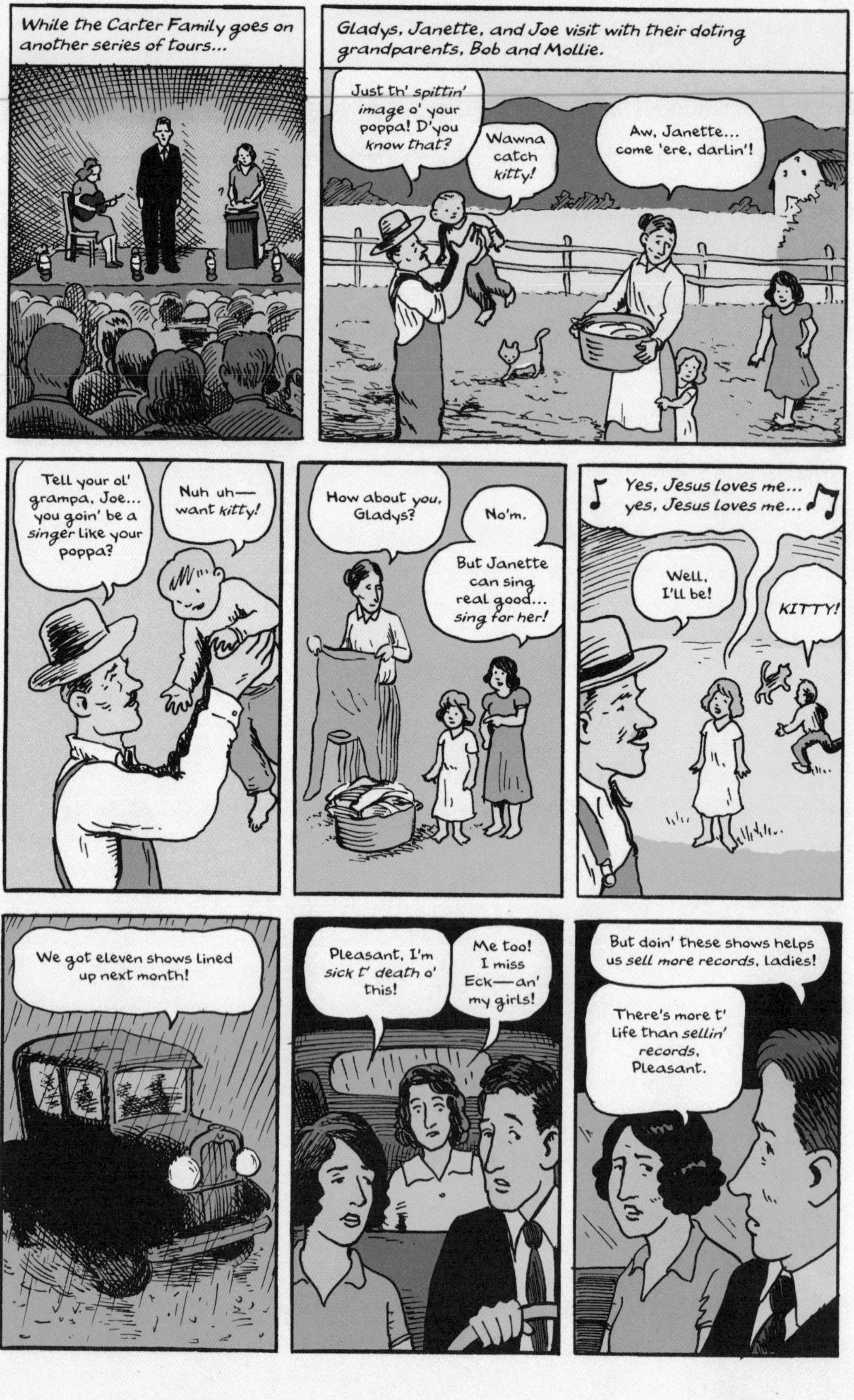
While the Carter Family goes on another series of tours...
Gladys, Janette, and Joe visit with their doting grandparents, Bob and Mollie.
Just th' spittin' image o' your poppa! D'you know that?
Wawna catch kitty!
Aw, Janette... come 'ere, darlin'!
Tell your ol' grampa, Joe... you goin' be a singer like your poppa?
Nuh uh— want kitty!
How about you, Gladys?
No'm.
But Janette can sing real good... sing for her!
Yes, Jesus loves me... yes, Jesus loves me...
Well, I'll be!
KITTY!
We got eleven shows lined up next month!
Pleasant, I'm sick t' death o' this!
Me too! I miss Eck—an' my girls!
But doin' these shows helps us sell more records, ladies!
There's more t' life than sellin' records, Pleasant.

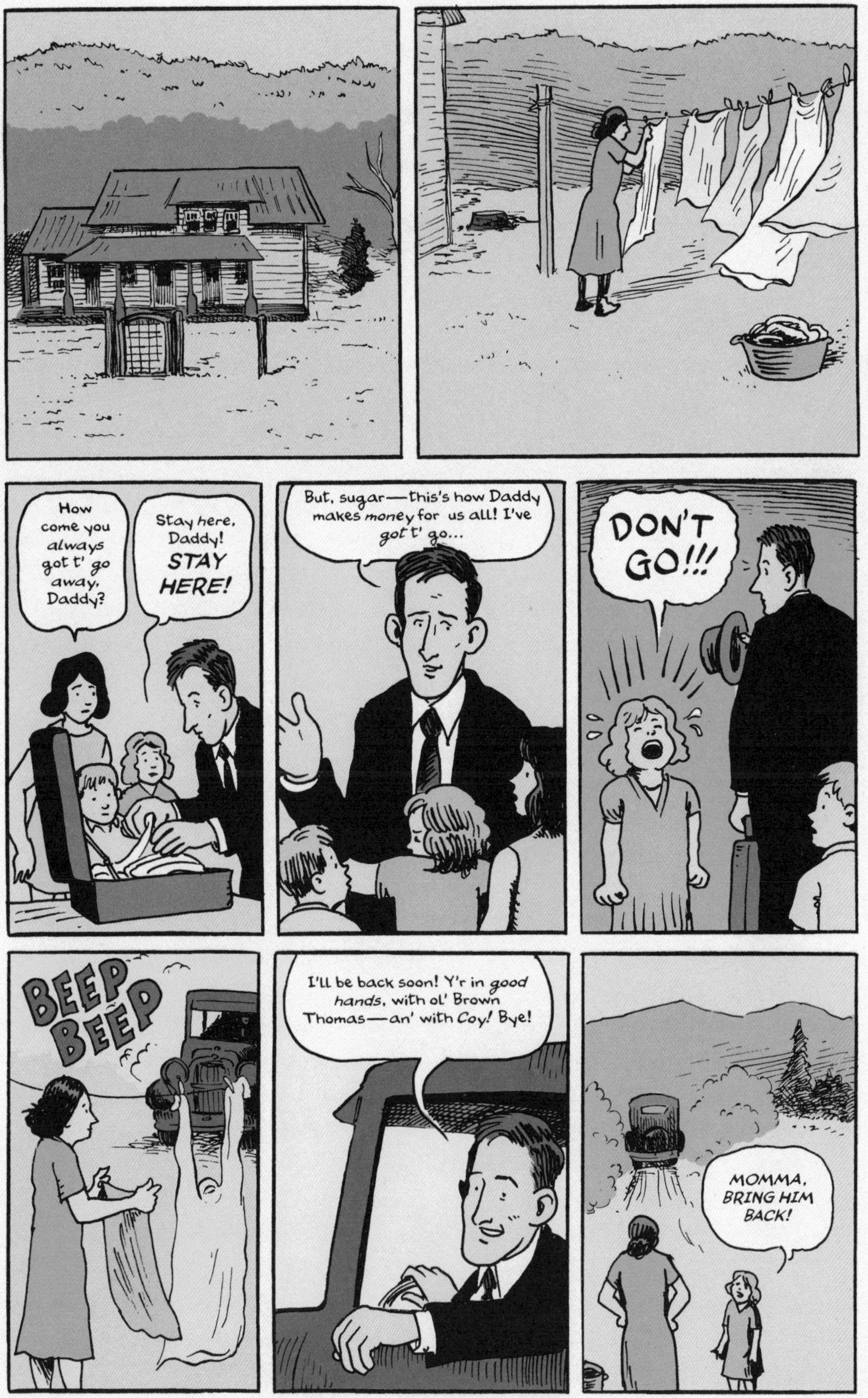
How come you always got t' go away, Daddy?
Stay here, Daddy! STAY HERE!
But, sugar—this's how Daddy makes money for us all! I've got t' go...
DON'T GO!!!
BEEP BEEP
I'll be back soon! Y'r in good hands, with ol' Brown Thomas—an' with Coy! Bye!
MOMMA, BRING HIM BACK!

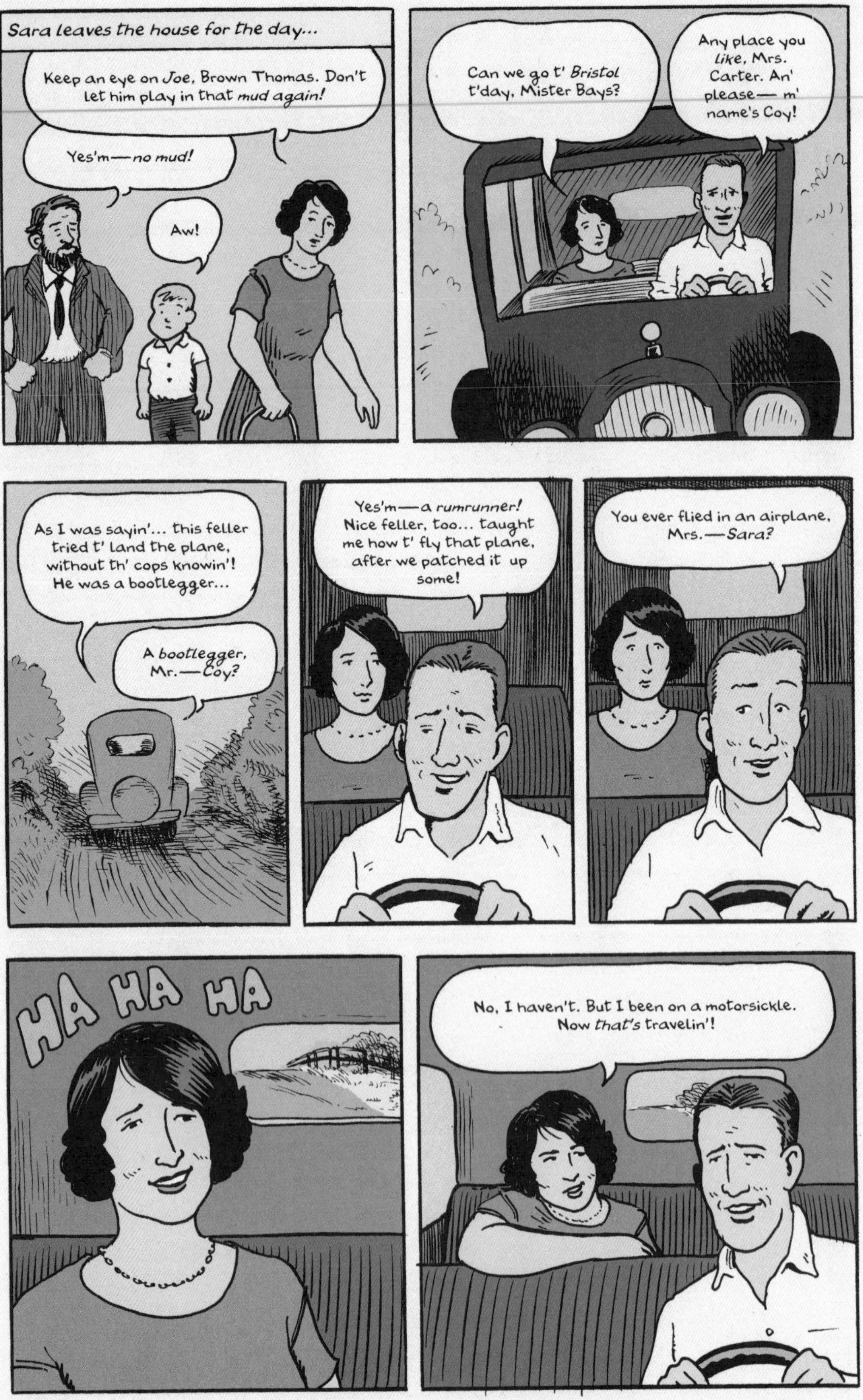
Sara leaves the house for the day...
Keep an eye on Joe, Brown Thomas. Don't let him play in that mud again!
Yes'm—no mud!
Aw!
Can we go t' Bristol t'day, Mister Bays?
Any place you like, Mrs. Carter. An' please— m' name's Coy!
As I was sayin'... this feller tried t' land the plane, without th' cops knowin'! He was a bootlegger...
A bootlegger, Mr.—Coy?
Yes'm—a rumrunner! Nice feller, too... taught me how t' fly that plane, after we patched it up some!
You ever flied in an airplane, Mrs.—Sara?
HA HA HA
No, I haven't. But I been on a motorsickle. Now that's travelin'!

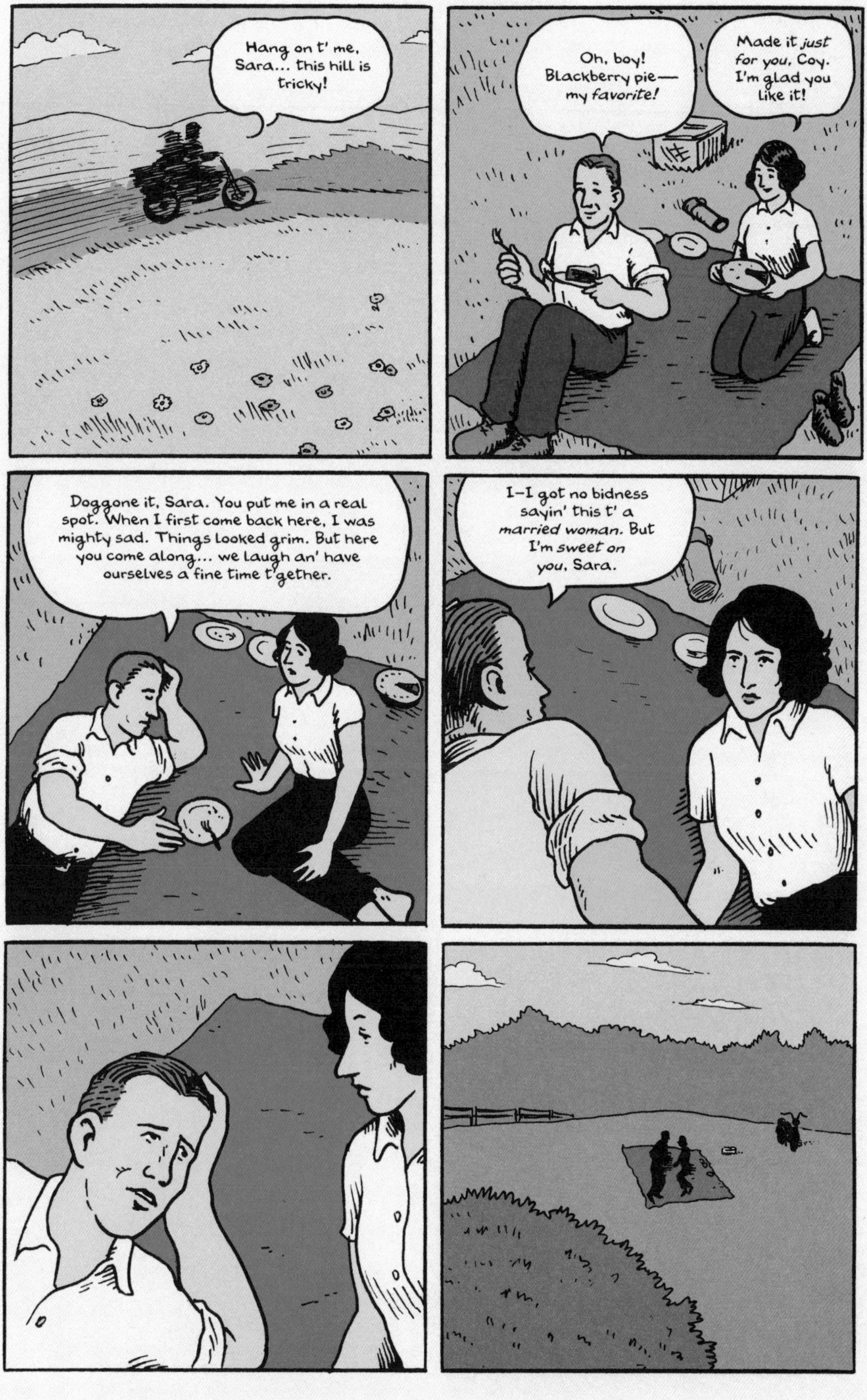
Hang on t' me, Sara... this hill is tricky!
Oh, boy! Blackberry pie— my *favorite!*
Made it *just* for you, Coy. I'm glad you like it!
Doggone it, Sara. You put me in a real spot. When I first come back here, I was mighty sad. Things looked grim. But here you come along... we laugh an' have ourselves a fine time t'gether.
I—I got no bidness sayin' this t' a *married woman.* But I'm *sweet* on you, Sara.

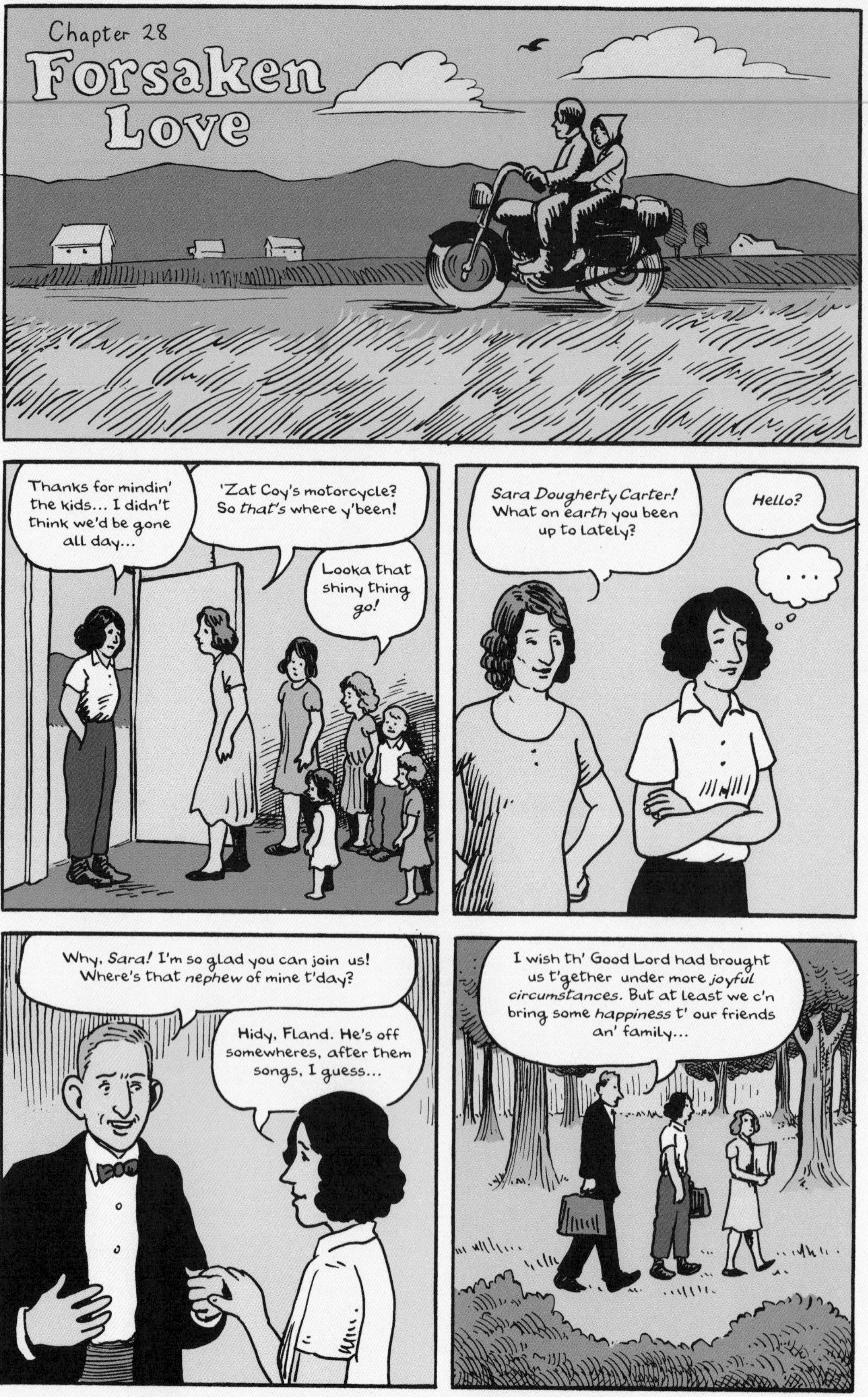
Chapter 28
Forsaken Love
Thanks for mindin' the kids... I didn't think we'd be gone all day...
'Zat Coy's motorcycle? So *that's* where y'been!
Looka that shiny thing *go!*
Sara Dougherty Carter! What on *earth* you been up to lately?
Hello?
. . .
Why, *Sara!* I'm so glad you can join us! Where's that *nephew* of mine t'day?
Hidy, Fland. He's off somewheres, after them songs, I guess...
I wish th' Good Lord had brought us t'gether under more *joyful circumstances.* But at least we c'n bring some *happiness* t' our friends an' family...

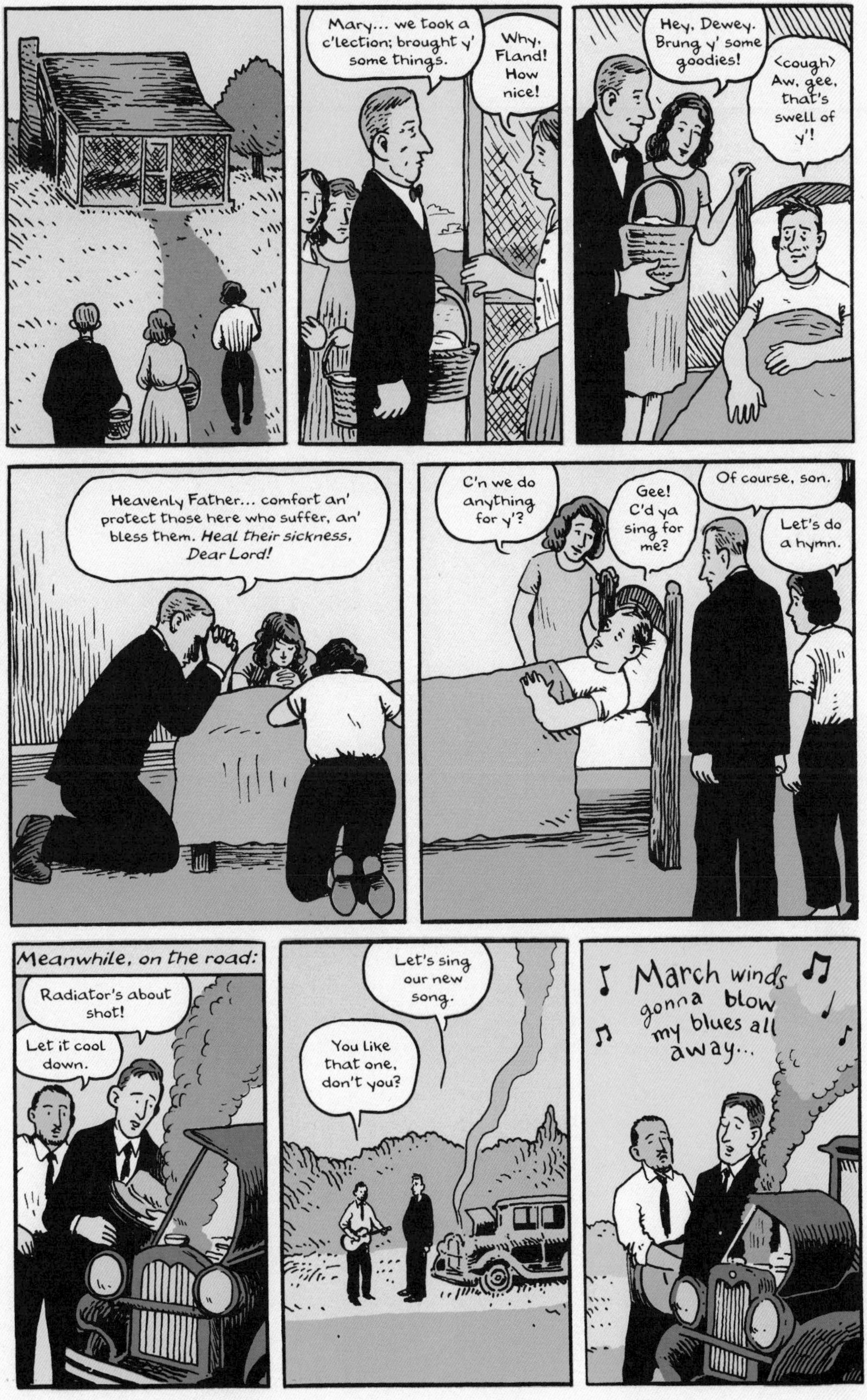
Mary... we took a c'lection; brought y' some things.
Why, Fland! How nice!
Hey, Dewey. Brung y' some goodies!
<cough> Aw, gee, that's swell of y'!
Heavenly Father... comfort an' protect those here who suffer, an' bless them. *Heal their sickness, Dear Lord!*
C'n we do anything for y'?
Gee! C'd ya sing for me?
Of course, son.
Let's do a hymn.
Meanwhile, on the road:
Radiator's about shot!
Let it cool down.
Let's sing our new song.
You like that one, don't you?
March winds gonna blow my blues all away...

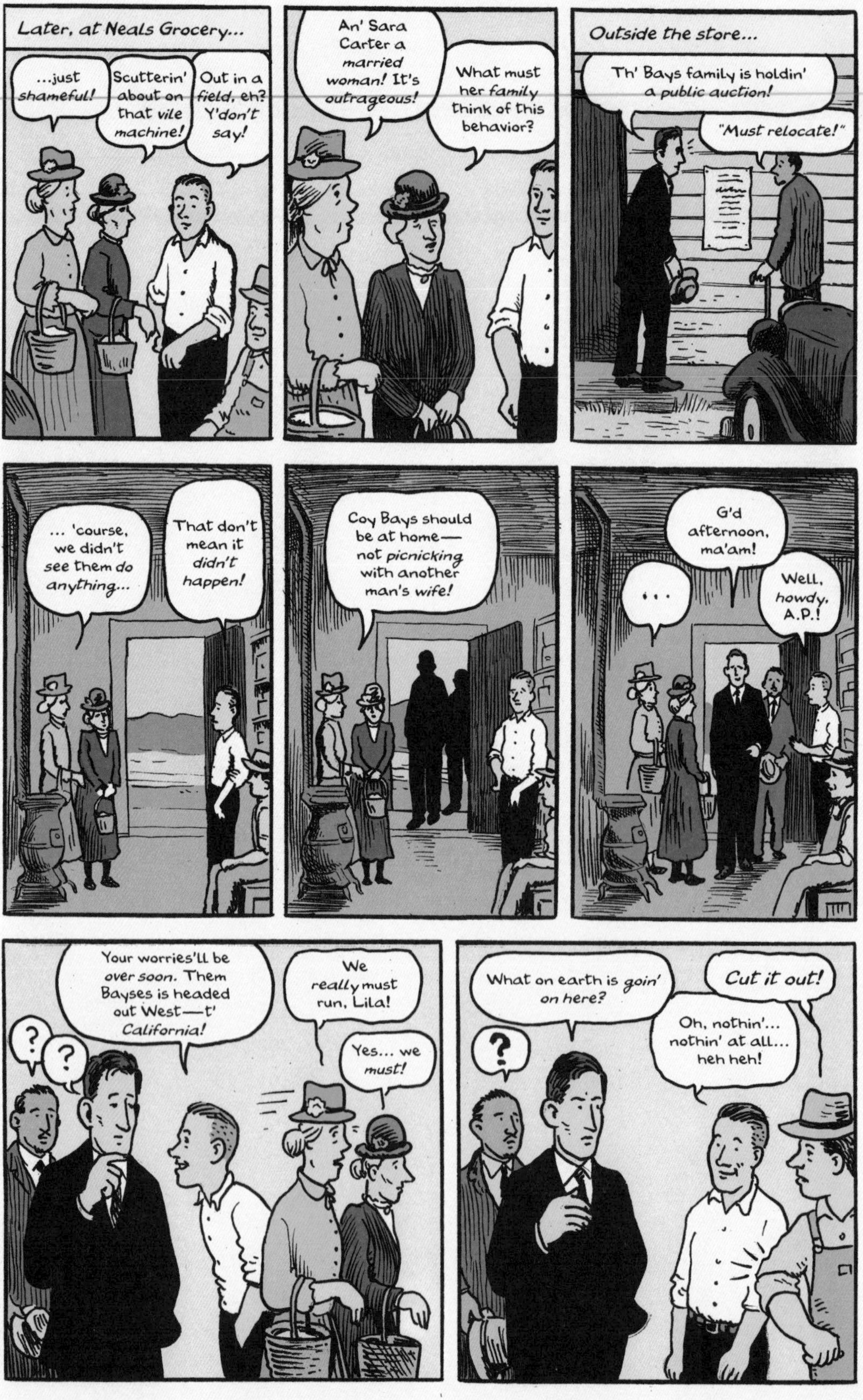

Later, at Neals Grocery...
...just shameful!
Scutterin' about on that vile machine!
Out in a field, eh? Y'don't say!
An' Sara Carter a married woman! It's outrageous!
What must her family think of this behavior?
Outside the store...
Th' Bays family is holdin' a public auction!
"Must relocate!"
... 'course, we didn't see them do anything...
That don't mean it didn't happen!
Coy Bays should be at home— not picnicking with another man's wife!
...
G'd afternoon, ma'am!
Well, howdy, A.P.!
?
?
Your worries'll be over soon. Them Bayses is headed out West—t' California!
We really must run, Lila!
Yes... we must!
?
What on earth is goin' on here?
Cut it out!
Oh, nothin'... nothin' at all... heh heh!

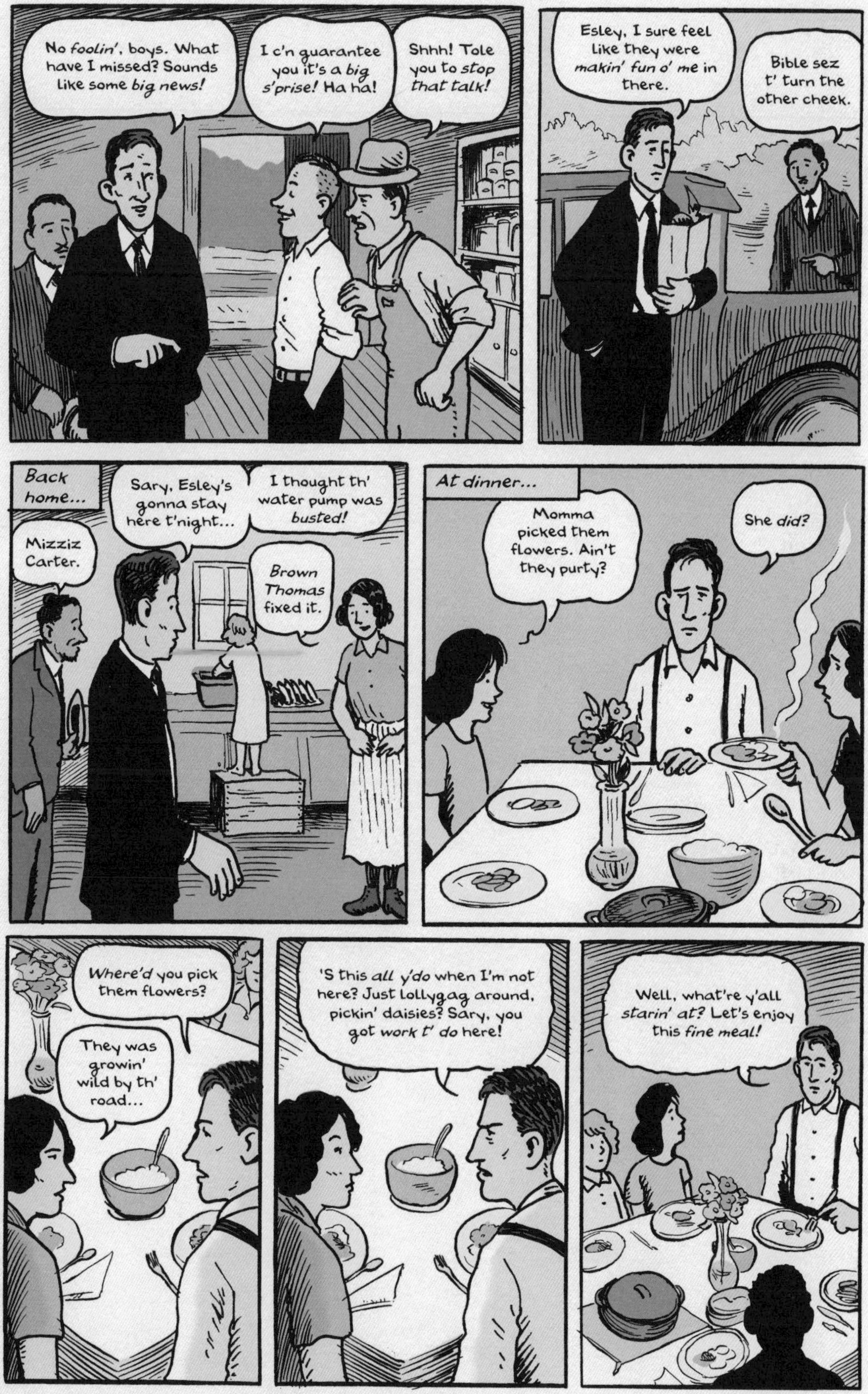
No *foolin'*, boys. What have I missed? Sounds like some *big news!*
I c'n guarantee you it's a *big s'prise!* Ha ha!
Shhh! Tole you to *stop that talk!*
Esley, I sure feel like they were *makin' fun o' me* in there.
Bible sez t' turn the other cheek.
Back home...
Mizziz Carter.
Sary, Esley's gonna stay here t'night...
I thought th' water pump was *busted!*
Brown Thomas fixed it.
At dinner...
Momma picked them flowers. Ain't they purty?
She *did?*
Where'd you pick them flowers?
They was growin' wild by th' road...
'S this *all y'do* when I'm not here? Just lollygag around, pickin' daisies? Sary, you got *work t' do* here!
Well, what're y'all *starin' at?* Let's enjoy this *fine meal!*

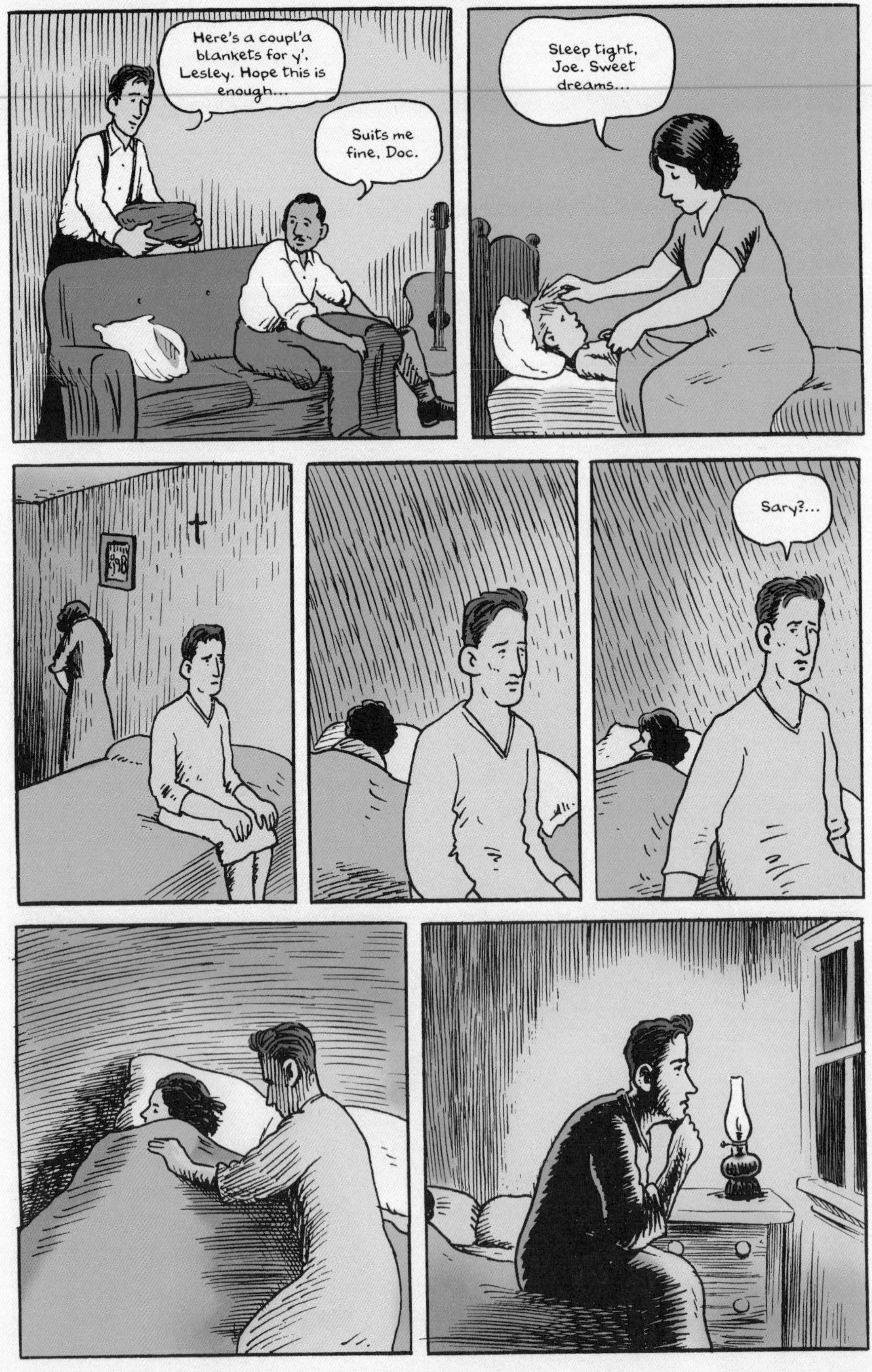
Here's a coupl'a blankets for y', Lesley. Hope this is enough...
Suits me fine, Doc.
Sleep tight, Joe. Sweet dreams...
Sary?...

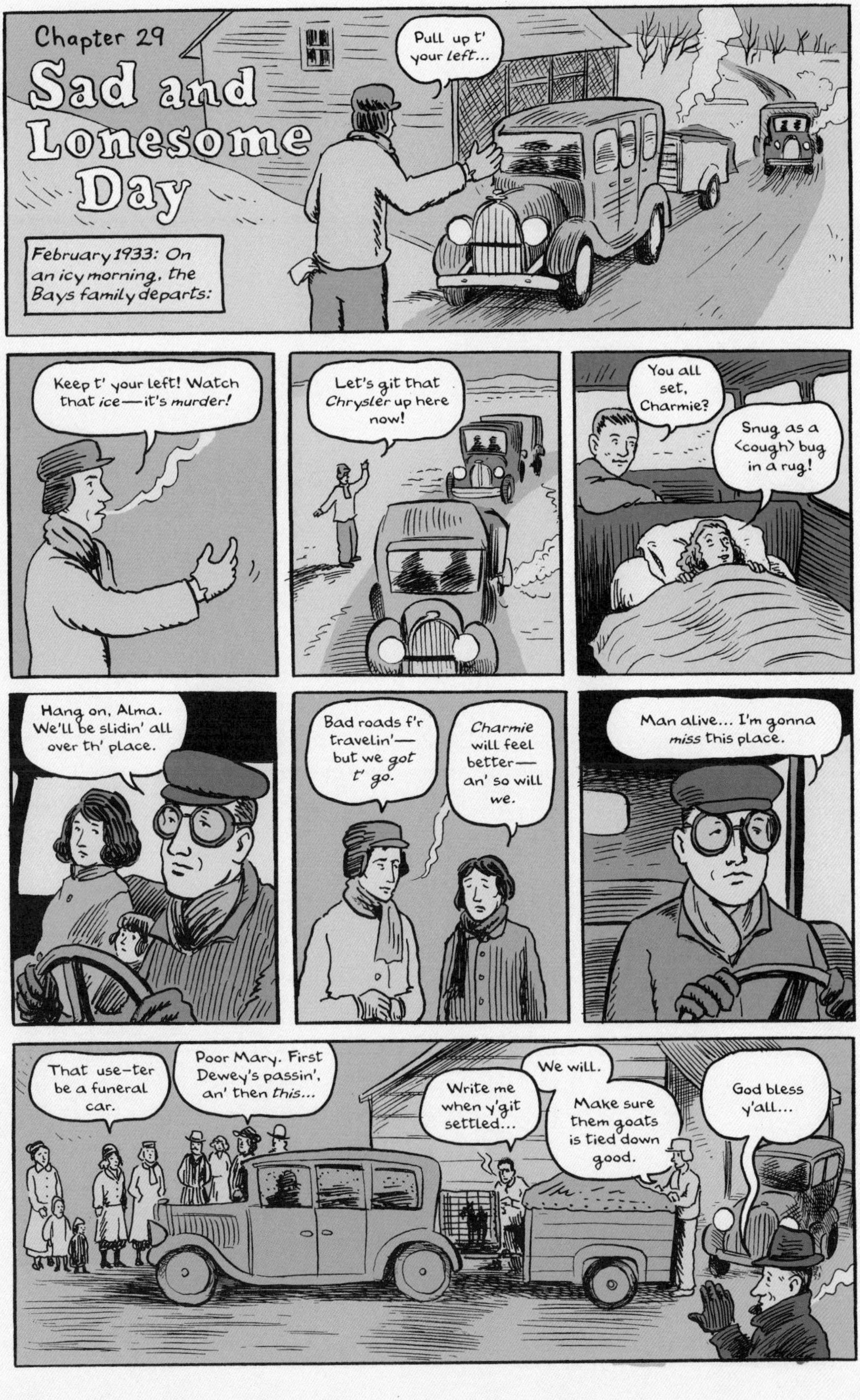
Chapter 29
Sad and Lonesome Day
February 1933: On an icy morning, the Bays family departs:
Pull up t' your *left*...
Keep t' your left! Watch that *ice*—it's *murder!*
Let's git that *Chrysler* up here now!
You all set, Charmie?
Snug as a <cough> bug in a rug!
Hang on, Alma. We'll be slidin' all over th' place.
Bad roads f'r travelin'—but we *got* t' go.
Charmie will feel better—an' so will we.
Man alive... I'm gonna *miss* this place.
That use-ter be a funeral car.
Poor Mary. First Dewey's passin', an' then *this*...
Write me when y'git settled...
We will.
Make sure them goats is tied down good.
God bless y'all...

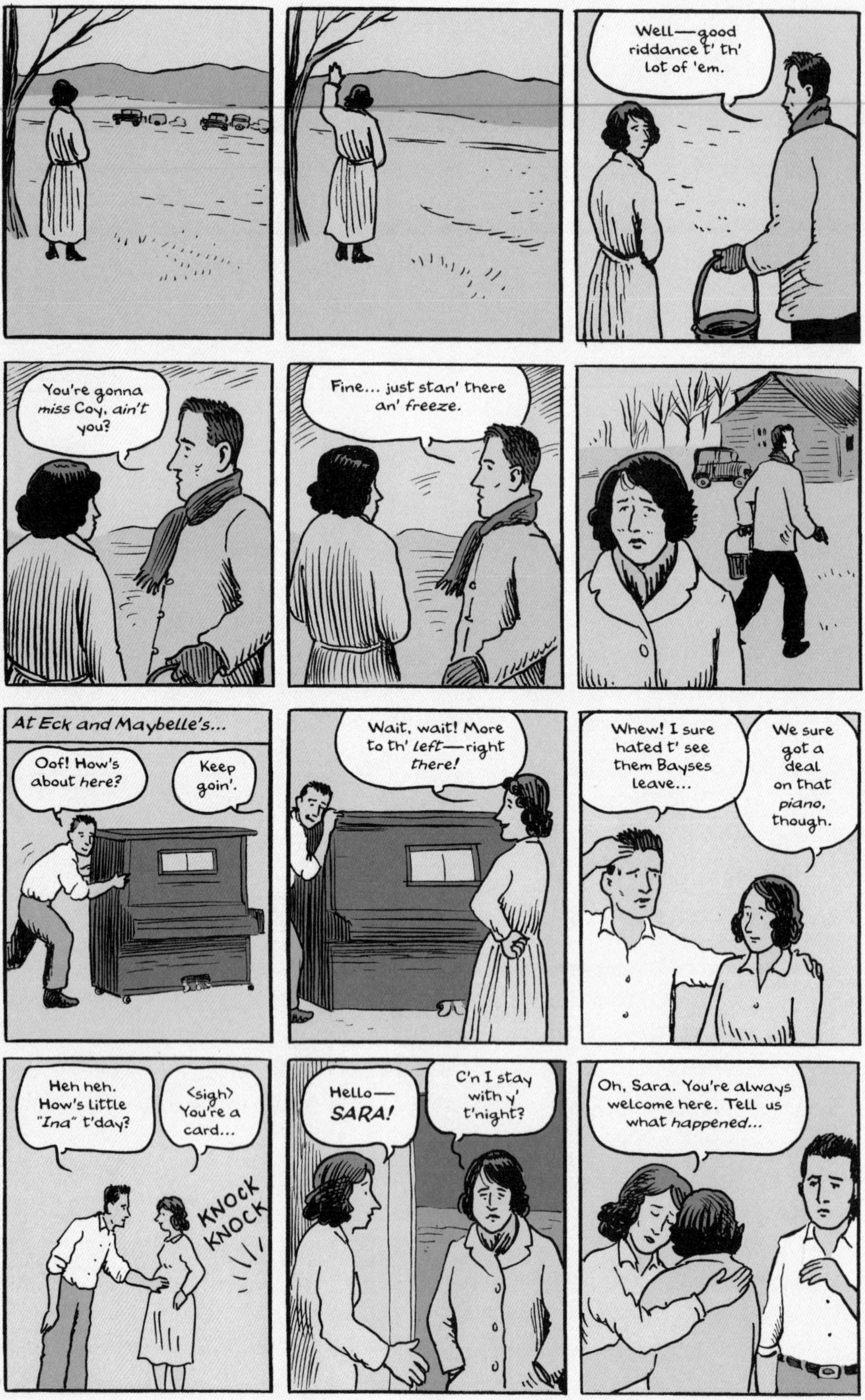
Well—good riddance t' th' lot of 'em.
You're gonna miss Coy, ain't you?
Fine... just stan' there an' freeze.
At Eck and Maybelle's...
Oof! How's about here?
Keep goin'.
Wait, wait! More to th' left—right there!
Whew! I sure hated t' see them Bayses leave...
We sure got a deal on that piano, though.
Heh heh. How's little "Ina" t'day?
<sigh> You're a card...
KNOCK KNOCK
Hello— SARA!
C'n I stay with y' t'night?
Oh, Sara. You're always welcome here. Tell us what happened...

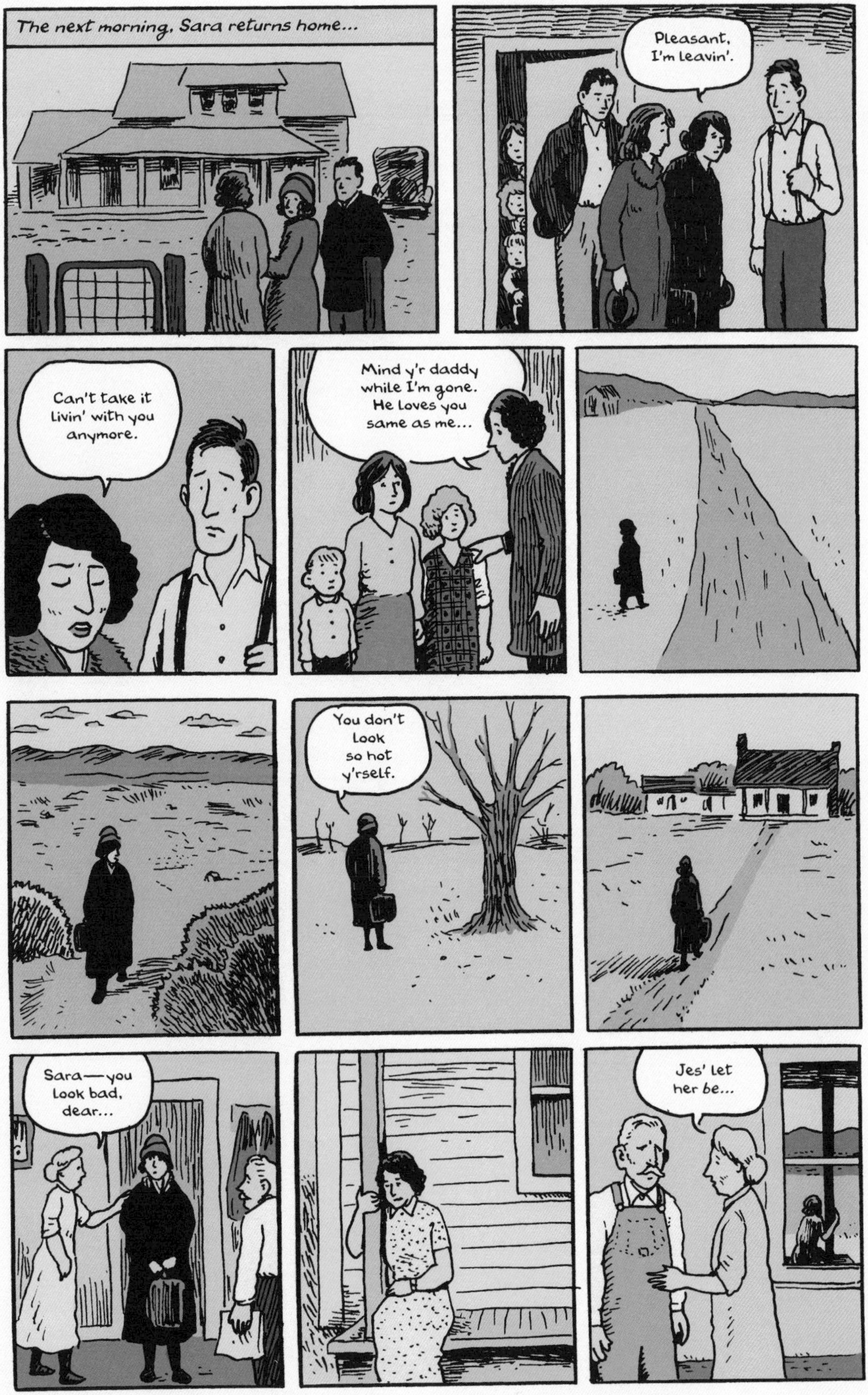
The next morning, Sara returns home...
Pleasant, I'm leavin'.
Can't take it livin' with you anymore.
Mind y'r daddy while I'm gone. He loves you same as me...
You don't look so hot y'rself.
Sara—you look bad, dear...
Jes' let her be...

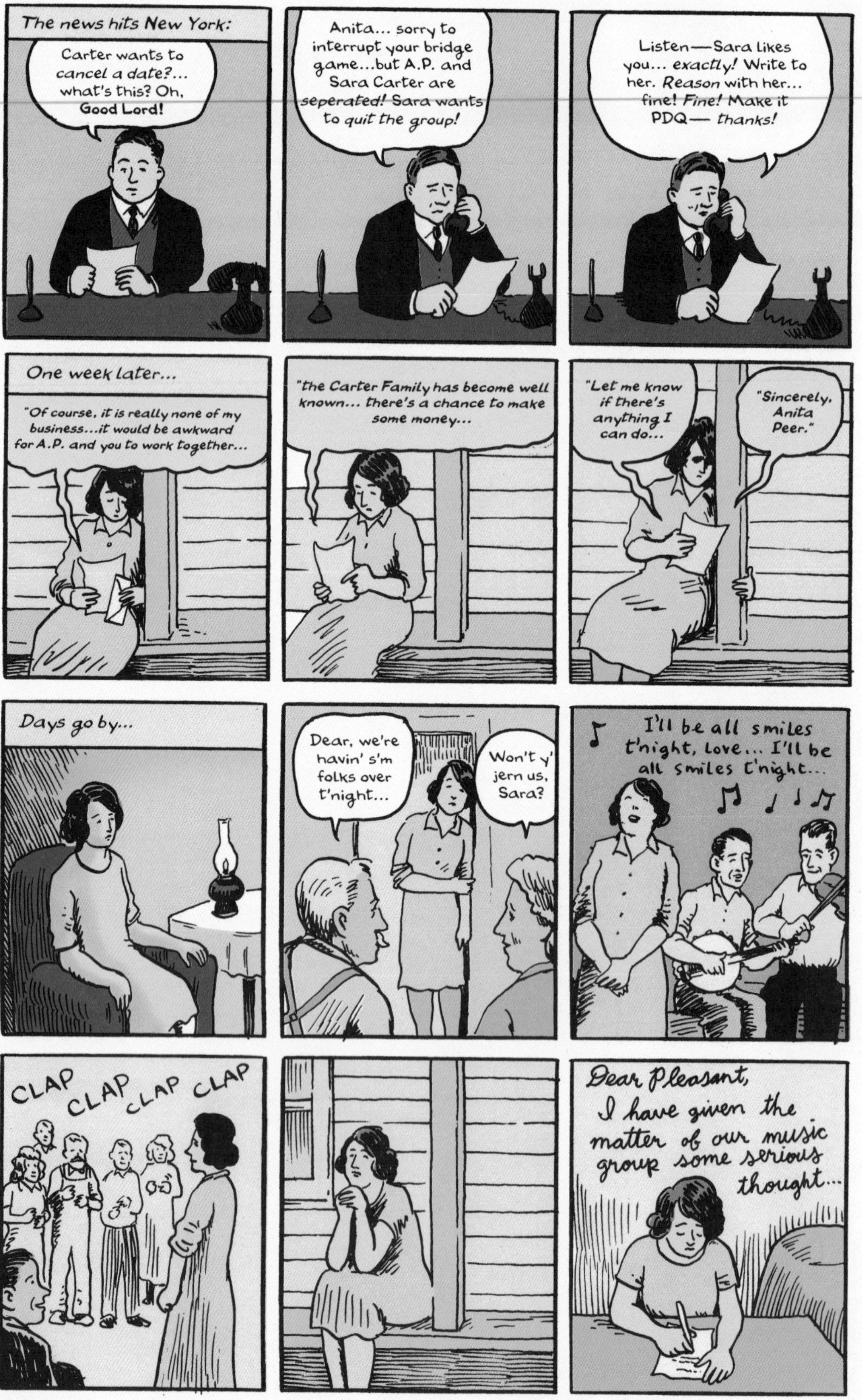
The news hits New York:
Carter wants to cancel a date?... what's this? Oh, Good Lord!
Anita... sorry to interrupt your bridge game...but A.P. and Sara Carter are seperated! Sara wants to quit the group!
Listen—Sara likes you... exactly! Write to her. Reason with her... fine! Fine! Make it PDQ— thanks!
One week later...
"Of course, it is really none of my business...it would be awkward for A.P. and you to work together...
"the Carter Family has become well known... there's a chance to make some money...
"Let me know if there's anything I can do...
"Sincerely, Anita Peer."
Days go by...
Dear, we're havin' s'm folks over t'night...
Won't y' jern us, Sara?
I'll be all smiles t'night, Love... I'll be all smiles t'night...
CLAP CLAP CLAP CLAP
Dear Pleasant,
I have given the matter of our music group some serious thought...

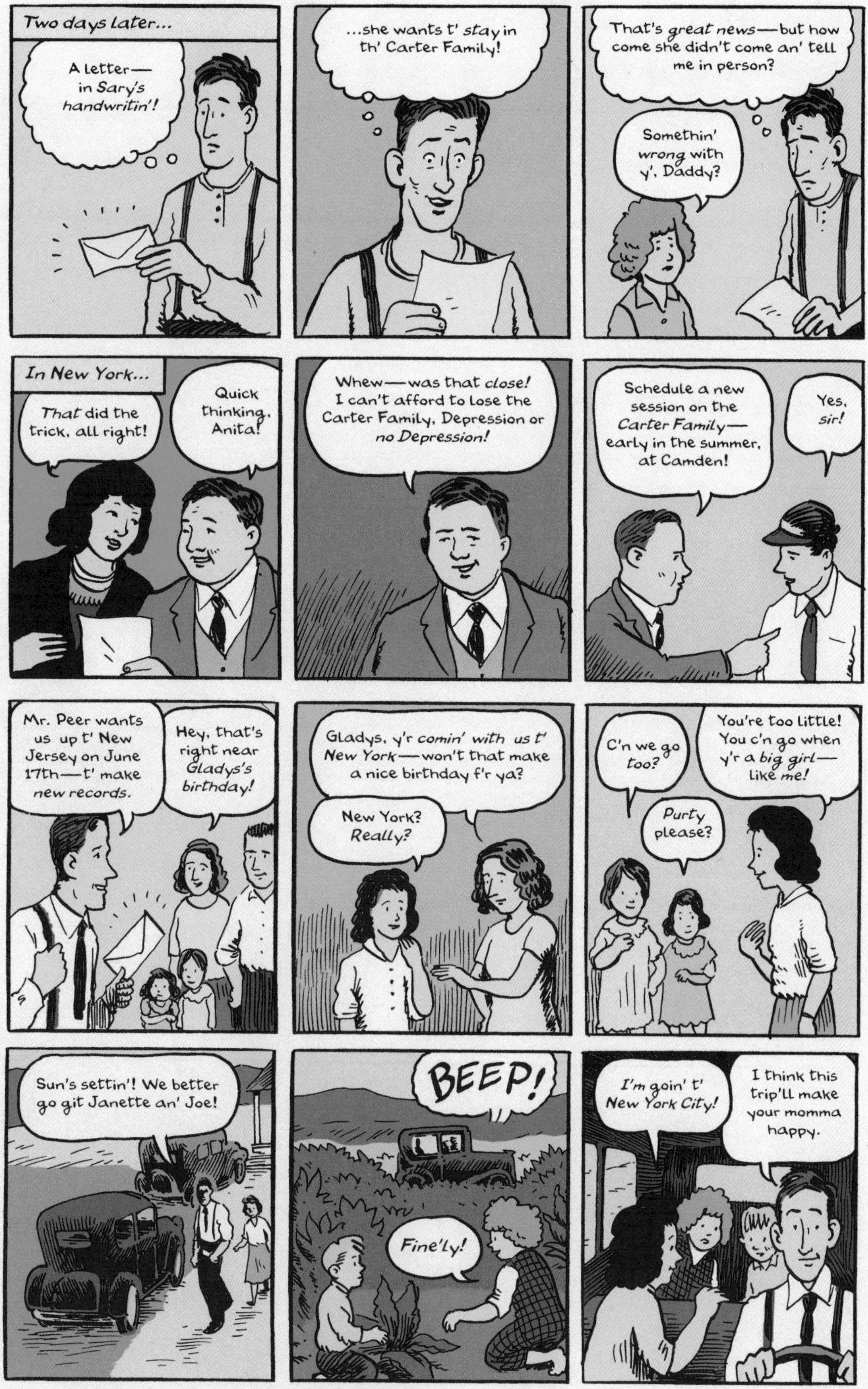
Two days later...
A letter— in Sary's handwritin'!
...she wants t' stay in th' Carter Family!
That's great news—but how come she didn't come an' tell me in person?
Somethin' wrong with y', Daddy?
In New York...
That did the trick, all right!
Quick thinking, Anita!
Whew—was that close! I can't afford to lose the Carter Family, Depression or no Depression!
Schedule a new session on the Carter Family— early in the summer, at Camden!
Yes, sir!
Mr. Peer wants us up t' New Jersey on June 17th—t' make new records.
Hey, that's right near Gladys's birthday!
Gladys, y'r comin' with us t' New York—won't that make a nice birthday f'r ya?
New York? Really?
C'n we go too?
You're too little! You c'n go when y'r a big girl— like me!
Purty please?
Sun's settin'! We better go git Janette an' Joe!
BEEP!
Fine'ly!
I'm goin' t' New York City!
I think this trip'll make your momma happy.

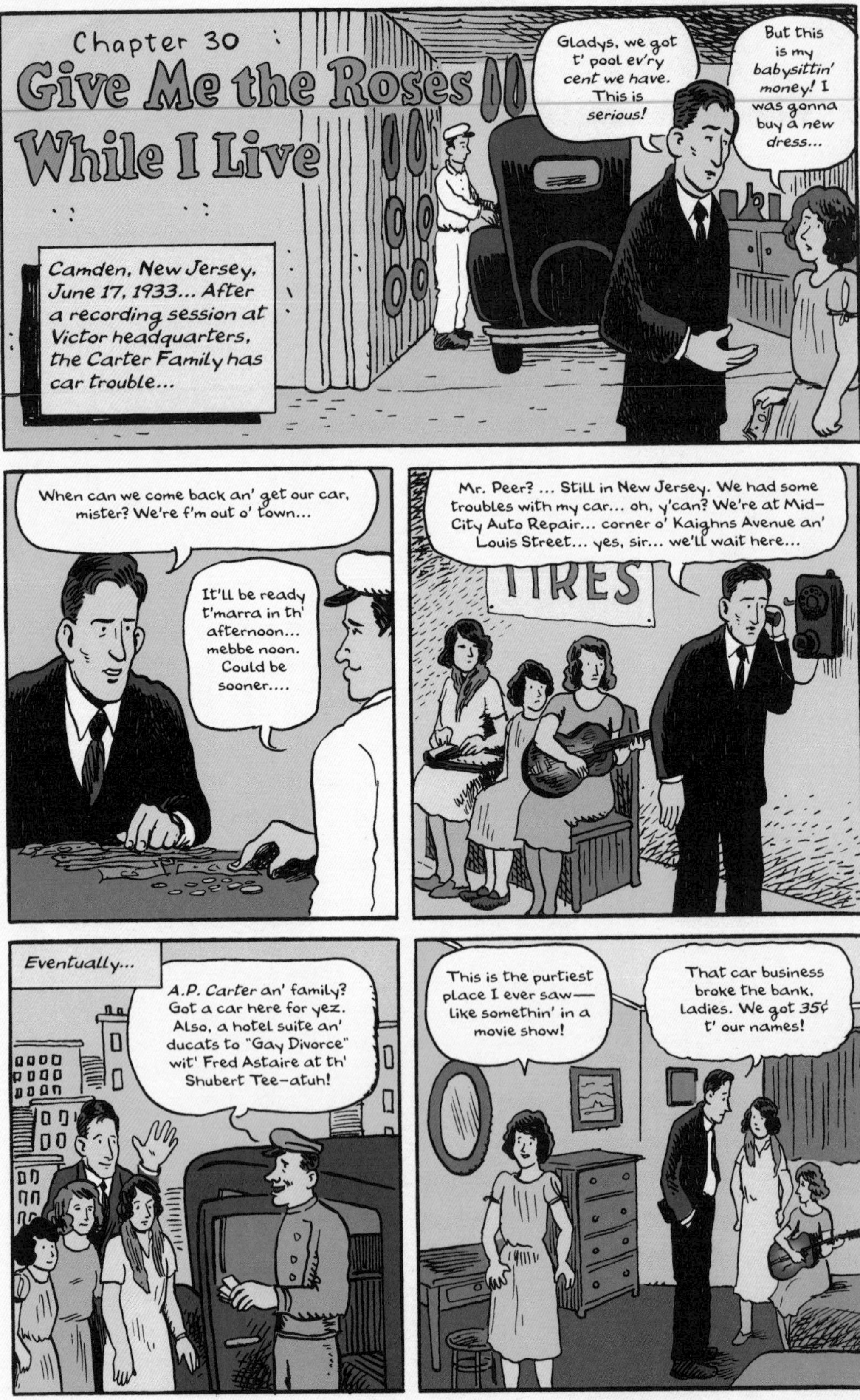
Chapter 30 :
Give Me the Roses While I Live
Camden, New Jersey, June 17, 1933... After a recording session at Victor headquarters, the Carter Family has car trouble...
Gladys, we got t' pool ev'ry cent we have. This is serious!
But this is my babysittin' money! I was gonna buy a new dress...
When can we come back an' get our car, mister? We're f'm out o' town...
It'll be ready t'marra in th' afternoon... mebbe noon. Could be sooner....
Mr. Peer? ... Still in New Jersey. We had some troubles with my car... oh, y'can? We're at Mid-City Auto Repair... corner o' Kaighns Avenue an' Louis Street... yes, sir... we'll wait here...
TIRES
Eventually...
A.P. Carter an' family? Got a car here for yez. Also, a hotel suite an' ducats to "Gay Divorce" wit' Fred Astaire at th' Shubert Tee-atuh!
This is the purtiest place I ever saw— like somethin' in a movie show!
That car business broke the bank, ladies. We got 35¢ t' our names!

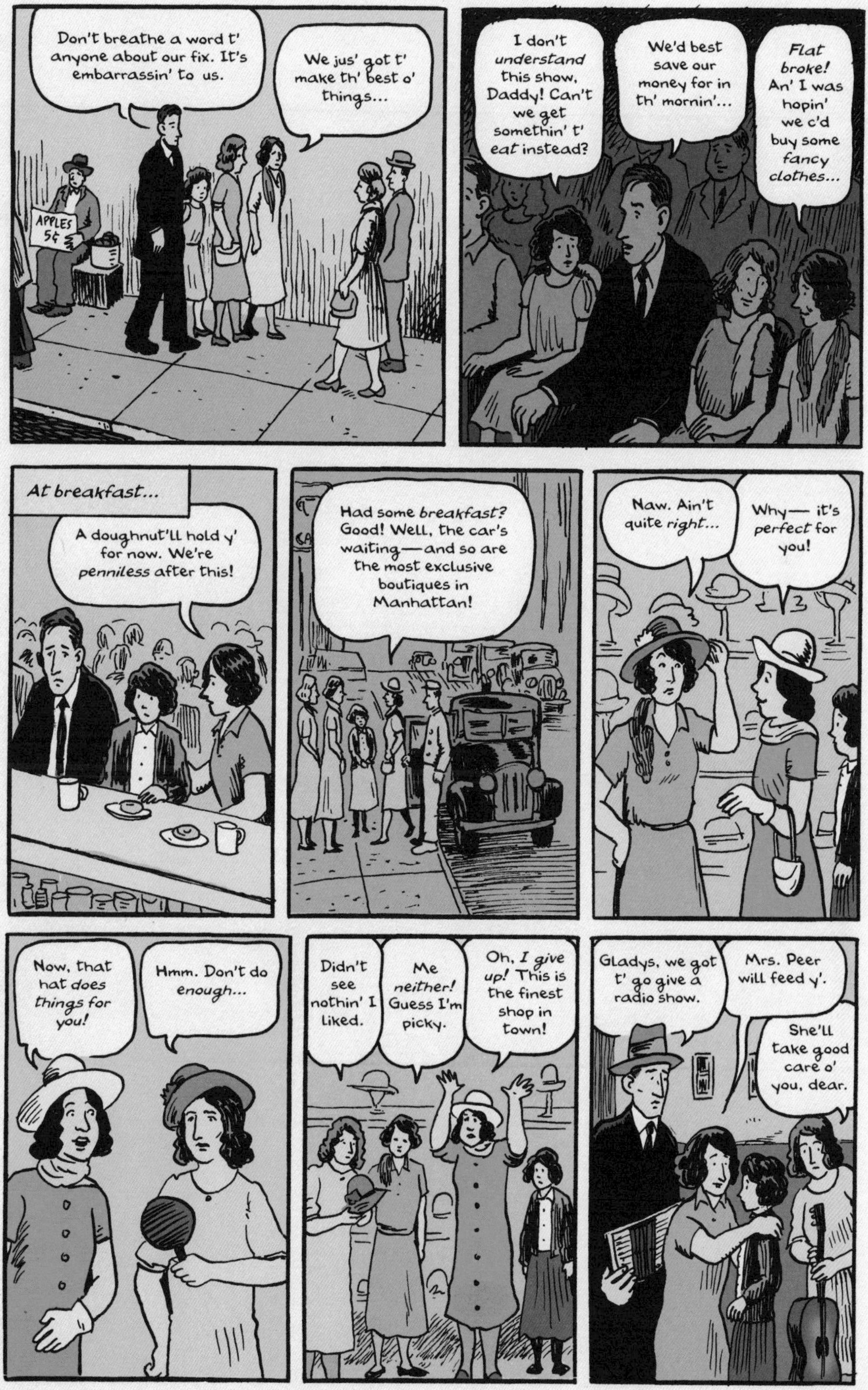
Don't breathe a word t' anyone about our fix. It's embarrassin' to us.
We jus' got t' make th' best o' things...
APPLES 5¢
I don't understand this show, Daddy! Can't we get somethin' t' eat instead?
We'd best save our money for in th' mornin'...
Flat broke! An' I was hopin' we c'd buy some fancy clothes...
At breakfast...
A doughnut'll hold y' for now. We're penniless after this!
Had some breakfast? Good! Well, the car's waiting—and so are the most exclusive boutiques in Manhattan!
Naw. Ain't quite right...
Why— it's perfect for you!
Now, that hat does things for you!
Hmm. Don't do enough...
Didn't see nothin' I liked.
Me neither! Guess I'm picky.
Oh, I give up! This is the finest shop in town!
Gladys, we got t' go give a radio show.
Mrs. Peer will feed y'.
She'll take good care o' you, dear.

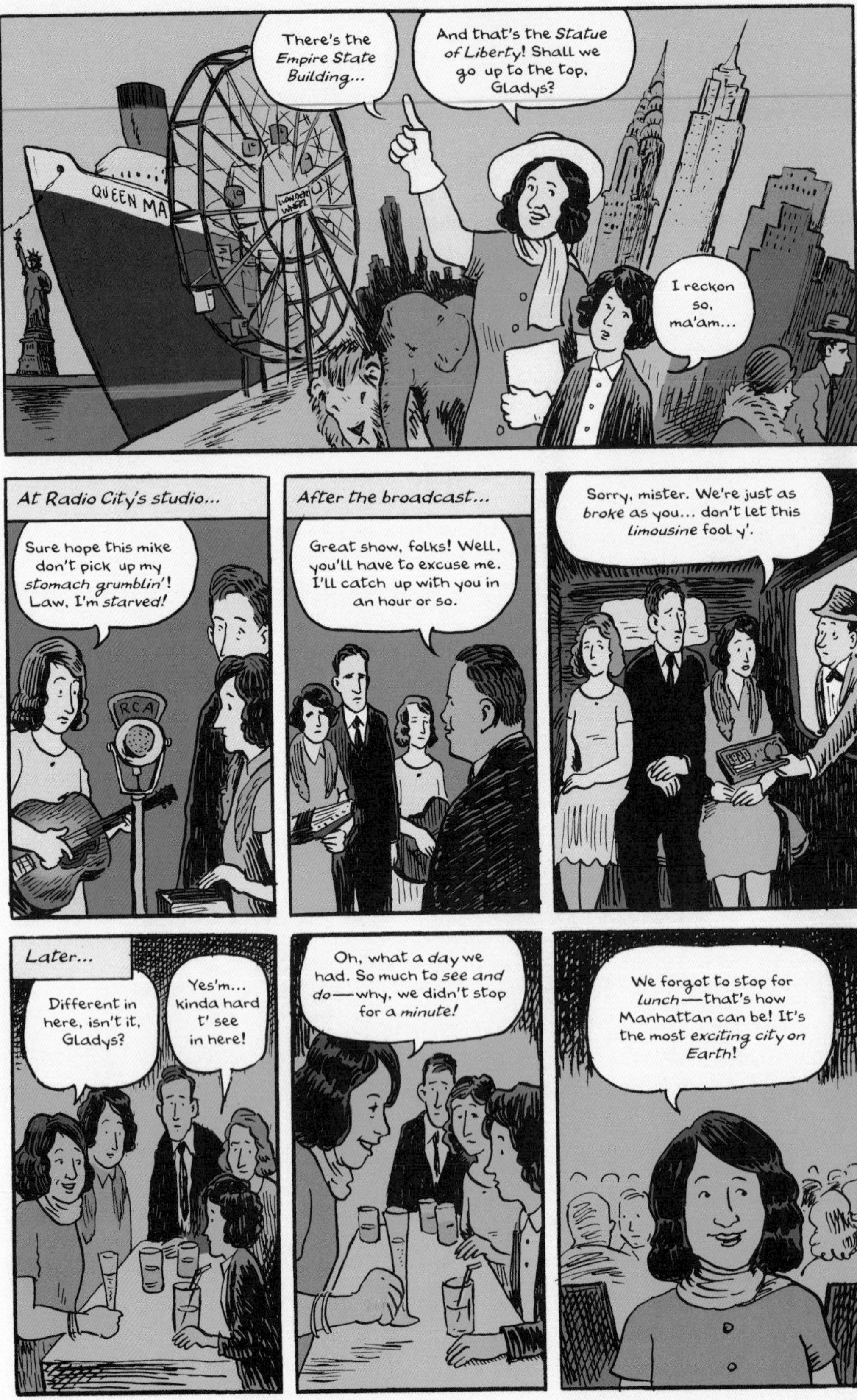
There's the *Empire State Building*...
And that's the *Statue of Liberty*! Shall we go up to the top, Gladys?
QUEEN MA
WONDER WHEEL
I reckon so, ma'am...
At Radio City's studio...
Sure hope this mike don't pick up my *stomach grumblin'*! Law, I'm *starved*!
RCA
After the broadcast...
Great show, folks! Well, you'll have to excuse me. I'll catch up with you in an hour or so.
Sorry, mister. We're just as *broke* as you... don't let this *limousine* fool y'.
Later...
Different in here, isn't it, Gladys?
Yes'm... kinda hard t' see in here!
Oh, what a *day* we had. So much to see *and do*—why, we didn't stop for a *minute!*
We forgot to stop for *lunch*—that's how Manhattan can be! It's the most *exciting city* on *Earth*!

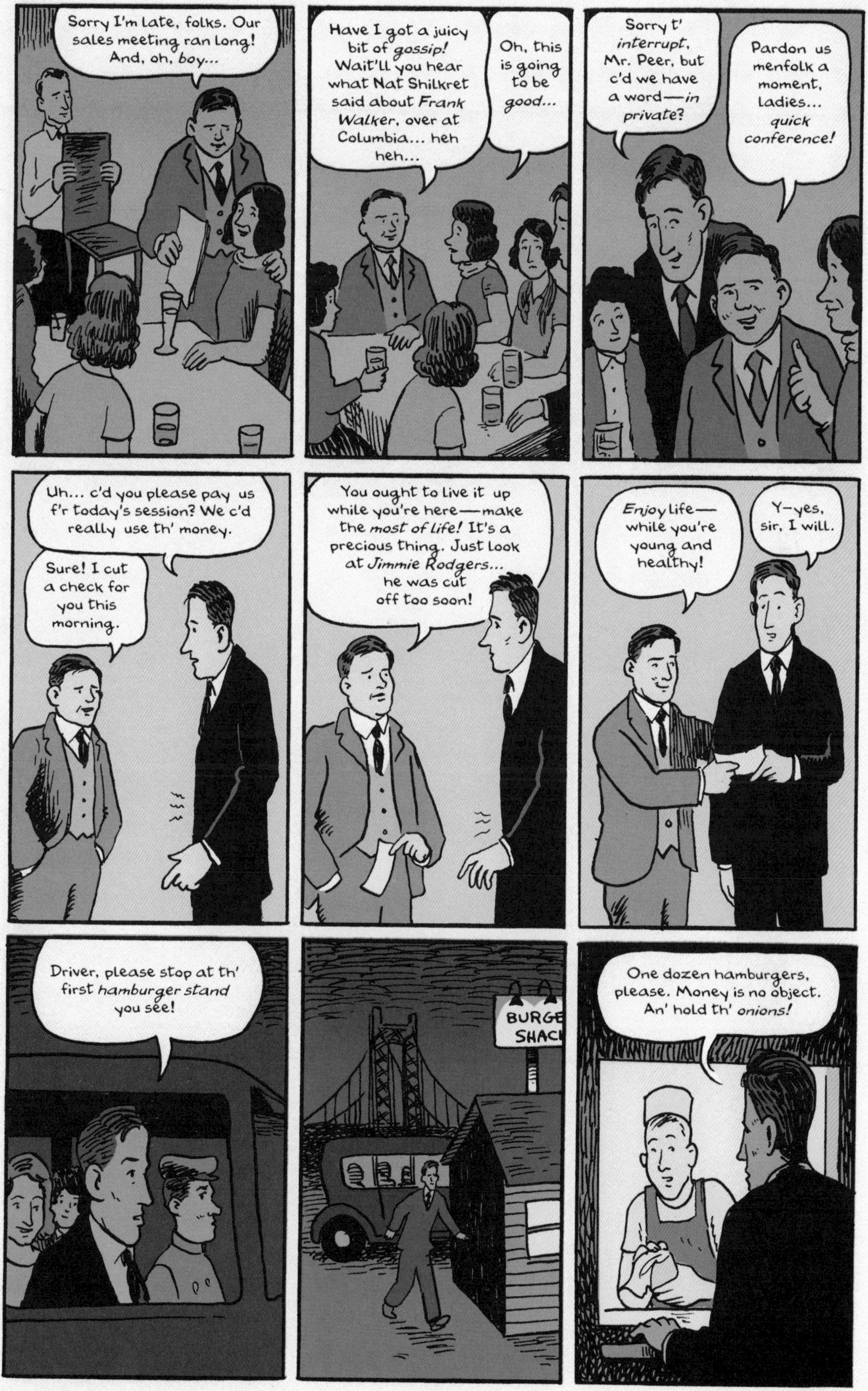
Sorry I'm late, folks. Our sales meeting ran long! And, oh, boy...
Have I got a juicy bit of gossip! Wait'll you hear what Nat Shilkret said about Frank Walker, over at Columbia... heh heh...
Oh, this is going to be good...
Sorry t' interrupt, Mr. Peer, but c'd we have a word—in private?
Pardon us menfolk a moment, ladies... quick conference!
Uh... c'd you please pay us f'r today's session? We c'd really use th' money.
Sure! I cut a check for you this morning.
You ought to live it up while you're here—make the most of life! It's a precious thing. Just look at Jimmie Rodgers... he was cut off too soon!
Enjoy life—while you're young and healthy!
Y-yes, sir, I will.
Driver, please stop at th' first hamburger stand you see!
BURGE
SHAC
One dozen hamburgers, please. Money is no object. An' hold th' onions!

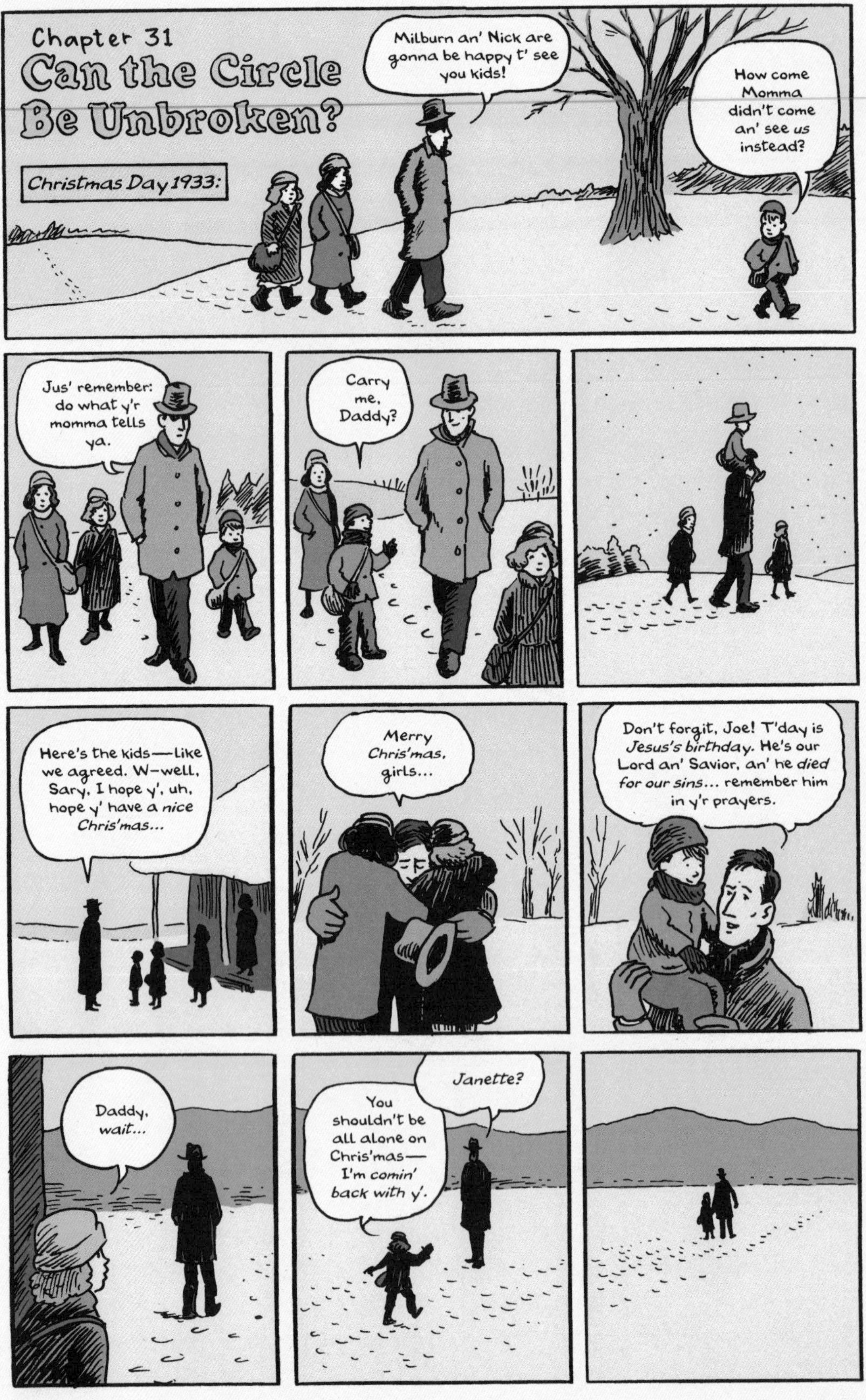
Chapter 31
Can the Circle Be Unbroken?
Christmas Day 1933:
Milburn an' Nick are gonna be happy t' see you kids!
How come Momma didn't come an' see *us* instead?
Jus' remember: do what y'r momma tells ya.
Carry me, Daddy?
Here's the kids—like we agreed. W-well, Sary, I hope y', uh, hope y' have a *nice Chris'mas*...
Merry *Chris'mas*, girls...
Don't forgit, Joe! T'day is *Jesus's birthday*. He's our Lord an' Savior, an' he *died* for our *sins*... remember him in y'r prayers.
Daddy, *wait*...
Janette?
You shouldn't be all alone on Chris'mas—I'm *comin'* back with y'.

Carter's Blues, 1934 Version

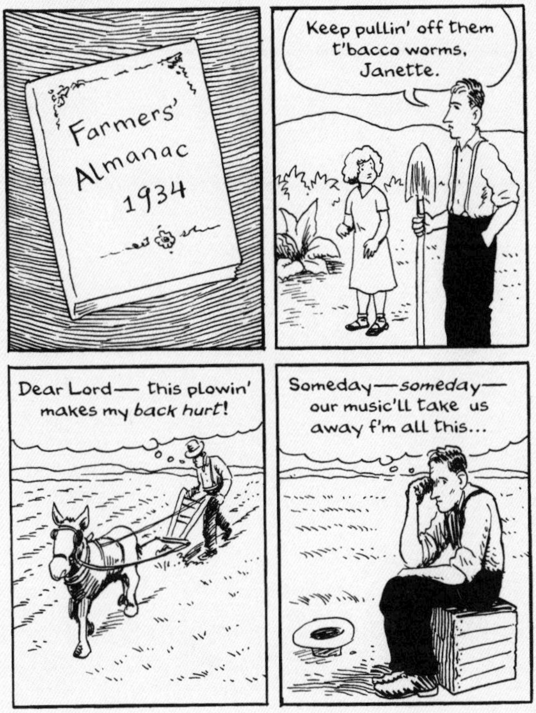
Farmers' Almanac 1934
Keep pullin' off them t'bacco worms, Janette.
Dear Lord— this plowin' makes my *back hurt*!
Someday—*someday*— our music'll take us away f'm all this...

A Stationary Position

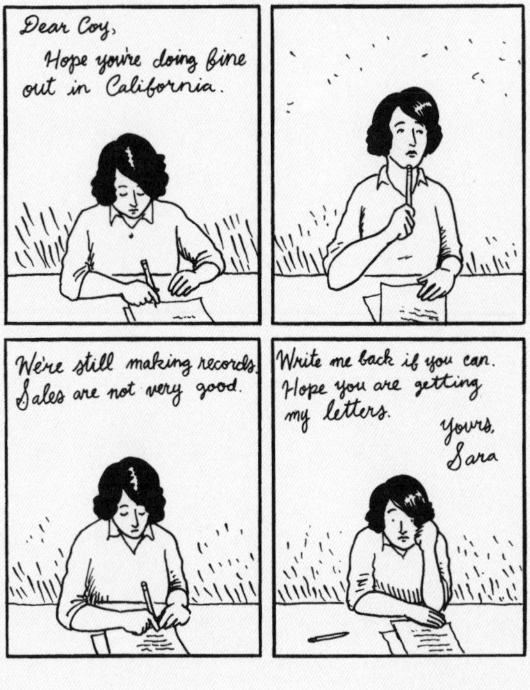
Dear Coy,
Hope you're doing fine out in California.
We're still making records. Sales are not very good.
Write me back if you can. Hope you are getting my letters.
Yours, Sara

Stew Ball

It's easy to cook you some food! I'll show you girls how.
Got us some veg'tables, a li'l bit o' meat, some salt...
Put 'em all in a pot. Boil it 'til it starts to bubble... stir it... then put a lid on it.
Hour from now, we'll have us a nice stew. Just in time for supper! Smells good already!

Song of Joy

There'll be joy, joy, joy...

From Hit to Flop

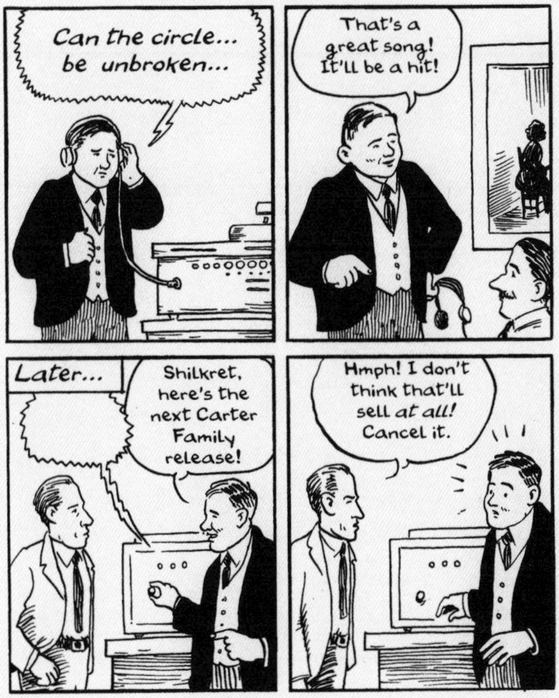
Can the circle... be unbroken...
That's a great song! It'll be a hit!
Later...
Shilkret, here's the next Carter Family release!
Hmph! I don't think that'll sell *at all!* Cancel it.

You Can Bank on It, Janette

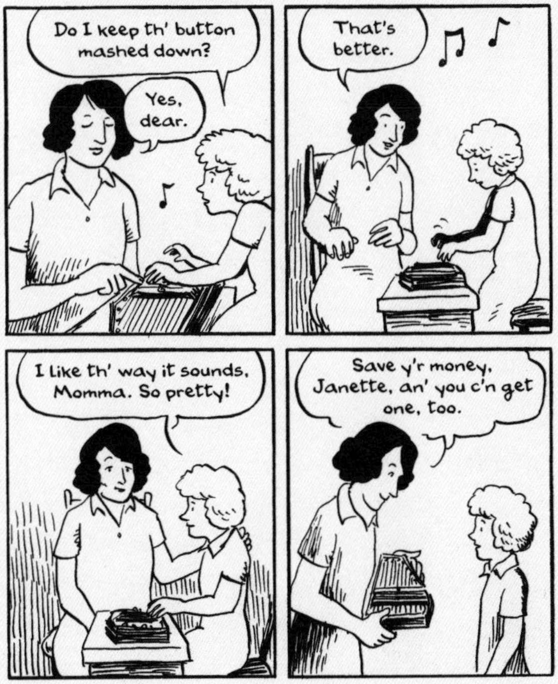
Do I keep th' button mashed down?
Yes, dear.
That's better.
I like th' way it sounds, Momma. So pretty!
Save y'r money, Janette, an' you c'n get one, too.

Old Familiar Tune

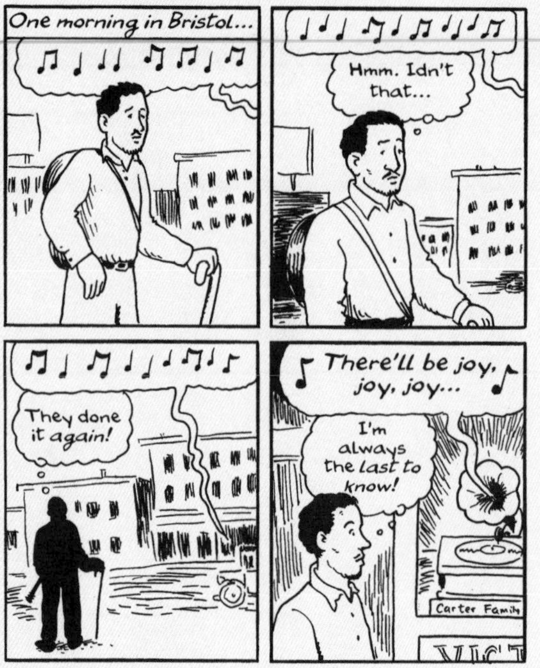
One morning in Bristol...
Hmm. Idn't that...
They done it again!
There'll be joy, joy, joy...
I'm always the last to know!
Carter Famil

There'll Be Some Changes Made

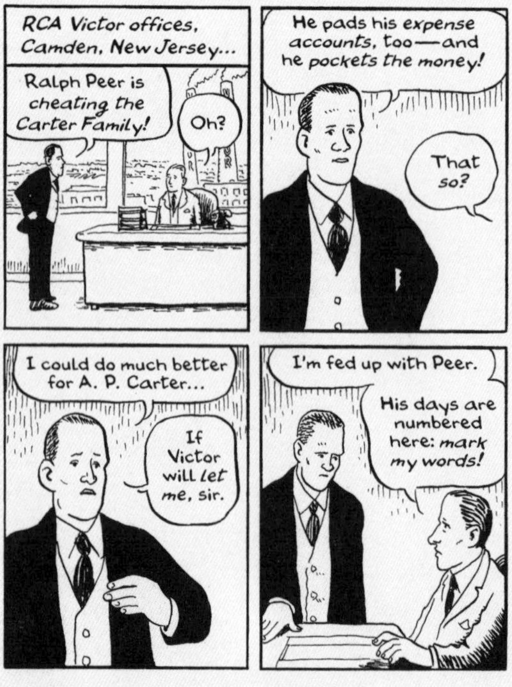
RCA Victor offices, Camden, New Jersey...
Ralph Peer is cheating the Carter Family!
Oh?
He pads his expense accounts, too—and he pockets the money!
That so?
I could do much better for A. P. Carter...
If Victor will let me, sir.
I'm fed up with Peer.
His days are numbered here: mark my words!

A Very Special Delivery

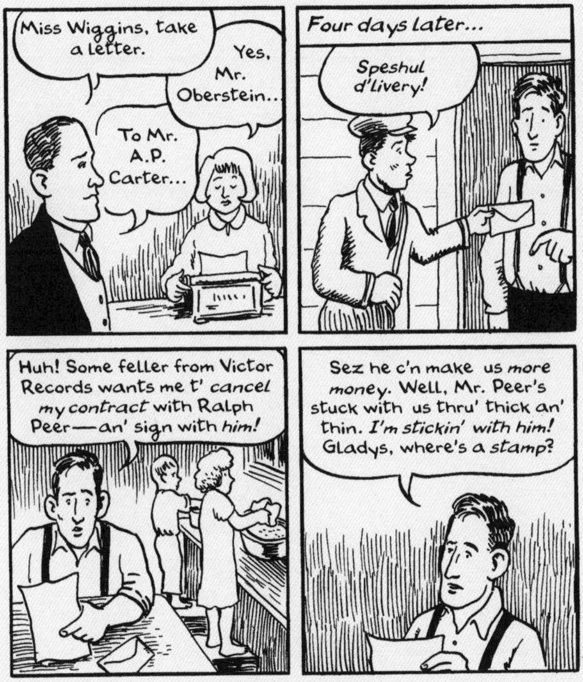
Miss Wiggins, take a letter.
Yes, Mr. Oberstein...
To Mr. A.P. Carter...
Four days later...
Speshul d'livery!
Huh! Some feller from Victor Records wants me t' *cancel my contract* with Ralph Peer—an' sign with *him!*
Sez he c'n make us *more money*. Well, Mr. Peer's stuck with us thru' thick an' thin. *I'm stickin' with him!* Gladys, where's a *stamp?*

Carting Off the Carters

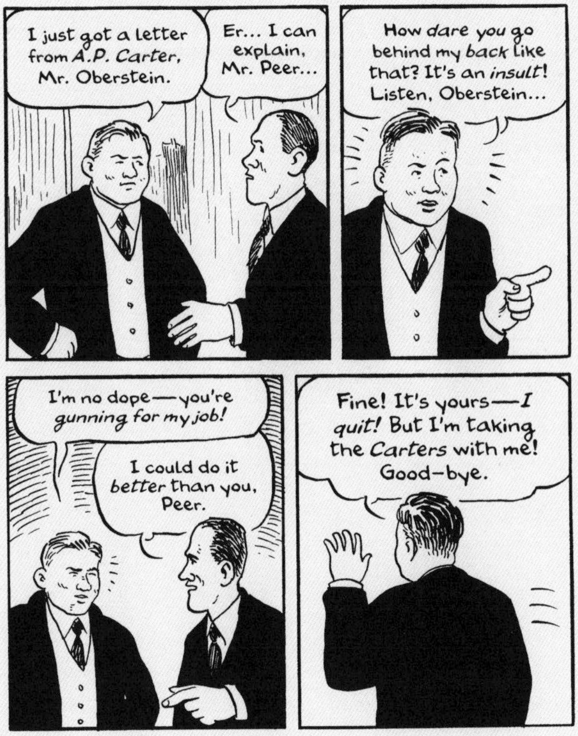
I just got a letter from *A.P. Carter*, Mr. Oberstein.
Er... I can explain, Mr. Peer...
How *dare* you go behind my *back* like that? It's an *insult!* Listen, Oberstein...
I'm no dope—you're *gunning for my job!*
I could do it *better* than you, Peer.
Fine! It's yours—*I quit!* But I'm taking the *Carters* with me! Good-bye.

A Taxing Waxing

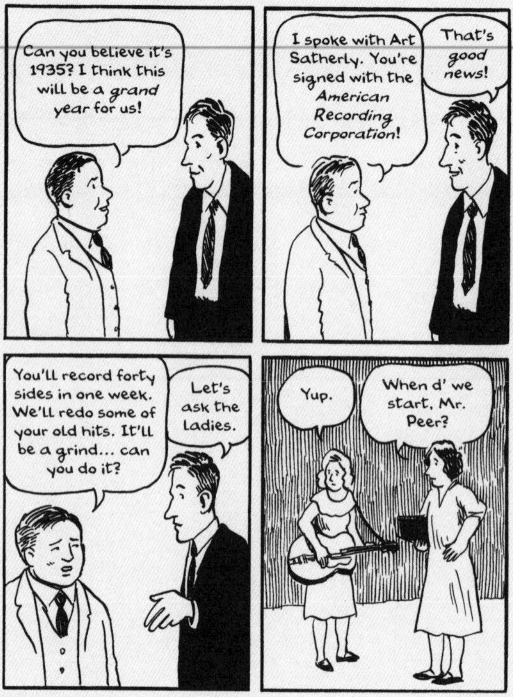
Can you believe it's 1935? I think this will be a *grand* year for us!
I spoke with Art Satherly. You're signed with the *American Recording Corporation*!
That's *good* news!
You'll record forty sides in one week. We'll redo some of your old hits. It'll be a grind... can you do it?
Let's ask the ladies.
Yup.
When d' we start, Mr. Peer?

It Sounded Fine to Me!

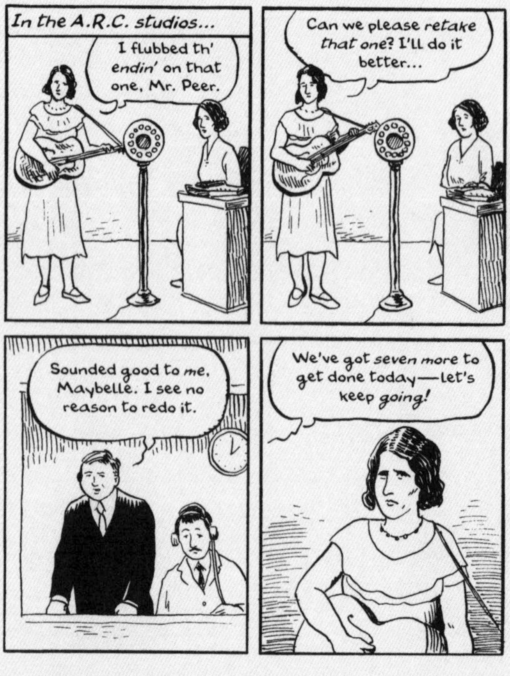
In the A.R.C. studios...
I flubbed th' *endin'* on that one, Mr. Peer.
Can we please *retake that one*? I'll do it better...
Sounded good to *me*, Maybelle. I see no reason to redo it.
We've got *seven more* to get done today—let's keep *going*!

A Bit of "Peer" Pressure

Eli Oberstein, please... Yes, I'll *hold*... (*Hmmm de dum...*)
Eli? Ralph Peer... Uh *huh*... uh *huh*... how's every little thing?
Just wanted you to know... that "Can the Circle" song? The one Victor *passed on* last year?
Well, I cut it with the Carters on A.R.C.—and it's *selling like hotcakes!*

Janette's Big Day!

Do I got enough? I oughta. Let's see...
$13! Now I c'n buy me an arter-harp!
Daddy, I saved 'nough. Will you buy one for me?
I'm goin' over to Bristol t'day.
Oh, I cain't wait... *I cain't wait!!*

There "Auto" Be a Harp!

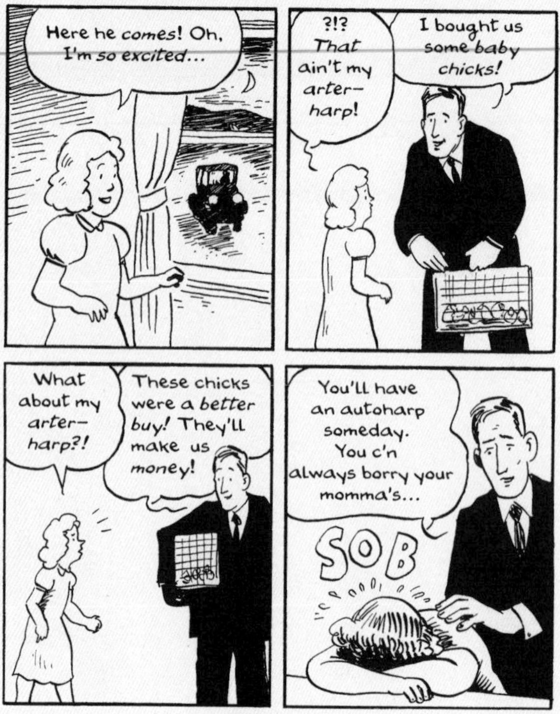
Here he comes! Oh, I'm so excited...
?!? That ain't my arter-harp!
I bought us some baby chicks!
What about my arter-harp?!
These chicks were a better buy! They'll make us money!
You'll have an autoharp someday. You c'n always borry your momma's...
SOB

A Mixed Message

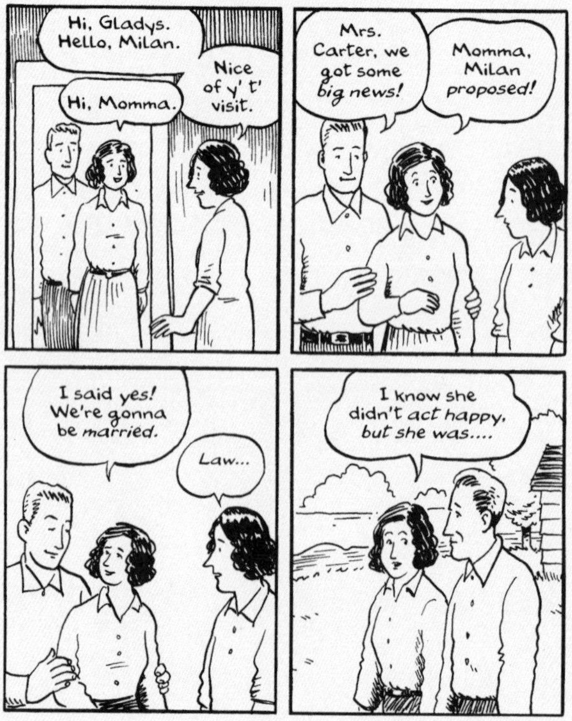
Hi, Gladys. Hello, Milan.
Hi, Momma.
Nice of y' t' visit.
Mrs. Carter, we got some big news!
Momma, Milan proposed!
I said yes! We're gonna be married.
Law...
I know she didn't act happy, but she was....

GOLD DIGGER OF 1936

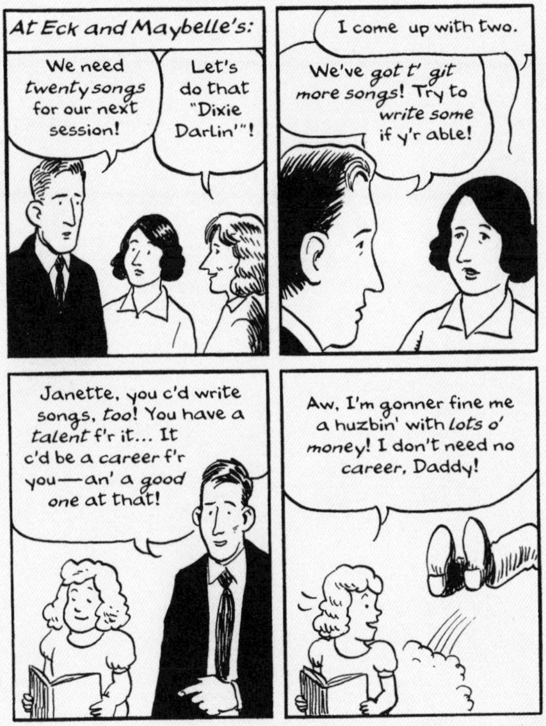
At Eck and Maybelle's:
We need twenty songs for our next session!
Let's do that "Dixie Darlin'"!
I come up with two.
We've got t' git more songs! Try to write some if y'r able!
Janette, you c'd write songs, too! You have a talent f'r it... It c'd be a career f'r you—an' a good one at that!
Aw, I'm gonner fine me a huzbin' with lots o' money! I don't need no career, Daddy!

APOLOGY NOT ACCEPTED

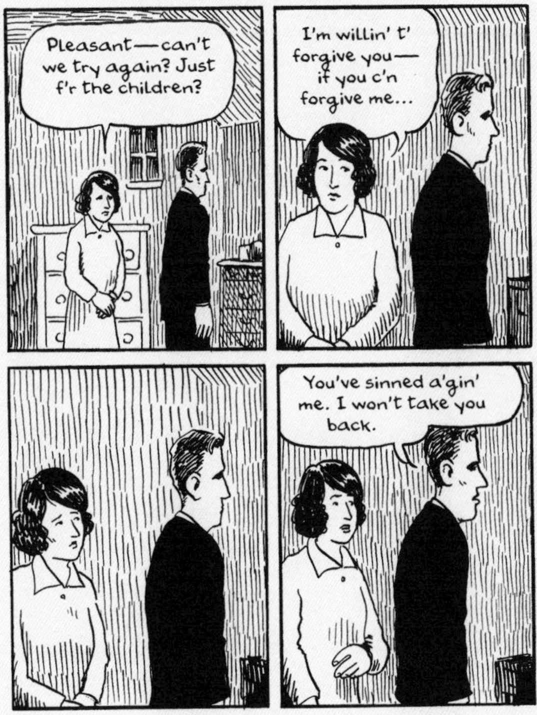
Pleasant—can't we try again? Just f'r the children?
I'm willin' t' forgive you— if you c'n forgive me...
You've sinned a'gin' me. I won't take you back.

THE LAST LETTER

Sary's filed for a divorce! She went over to Gate City an' got a lawyer! Well...
Dear mr.Bond,
In Reply.to your.
letter.
1.Will.Not.Sue for.
Divorce. If.Sara.
Wants to Divorce
Me.1.Will.
Contest it
...
Sary, what's gonna become of us?

THIS MAKES IT FINAL!

...custody of the children shall be awarded to the defendant, A.P. Carter...
Sara Carter will be permitted to see said children at seasonal times and intervals....
Has the defendant anything to say on his behalf?
N-no, Y'r Honor.
Divorce is hereby granted...

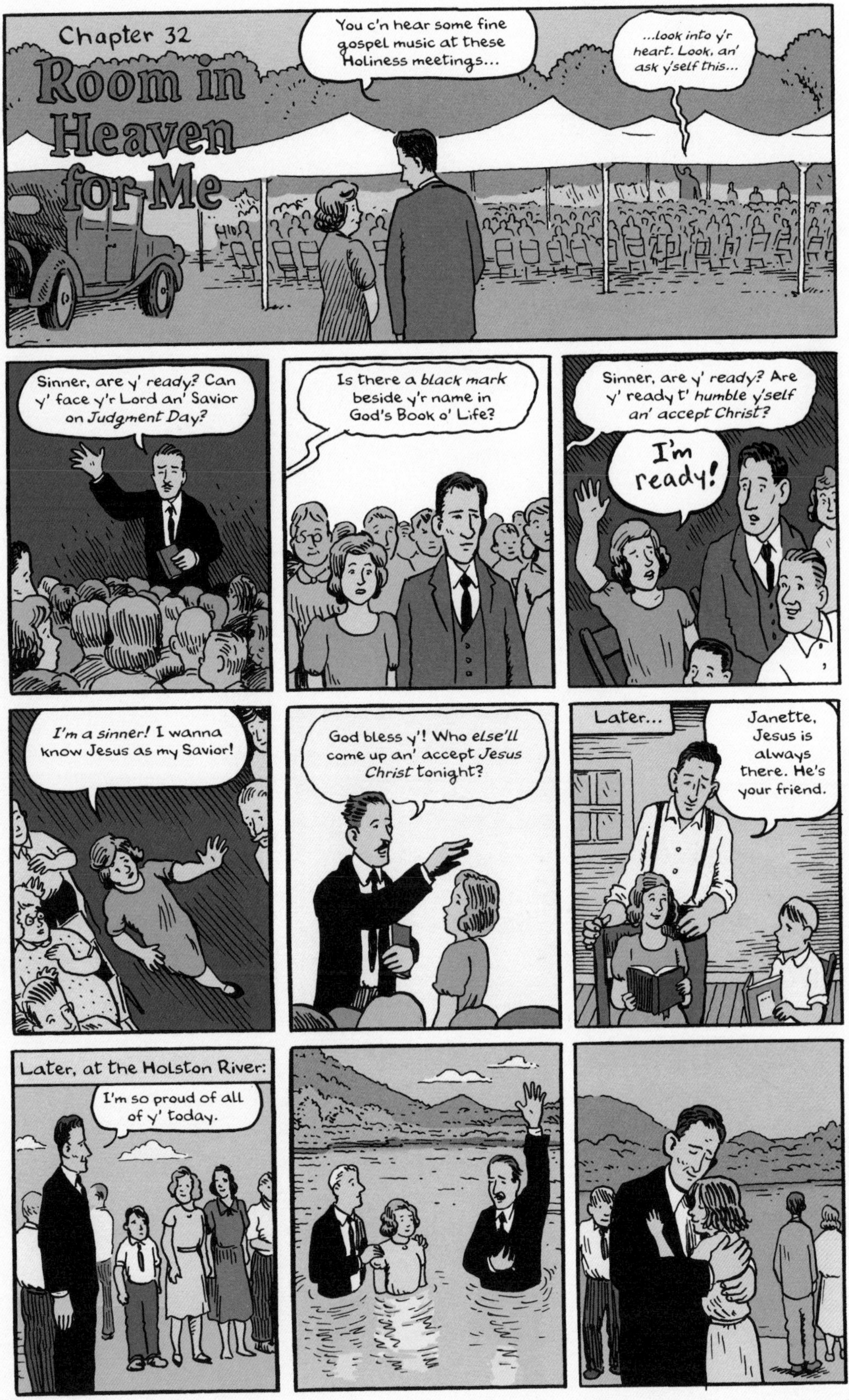
Chapter 32
Room in Heaven for Me
You c'n hear some fine gospel music at these Holiness meetings...
...look into y'r heart. Look, an' ask y'self this...
Sinner, are y' *ready*? Can y' face y'r Lord an' Savior on *Judgment Day*?
Is there a *black mark* beside y'r name in God's Book o' Life?
Sinner, are y' *ready*? Are y' ready t' *humble y'self an' accept Christ*?
I'm ready!
I'm a sinner! I wanna know Jesus as my Savior!
God bless y'! Who *else'll* come up an' accept *Jesus Christ* tonight?
Later...
Janette, Jesus is always there. He's your friend.
Later, at the Holston River:
I'm so proud of all of y' today.

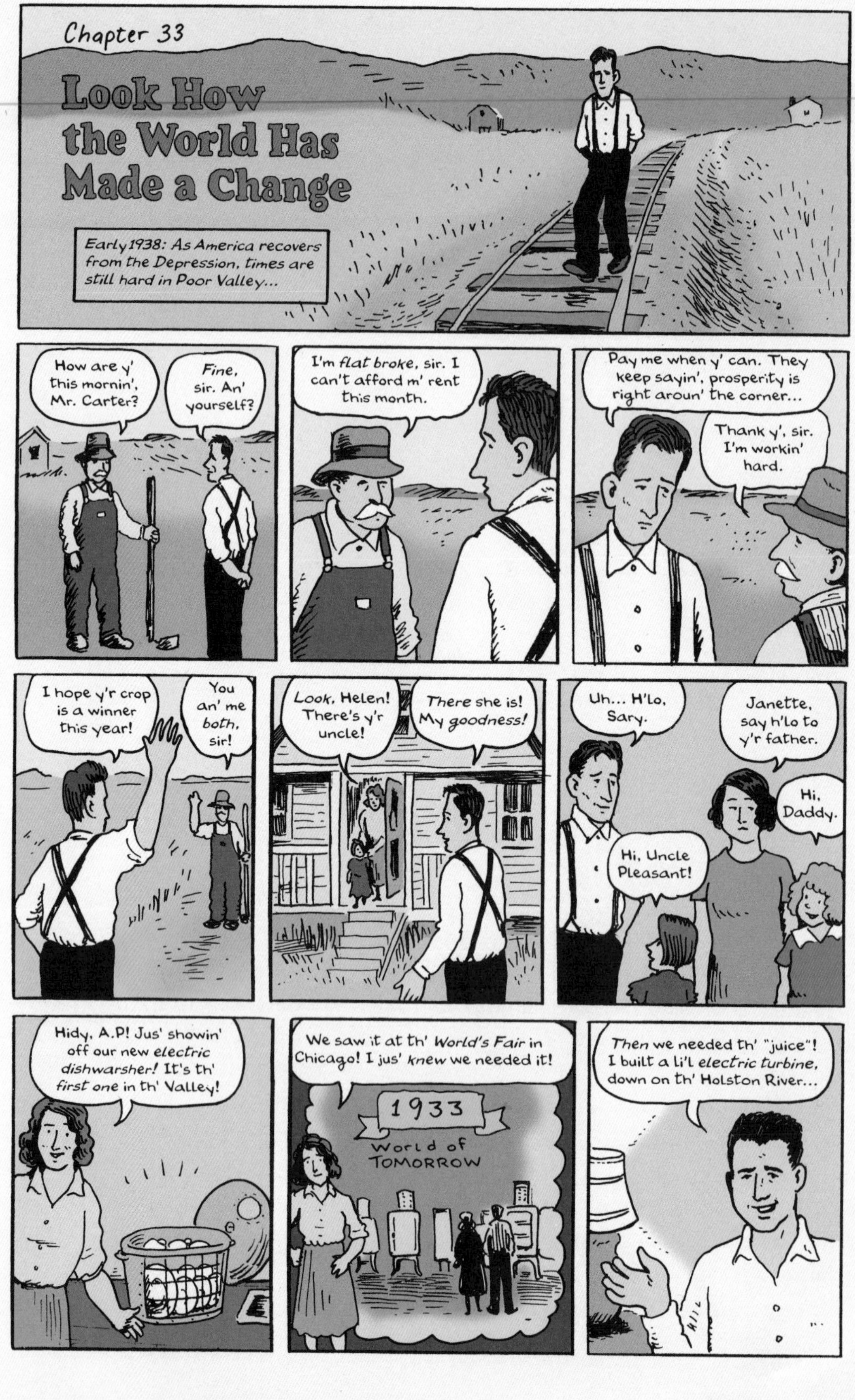
Chapter 33
Look How the World Has Made a Change
Early 1938: As America recovers from the Depression, times are still hard in Poor Valley...
How are y' this mornin', Mr. Carter?
Fine, sir. An' yourself?
I'm *flat broke*, sir. I can't afford m' rent this month.
Pay me when y' can. They keep sayin', prosperity is right aroun' the corner...
Thank y', sir. I'm workin' hard.
I hope y'r crop is a winner this year!
You an' me *both*, sir!
Look, Helen! There's y'r uncle!
There she is! My *goodness*!
Uh... H'lo, Sary.
Janette, say h'lo to y'r father.
Hi, Daddy.
Hi, Uncle Pleasant!
Hidy, A.P! Jus' showin' off our new *electric dishwarsher*! It's th' *first one* in th' Valley!
We saw it at th' *World's Fair* in Chicago! I jus' *knew* we needed it!
1933
World of TOMORROW
Then we needed th' "juice"! I built a li'l *electric turbine*, down on th' Holston River...

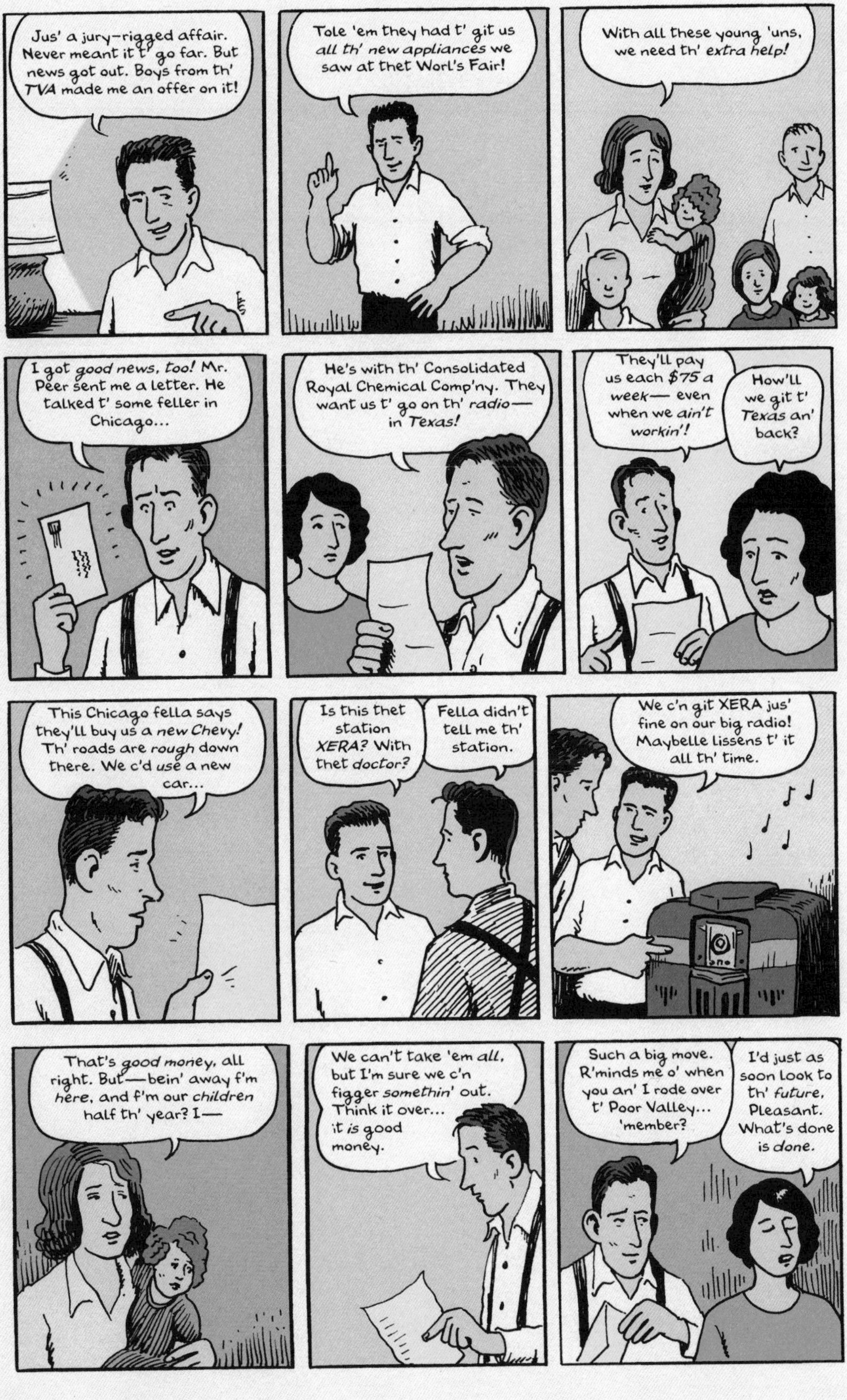
Jus' a jury-rigged affair. Never meant it t' go far. But news got out. Boys from th' TVA made me an offer on it!
Tole 'em they had t' git us all th' new appliances we saw at thet Worl's Fair!
With all these young 'uns, we need th' extra help!
I got good news, too! Mr. Peer sent me a letter. He talked t' some feller in Chicago...
He's with th' Consolidated Royal Chemical Comp'ny. They want us t' go on th' radio— in Texas!
They'll pay us each $75 a week— even when we ain't workin'!
How'll we git t' Texas an' back?
This Chicago fella says they'll buy us a new Chevy! Th' roads are rough down there. We c'd use a new car...
Is this thet station XERA? With thet doctor?
Fella didn't tell me th' station.
We c'n git XERA jus' fine on our big radio! Maybelle lissens t' it all th' time.
That's good money, all right. But—bein' away f'm here, and f'm our children half th' year? I—
We can't take 'em all, but I'm sure we c'n figger somethin' out. Think it over... it is good money.
Such a big move. R'minds me o' when you an' I rode over t' Poor Valley... 'member?
I'd just as soon look to th' future, Pleasant. What's done is done.

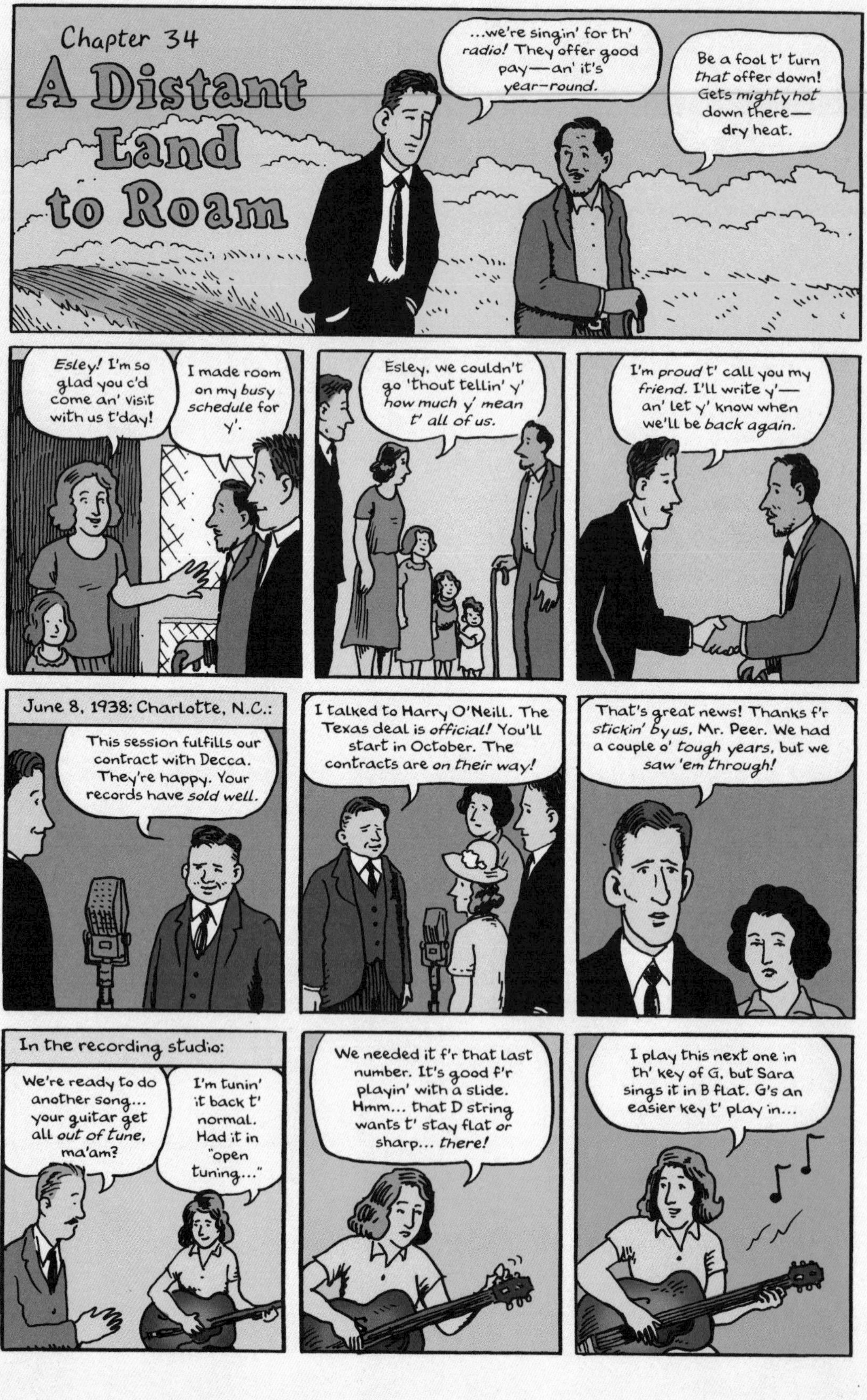
Chapter 34
A Distant Land to Roam
...we're singin' for th' radio! They offer good pay—an' it's year-round.
Be a fool t' turn that offer down! Gets mighty hot down there—dry heat.
Esley! I'm so glad you c'd come an' visit with us t'day!
I made room on my busy schedule for y'.
Esley, we couldn't go 'thout tellin' y' how much y' mean t' all of us.
I'm proud t' call you my friend. I'll write y'—an' let y' know when we'll be back again.
June 8, 1938: Charlotte, N.C.:
This session fulfills our contract with Decca. They're happy. Your records have sold well.
I talked to Harry O'Neill. The Texas deal is official! You'll start in October. The contracts are on their way!
That's great news! Thanks f'r stickin' by us, Mr. Peer. We had a couple o' tough years, but we saw 'em through!
In the recording studio:
We're ready to do another song... your guitar get all out of tune, ma'am?
I'm tunin' it back t' normal. Had it in "open tuning..."
We needed it f'r that last number. It's good f'r playin' with a slide. Hmm... that D string wants t' stay flat or sharp... there!
I play this next one in th' key of G, but Sara sings it in B flat. G's an easier key t' play in...

So I'll put on this little gadget. I call 'er a "cheater," but th' real name is a "capo"!

I like it 'cause it makes th' guitar sound *brighter*—I'm playin' up higher on th' frets! An' now I can play *better*, an' Sara can sing in th' key that *suits her voice*...

That's *something!* So what's our next one?

This one's called "You Are My Flower."

And on August 30, 1938...

...healthy li'l baby girl! You c'n see th' mother an' child now.

Law, Pleasant. We're... grandparents!

She's... she's *beautiful.* What d'y' call 'er?

Her name is Nancy Flo.

God bless y'all! *Congratulations,* Milan!

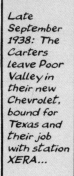

Late September 1938: The Carters leave Poor Valley in their new Chevrolet, bound for Texas and their job with station XERA...

Th' girls gunna miss you!

I'll be back 'fore y' know it, dears!

We gotta git movin'!

Gladys, watch after Joe f'r me.

We'll see y' soon, brother.

This is a swell car. Have a safe trip.

I'll be in Texas soon as th' railroad can arrange it. Law, I'll *miss* you...

I'll write you once we git there.

Pleasant, it's nearly *midnight.* Ain't y' *tired?*

Aw, I c'n sleep when we *get* there!

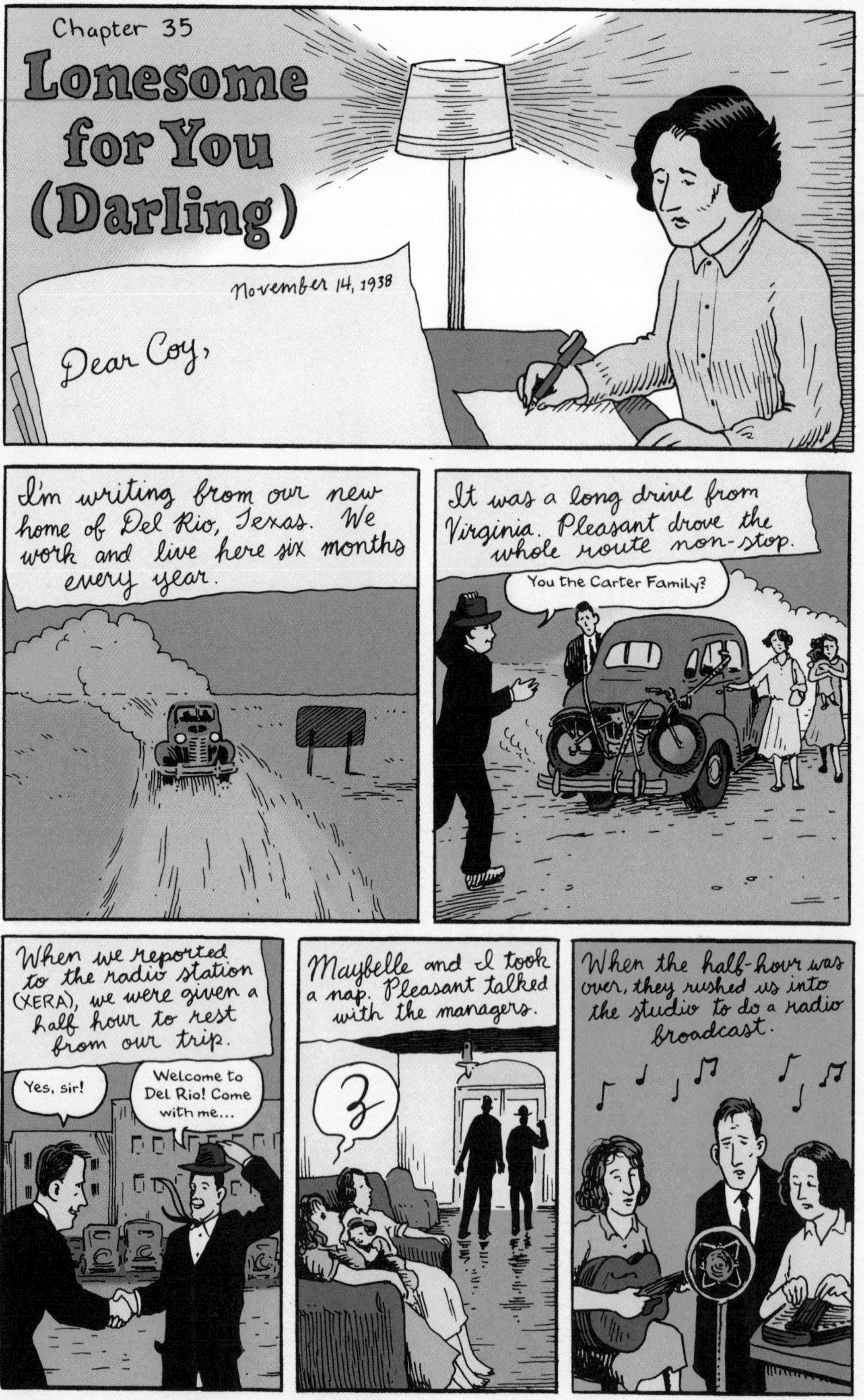
Chapter 35
Lonesome for You (Darling)
November 14, 1938
Dear Coy,
I'm writing from our new home of Del Rio, Texas. We work and live here six months every year.
It was a long drive from Virginia. Pleasant drove the whole route non-stop.
You the Carter Family?
When we reported to the radio station (XERA), we were given a half hour to rest from our trip.
Yes, sir!
Welcome to Del Rio! Come with me...
Maybelle and I took a nap. Pleasant talked with the managers.
Z
When the half-hour was over, they rushed us into the studio to do a radio broadcast.

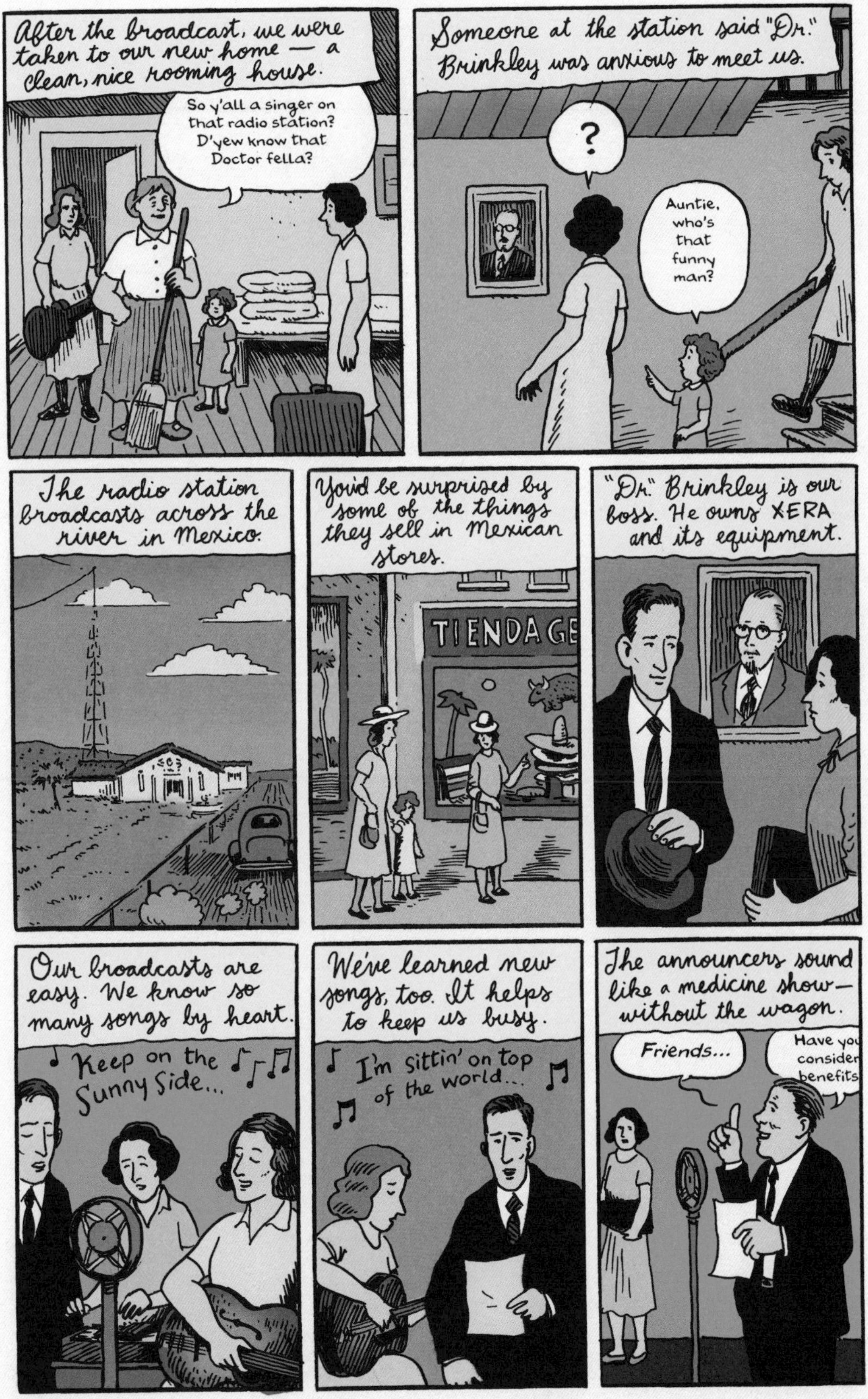
After the broadcast, we were taken to our new home — a clean, nice rooming house.
So y'all a singer on that radio station? D'yew know that Doctor fella?
Someone at the station said "Dr." Brinkley was anxious to meet us.
?
Auntie, who's that funny man?
The radio station broadcasts across the river in Mexico.
You'd be surprised by some of the things they sell in Mexican stores.
TIENDAGE
"Dr." Brinkley is our boss. He owns XERA and its equipment.
Our broadcasts are easy. We know so many songs by heart.
Keep on the Sunny Side...
We've learned new songs, too. It helps to keep us busy.
I'm sittin' on top of the world...
The announcers sound like a medicine show— without the wagon.
Friends...
Have you consider benefits

They play "Dr." Brinkley's talks on loudspeakers all over the station.

Do you want to be a man... or a capon? The choice is yours—

They have cowboy singers and other string bands on the air too.

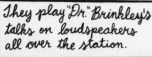

ON AIR

A woman named Rose Dawn tells horoscopes on the air. I can't understand a word she says.

...Venus is still in retrograde. Librans, beware the shadow of Mars! It may manifest itself in several ways...

One morning, we got word "Dr." Brinkley was in Del Rio. He wanted to meet us at once.

AIR

He's waiting for you at his estate.

Be ready to go in ten minutes.

We were taken to his home. It looks like a Spanish palace.

The doorman will open the gates...

How d'we get in there, mister?

DOCTOR BRINKLEY

A butler met us at the door. He brought us into a room full of mirrors and clocks.

His house is full of pictures and paintings and statues. Nice if you care for that sort of thing.

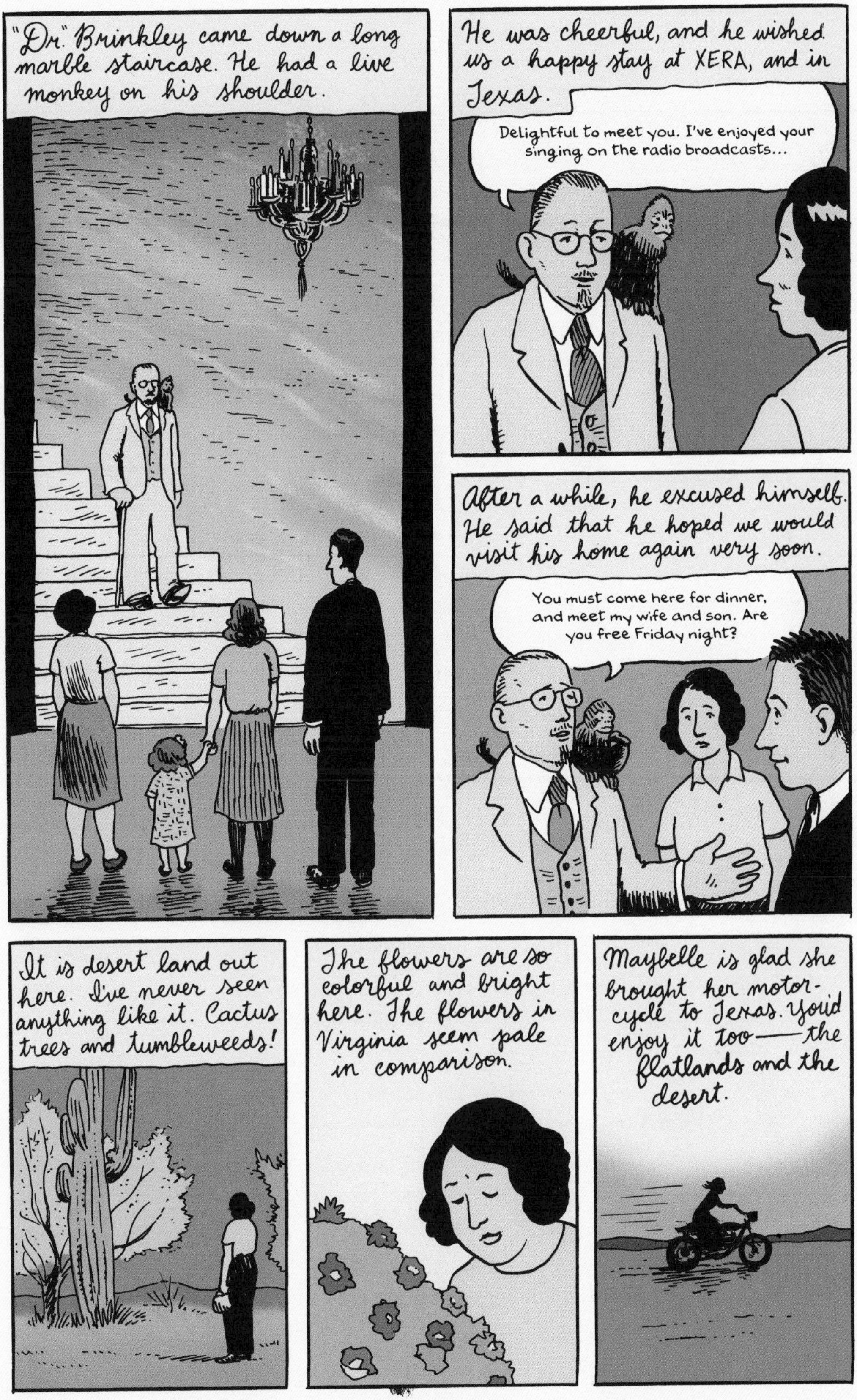
"Dr." Brinkley came down a long marble staircase. He had a live monkey on his shoulder.
He was cheerful, and he wished us a happy stay at XERA, and in Texas.
Delightful to meet you. I've enjoyed your singing on the radio broadcasts...
After a while, he excused himself. He said that he hoped we would visit his home again very soon.
You must come here for dinner, and meet my wife and son. Are you free Friday night?
It is desert land out here. I've never seen anything like it. Cactus trees and tumbleweeds!
The flowers are so colorful and bright here. The flowers in Virginia seem pale in comparison.
Maybelle is glad she brought her motor-cycle to Texas. You'd enjoy it too—the flatlands and the desert.

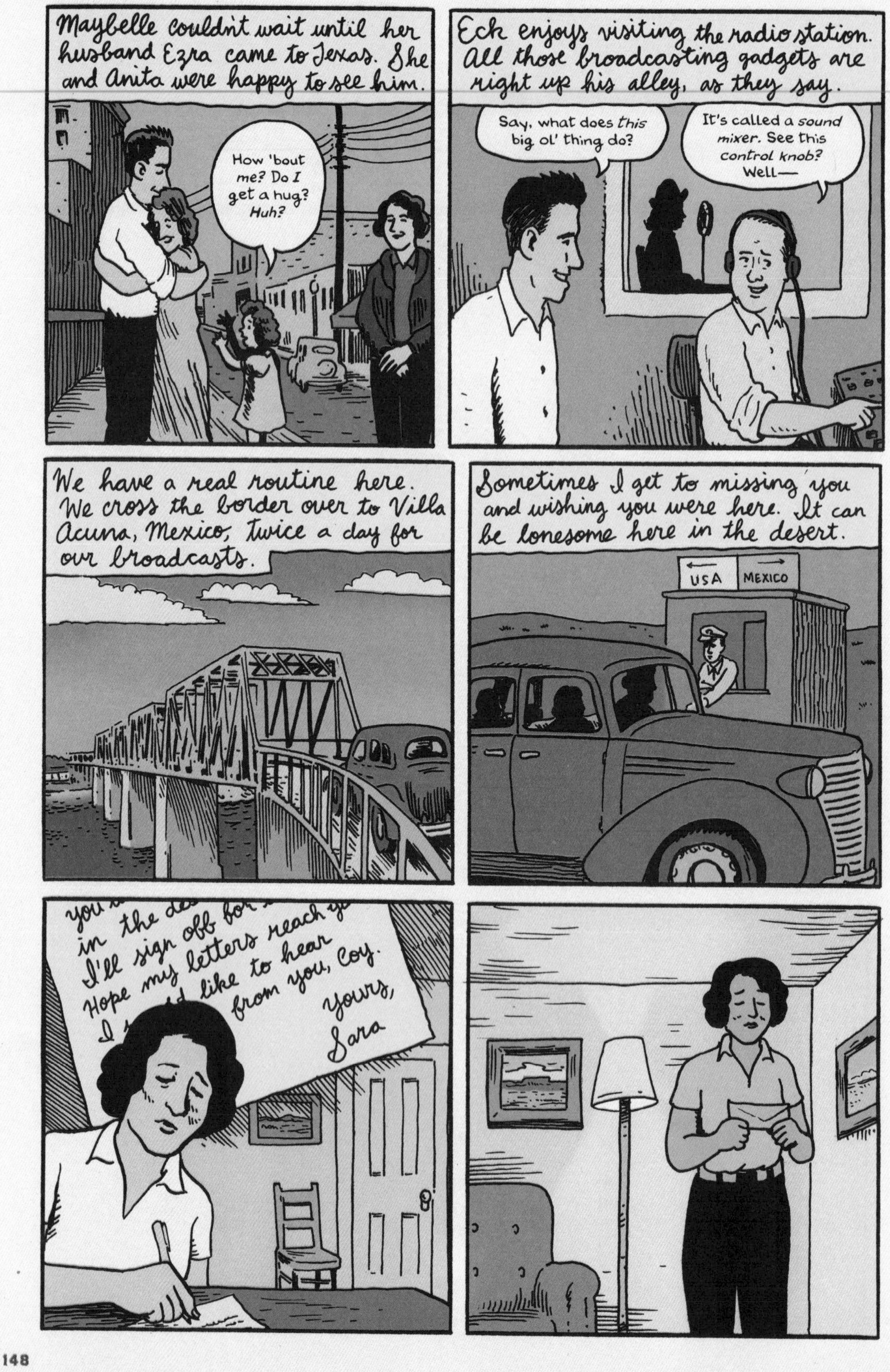
Maybelle couldn't wait until her husband Ezra came to Texas. She and Anita were happy to see him.
How 'bout me? Do I get a hug? Huh?
Eck enjoys visiting the radio station. All those broadcasting gadgets are right up his alley, as they say.
Say, what does *this* big ol' thing do?
It's called a *sound mixer*. See this control knob? Well—
We have a real routine here. We cross the border over to Villa Acuna, Mexico, twice a day for our broadcasts.
Sometimes I get to missing you and wishing you were here. It can be lonesome here in the desert.
USA
MEXICO
in the
I'll sign off for
Hope my letters reach
like to hear
from you, Coy.
Yours,
Sara

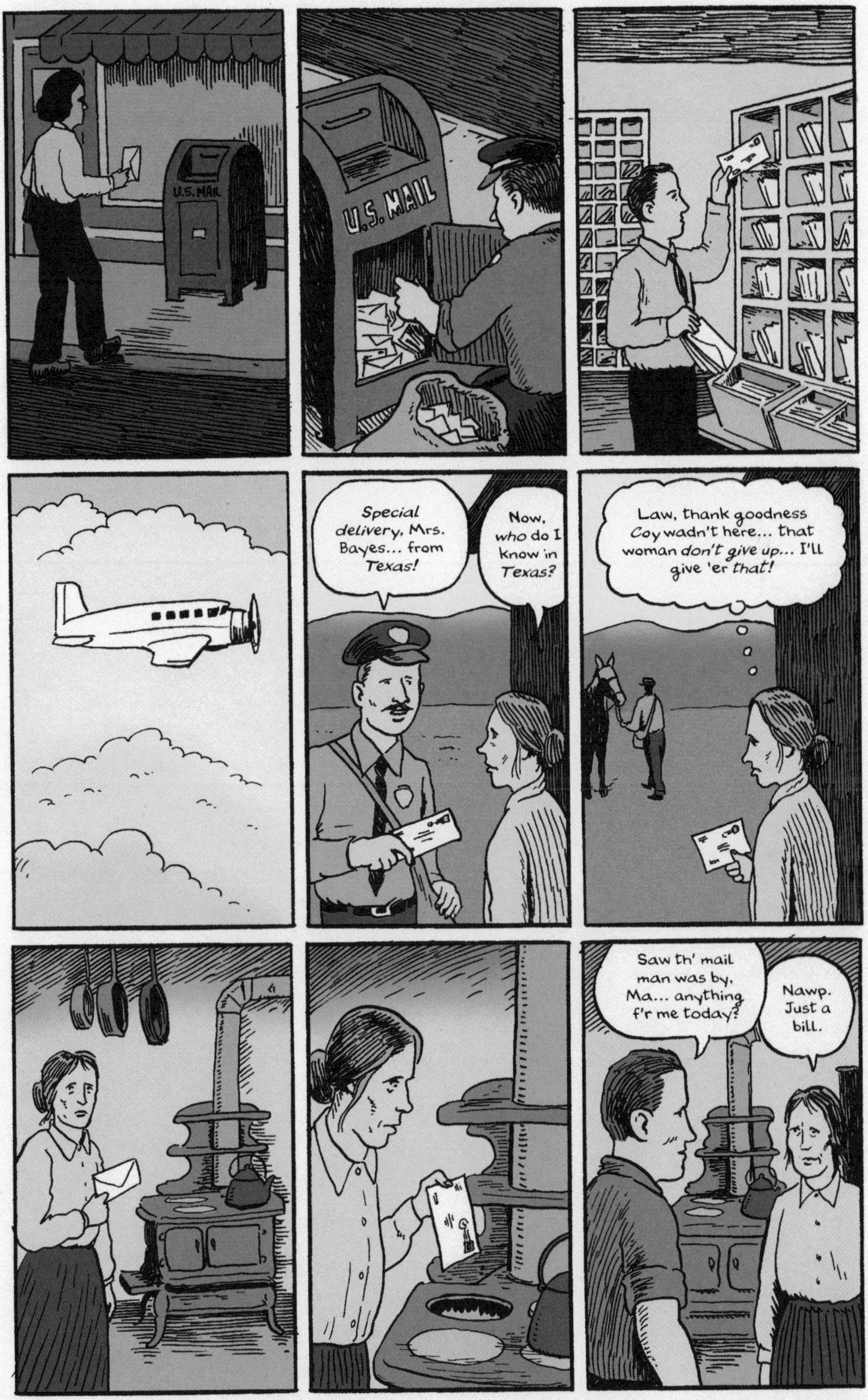
U.S. MAIL
U.S. MAIL
Special delivery, Mrs. Bayes... from Texas!
Now, who do I know in Texas?
Law, thank goodness Coy wadn't here... that woman don't give up... I'll give 'er that!
Saw th' mail man was by, Ma... anything f'r me today?
Nawp. Just a bill.

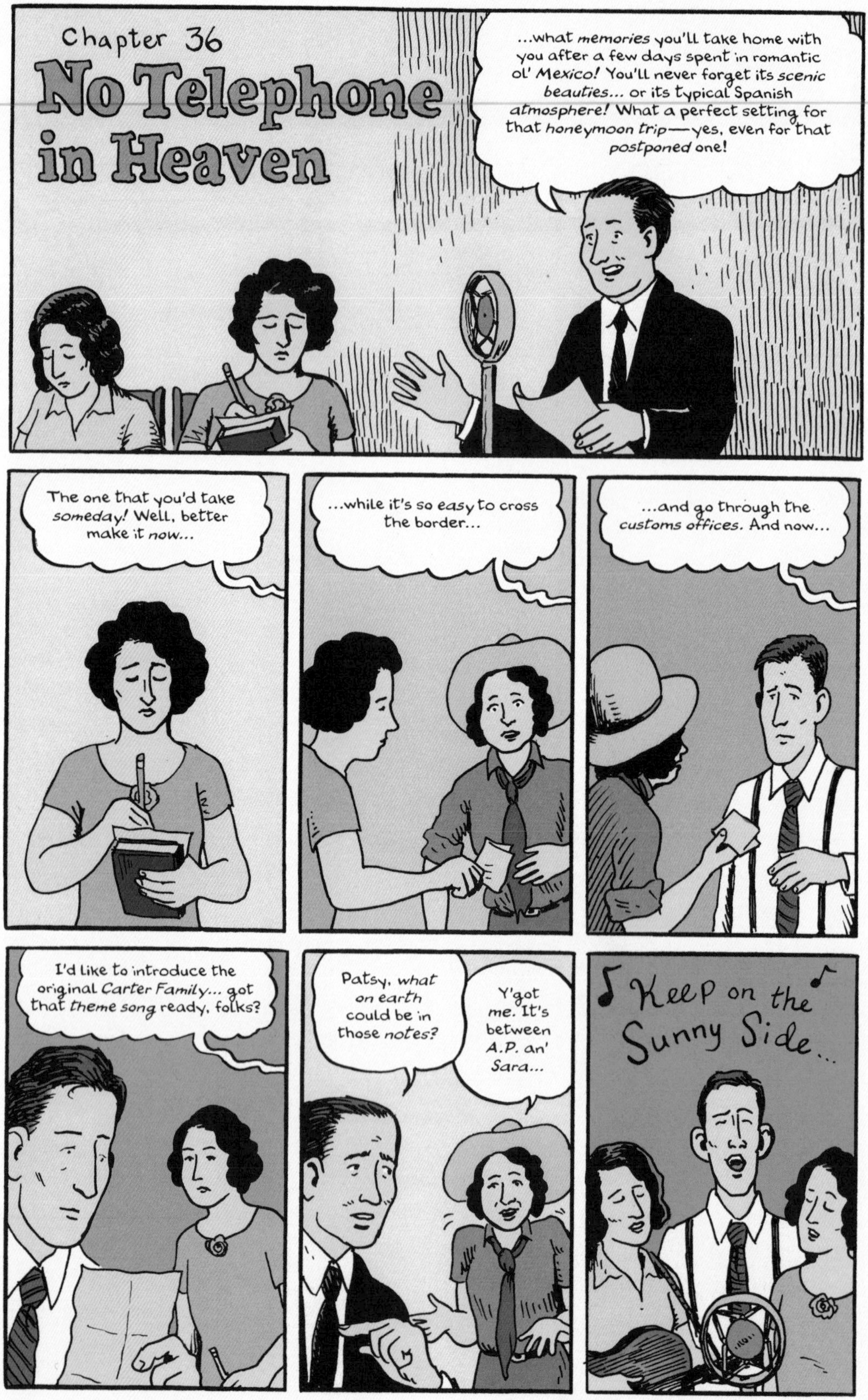
Chapter 36
No Telephone in Heaven
...what memories you'll take home with you after a few days spent in romantic ol' Mexico! You'll never forget its scenic beauties... or its typical Spanish atmosphere! What a perfect setting for that honeymoon trip—yes, even for that postponed one!
The one that you'd take someday! Well, better make it now...
...while it's so easy to cross the border...
...and go through the customs offices. And now...
I'd like to introduce the original Carter Family... got that theme song ready, folks?
Patsy, what on earth could be in those notes?
Y'got me. It's between A.P. an' Sara...
Keep on the Sunny Side...

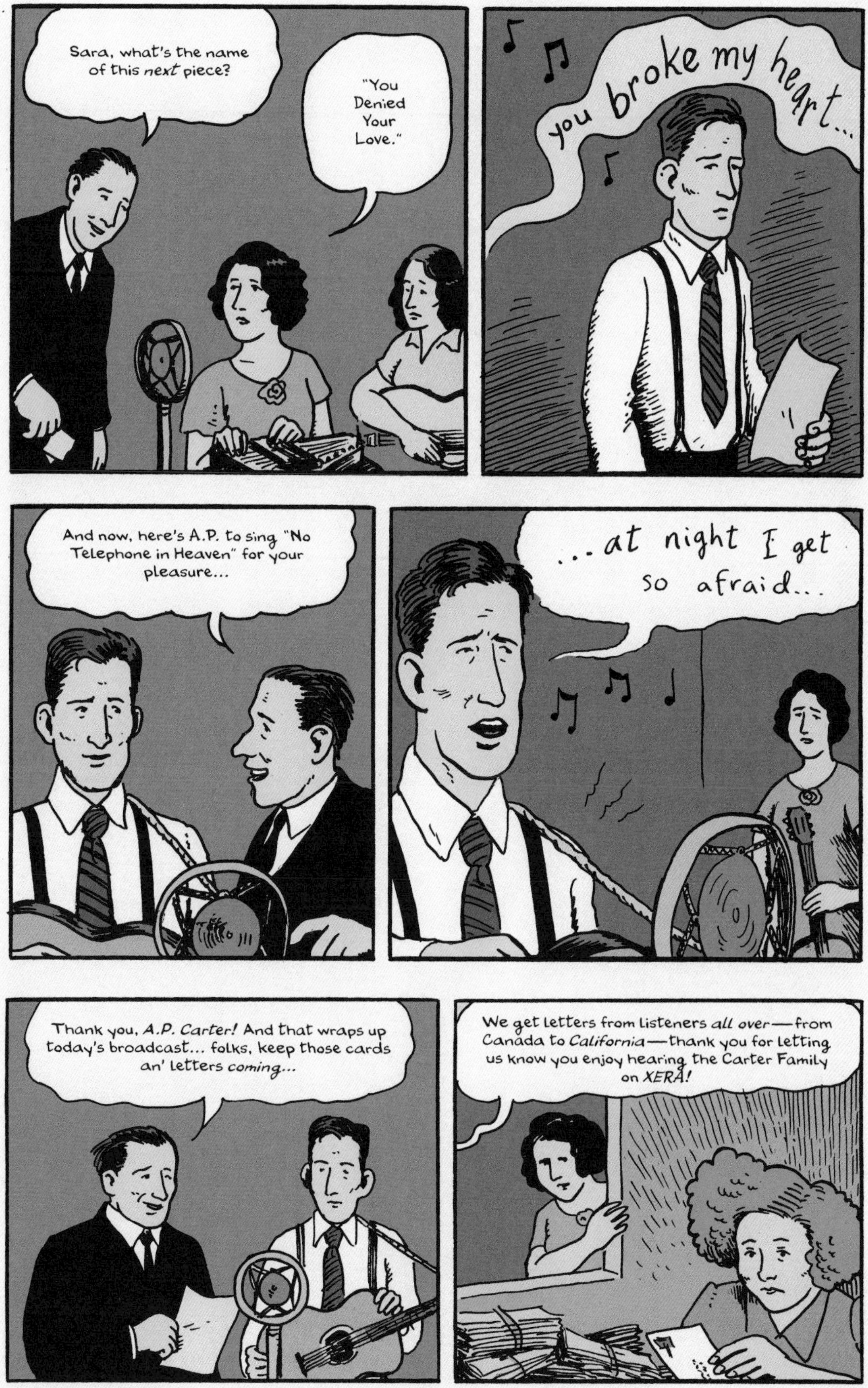
Sara, what's the name of this *next* piece?
"You Denied Your Love."
you broke my heart...
And now, here's A.P. to sing "No Telephone in Heaven" for your pleasure...
...at night I get so afraid...
Thank you, *A.P. Carter!* And that wraps up today's broadcast... folks, keep those cards an' letters *coming*...
We get letters from listeners *all over*—from Canada to *California*—thank you for letting us know you enjoy hearing the Carter Family on *XERA!*

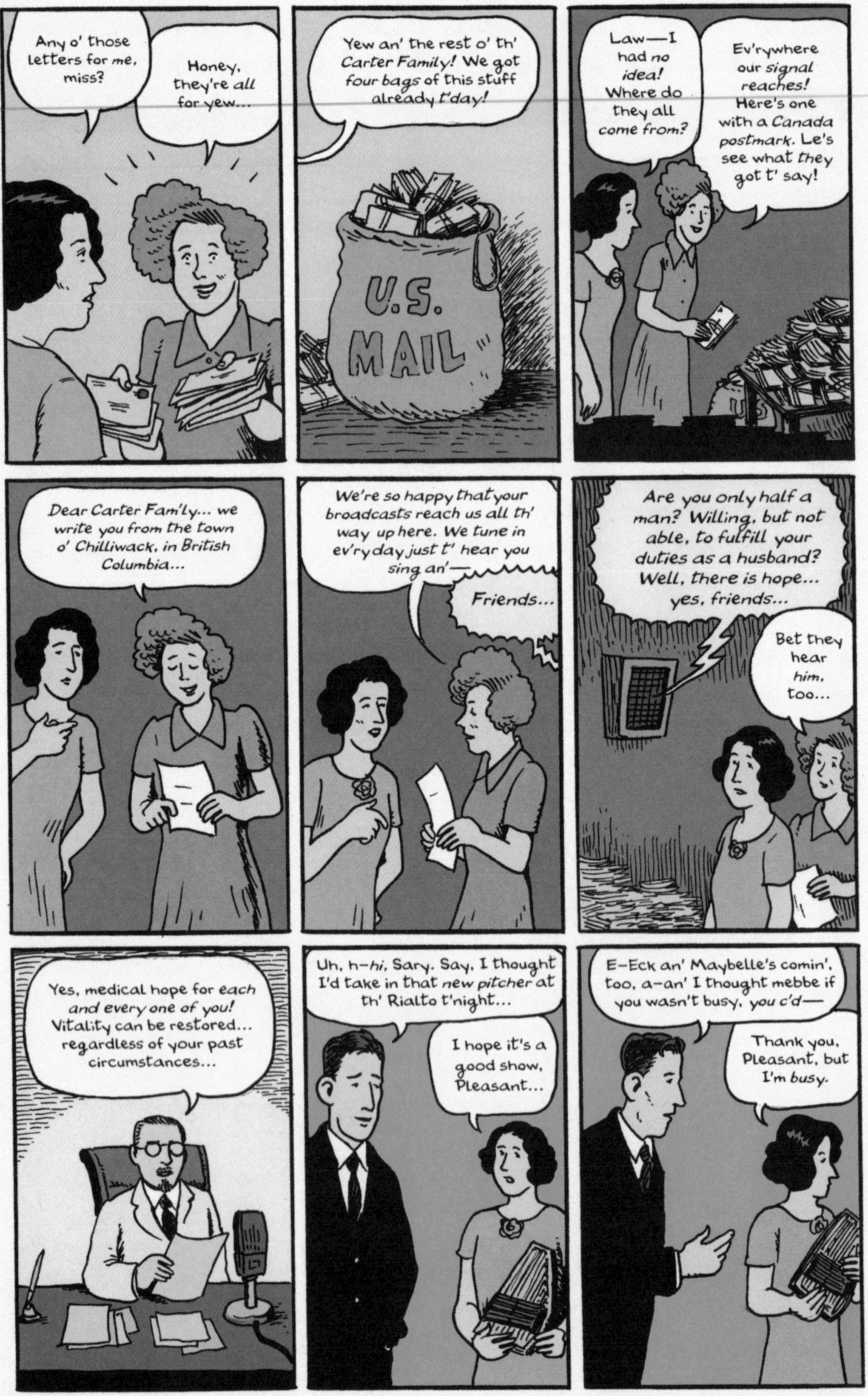
Any o' those letters for *me*, miss?
Honey, they're *all* for yew...
Yew an' the rest o' th' *Carter Family*! We got four *bags* of this stuff already *t'day*!
U.S. MAIL
Law—I had *no idea*! Where do they all come from?
Ev'rywhere our *signal* reaches! Here's one with a *Canada postmark*. Le's see what *they* got t' say!
Dear Carter Fam'ly... we write you from the town o' Chilliwack, in British Columbia...
We're so happy that your broadcasts reach us all th' way up here. We tune in ev'ryday just t' hear you sing an'—
Friends...
Are you only half a man? Willing, but not able, to fulfill your duties as a husband? Well, there is hope... yes, friends...
Bet they hear *him*, too...
Yes, medical hope for each and every one of you! Vitality can be restored... regardless of your past circumstances...
Uh, h–*hi*, Sary. Say, I thought I'd take in that *new pitcher* at th' Rialto t'night...
I hope it's a good show, Pleasant...
E–Eck an' Maybelle's comin', too, a–an' I thought mebbe if you wasn't busy, *you c'd*—
Thank you, Pleasant, but I'm *busy*.

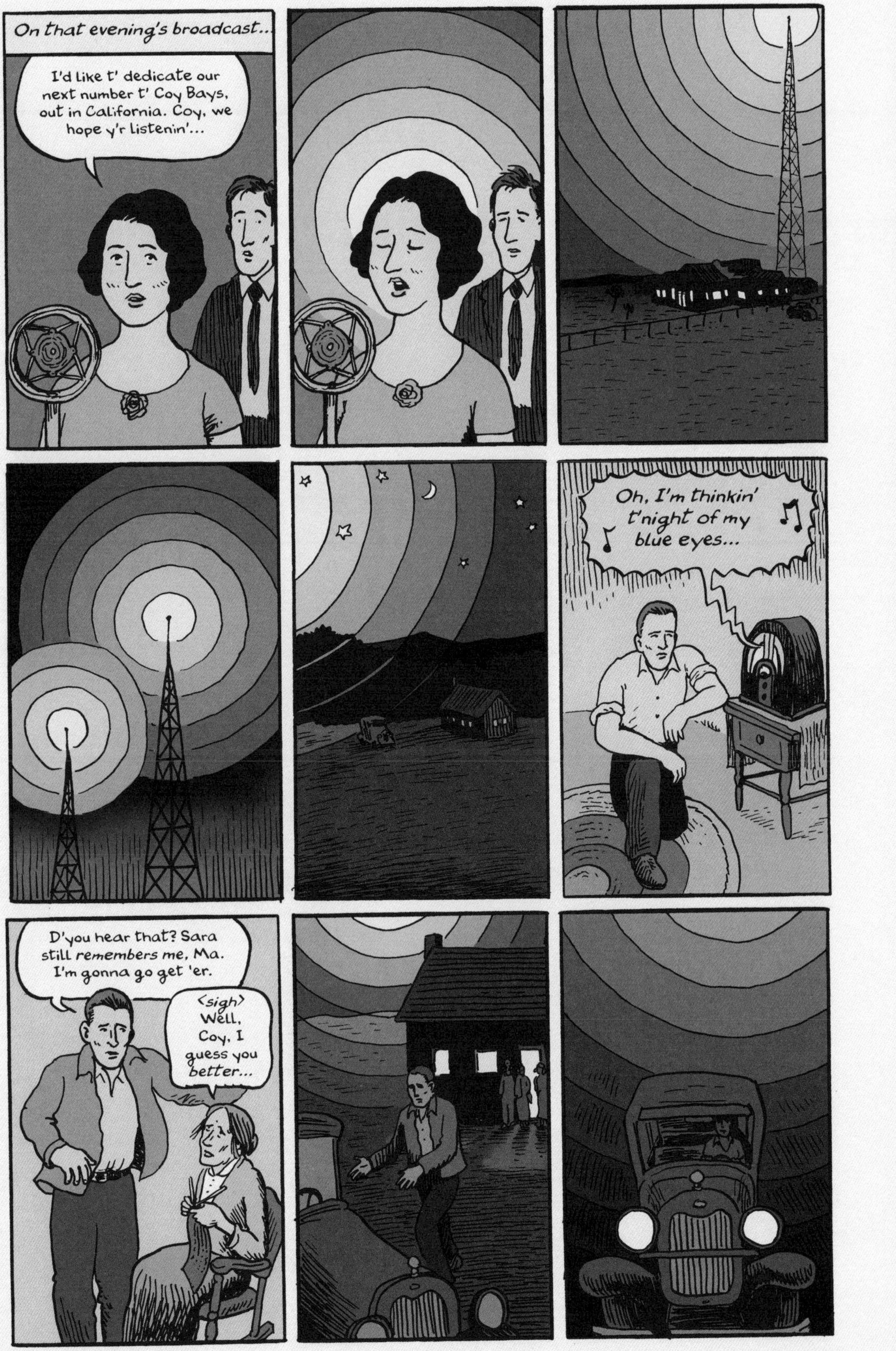
On that evening's broadcast...
I'd like t' dedicate our next number t' Coy Bays, out in California. Coy, we hope y'r listenin'...
Oh, I'm thinkin' t'night of my blue eyes...
D'you hear that? Sara still *remembers* me, Ma. I'm gonna go get 'er.
<*sigh*> Well, Coy, I guess you *better*...

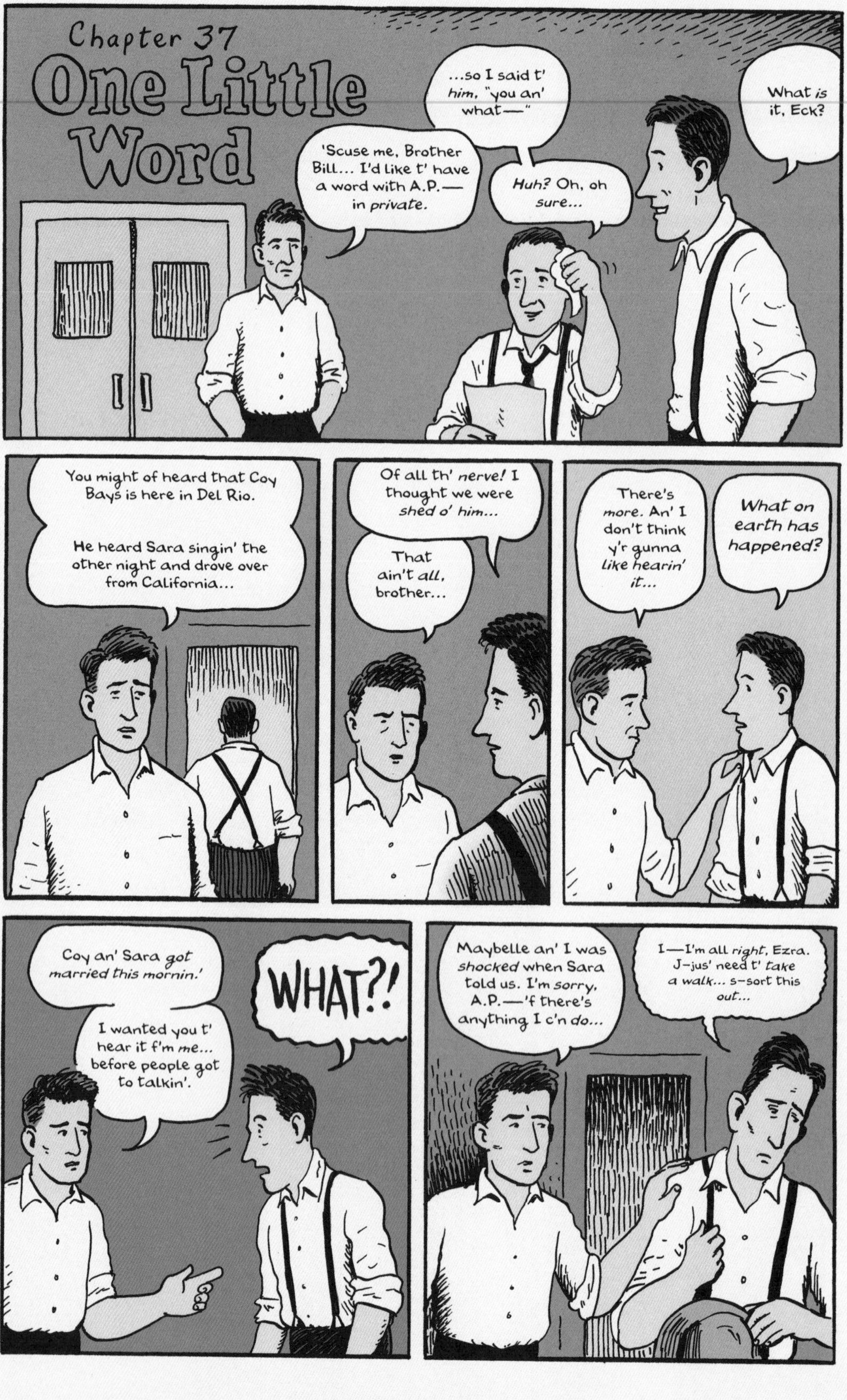
Chapter 37
One Little Word
'Scuse me, Brother Bill... I'd like t' have a word with A.P.— in *private*.
...so I said t' *him*, "you an' what—"
Huh? Oh, oh sure...
What *is* it, Eck?
You might of heard that Coy Bays is here in Del Rio.
He heard Sara singin' the other night and drove over from California...
Of all th' *nerve!* I thought we were *shed o' him...*
That ain't *all*, brother...
There's *more*. An' I don't think y'r gunna *like hearin' it...*
What on earth has happened?
Coy an' Sara *got married this mornin.'*
I wanted you t' hear it f'm *me*... before people got to talkin'.
WHAT?!
Maybelle an' I was *shocked* when Sara told us. I'm *sorry*, A.P.—'f there's anything I c'n *do*...
I—I'm all *right*, Ezra. J-jus' need t' *take a walk*... s-sort this *out*...

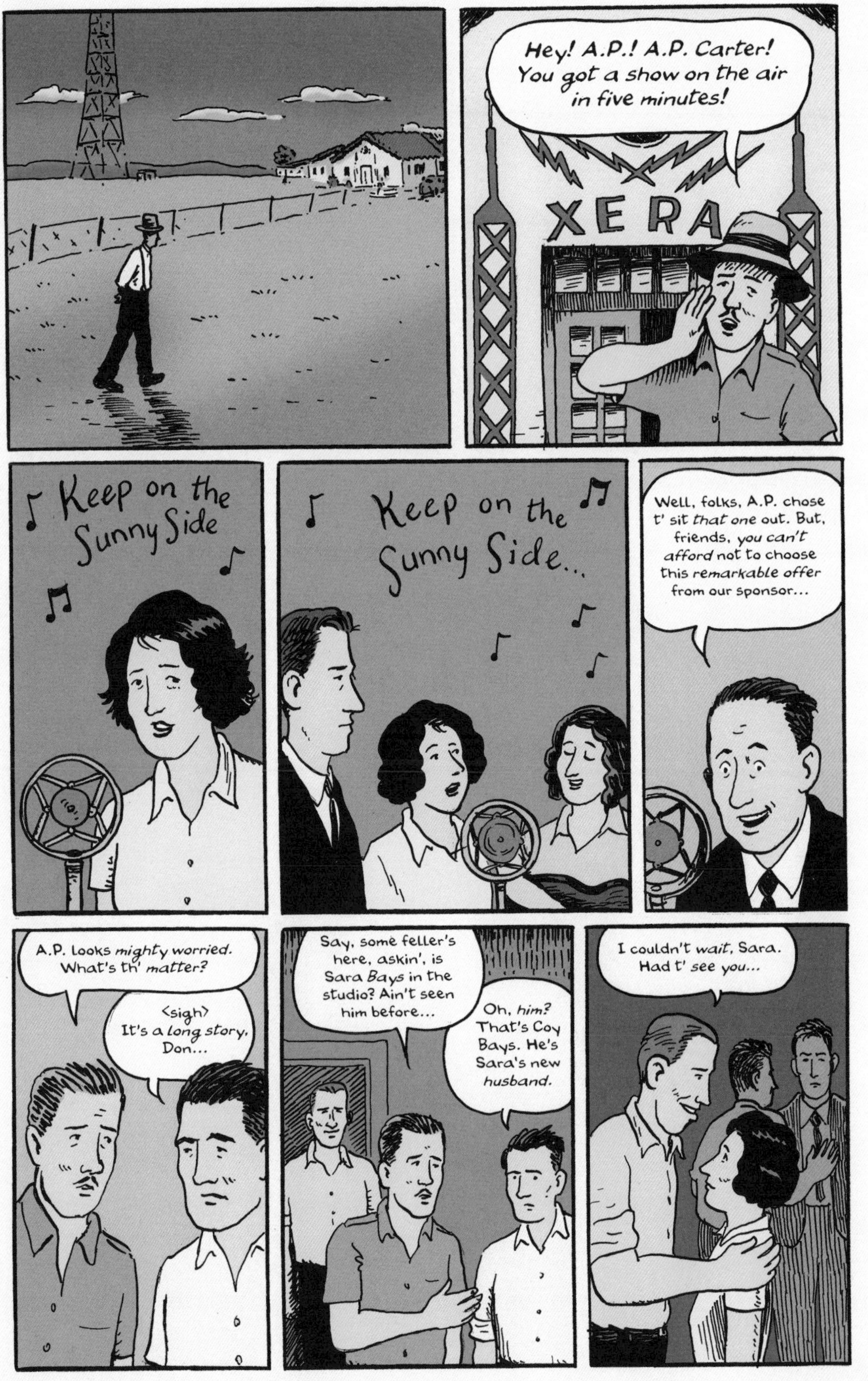
Hey! A.P.! A.P. Carter! You got a show on the air in five minutes!
XERA
Keep on the Sunny Side
Keep on the Sunny Side...
Well, folks, A.P. chose t' sit *that* one out. But, friends, *you can't afford* not to choose this *remarkable* offer from our sponsor...
A.P. Looks *mighty* worried. What's th' *matter*?
<sigh> It's a *long story*, Don...
Say, some feller's here, askin', is Sara *Bays* in the studio? Ain't seen him before...
Oh, *him*? That's Coy Bays. He's Sara's new *husband*.
I couldn't *wait*, Sara. Had t' *see* you...

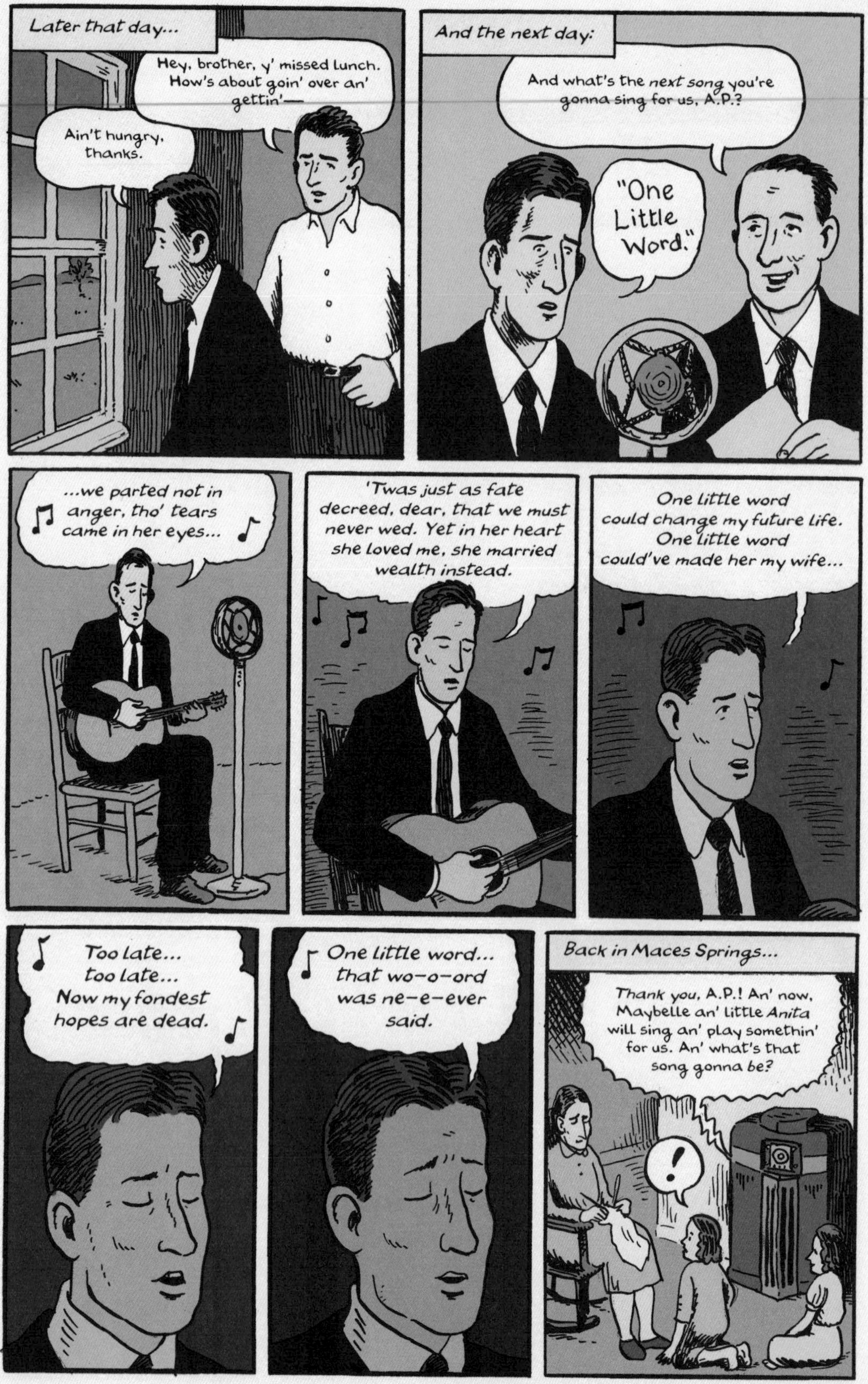
Later that day...
Hey, brother, y' missed lunch. How's about goin' over an' gettin'—
Ain't hungry, thanks.
And the next day:
And what's the next song you're gonna sing for us, A.P.?
"One Little Word."
...we parted not in anger, tho' tears came in her eyes...
'Twas just as fate decreed, dear, that we must never wed. Yet in her heart she loved me, she married wealth instead.
One little word could change my future life. One little word could've made her my wife...
Too late... too late... Now my fondest hopes are dead.
One little word... that wo-o-ord was ne-e-ever said.
Back in Maces Springs...
Thank you, A.P.! An' now, Maybelle an' little Anita will sing an' play somethin' for us. An' what's that song gonna be?
!

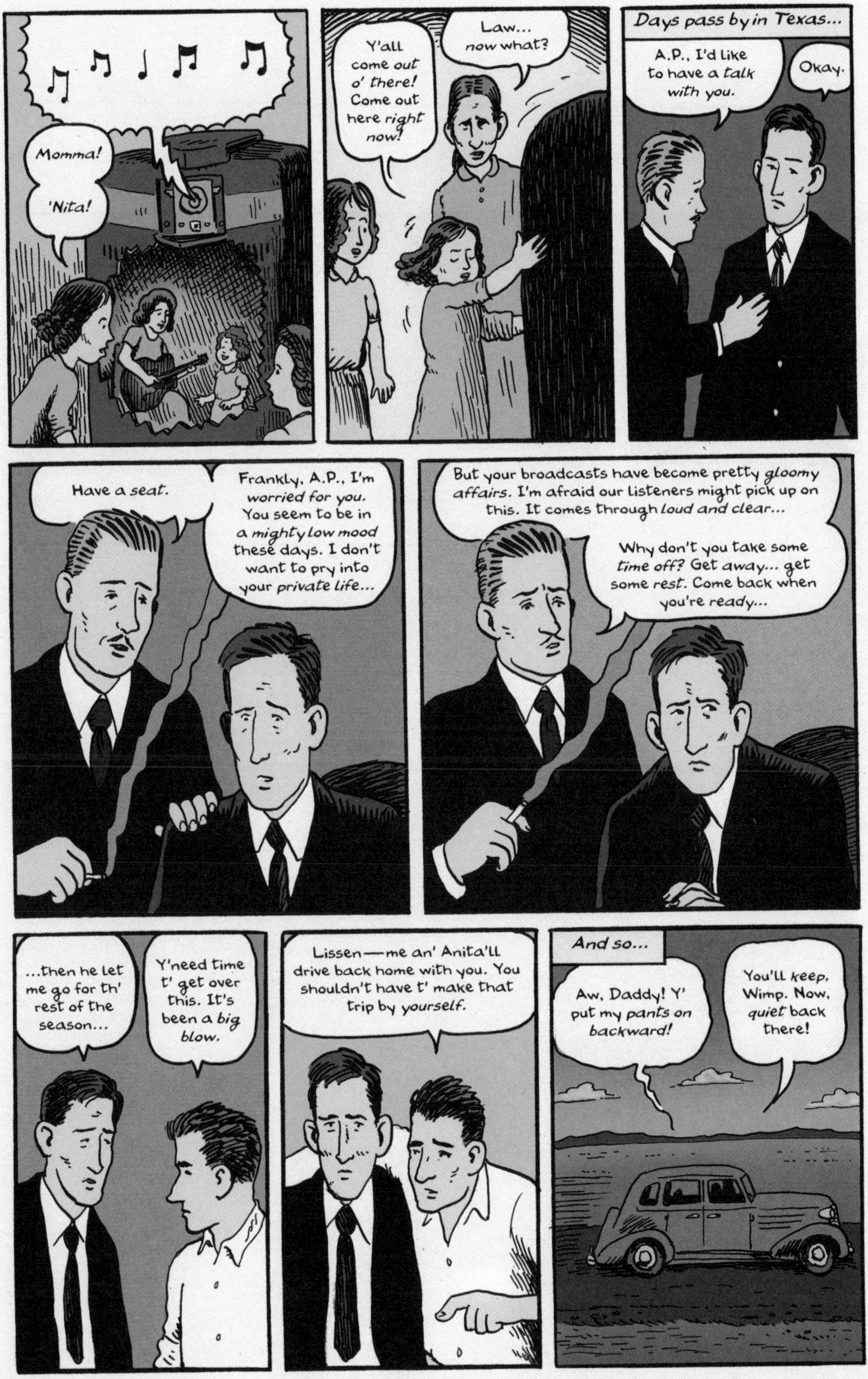
Momma!
'Nita!
Y'all come out o' there! Come out here right now!
Law... now what?
Days pass by in Texas...
A.P., I'd like to have a talk with you.
Okay.
Have a seat.
Frankly, A.P., I'm worried for you. You seem to be in a mighty low mood these days. I don't want to pry into your private life...
But your broadcasts have become pretty gloomy affairs. I'm afraid our listeners might pick up on this. It comes through loud and clear...
Why don't you take some time off? Get away... get some rest. Come back when you're ready...
...then he let me go for th' rest of the season...
Y'need time t' get over this. It's been a big blow.
Lissen—me an' Anita'll drive back home with you. You shouldn't have t' make that trip by yourself.
And so...
Aw, Daddy! Y' put my pants on backward!
You'll keep, Wimp. Now, quiet back there!

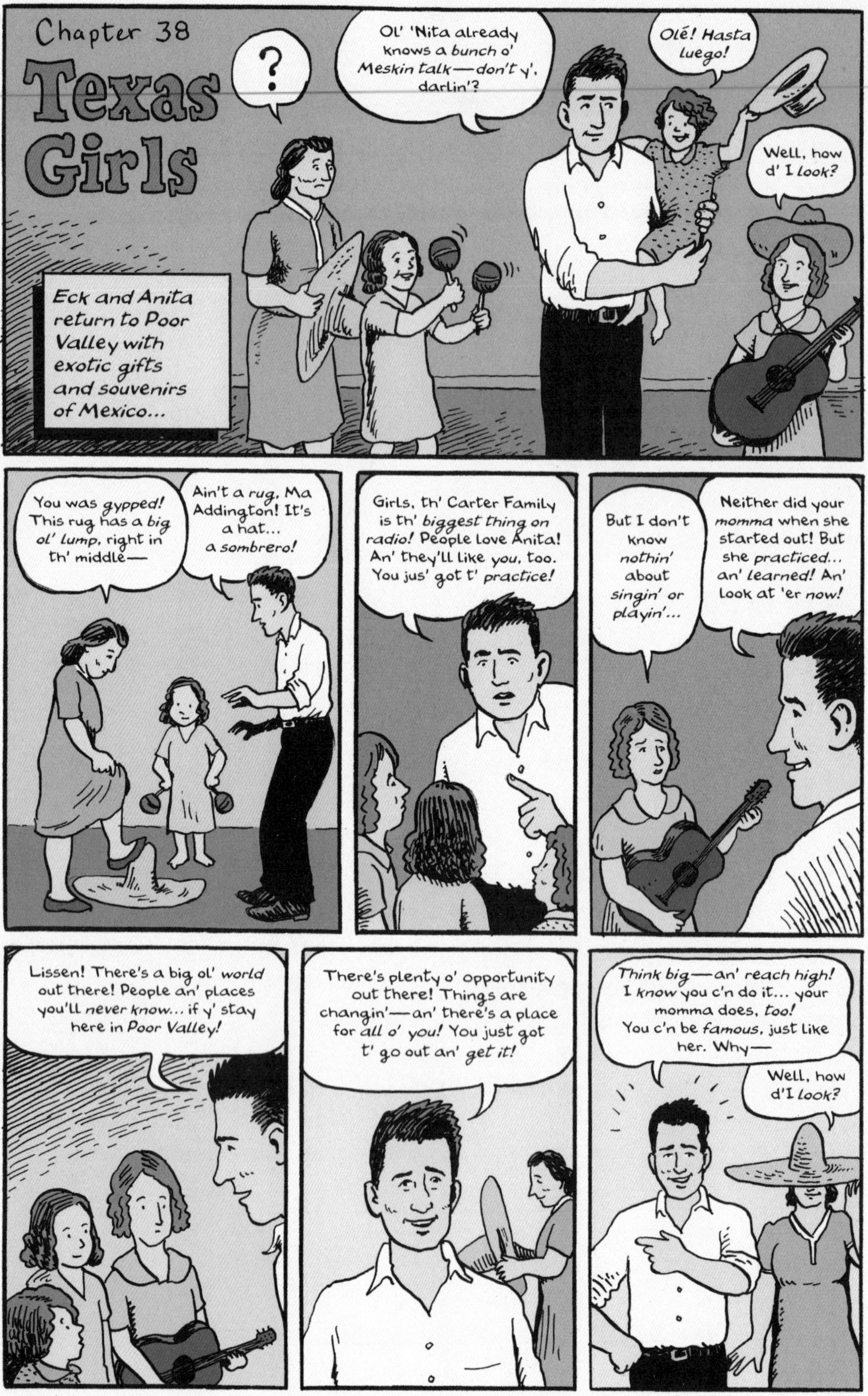
Chapter 38
Texas Girls
?
Ol' 'Nita already knows a *bunch o' Meskin talk*—*don't* y', darlin'?
Olé! Hasta luego!
Well, how d' I *look*?
Eck and Anita return to Poor Valley with exotic gifts and souvenirs of Mexico...
You was *gypped!* This rug has a *big ol' lump*, right in th' middle—
Ain't a *rug*, Ma Addington! It's a hat... a *sombrero!*
Girls, th' Carter Family is th' *biggest thing* on *radio!* People love Anita! An' they'll like *you*, too. You jus' got t' *practice!*
But I don't know *nothin'* about *singin'* or *playin'*...
Neither did your *momma* when she started out! But she *practiced*... an' *learned!* An' look at 'er *now!*
Lissen! There's a big ol' *world* out there! People an' places you'll *never know*... if y' stay here in *Poor Valley!*
There's plenty o' opportunity out there! Things are *changin'*—an' there's a place for *all* o' you! You just got t' go out an' *get it!*
Think big—an' *reach high!* I *know* you c'n do it... your momma does, *too!* You c'n be *famous*, just like her. Why—
Well, how d'I *look*?

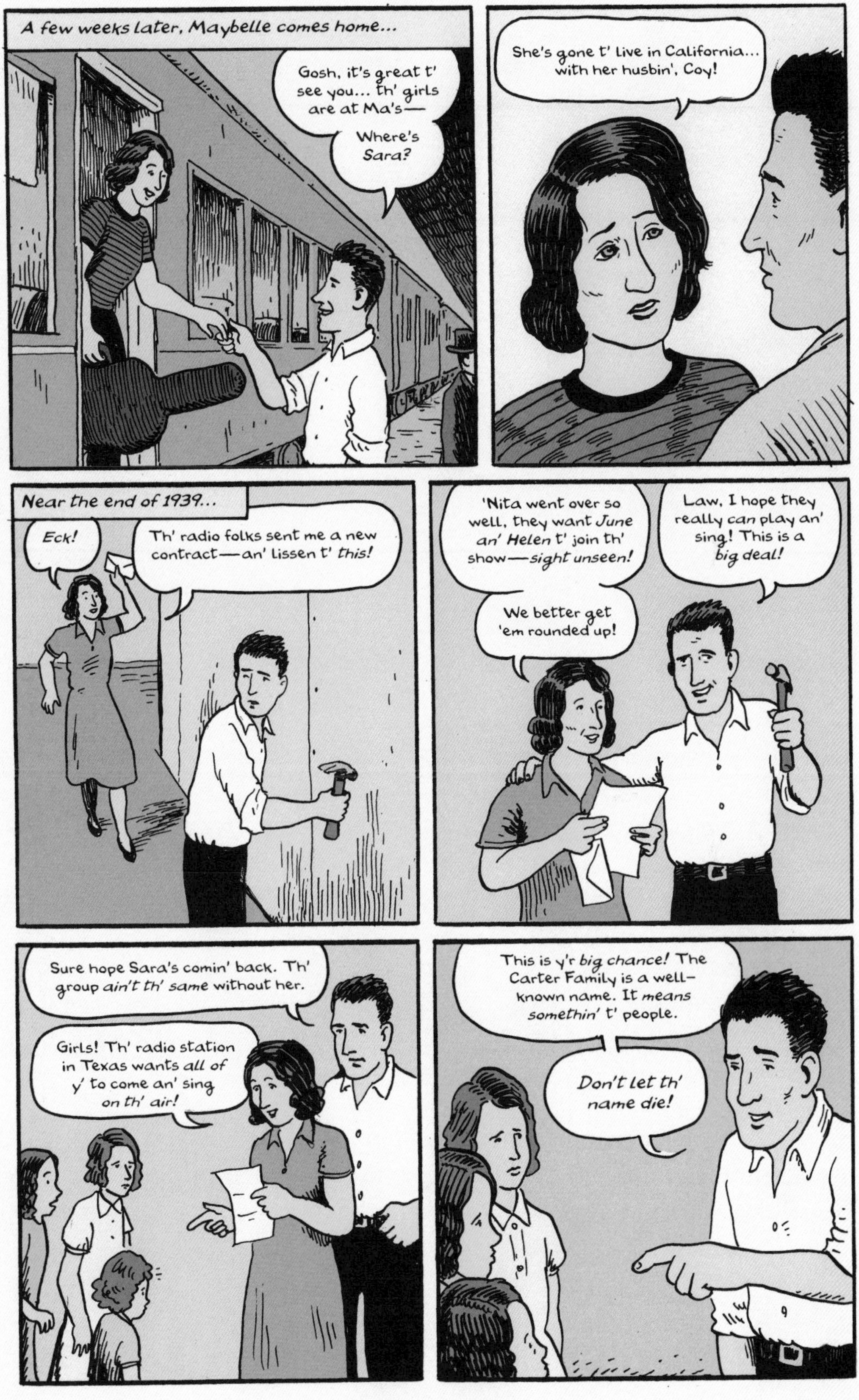
A few weeks later, Maybelle comes home...
Gosh, it's great t' see you... th' girls are at Ma's—
Where's Sara?
She's gone t' live in California... with her husbin', Coy!
Near the end of 1939...
Eck!
Th' radio folks sent me a new contract—an' lissen t' this!
'Nita went over so well, they want June an' Helen t' join th' show—sight unseen!
We better get 'em rounded up!
Law, I hope they really can play an' sing! This is a big deal!
Sure hope Sara's comin' back. Th' group ain't th' same without her.
Girls! Th' radio station in Texas wants all of y' to come an' sing on th' air!
This is y'r big chance! The Carter Family is a well-known name. It means somethin' t' people.
Don't let th' name die!

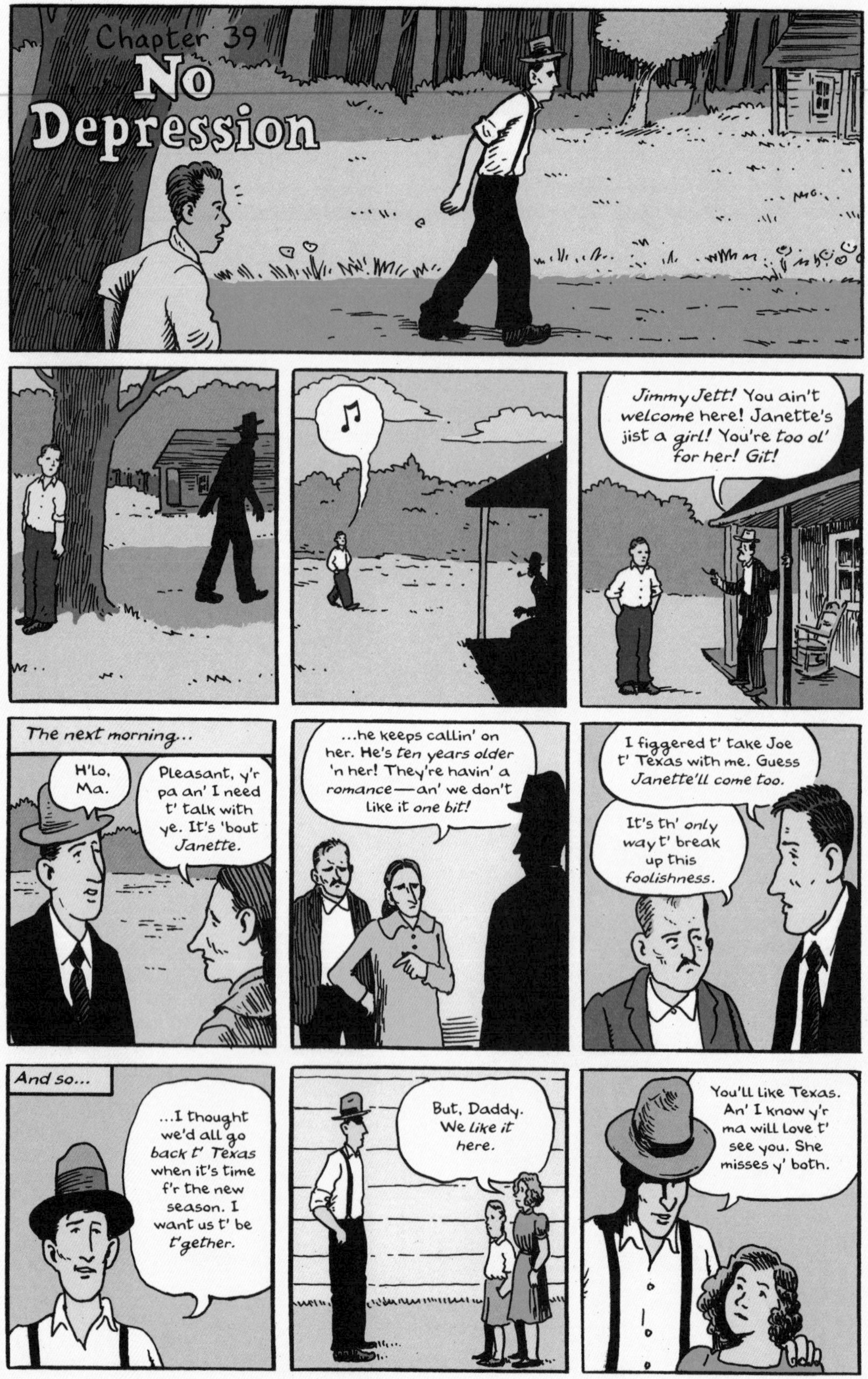
Chapter 39
No Depression
♪
Jimmy Jett! You ain't welcome here! Janette's jist a girl! You're too ol' for her! Git!
The next morning...
H'lo, Ma.
Pleasant, y'r pa an' I need t' talk with ye. It's 'bout Janette.
...he keeps callin' on her. He's ten years older 'n her! They're havin' a romance—an' we don't like it one bit!
I figgered t' take Joe t' Texas with me. Guess Janette'll come too.
It's th' only way t' break up this foolishness.
And so...
...I thought we'd all go back t' Texas when it's time f'r the new season. I want us t' be t'gether.
But, Daddy. We like it here.
You'll like Texas. An' I know y'r ma will love t' see you. She misses y' both.

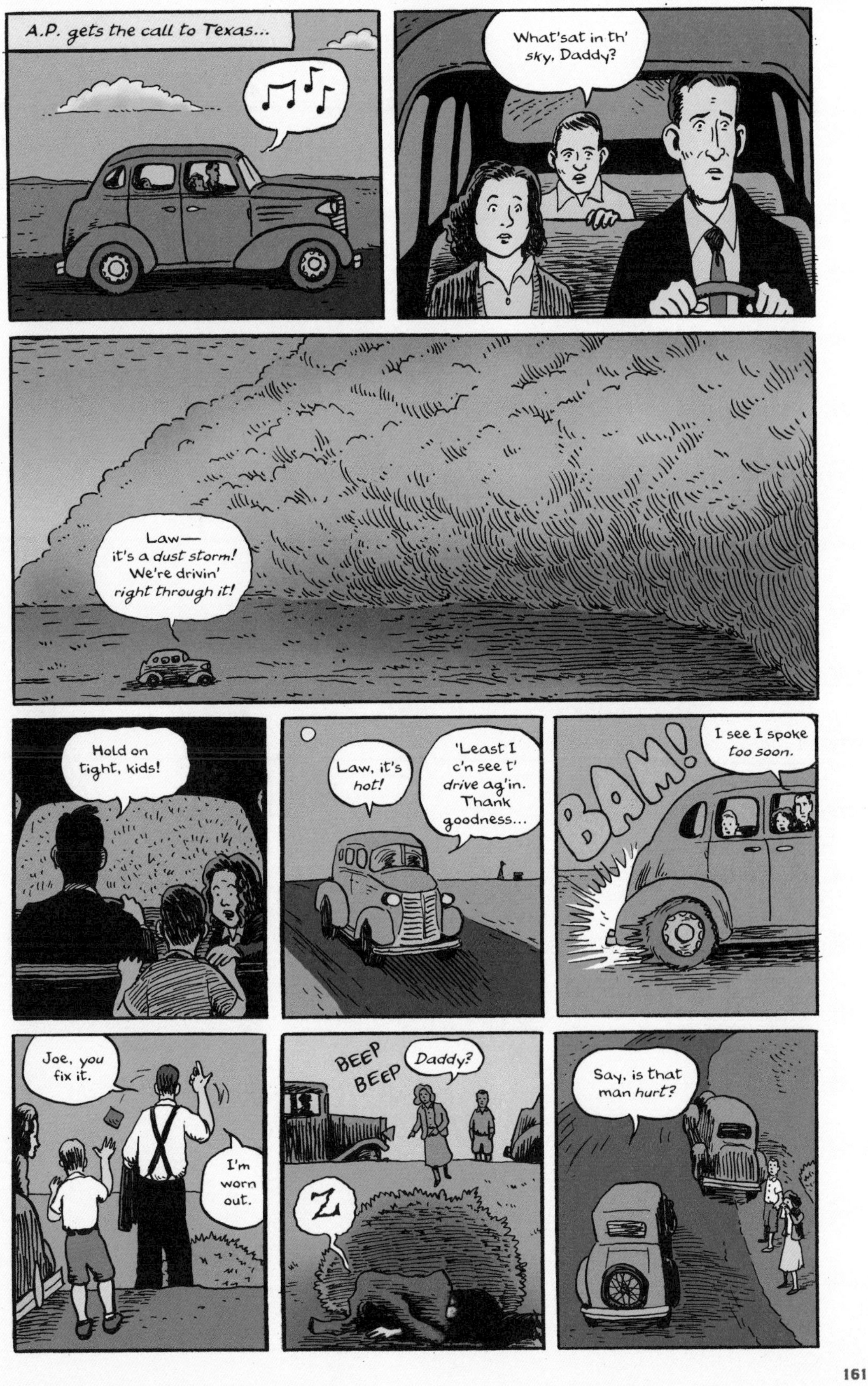
A.P. gets the call to Texas...
What'sat in th' sky, Daddy?
Law— it's a dust storm! We're drivin' right through it!
Hold on tight, kids!
Law, it's hot!
'Least I c'n see t' drive ag'in. Thank goodness...
BAM!
I see I spoke too soon.
Joe, you fix it.
I'm worn out.
BEEP BEEP
Daddy?
Z
Say, is that man hurt?

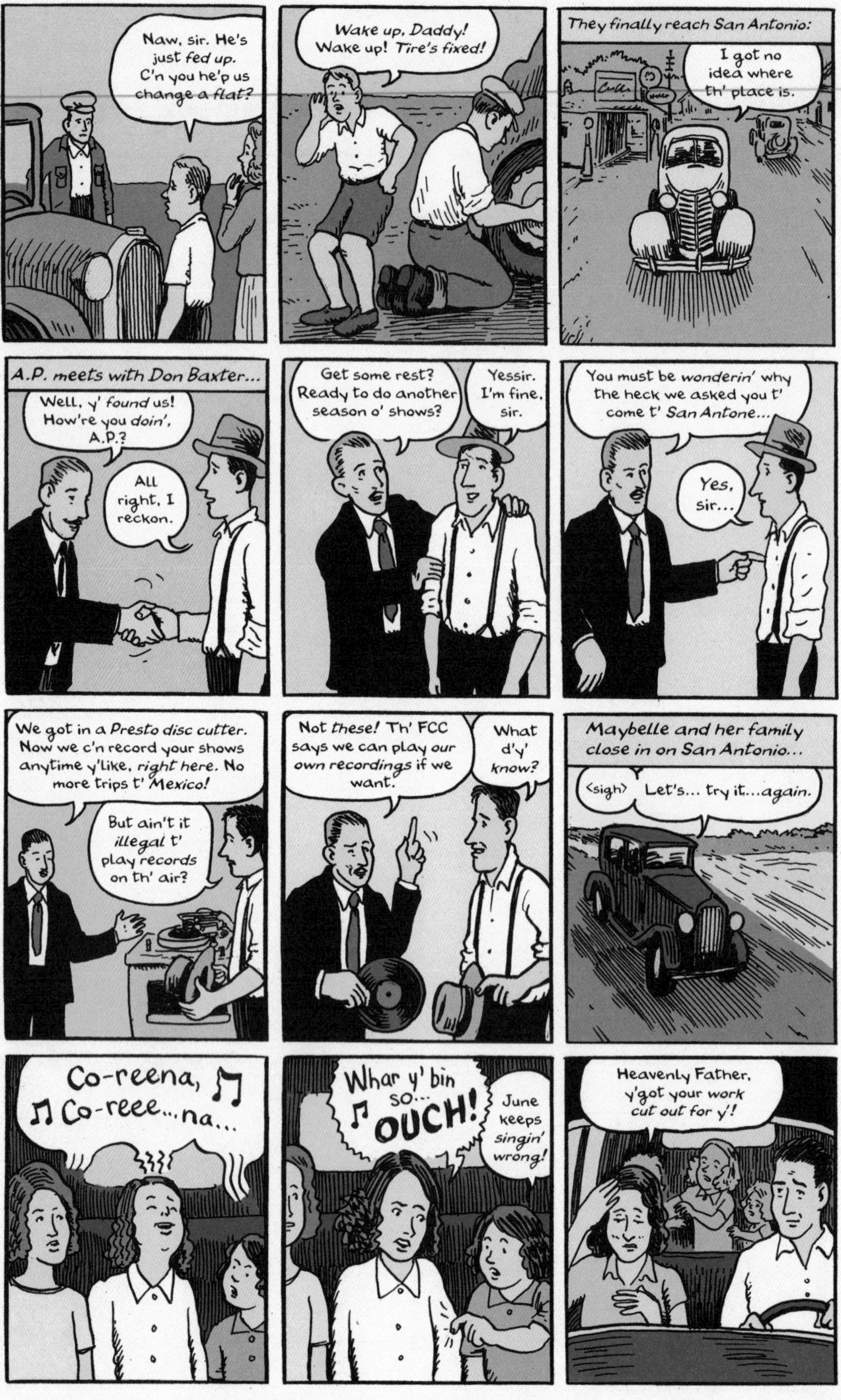
Naw, sir. He's just fed up. C'n you he'p us change a flat?
Wake up, Daddy! Wake up! Tire's fixed!
They finally reach San Antonio:
I got no idea where th' place is.
A.P. meets with Don Baxter...
Well, y' found us! How're you doin', A.P.?
All right, I reckon.
Get some rest? Ready to do another season o' shows?
Yessir. I'm fine, sir.
You must be wonderin' why the heck we asked you t' come t' San Antone...
Yes, sir...
We got in a Presto disc cutter. Now we c'n record your shows anytime y'like, right here. No more trips t' Mexico!
But ain't it illegal t' play records on th' air?
Not these! Th' FCC says we can play our own recordings if we want.
What d'y' know?
Maybelle and her family close in on San Antonio...
<sigh> Let's... try it...again.
Co-reena, ♫ ♫ Co-reee...na...
Whar y' bin so... ♫ OUCH!
June keeps singin' wrong!
Heavenly Father, y'got your work cut out for y'!

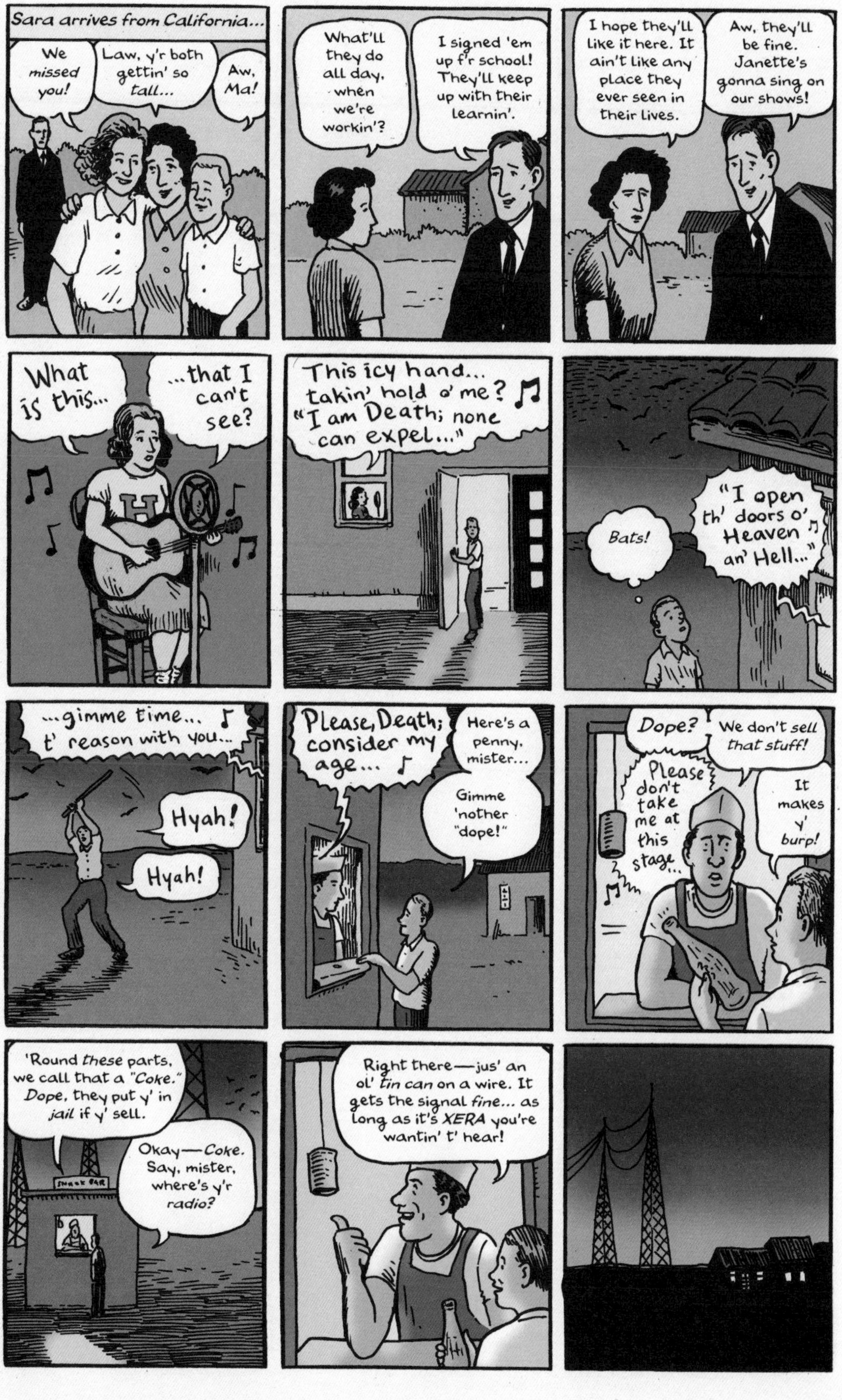
Sara arrives from California...
We missed you!
Law, y'r both gettin' so tall...
Aw, Ma!
What'll they do all day, when we're workin'?
I signed 'em up f'r school! They'll keep up with their learnin'.
I hope they'll like it here. It ain't like any place they ever seen in their lives.
Aw, they'll be fine. Janette's gonna sing on our shows!
What is this...
...that I can't see?
This icy hand... takin' hold o' me? "I am Death; none can expel..."
Bats!
"I open th' doors o' Heaven an' Hell..."
...gimme time... t' reason with you...
Hyah!
Hyah!
Please, Death; consider my age...
Here's a penny, mister...
Gimme 'nother "dope!"
Dope?
We don't sell that stuff!
Please don't take me at this stage...
It makes y' burp!
'Round these parts, we call that a "Coke." Dope, they put y' in jail if y' sell.
Okay—Coke. Say, mister, where's y'r radio?
Right there—jus' an ol' tin can on a wire. It gets the signal fine... as long as it's XERA you're wantin' t' hear!

Janette and Joe attend school...

'Ere's 'at hillbilly!

She tawks funneh!

Daddy, I hate Texas! I wanna go back t' Virginia!

But, Janette, honey...

Th' Good Lord has blessed us here. We're makin' money... an' you're doin' fine on th' radio! We're all happy here.

I'm not happy.

'F you'd buy a gittar, you c'd be a regular on th' radio with us! Y'r a fine singer an' songwriter. Th' Lord has blessed you with talent!

Listen: give me th' money you've saved. I'll buy you a gittar. If you're still unhappy, come Christmas, I'll buy you a ticket back t' Virginia!

Sniff Sniff

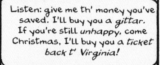

Meanwhile, in California...

Wait'll Sara reads this!

Coy's letter reaches Texas:

...I'm coming to set up housekeeping with you in San Antone...

Hi, Sary! Is that some fan mail?

In a manner o' speakin'.

At last—the Carter Sisters audition for XERA!

♪ Those chime bells ring— yodel-ay, odel-eee...

♪ Those mockin'- birds sing, yodel-ay, odel-eee...

Wonderful! Our listeners will just love you girls! Let's get you on the air tonight!

!

Sorry we're late. How'd it go?

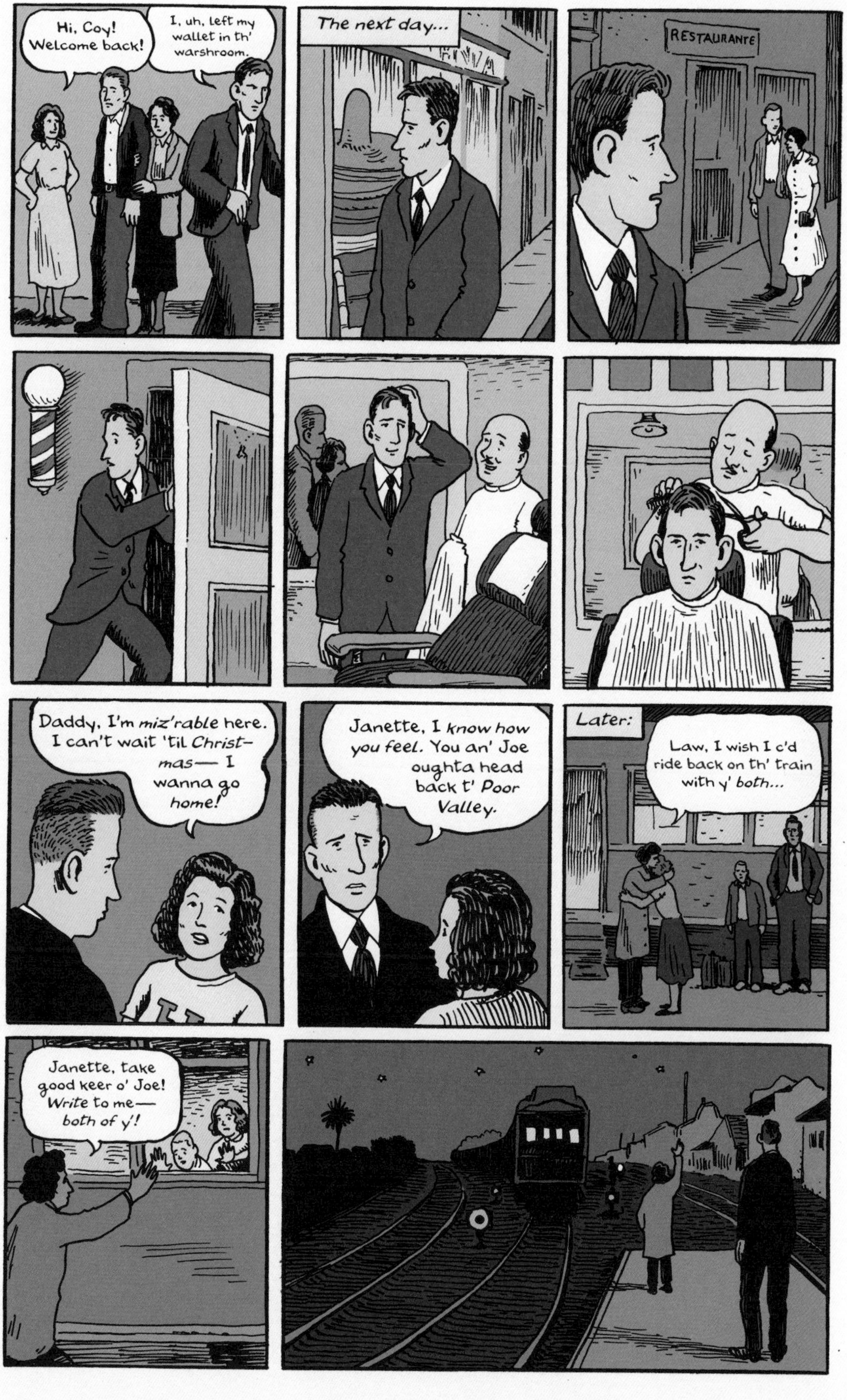
Hi, Coy! Welcome back!
I, uh, left my wallet in th' warshroom.
The next day...
RESTAURANTE
Daddy, I'm miz'rable here. I can't wait 'til Christ-mas— I wanna go home!
Janette, I know how you feel. You an' Joe oughta head back t' Poor Valley.
Later:
Law, I wish I c'd ride back on th' train with y' both...
Janette, take good keer o' Joe! Write to me— both of y'!

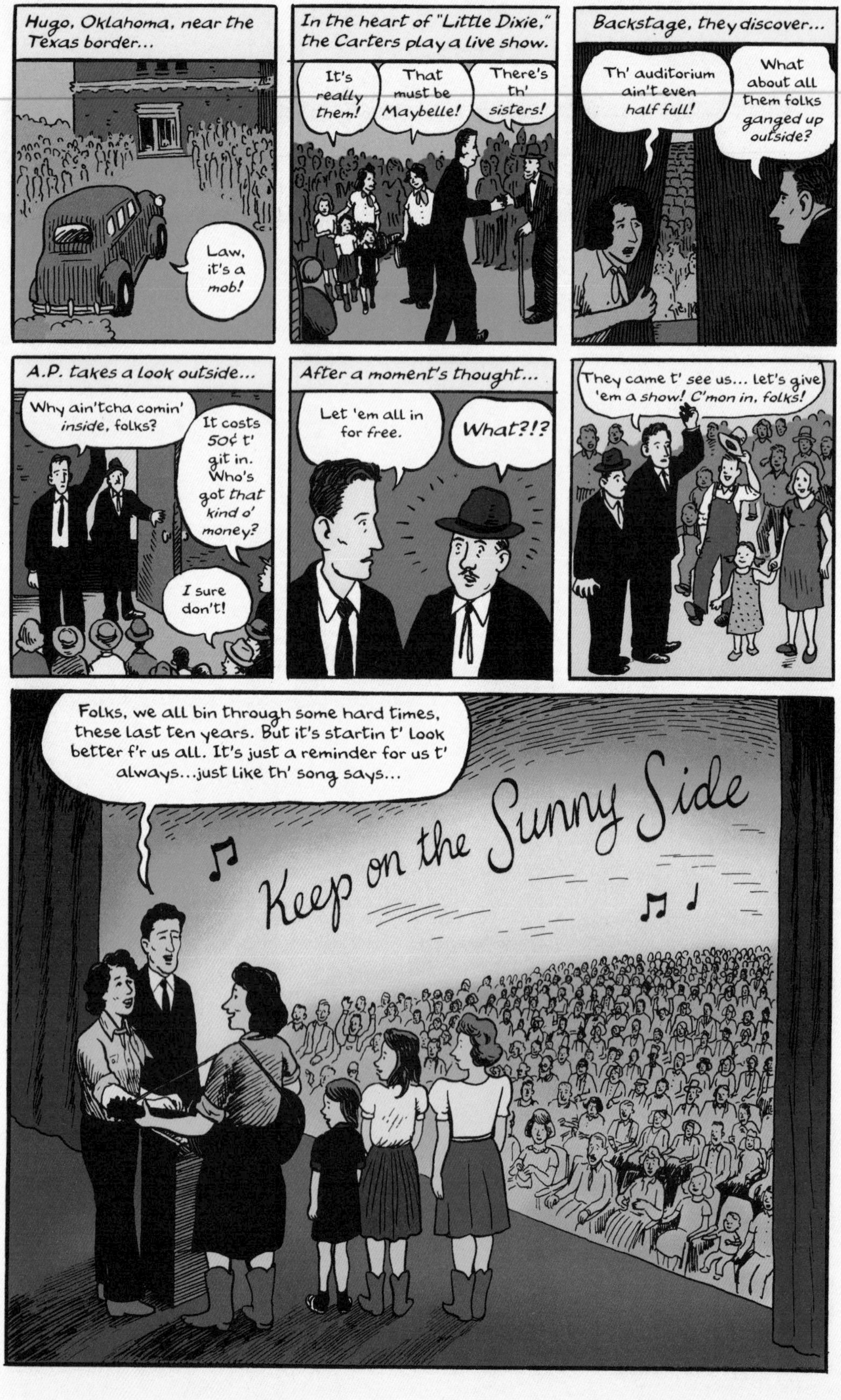
Hugo, Oklahoma, near the Texas border...
Law, it's a mob!
In the heart of "Little Dixie," the Carters play a live show.
It's really them!
That must be Maybelle!
There's th' sisters!
Backstage, they discover...
Th' auditorium ain't even half full!
What about all them folks ganged up outside?
A.P. takes a look outside...
Why ain'tcha comin' inside, folks?
It costs 50¢ t' git in. Who's got that kind o' money?
I sure don't!
After a moment's thought...
Let 'em all in for free.
What?!?
They came t' see us... let's give 'em a show! C'mon in, folks!
Folks, we all bin through some hard times, these last ten years. But it's startin t' look better f'r us all. It's just a reminder for us t' always...just like th' song says...
Keep on the Sunny Side

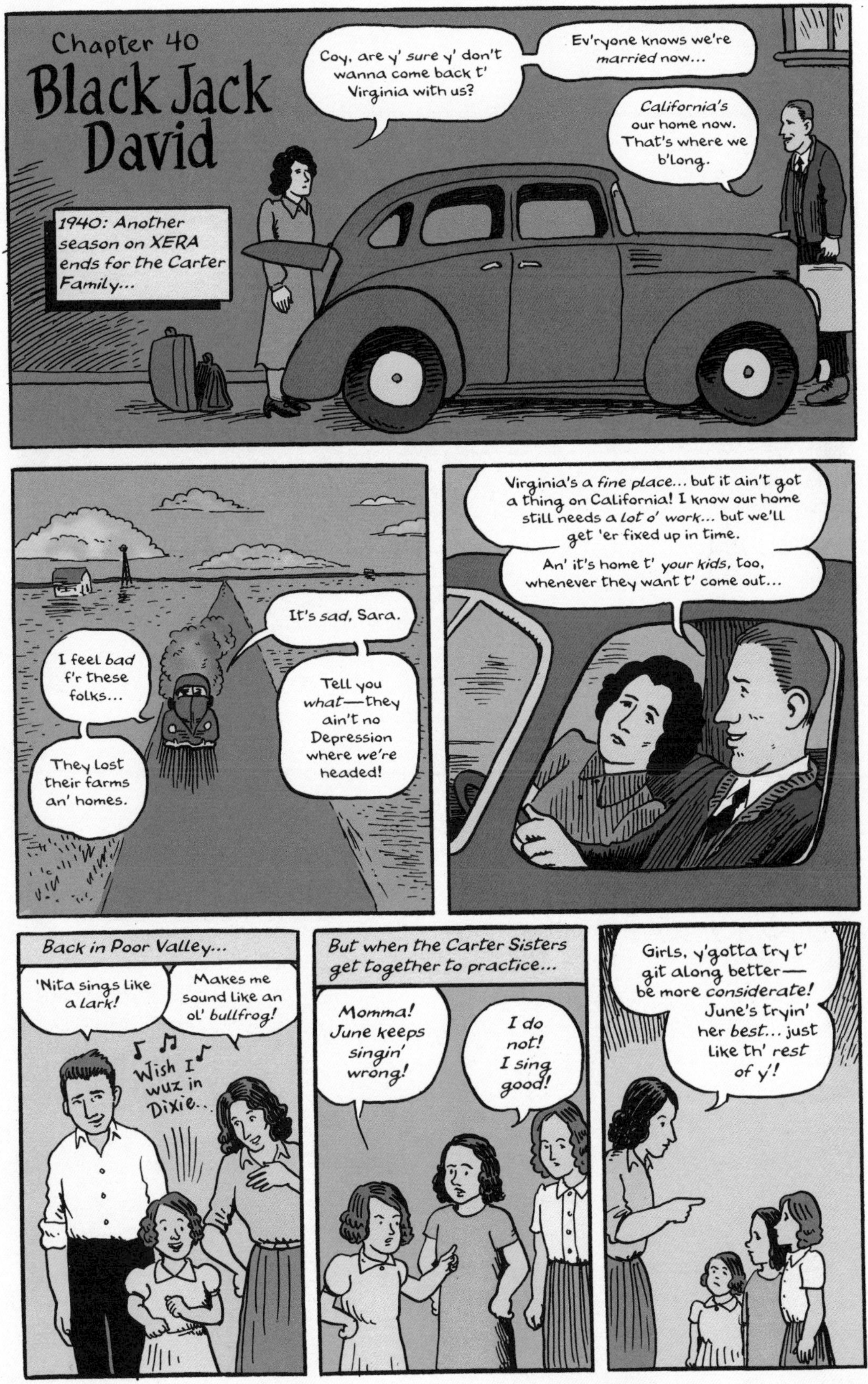
Chapter 40
Black Jack David
1940: Another season on XERA ends for the Carter Family...
Coy, are y' sure y' don't wanna come back t' Virginia with us?
Ev'ryone knows we're married now...
California's our home now. That's where we b'long.
I feel bad f'r these folks...
They lost their farms an' homes.
It's sad, Sara.
Tell you what—they ain't no Depression where we're headed!
Virginia's a fine place... but it ain't got a thing on California! I know our home still needs a lot o' work... but we'll get 'er fixed up in time.
An' it's home t' your kids, too, whenever they want t' come out...
Back in Poor Valley...
'Nita sings like a lark!
Makes me sound like an ol' bullfrog!
Wish I wuz in Dixie...
But when the Carter Sisters get together to practice...
Momma! June keeps singin' wrong!
I do not! I sing good!
Girls, y'gotta try t' git along better—be more considerate! June's tryin' her best... just like th' rest of y'!

And over at A.P.'s house...

Lonesome here, without Joe an' Janette under foot. <sigh> Used t' be so much goin' on around here...

KNOCK KNOCK

Gladys! What a s'prise! C'mon in!

Hi, Daddy.

How's Joe doin'? An' that little Nancy Flo?

Aw, they're fine. 'Fraid I got some bad news for y', Daddy. It's about Janette...

She's gittin' married t' Jimmy Jett. They got th' date set for th' end of May. She ast me t' ask you, would you give her away at th' altar...

What?!

Has Janette lost her mind? We've tole her over an' over: she's too young!

She's settin' herself up for a terrible fall!

Well—I hope she'll have some happiness in her life.

She ain't had much, so far...

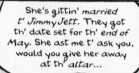

June visits with her cousin Fern one afternoon...

They got cactuses an' coyotes in th' desert— jus' like in th' movies!

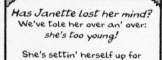

Now that I bin t' Texas, I wanna see more o' th' world!

An' I'm gunna do it, Fern!

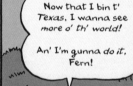

I'm gunna meet kings an' queens! Jus' you wait an' see!

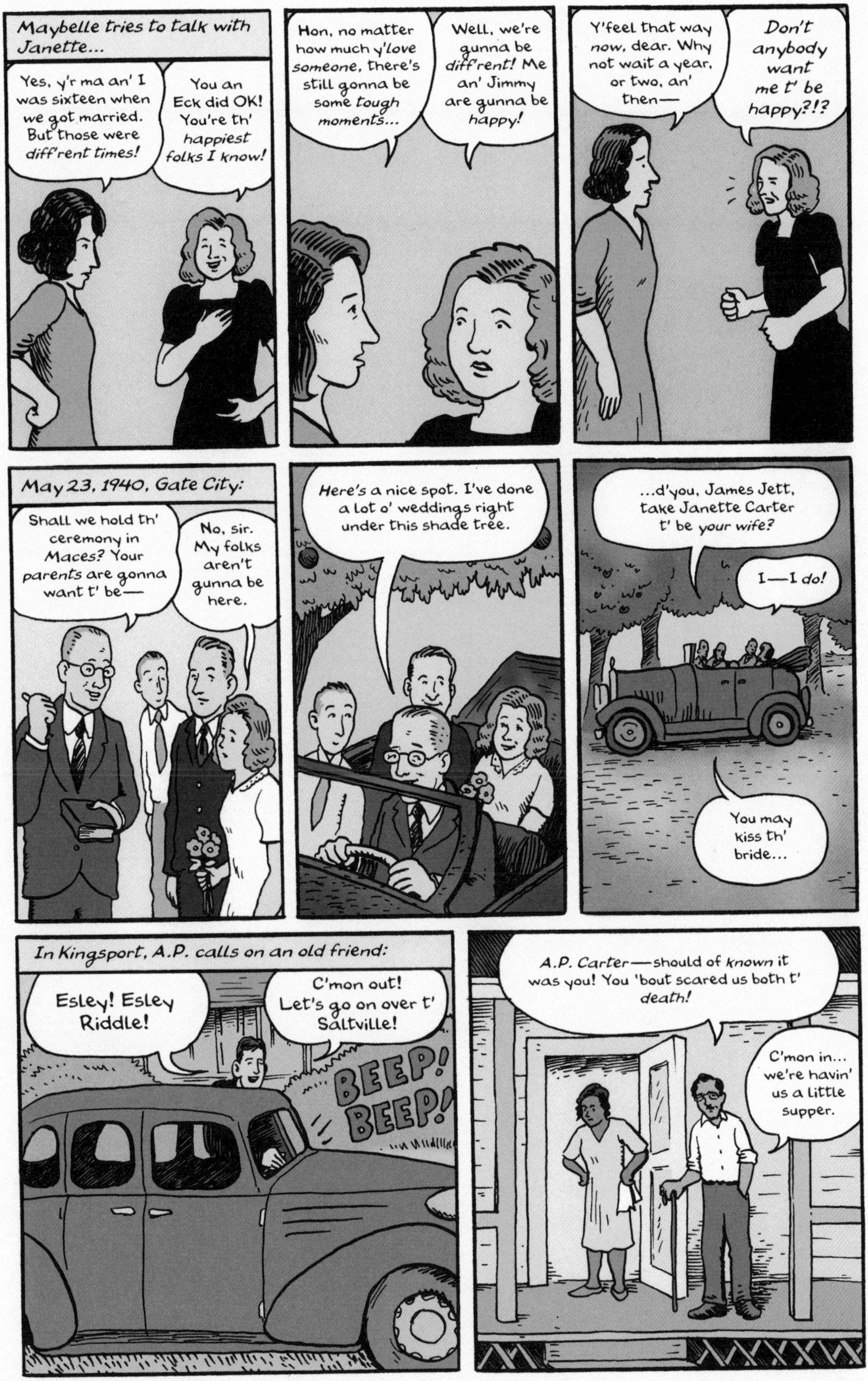
Maybelle tries to talk with Janette...
Yes, y'r ma an' I was sixteen when we got married. But those were diff'rent times!
You an Eck did OK! You're th' happiest folks I know!
Hon, no matter how much y'love someone, there's still gonna be some tough moments...
Well, we're gunna be diff'rent! Me an' Jimmy are gunna be happy!
Y'feel that way now, dear. Why not wait a year, or two, an' then—
Don't anybody want me t' be happy?!?
May 23, 1940, Gate City:
Shall we hold th' ceremony in Maces? Your parents are gonna want t' be—
No, sir. My folks aren't gunna be here.
Here's a nice spot. I've done a lot o' weddings right under this shade tree.
...d'you, James Jett, take Janette Carter t' be your wife?
I—I do!
You may kiss th' bride...
In Kingsport, A.P. calls on an old friend:
Esley! Esley Riddle!
C'mon out! Let's go on over t' Saltville!
BEEP! BEEP!
A.P. Carter—should of known it was you! You 'bout scared us both t' death!
C'mon in... we're havin' us a little supper.

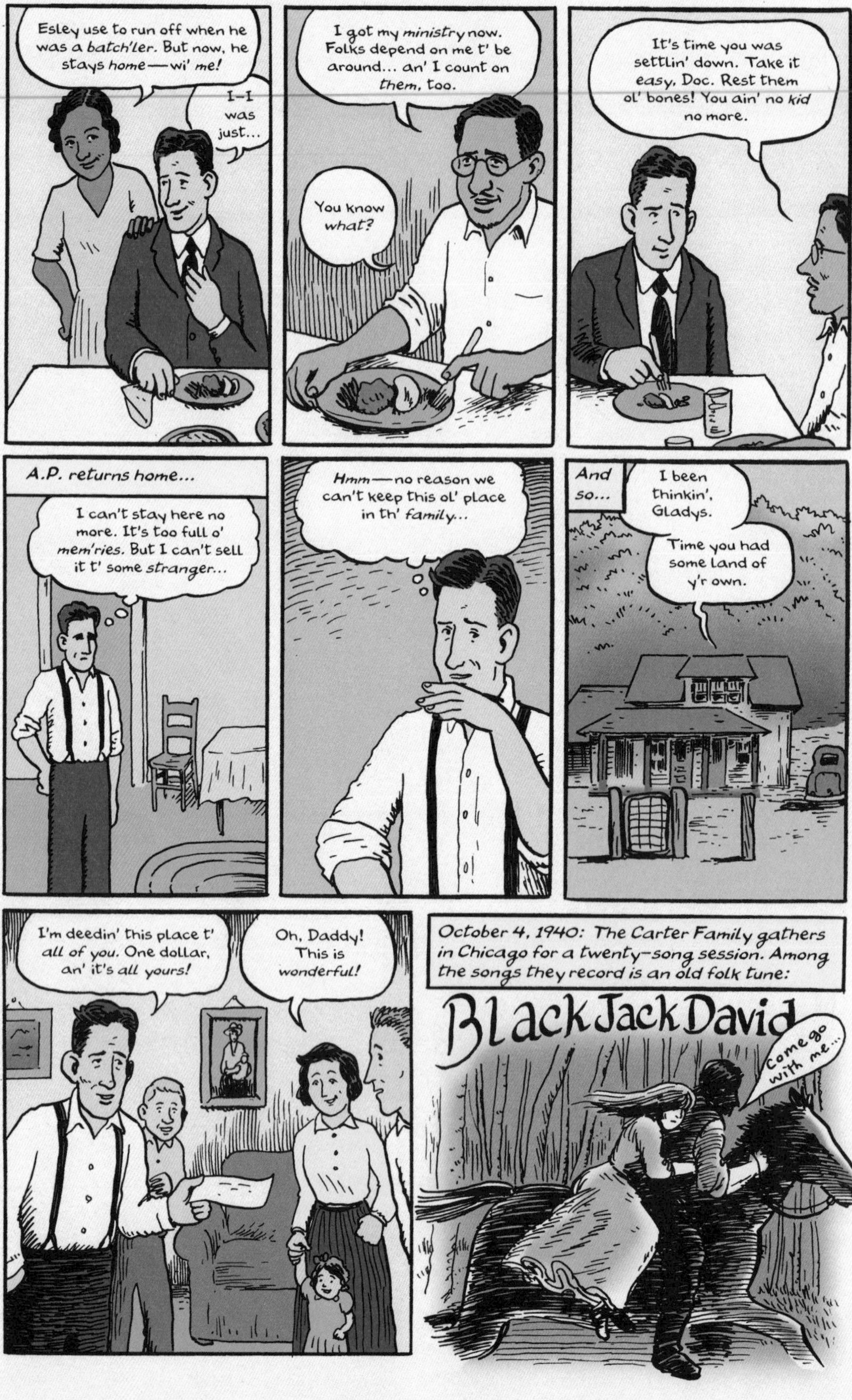
Esley use to run off when he was a *batch'ler*. But now, he stays *home*—wi' *me!*
I–I was just...
I got my *ministry* now. Folks depend on me t' be around... an' I count on *them*, too.
You know *what?*
It's time you was settlin' down. Take it easy, Doc. Rest them ol' bones! You ain' no *kid* no more.
A.P. returns home...
I can't stay here no more. It's too full o' *mem'ries*. But I can't sell it t' some *stranger*...
Hmm—no reason we can't keep this ol' place in th' *family*...
And so...
I been thinkin', Gladys.
Time you had some land of y'r own.
I'm deedin' this place t' all of you. One dollar, an' it's *all* yours!
Oh, Daddy! This is *wonderful!*
October 4, 1940: The Carter Family gathers in Chicago for a twenty-song session. Among the songs they record is an old folk tune:
Black Jack David
Come go with me...

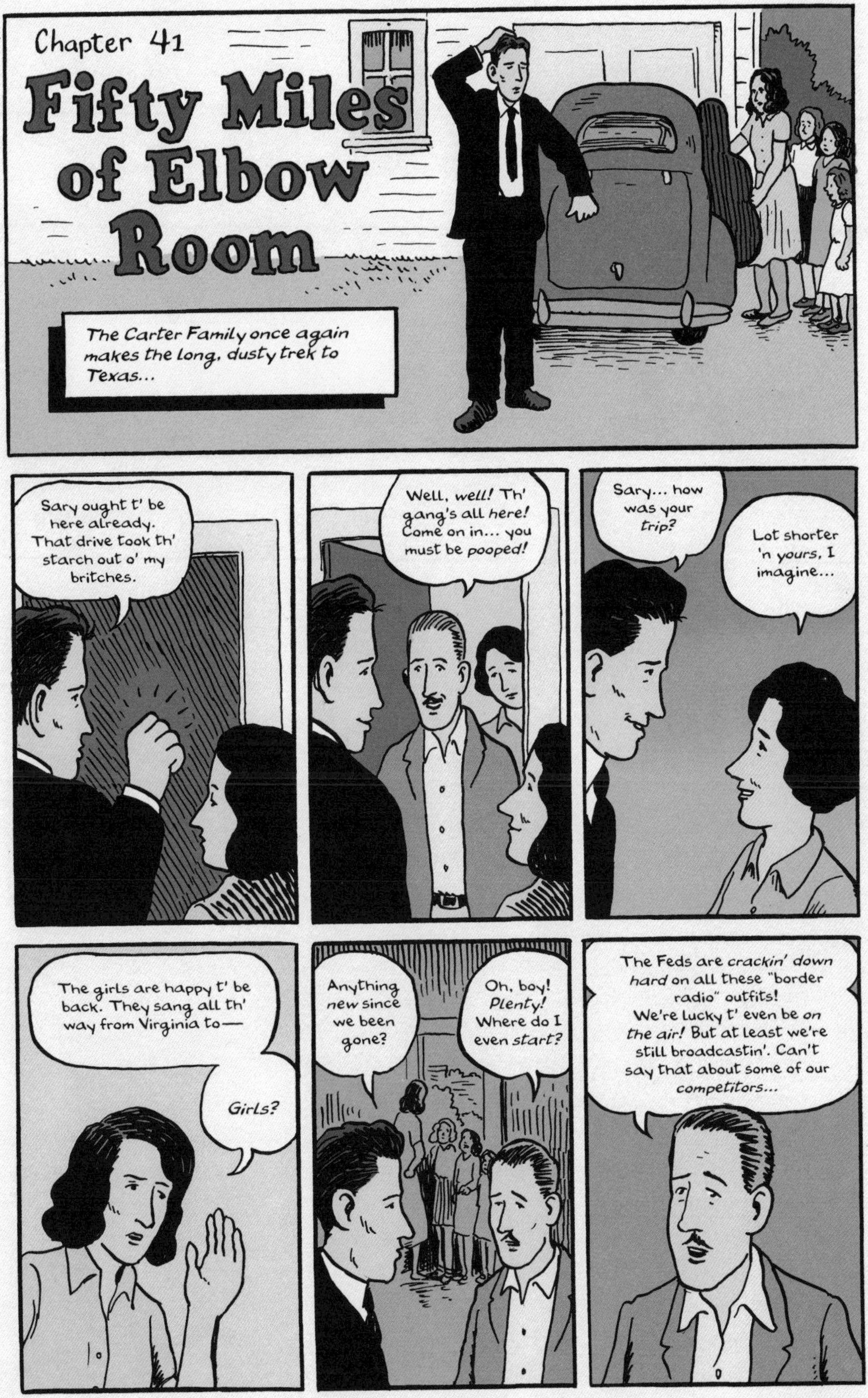
Chapter 41
Fifty Miles of Elbow Room
The Carter Family once again makes the long, dusty trek to Texas...
Sary ought t' be here already. That drive took th' starch out o' my britches.
Well, *well!* Th' gang's all *here!* Come on in... you must be *pooped!*
Sary... how was your *trip?*
Lot shorter 'n yours, I imagine...
The girls are happy t' be back. They sang all th' way from Virginia to—
Girls?
Anything *new* since we been gone?
Oh, boy! *Plenty!* Where do I even *start?*
The Feds are *crackin' down hard* on all these "border radio" outfits! We're lucky t' even be *on the air!* But at least we're still broadcastin'. Can't say that about some of our *competitors...*

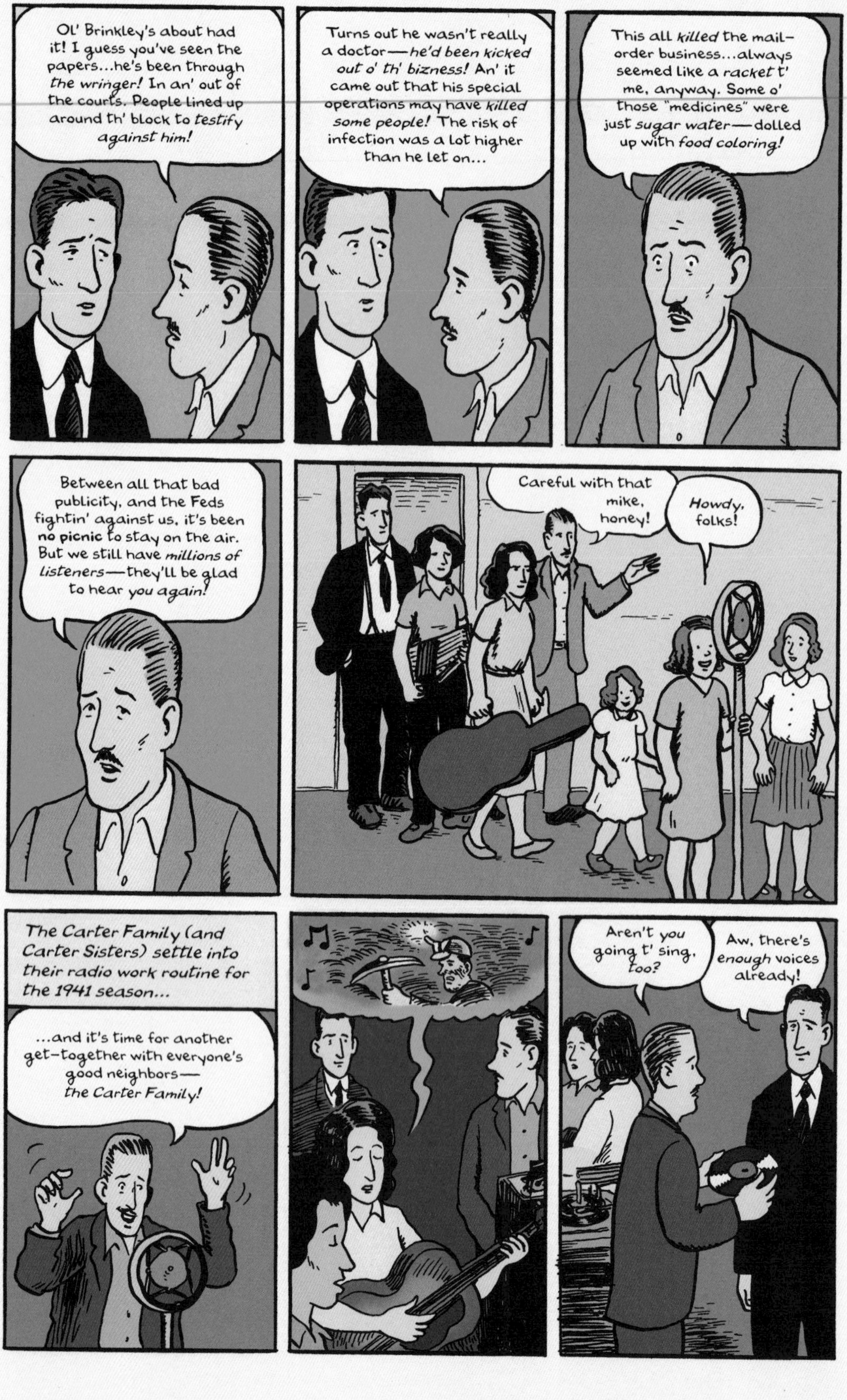
Ol' Brinkley's about had it! I guess you've seen the papers...he's been through the wringer! In an' out of the courts. People lined up around th' block to testify against him!
Turns out he wasn't really a doctor—he'd been kicked out o' th' bizness! An' it came out that his special operations may have killed some people! The risk of infection was a lot higher than he let on...
This all killed the mail-order business...always seemed like a racket t' me, anyway. Some o' those "medicines" were just sugar water—dolled up with food coloring!
Between all that bad publicity, and the Feds fightin' against us, it's been no picnic to stay on the air. But we still have millions of listeners—they'll be glad to hear you again!
Careful with that mike, honey!
Howdy, folks!
The Carter Family (and Carter Sisters) settle into their radio work routine for the 1941 season...
...and it's time for another get-together with everyone's good neighbors— the Carter Family!
Aren't you going t' sing, too?
Aw, there's enough voices already!

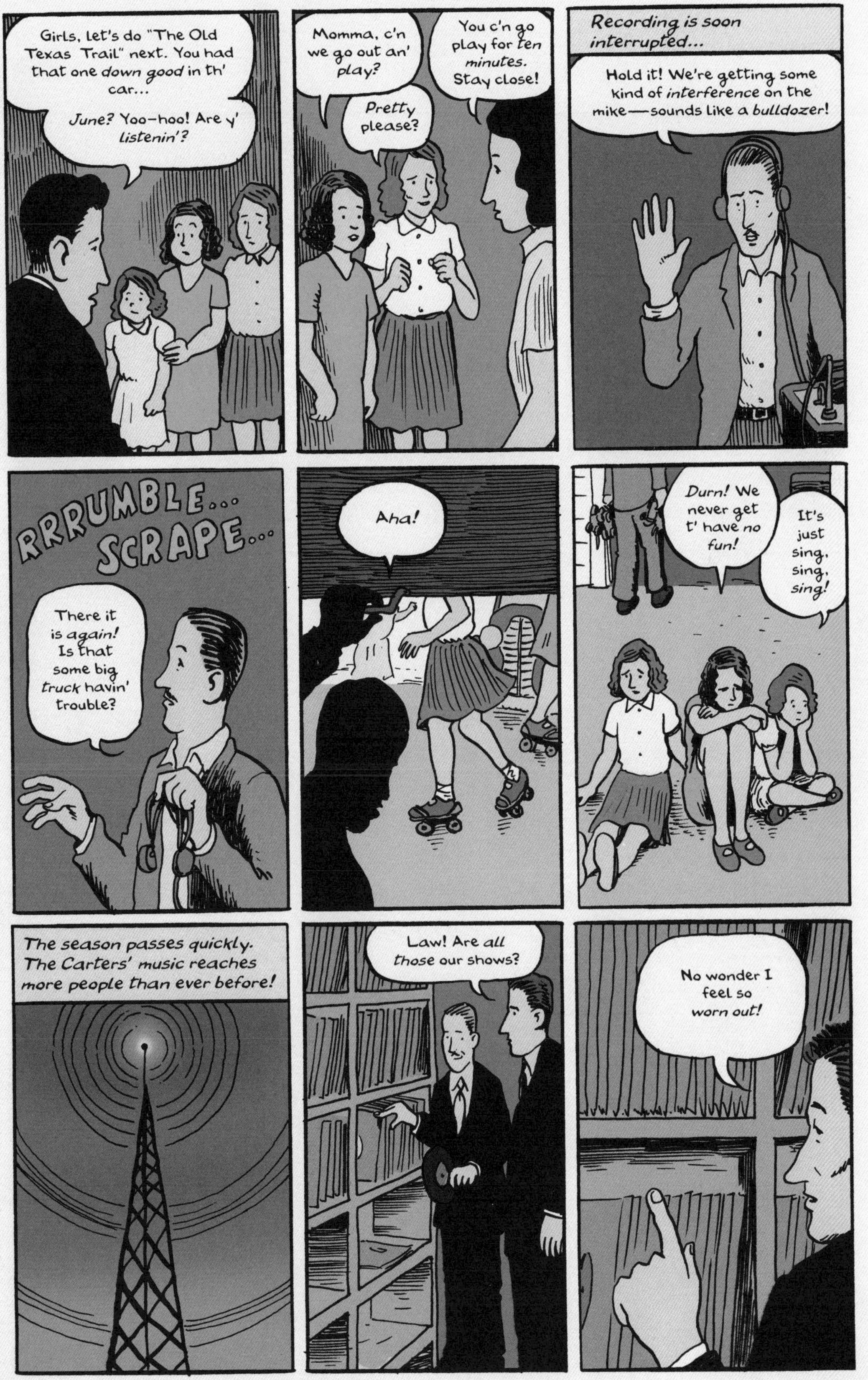
Girls, let's do "The Old Texas Trail" next. You had that one *down good* in th' car...
June? Yoo-hoo! Are y' *listenin'*?
Momma, c'n we go out an' play?
You c'n go play for *ten minutes.* Stay close!
Pretty please?
Recording is soon interrupted...
Hold it! We're getting some kind of *interference* on the mike—sounds like a *bulldozer*!
RRRUMBLE... SCRAPE...
There it is *again*! Is that some big *truck* havin' trouble?
Aha!
Durn! We never get t' have *no fun*!
It's just sing, sing, *sing*!
The season passes quickly. The Carters' music reaches more people than ever before!
Law! Are *all* those our shows?
No wonder I feel so *worn out*!

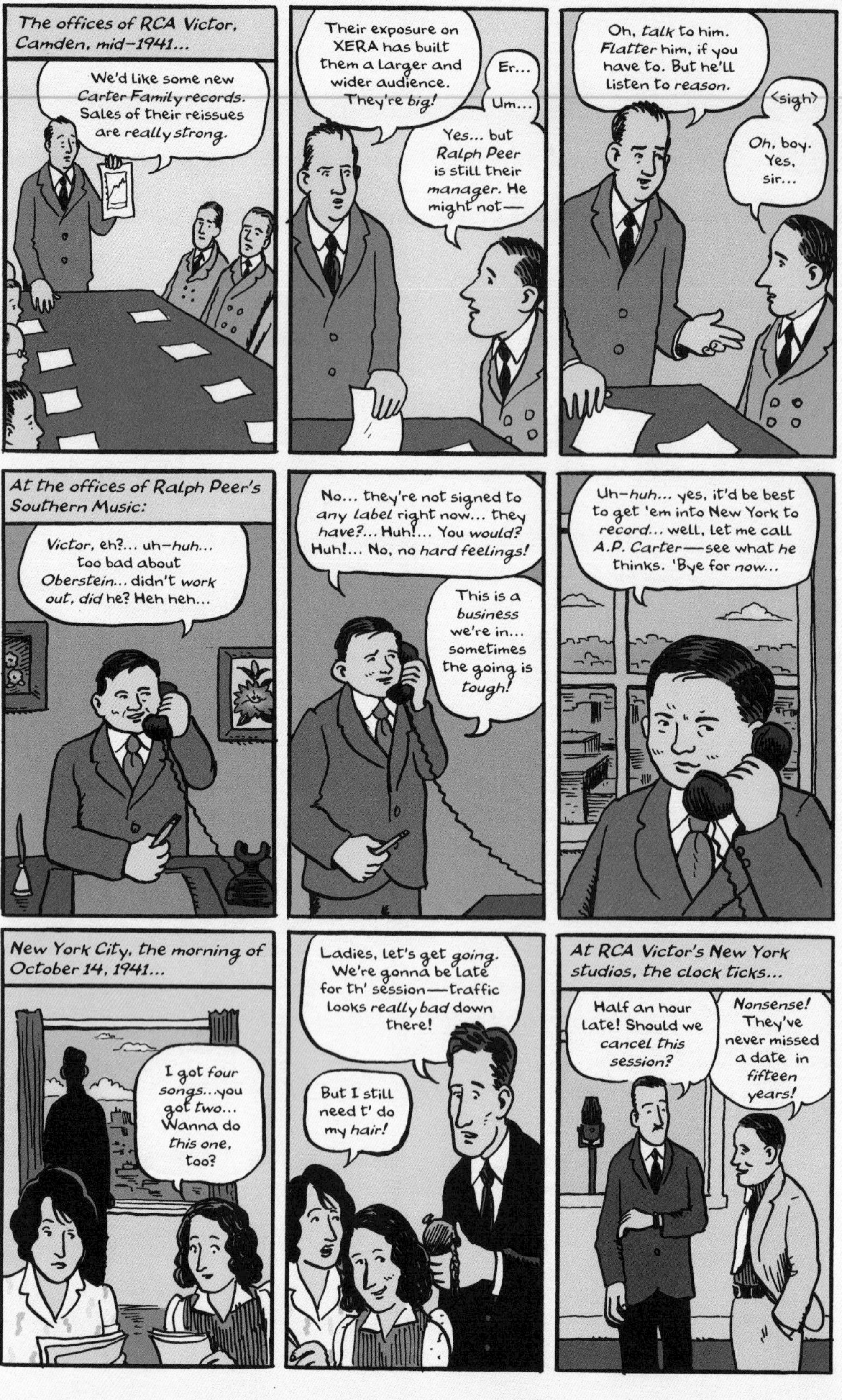
The offices of RCA Victor, Camden, mid-1941...
We'd like some new *Carter Family* records. Sales of their reissues are *really strong*.
Their exposure on XERA has built them a larger and wider audience. They're *big!*
Er...
Um...
Yes... but *Ralph Peer* is still their *manager*. He might not—
Oh, *talk* to him. *Flatter* him, if you have to. But he'll listen to *reason*.
<sigh>
Oh, boy. Yes, sir...
At the offices of Ralph Peer's Southern Music:
Victor, eh?... uh-*huh*... too bad about Oberstein... didn't *work* out, *did* he? Heh heh...
No... they're not signed to *any label* right now... they *have*?... Huh!... You *would*? Huh!... No, no *hard feelings!*
This is a *business* we're in... sometimes the going is *tough!*
Uh-*huh*... yes, it'd be best to get 'em into New York to *record*... well, let me call *A.P. Carter*—see what *he* thinks. 'Bye for *now*...
New York City, the morning of October 14, 1941...
I got four songs...you got two... Wanna do *this one*, too?
Ladies, let's get *going*. We're gonna be late for th' session—traffic looks *really bad* down there!
But I still need t' do my *hair!*
At RCA Victor's New York studios, the clock ticks...
Half an hour late! Should we cancel *this* session?
Nonsense! They've never missed a date in fifteen years!

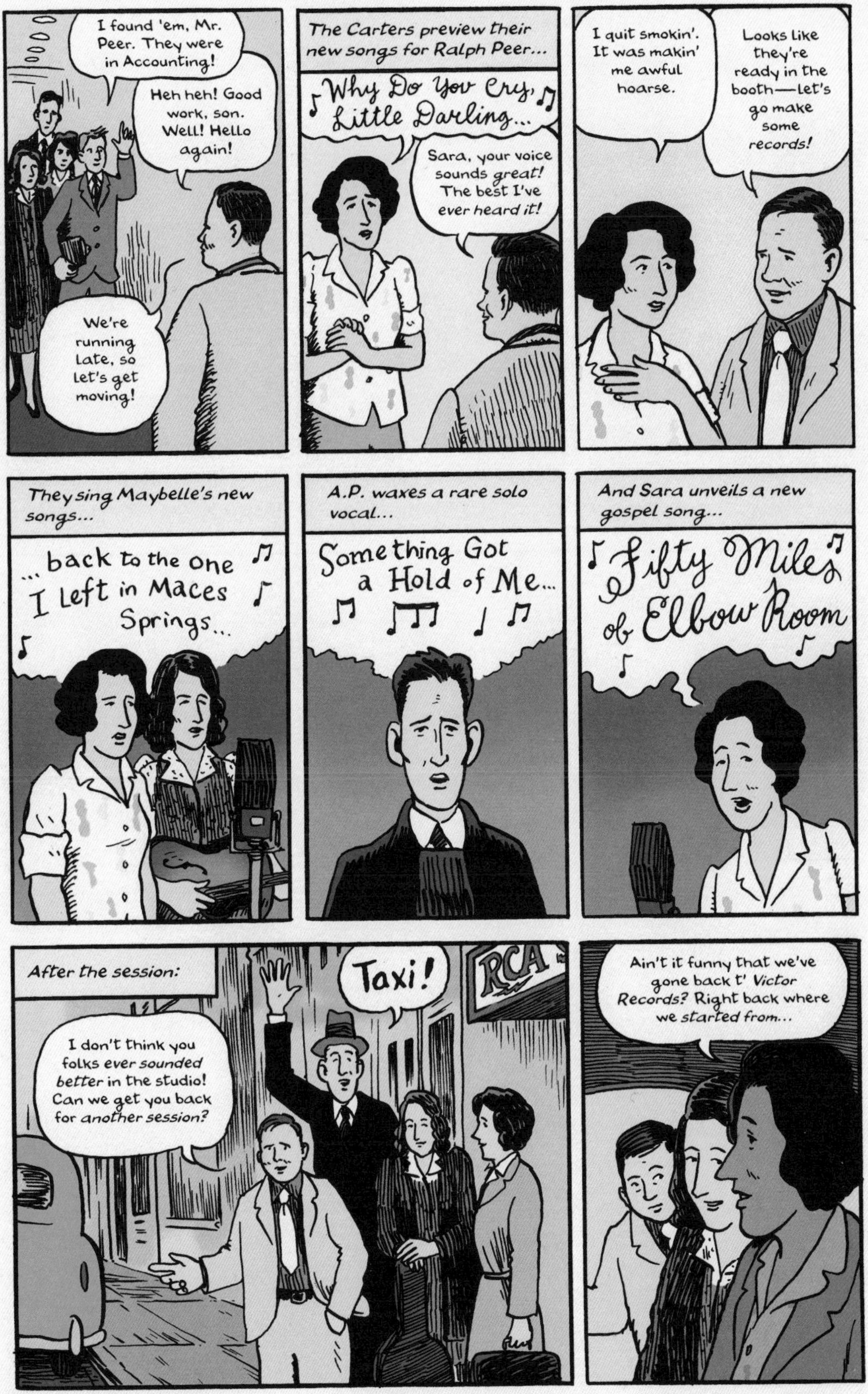

I found 'em, Mr. Peer. They were in Accounting!
Heh heh! Good work, son. Well! Hello again!
We're running late, so let's get moving!
The Carters preview their new songs for Ralph Peer...
Why Do You Cry, Little Darling...
Sara, your voice sounds great! The best I've ever heard it!
I quit smokin'. It was makin' me awful hoarse.
Looks like they're ready in the booth—let's go make some records!
They sing Maybelle's new songs...
... back to the one I left in Maces Springs...
A.P. waxes a rare solo vocal...
Something Got a Hold of Me...
And Sara unveils a new gospel song...
Fifty Miles of Elbow Room
After the session:
Taxi!
RCA
I don't think you folks ever sounded better in the studio! Can we get you back for another session?
Ain't it funny that we've gone back t' Victor Records? Right back where we started from...

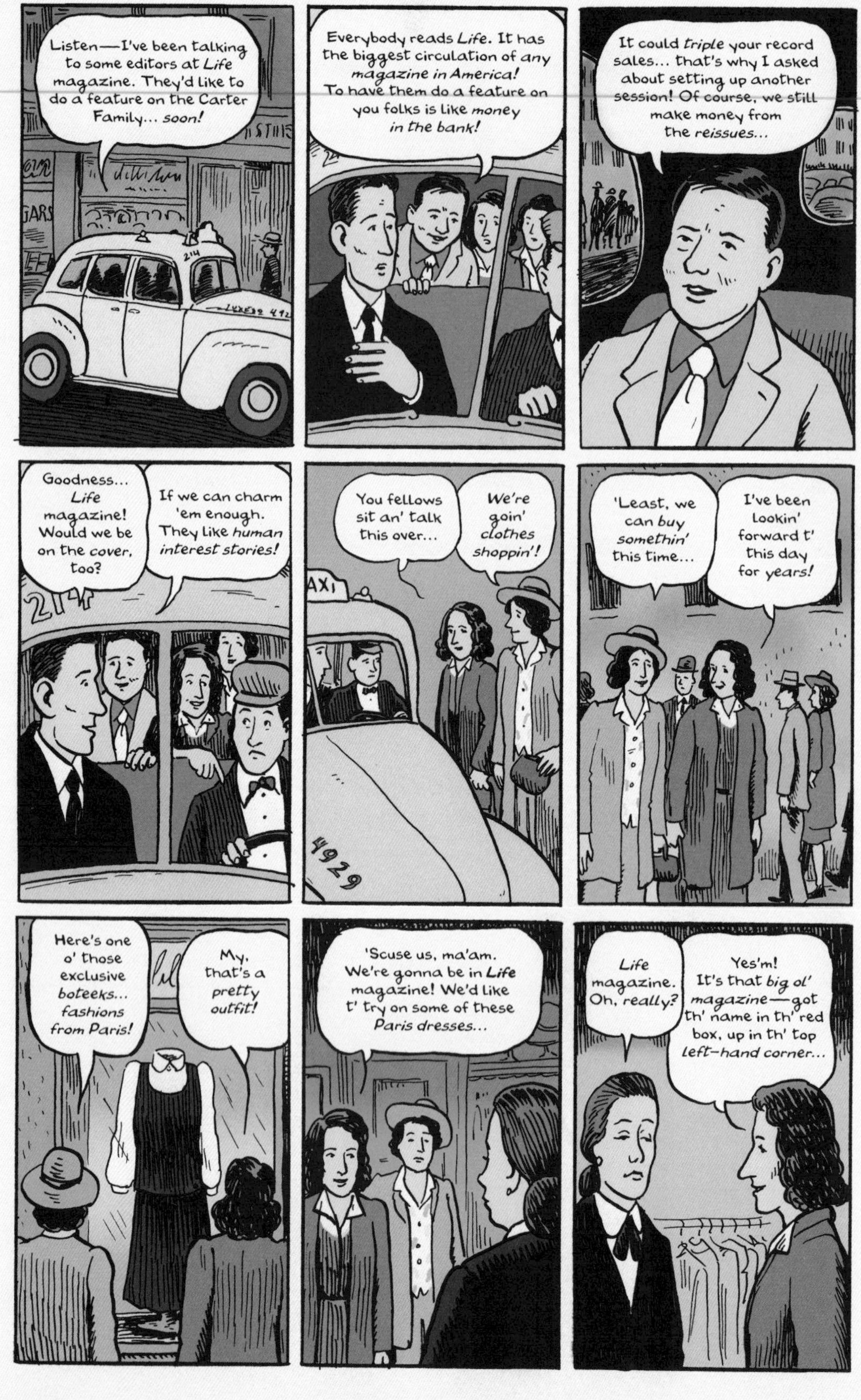

Listen—I've been talking to some editors at *Life* magazine. They'd like to do a feature on the Carter Family... *soon!*
Everybody reads *Life*. It has the biggest circulation of *any magazine in America!* To have them do a feature on you folks is like *money in the bank!*
It could *triple* your record sales... that's why I asked about setting up another session! Of course, we still make money from the *reissues*...
Goodness... *Life* magazine! Would we be on the cover, too?
If we can charm 'em enough. They like *human interest stories!*
You fellows sit an' talk this over...
We're *goin' clothes shoppin'!*
'Least, we can *buy somethin'* this time...
I've been lookin' forward t' this day *for years!*
Here's one o' those exclusive *boteeks... fashions from Paris!*
My, that's a *pretty outfit!*
'Scuse us, ma'am. We're gonna be in *Life* magazine! We'd like t' try on some of these *Paris dresses*...
Life magazine. Oh, *really?*
Yes'm! It's that *big ol' magazine*—got th' name in th' red box, up in th' top *left-hand corner*...

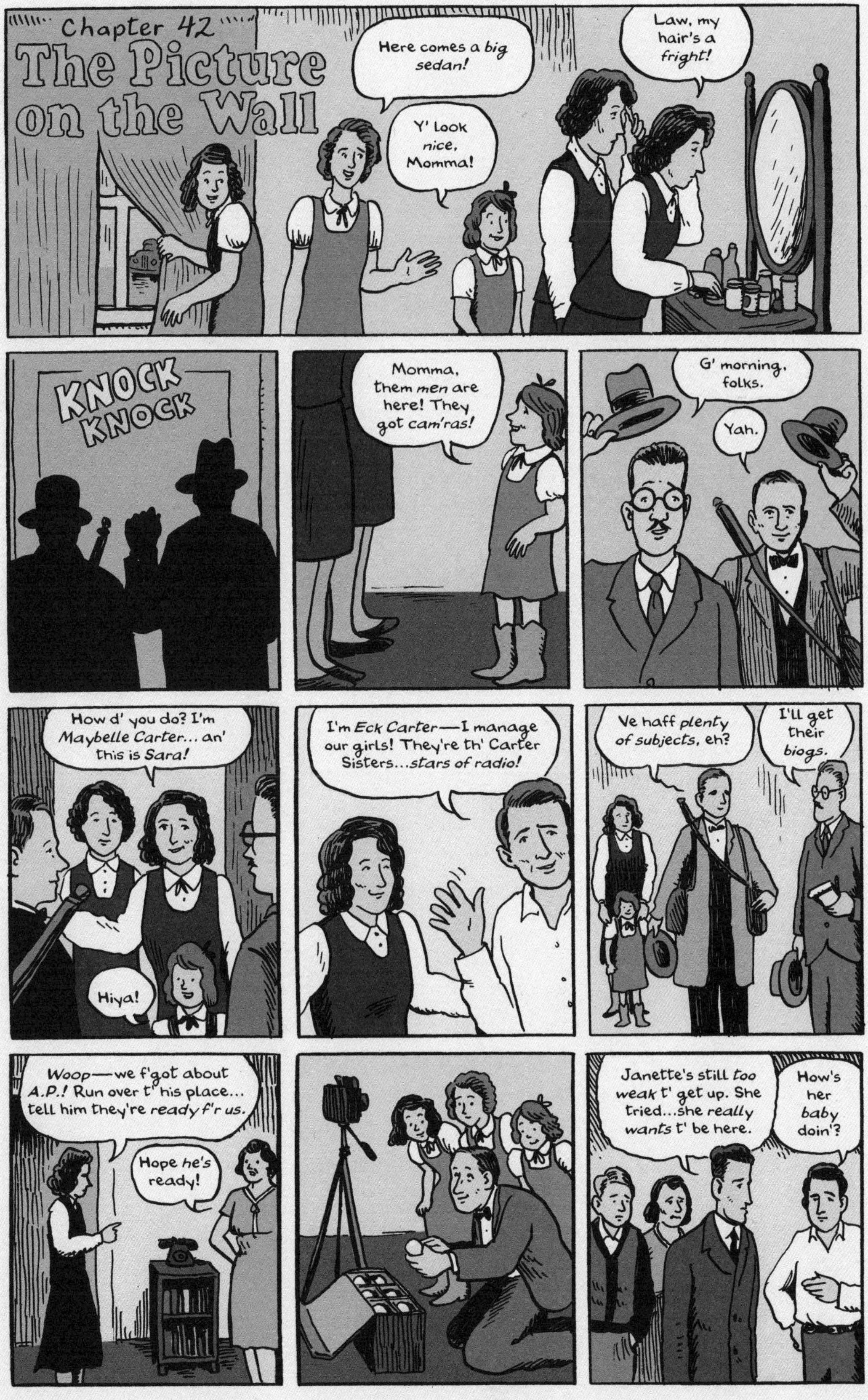
Chapter 42
The Picture on the Wall
Here comes a big sedan!
Law, my hair's a fright!
Y' look nice, Momma!
KNOCK KNOCK
Momma, them men are here! They got cam'ras!
G' morning, folks.
Yah.
How d' you do? I'm Maybelle Carter... an' this is Sara!
Hiya!
I'm Eck Carter—I manage our girls! They're th' Carter Sisters... stars of radio!
Ve haff plenty of subjects, eh?
I'll get their biogs.
Woop—we f'got about A.P.! Run over t' his place... tell him they're ready f'r us.
Hope he's ready!
Janette's still too weak t' get up. She tried... she really wants t' be here.
How's her baby doin'?

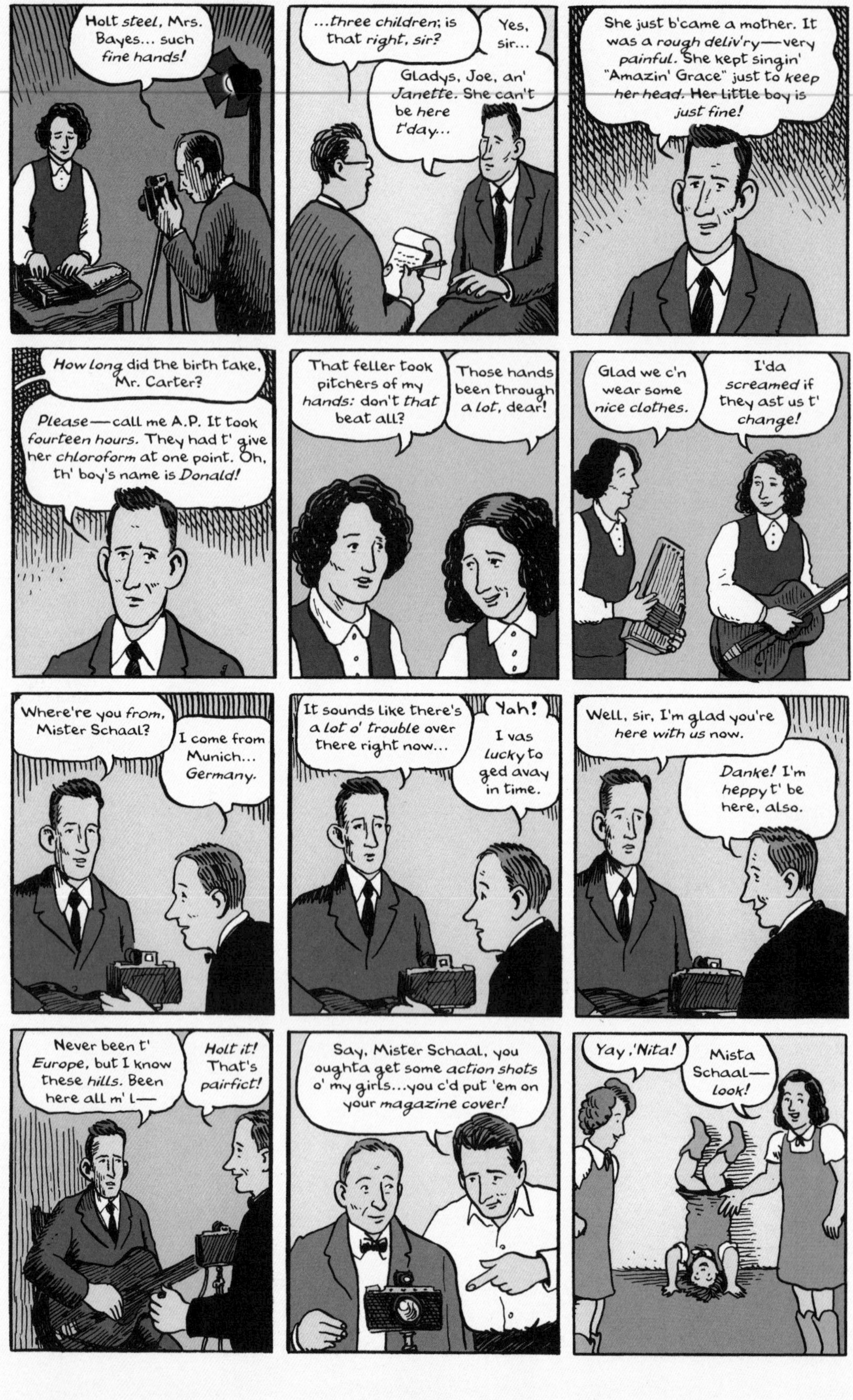
Holt steel, Mrs. Bayes... such fine hands!
...three children; is that right, sir?
Yes, sir...
Gladys, Joe, an' Janette. She can't be here t'day...
She just b'came a mother. It was a rough deliv'ry—very painful. She kept singin' "Amazin' Grace" just to keep her head. Her little boy is just fine!
How long did the birth take, Mr. Carter?
Please—call me A.P. It took fourteen hours. They had t' give her chloroform at one point. Oh, th' boy's name is Donald!
That feller took pitchers of my hands: don't that beat all?
Those hands been through a lot, dear!
Glad we c'n wear some nice clothes.
I'da screamed if they ast us t' change!
Where're you from, Mister Schaal?
I come from Munich... Germany.
It sounds like there's a lot o' trouble over there right now...
Yah!
I vas lucky to ged avay in time.
Well, sir, I'm glad you're here with us now.
Danke! I'm heppy t' be here, also.
Never been t' Europe, but I know these hills. Been here all m' l—
Holt it! That's pairfict!
Say, Mister Schaal, you oughta get some action shots o' my girls...you c'd put 'em on your magazine cover!
Yay, 'Nita!
Mista Schaal—look!

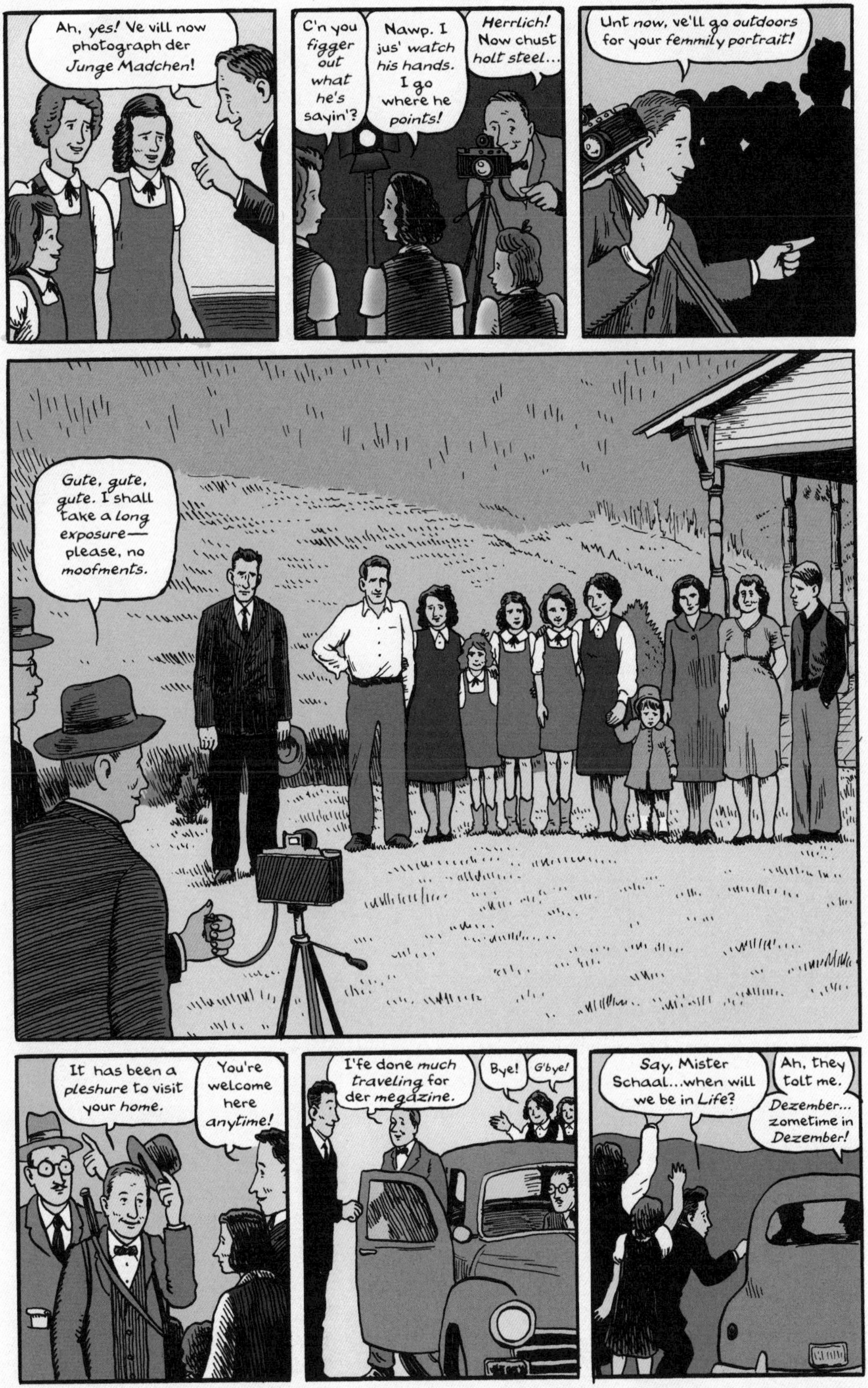
Ah, yes! Ve vill now photograph der Junge Madchen!
C'n you figger out what he's sayin'?
Nawp. I jus' watch his hands. I go where he points!
Herrlich! Now chust holt steel...
Unt now, ve'll go outdoors for your femmily portrait!
Gute, gute, gute. I shall take a long exposure—please, no moofments.
It has been a pleshure to visit your home.
You're welcome here anytime!
I'fe done much traveling for der megazine.
Bye!
G'bye!
Say, Mister Schaal...when will we be in Life?
Ah, they tolt me.
Dezember... zometime in Dezember!

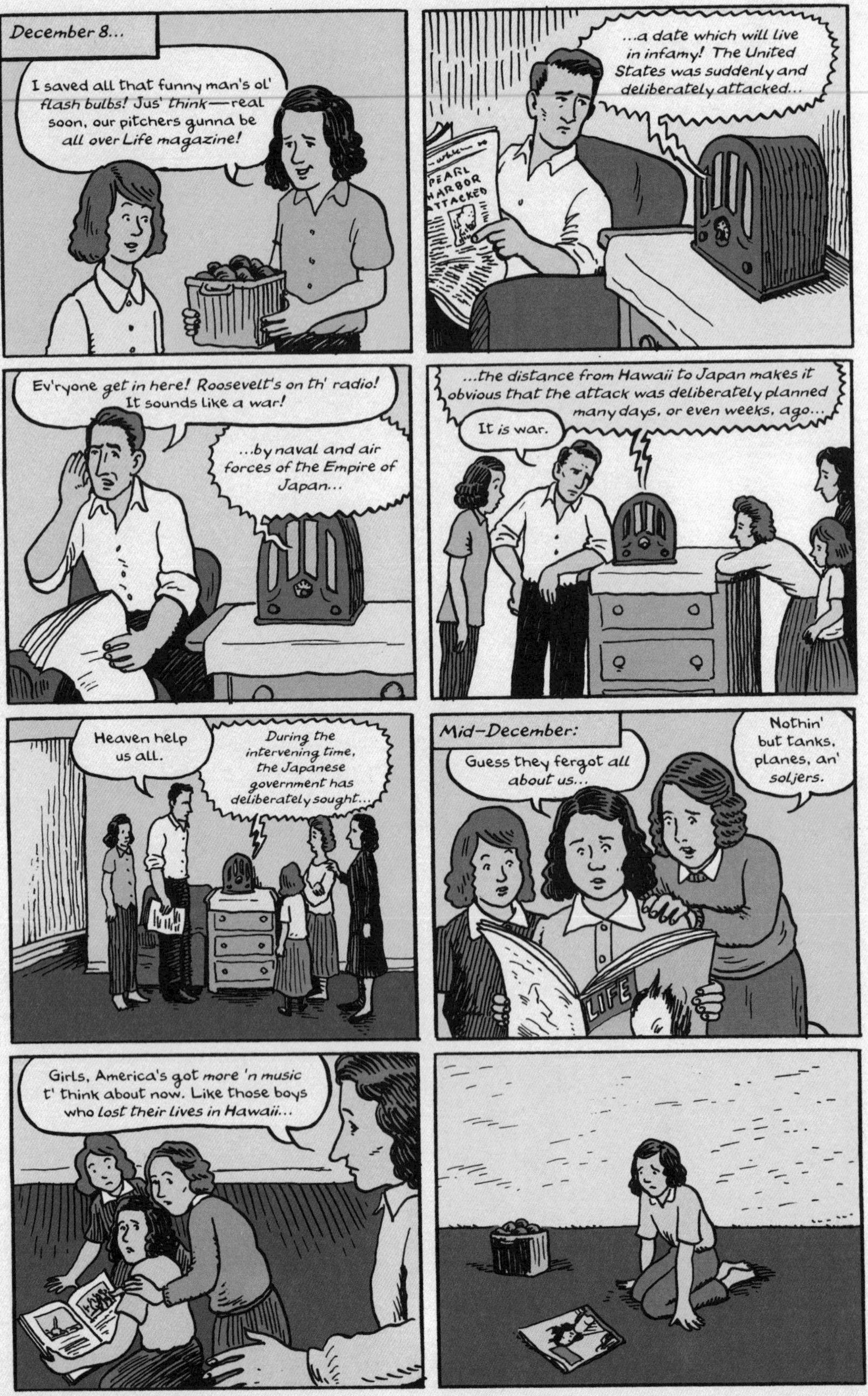
December 8...
I saved all that funny man's ol' flash bulbs! Jus' think—real soon, our pitchers gunna be all over Life magazine!
...a date which will live in infamy! The United States was suddenly and deliberately attacked...
PEARL HARBOR ATTACKED
Ev'ryone get in here! Roosevelt's on th' radio! It sounds like a war!
...by naval and air forces of the Empire of Japan...
...the distance from Hawaii to Japan makes it obvious that the attack was deliberately planned many days, or even weeks, ago...
It is war.
Heaven help us all.
During the intervening time, the Japanese government has deliberately sought...
Mid-December:
Guess they fergot all about us...
Nothin' but tanks, planes, an' soljers.
LIFE
Girls, America's got more 'n music t' think about now. Like those boys who lost their lives in Hawaii...

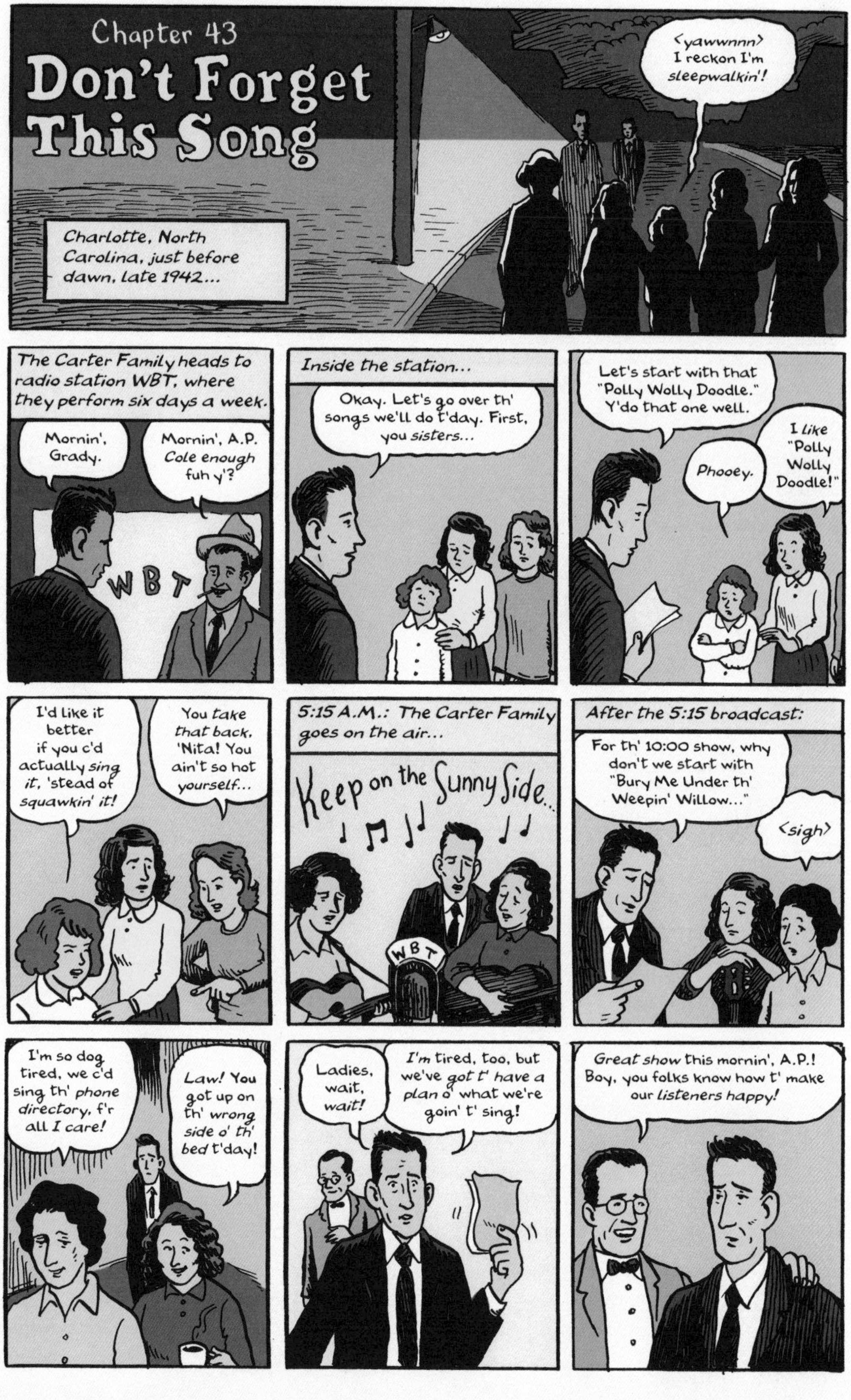
Chapter 43
Don't Forget This Song
<yawwnnn> I reckon I'm sleepwalkin'!
Charlotte, North Carolina, just before dawn, late 1942...
The Carter Family heads to radio station WBT, where they perform six days a week.
Mornin', Grady.
Mornin', A.P. Cole enough fuh y'?
WBT
Inside the station...
Okay. Let's go over th' songs we'll do t'day. First, you sisters...
Let's start with that "Polly Wolly Doodle." Y'do that one well.
Phooey.
I like "Polly Wolly Doodle!"
I'd like it better if you c'd actually sing it, 'stead of squawkin' it!
You take that back, 'Nita! You ain't so hot yourself...
5:15 A.M.: The Carter Family goes on the air...
Keep on the Sunny Side...
WBT
After the 5:15 broadcast:
For th' 10:00 show, why don't we start with "Bury Me Under th' Weepin' Willow..."
<sigh>
I'm so dog tired, we c'd sing th' phone directory, f'r all I care!
Law! You got up on th' wrong side o' th' bed t'day!
Ladies, wait, wait!
I'm tired, too, but we've got t' have a plan o' what we're goin' t' sing!
Great show this mornin', A.P.! Boy, you folks know how t' make our listeners happy!

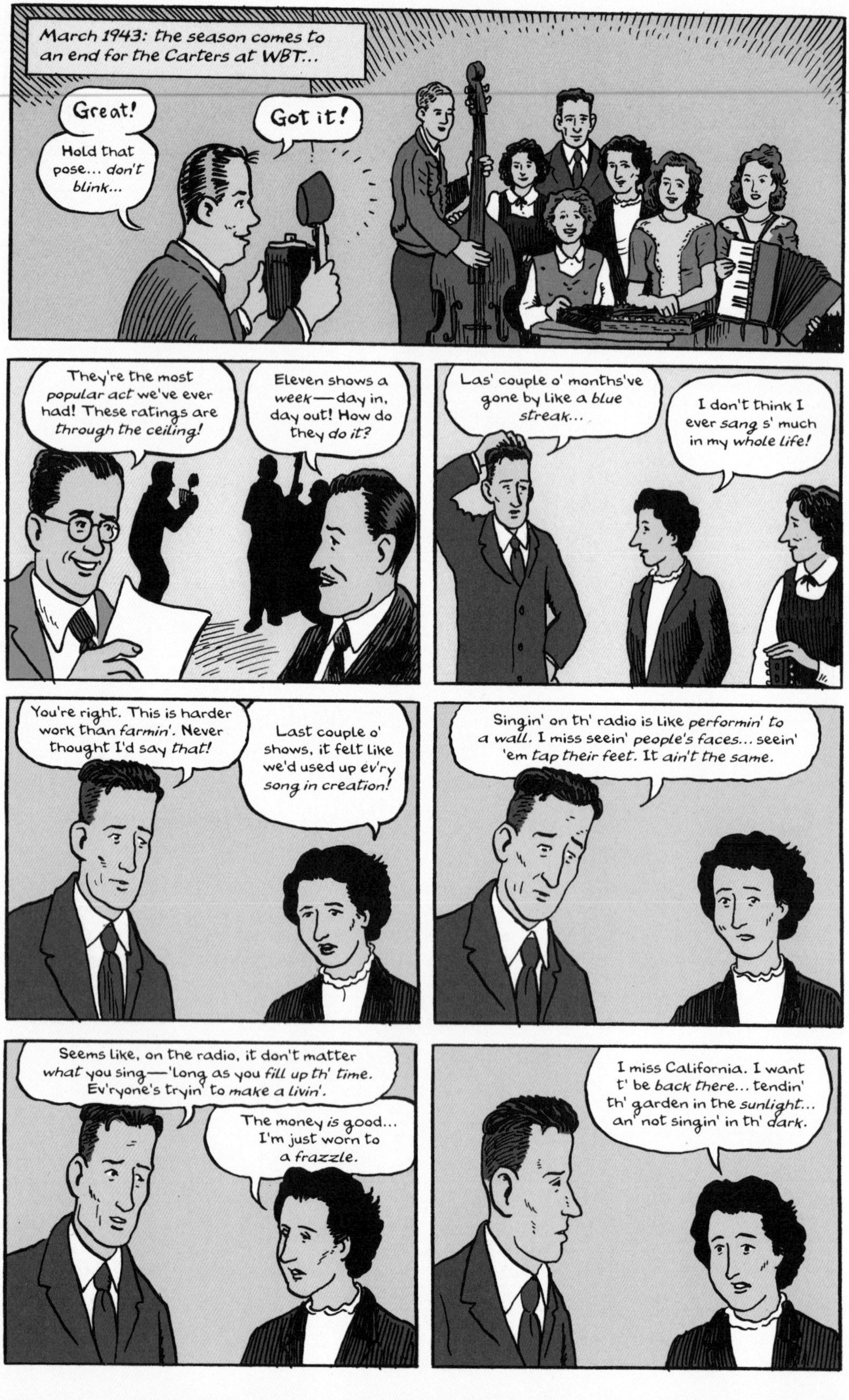
March 1943: the season comes to an end for the Carters at WBT...
Great!
Hold that pose... don't blink...
Got it!
They're the most popular act we've ever had! These ratings are through the ceiling!
Eleven shows a week—day in, day out! How do they do it?
Las' couple o' months've gone by like a blue streak...
I don't think I ever sang s' much in my whole life!
You're right. This is harder work than farmin'. Never thought I'd say that!
Last couple o' shows, it felt like we'd used up ev'ry song in creation!
Singin' on th' radio is like performin' to a wall. I miss seein' people's faces... seein' 'em tap their feet. It ain't the same.
Seems like, on the radio, it don't matter what you sing—'long as you fill up th' time. Ev'ryone's tryin' to make a livin'.
The money is good... I'm just worn to a frazzle.
I miss California. I want t' be back there... tendin' th' garden in the sunlight... an' not singin' in th' dark.

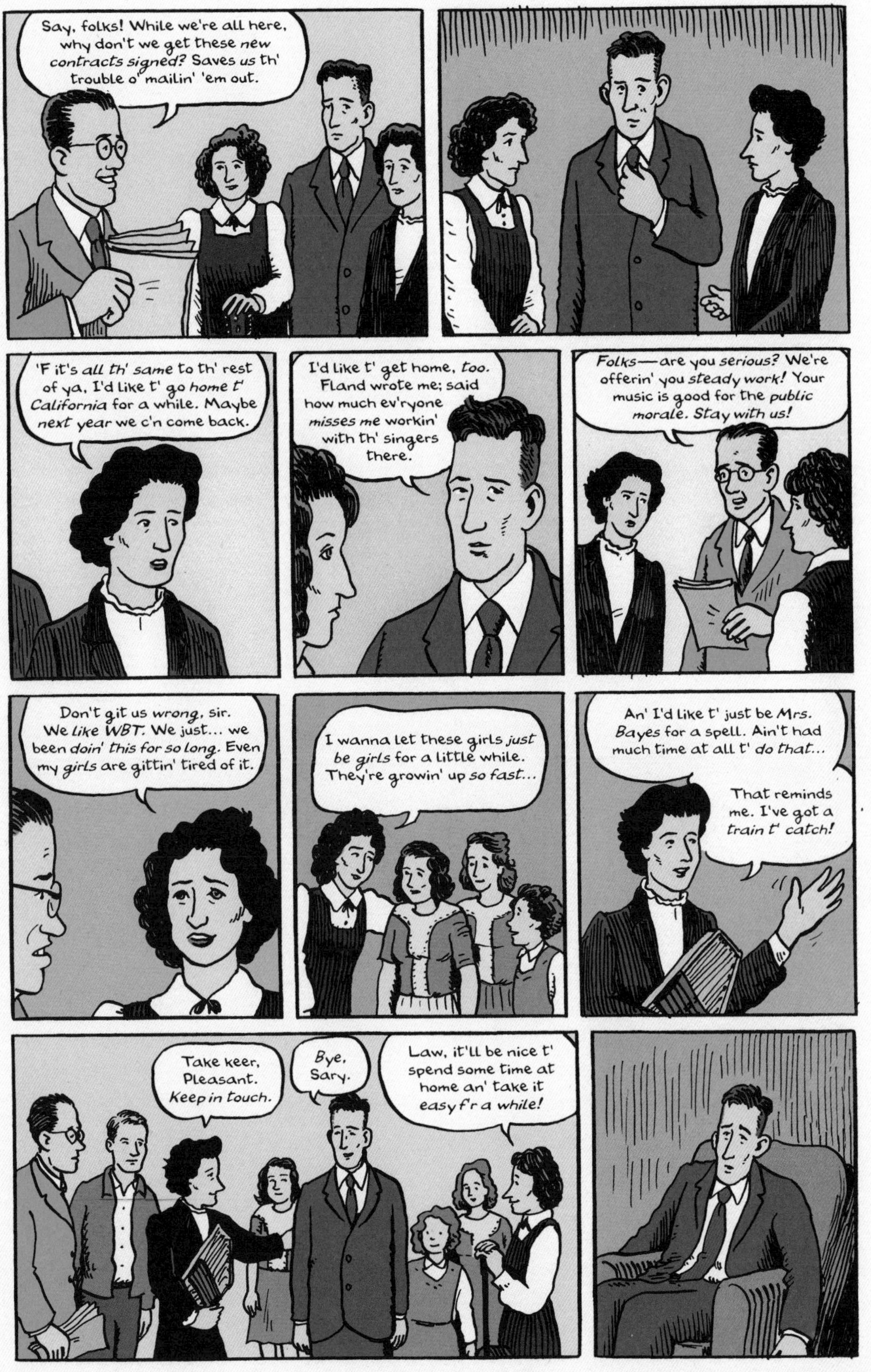
Say, folks! While we're all here, why don't we get these new contracts signed? Saves us th' trouble o' mailin' 'em out.
'F it's all th' same to th' rest of ya, I'd like t' go home t' California for a while. Maybe next year we c'n come back.
I'd like t' get home, too. Fland wrote me; said how much ev'ryone misses me workin' with th' singers there.
Folks—are you serious? We're offerin' you steady work! Your music is good for the public morale. Stay with us!
Don't git us wrong, sir. We like WBT. We just... we been doin' this for so long. Even my girls are gittin' tired of it.
I wanna let these girls just be girls for a little while. They're growin' up so fast...
An' I'd like t' just be Mrs. Bayes for a spell. Ain't had much time at all t' do that...
That reminds me. I've got a train t' catch!
Take keer, Pleasant. Keep in touch.
Bye, Sary.
Law, it'll be nice t' spend some time at home an' take it easy f'r a while!

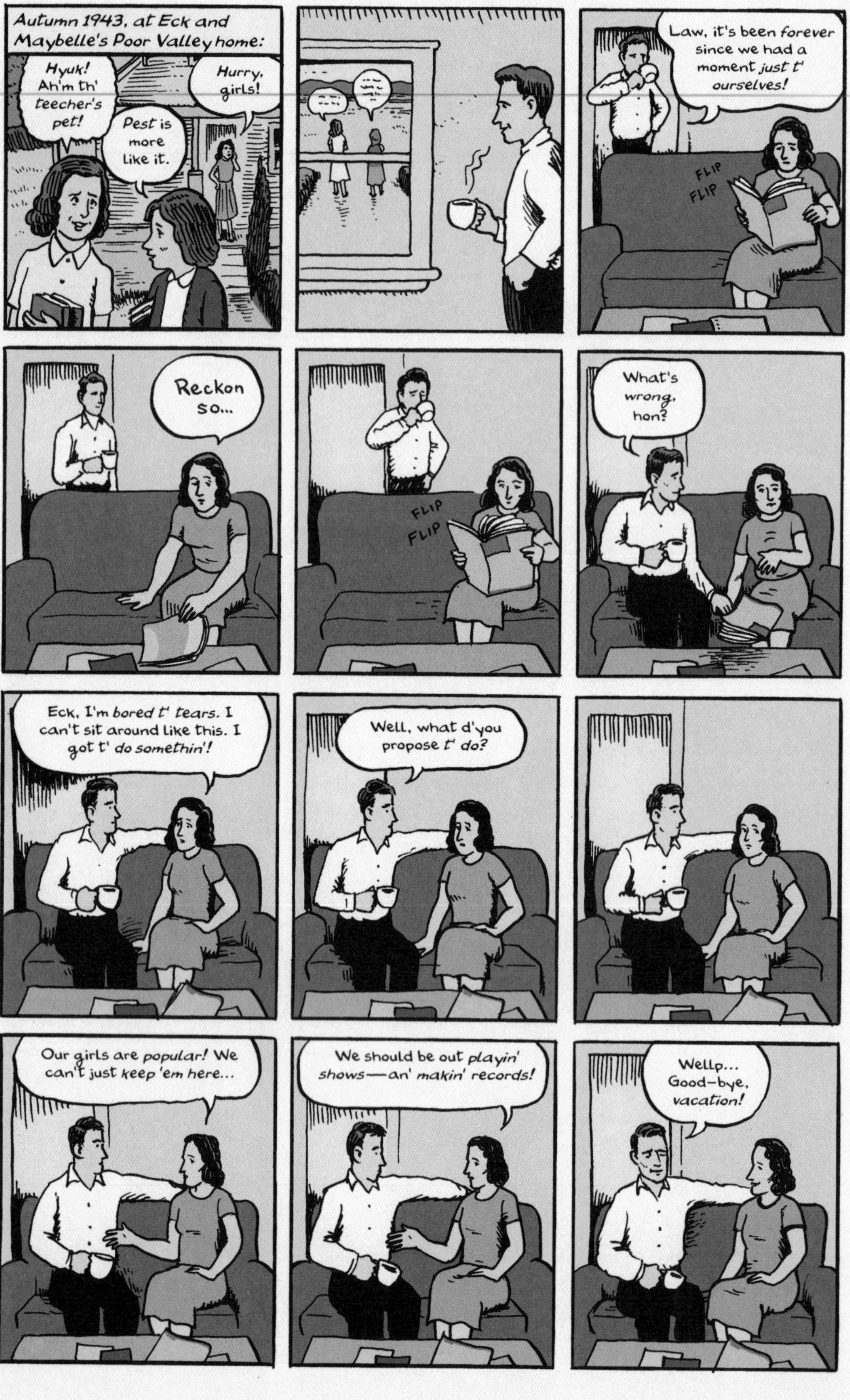
Autumn 1943, at Eck and Maybelle's Poor Valley home:
Hyuk! Ah'm th' teecher's pet!
Pest is more like it.
Hurry, girls!
Law, it's been forever since we had a moment just t' ourselves!
FLIP FLIP
Reckon so...
FLIP FLIP
What's wrong, hon?
Eck, I'm bored t' tears. I can't sit around like this. I got t' do somethin'!
Well, what d'you propose t' do?
Our girls are popular! We can't just keep 'em here...
We should be out playin' shows—an' makin' records!
Wellp... Good-bye, vacation!

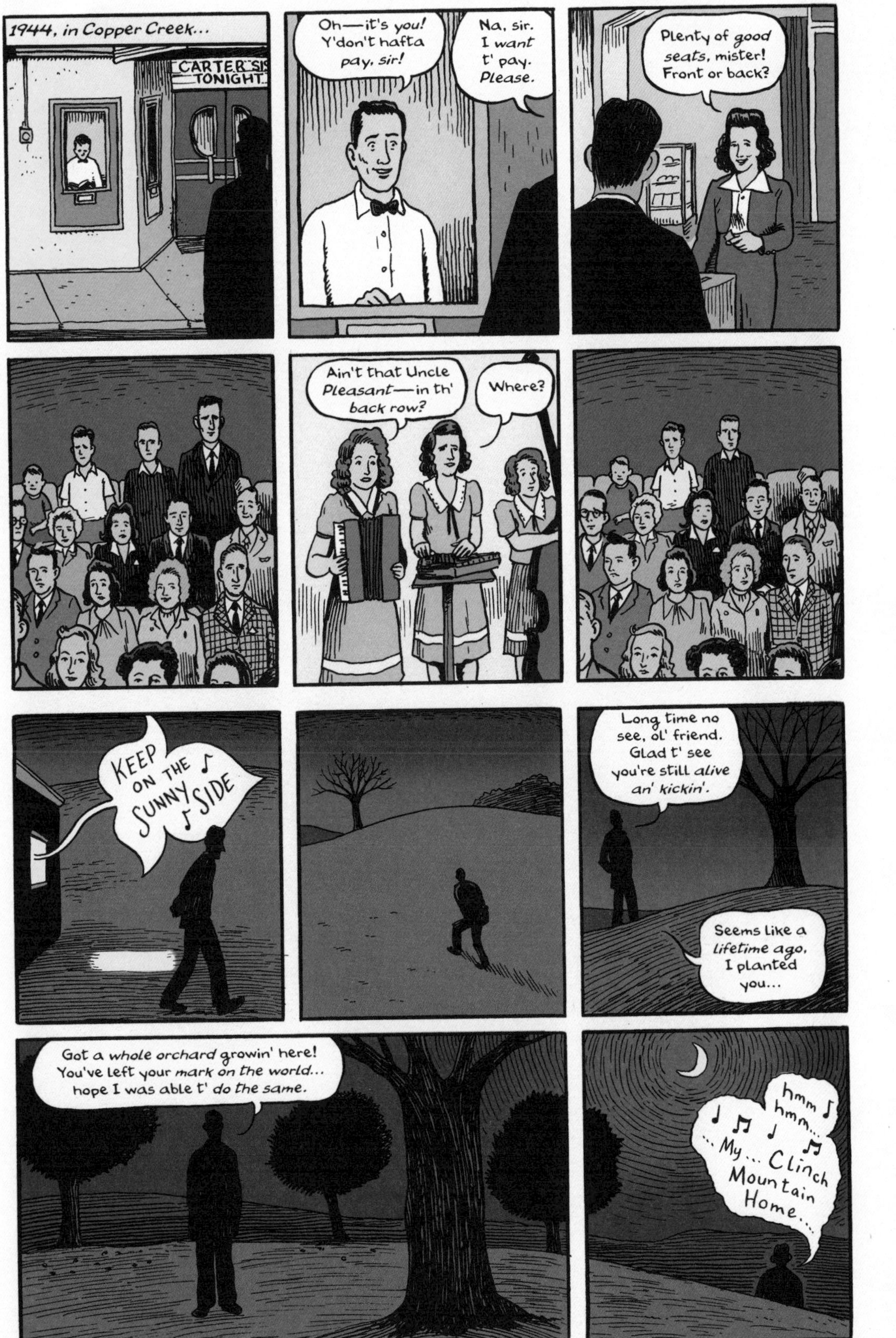
1944, in Copper Creek...
CARTER SIS
TONIGHT
Oh—it's you! Y'don't hafta pay, sir!
Na, sir. I want t' pay. Please.
Plenty of good seats, mister! Front or back?
Ain't that Uncle Pleasant—in th' back row?
Where?
KEEP ON THE SUNNY SIDE
Long time no see, ol' friend. Glad t' see you're still alive an' kickin'.
Seems like a lifetime ago, I planted you...
Got a whole orchard growin' here! You've left your mark on the world... hope I was able t' do the same.
hmm hmm...
... My ... Clinch Mountain Home...

Selected Bibliography

Many books, articles, and interviews informed this graphic novel, which has taken years of research. Each of these added to our understanding of the Carter Family's career, their lives, and the world they inhabited. We could not have completed this book without the following sources:

INTERVIEWS

Conducted by Frank M. Young:

    Bill Clifton (April 2009)

    Rita Forrester (March 18, 2009)

    Peggy Marsheck (March 29, 2009)

    Ralph Peer II (March 24, 2009)

    Mike Seeger (April 7, 2009, and April 11, 2009)

From the Southern Folklife Collection, University of North Carolina at Chapel Hill:

    Lillian Borgeson: Interview with Ralph Peer, 1958 (six CDs)

    Ed Kahn Collection: Interview with Virgie Hobbs, August 11, 1963 (three CDs)

    Mike Seeger Collection: Interview with Lesley Riddle, October 27, 1963 (two CDs)

With Sara and Maybelle Carter:

    Disc 12 of *The Carter Family: In the Shadow of Clinch Mountain*. Germany: Bear Family Records, 2000.

With Janette and Joe Carter by Kip Lornell:

    Available online at the Digital Library of Appalachia (aca-dla.org/index.php).

The American Experience: The Carter Family—Will the Circle Be Unbroken, directed by Cathy Conkright. PBS Home Video, 2005.

The Archie Green Papers at the University of North Carolina. Chapel Hill, NC.

Atkins, John, ed. *The Carter Family*. Old Time Music Booklet No. 1. London: Old Time Music, 1973.

Barnum, Frederick O. "His Master's Voice" in *America: Ninety Years of Communications Pioneering and Progress*. Camden, NJ: General Electric Company, 1991.

Bufwack, Mary, and Robert Oermann. *Finding Her Voice: The Illustrated History of Women in Country Music*. New York: Henry Holt, 1995.

Carr, Patrick, ed. *The Illustrated History of Country Music*. New York: Country Music Magazine Press Books/Doubleday, 1979.

Carter, Janette. *Living with Memories*. Carter Family Memorial Music Center. Hiltons, VA, 1983.

Carter, Janette. *My Clinch Mountain Home*. Carter Family Music Center. Hiltons, VA, 2005.

Carter Cash, John. *Anchored in Love: An Intimate Portrait of June Carter Cash*. Nashville, TN: Thomas Nelson, 2007.

Carter Cash, June. *Among My Klediments*. Peabody, MA: Zondervan Publishing, 1981.

Dew, Joan. *Singers & Sweethearts: The Women of Country Music*. New York: Country Music Magazine Press, A Doubleday Dolphin Book, 1977.

The Ed Kahn Collection at the University of North Carolina. Chapel Hill, NC.

Fowler, Gene, and Bill Crawford. *Border Radio*. Austin, TX: Texas Monthly Press, 1987.

Hirshberg, Charles. "The Ballad of A.P. Carter." *Life*, December 1991.

Kahn, Ed. Liner notes to three-CD series, *The Carter Family on Border Radio*. El Cerrito, CA: Arhoolie Records, 1995–99.

Kephart, Horace. *Our Southern Highlanders*. Alexander, NC: Land of the Sky Books, 1922, 2001.

Kingsbury, Paul, and Alanna Nash, editors. *Will the Circle Be Unbroken*. New York: Dorling Kindersley, 2006.

Lee, R. Alton. *The Bizarre Careers of John R. Brinkley*. Lexington, KY: University Press of Kentucky, 2002.

O'Connell, Barry. Liner notes to *Step by Step: Lesley Riddle Meets the Carter Family: Blues, Country, and Sacred Songs*. Burlington, MA: Rounder Records, 1993.

Oermann, Robert K. "June Carter Remembers Her Family's Legacy." *The Journal*, 1999.

Porterfield, Nolan. *Jimmie Rodgers: The Life and Times of America's Blue Yodeler*. Champaign, IL: University of Illinois Press, 1979.

Ramsey, Jr., Frederic. *Been Here and Gone*. Rutgers, NJ: Rutgers University Press, 1960.

Richards, Marlee. *America in the 1910s*. Minneapolis, MN: Twenty-First Century Books, 2010.

Russell, Tony. *Country Music Records: A Discography, 1922–1942*. New York: Oxford University Press, 2008.

Russell, Tony. *Country Music Originals: The Legends and the Lost*. New York: Oxford University Press, 2010.

Tosches, Nick. *Country: The Biggest Music in America*. New York: Stein & Day, 1977.

Tosches, Nick. *Where Dead Voices Gather*. Boston, MA: Little, Brown, 2001.

Wigginton, Eliot, ed. *The Foxfire Book*. New York: Anchor Books, 1972.

Wolfe, Charles. *The Carter Family: Their Complete Victor Recordings, Volumes 1–9*. Liner notes. Burlington, MA: Rounder Records, 1992–98.

Wolfe, Charles. *Classic Country: Legends of Country Music*. New York: Routledge Press, 2000.

Wolfe, Charles. *The Carter Family: In the Shadow of Clinch Mountain*. Liner notes for CD box set. Germany: Bear Family Records, 2001.

Wolfe, Charles, and Ted Olson, editors. *The Bristol Sessions: Writings About the Big Bang of Country Music*. Jefferson, NC: McFarland, 2005. This volume of essays includes Gladys [Millard] Carter's remarkable short memoir, "I Remember Daddy."

Zwonitzer, Mark, with Charles Hirshberg. *Will You Miss Me When I'm Gone? The Carter Family & Their Legacy in American Music*. New York: Simon & Schuster, 2002.

Acknowledgments

For their early encouragement, thanks to: Ilse Thompson-Driggs, Sammy Harkham, Tom Hart and Leela Corman, Nick Bertozzi, Ellen Lindner, Bob Mecoy, and Charles Kochman.

An essential thank you goes to Frank M. Young, for turning an idea into a vision, and then agreeing to make our shared vision into a full-color graphic novel.

Throughout the process of creating the book, friends old and new stepped in to lend their support, advice, and sometimes furniture. There are so many people to thank, but these names come especially mind: Coby Lorang and Korinna Marks, the Benincasa Family, Elizabeth Shieldkret, Paul Tumey, Priscilla Alice Bowen, Roberta Gregory, Robert Crumb, Laura Park, Beth Harrington, William S. Blackwell, Jeff Sadler, Dalton Webb, Tom Spurgeon, and, for lending his time and considerable talents, Jim Gill.

Thanks to all my comics world friends who talked with me at various times about this project (you are too numerous to list, but please know that I am grateful).

A big thanks to my mother, Barbara Lasky, to my father, David E. Lasky and his wife Mary, and to my brother Jason and his family.

Thanks to everyone who gave me freelance assignments and teaching gigs while I was working on this book, including (but not limited to): Lydia McIntosh, Patton Oswalt, Paul Buhle, Russ Kick, King County Public Health, LitA, ZAPP and Richard Hugo House, Arts Corps, the Seattle Public Library, King County Libraries, and *The Stranger*.

Special thanks to Sean Robinson for his invaluable background inking on certain pages. Thank you Dalton Webb, Carl Nelson, Tom Dougherty, and Vince Aparo for their valiant eleventh-hour background inking assistance.

We are grateful to all of our generous and supportive Kickstarter backers.

Frank and I are extremely grateful to those who consented to be interviewed: Rita Forrester, Mike Seeger, Bill Clifton, Peggy Marsheck, and Kip Lornell. Thank you John Maeder, Ron McConnell, and Ron Penix for answering questions that most other people would not know the answers to. Special thanks to volunteer researcher Susan Gale. Thanks to Mark Zwonitzer and Charles Hirshberg for writing the definitive book on the Carter Family. And thanks to Ed Kahn, Mike Seeger, Archie Green, and others who did pioneering research on the Carters.

Along with editor Charles Kochman, thanks to Neil Egan, Sara Corbett, and Chad Beckerman (designers); Tamara Arellano (managing editor); and Alison Gervais (production).

The biggest thanks goes to my patient and supportive significant other, Leeann Bowen.

And thank you, Carter Family, for all the music.

—D.L.

My collaborator, David Lasky, tops this list. I'm in awe of his talent as an expressive, sensitive artist. He has made the characters of this story come to life, and has enriched every moment of the book with his gifts. We've been through endless drafts, rewrites, rethinks, and emerged from seeming dead ends with great ideas. He's also helped me learn InDesign, and taught me a lot of Photoshop tricks I didn't know.

The following kind folks contributed to this project via good advice, technical expertise, access to historical data, and constant encouragement. Without them, David and I could not have created (or completed) *Don't Forget This Song*.

Cori Antaya, my dear sister; Thomas Brown and Allen Watkins, good friends and aficionados of the history of American recorded music; Mark Campos; Bruce and Joan Chrislip; Gabriel Corbera; Dana Countryman, whose good humor, creativity, and encouragement are an inspiration to me; Robert Crumb; Kim Deitch; Tom Devlin; Eubie Cat (R.I.P.); Jerit Fourman; Roberta Gregory; Bill Grose; Jason Gutz; Beth Harrington; Ira J. Katz; Michael Komlos, for his unending friendship and generosity; Thad Komorowski, for his friendship and support (and that complete set of Warner Bros. cartoons on DVD!); Lesli Larson and the staff at the Knight Reference Library of Oregon State University; Kip Lornell; John Maeder; Michael McCarty; Bob Mecoy, my long-suffering literary agent; Françoise Mouly; Naraya (R.I.P.); Peter Pentz; Nolan Porterfield, one of our finest writers and scholars on country music; Lois Regen, for her unending friendship and generosity; Don V. Roff; Teddy the Pug; Kob Tiptus; Gordon and Margaret Watkins; Charles Wolfe (R.I.P.); David A. Young, who gave me shelter when I'd otherwise have been on the streets; Mark Zwonitzer; and the kind supporters of our Kickstarter campaign.

Special thanks to James L. Gill's assist with the grunt work of coloring; to Sean Robinson for his brilliant ink work; to Carl Nelson, Tom Dougherty, and Dalton Webb, for also assisting with their fine ink work; to Paul Tumey, for his kindness, friendship, support, and feedback; to Art Spiegelman, for reaching out and gifting us with the benefit of his wisdom and experience, and to Charles Kochman and his team at Abrams ComicArts: Neil Egan, Sara Corbett, Chad Beckerman, Tamara Arellano, and Alison Gervais.

And, to echo David, thanks to A.P., Sara, and Maybelle for the timeless, haunting music that inspired the making of this graphic novel.

—F.M.Y.

We began work on this graphic novel with our publisher in the fall of 2007. In the fall of 2011 we launched a Kickstarter campaign to help us bring this project to completion. Thank you for your patience— and support.

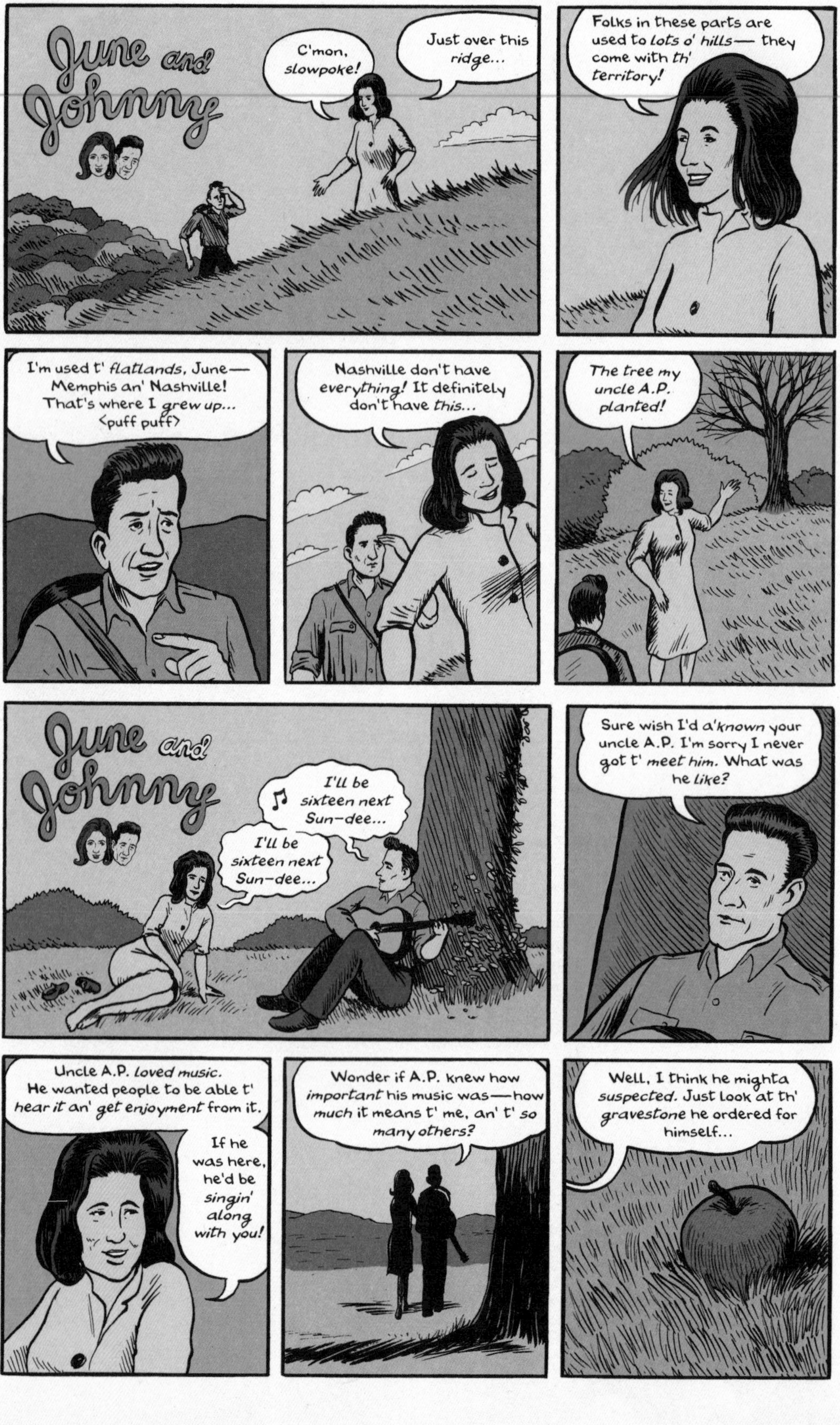
June and Johnny
Just over this ridge...
C'mon, slowpoke!
Folks in these parts are used to lots o' hills— they come with th' territory!
I'm used t' flatlands, June— Memphis an' Nashville! That's where I grew up... <puff puff>
Nashville don't have everything! It definitely don't have this...
The tree my uncle A.P. planted!
June and Johnny
I'll be sixteen next Sun-dee...
I'll be sixteen next Sun-dee...
Sure wish I'd a'known your uncle A.P. I'm sorry I never got t' meet him. What was he like?
Uncle A.P. loved music. He wanted people to be able t' hear it an' get enjoyment from it.
If he was here, he'd be singin' along with you!
Wonder if A.P. knew how important his music was—how much it means t' me, an' t' so many others?
Well, I think he mighta suspected. Just look at th' gravestone he ordered for himself...